TEACHING AND TESTIMONY

INTERRUPTIONS: Border Testimony(ies) and Critical Discourse/s
Henry A. Giroux, editor

TEACHING AND TESTIMONY

*Rigoberta Menchú and
the North American Classroom*

Edited by
Allen Carey-Webb
Stephen Benz

STATE UNIVERSITY OF NEW YORK PRESS

Chapter 23 was reprinted from *College Literature* 19.3/20.1 (1992/93): 162–69, by permission of the publisher.

Published by
State University of New York Press, Albany

Printed in the United States of America

LB
1029
, B55
T425
1996
Sept. 2008

For information, address State University of New York Press,
State University Plaza, Albany, N.Y., 12246

Production by Marilyn Semerad
Marketing by Theresa Abad Swierzowski

Library of Congress Cataloging-in-Publication Data

Teaching and testmimony : Rigoberta Menchú and the North American
    classroom / edited by Allen Carey-Webb, Stephen Benz.
        p.   cm. — (Interruptions)
    Includes bibliographical references (p.   ) and index.
    ISBN 0–7914–3013–8 (alk. paper). — ISBN 0–7914–3014–6 (pbk. :
alk. paper)
        1. Education—Biographical methods. 2. Menchú, Rigobert Me llamo
Rigoberta Menchú y así me nació la conciencia. 3. Quiché Indians–
–Study and teaching. 4. Human rights workers—Guatemala—Study and
teaching. 5. Latin America—Civilization—Study and teaching.
6. Multicultural education. 7. Critical pedagogy. I. Carey-Webb,
Allen, 1957– II. Benz, Stephen Connely, 1958– . III. Series.
LB1029.B55T425   1996
370.11'5—dc20   96–592
                                                            CIP

10 9 8 7 6 5 4 3 2 1

CONTENTS

INTRODUCTION

TRANSFORMATIVE VOICES

ALLEN CAREY-WEBB

Teaching and Testimony is about the power of the word and transformative possibilities of inviting previously marginalized voices into classroom discourse. The activity of teaching testimonial narrative in its broadest sense brings to the center of attention the experience and perspective of the presumably voiceless, the peripheral, the unlettered, or the oppressed. Ranging from high school to graduate school, from inner-city immigrants in the Bronx to Freshman Composition students in Arizona, from an adolescent treatment facility in Minnesota to Women's Studies in Pennsylvania, *Teaching and Testimony* documents the efforts in the early 1990s of a remarkable diversity of teachers to incorporate testimonial narrative into classroom teaching. Indeed *Teaching and Testimony* is itself a testimony to a spontaneous, diverse, grassroots, politically and pedagogically conscious, counterhegemonic educational initiative cutting across levels and disciplines. Drawing on the words of Rigoberta Menchú, the contributors to this volume have confronted an imperial North American indifference and violence toward Central America, challenged prescribed curricular boundaries and official definitions of knowledge, and (dis)located North American students socially, culturally, historically, and politically. The chapters in *Teaching and Testimony* make evident that—in an inimical period of American history—teachers are still developing and deepening their students' and their own commitment to compassion, democracy, and mutual understanding.

Assembled in a spirit of support and encouragement for those teachers who are already engaged in the undertaking of bringing testimony into the classroom, *Teaching and Testimony* offers an invitation to other teachers to consider experimenting with some of the same materials and approaches. Today when the power and meaning of teaching and learning is often sapped by imposed, "trickle down" curriculums, legislated objectives, pedantic ivory tower infighting, funding shortfalls, standardized testing, and top-down, "scientific" management, the teachers in this book offer bottom-up narratives of vital classroom experiences that can and should serve as jumping off points for educational renewal and change at all levels. Energized by the teaching of testimonial narrative these teachers let their guard down, wrestle with the immediate difficulties and possibilities of classroom teaching, and speak with passion about the importance of what they and their students are learning. By turning to the rich, varied, and complex experience and wisdom of Rigoberta Menchú and the Quiché peoples, the teaching described in these pages aims at a truly meaningful multicultural pedagogy willing to rethink established frameworks of learning.

When Menchú was awarded the Nobel Peace Prize in 1992, worldwide attention was drawn to the indigenous peoples of the Americas and, in particular, to their life-and-death struggle in Guatemala. In the 1960s and 70s Rigoberta Menchú grew up in the dire poverty, backbreaking plantation labor, virulent racism, and horrific military violence that condition the lives of indigenous Guatemalans. Despite unrelenting repression, the modern-day descendants of the Maya have strategically adapted and maintained their languages, traditions, and communities. Menchú's own family attempted to evade oppression by founding a village in the north central highlands. Thwarted by violence and legal chicanery, Vicente Menchú, Rigoberta's father, was forced to undertake exhausting efforts to establish security for his community, efforts that eventually positioned him as leader in an emerging peasants' rights movement. To this movement the Guatemalan military—supported by the United States government—responded with devastating force, murdering upwards of 100,000 people between 1980 and 1983, including Rigoberta Menchú's brother and both of her parents. By the time she reached her early twenties, Rigoberta Menchú had worked as a field laborer, been a maid in the capital city, participated in her father's organizing efforts, learned Spanish, become an organizer in her own right, witnessed the murder of family members, been hunted by the army, and fled to Mexico to join an opposition movement in exile.

On a trip for this group she traveled to Europe in 1981 where she collaborated with Elisabeth Burgos, an activist ethnologist, to record and publish her life story. Appearing first in Mexico (1983) as *Me llamo Rigoberta Menchú y asi me nació la consciencia* (My name is Rigoberta Menchú and this is how my conscience/consciousness was born) Menchú's compelling book won the prestigious Casa de Las Americas Prize as the outstanding testimonial work of 1983. Translated by Ann Wright into English as *I, Rigoberta Menchú: An Indian Woman of Guatemala,* the work began to be read and taught at North American universities. By the mid-1990s Menchú's book achieved the status of a minor classic. Vilified in a chapter of Dinesh D'Souza's best-selling polemic *Illiberal Education,* and boosted by the Nobel Peace Prize, *I, Rigoberta Menchú* is increasingly read in Humanities, Spanish, Writing, Women's Studies, Comparative Literature, Anthropology, and Political Science courses. It has recently begun to be used either in whole or part in secondary schools.

If readers of *Teaching and Testimony* have not yet read Menchú's words it will be hard to understand the commitment, energy, and heterogeneity of the teaching set forth in these pages. It might be difficult for those unacquainted with Menchú to comprehend why the oral narrative of an illiterate Guatemalan servant girl should stimulate and connect the variety of classrooms, disciplines, and levels recounted here. Thus, it is incumbent on our readers who have not read Rigoberta Menchú's story to turn first to her words, however mediated by the form in which they are found. If after hearing Rigoberta Menchú you find yourself moved, if you want to think about the importance and possibility of passing on what she has to say, if you want to consider the complex possible meanings that her words and other testimonials like hers might have for North Americans, and particularly for North American students, then read on, your questions will be considered and addressed.

When I first heard Rigoberta Menchú speak in the fall of 1988 at the University of Oregon, she talked about the desperate plight of her people, of their terrible suffering and of the beauty and wisdom they had to offer humanity. Menchú was deeply concerned that the savage genocide still ongoing in Guatemala was being ignored by the world. With George Bush newly elected and American foreign policy in Central America still fixated on a cold warrior anti-communism, those of us involved in Central American solidarity work were desperate to get word out to the American people about what was really going on. That semester, in the introductory course that I taught as a graduate student, *I, Rigoberta Menchú* had a particular urgency. We talked about the way that our government was involved in the region, not only in overthrowing the Arbenz regime in Guatemala in 1954, but in the present-day military support and training, in the propping up of neofascist regimes, in the preparation of "interrogators"—the very torturers who murdered Menchú's brother and mother. In the years since 1988 I have continued to teach *I, Rigoberta Menchú* and found it a crucial text in a variety of courses, especially courses for the training of teachers. Today, in 1995, some of the issues have changed. The oppression of Guatemalan Mayan people has received increased international recognition through the award of the Nobel Peace Prize to Rigoberta Menchú and, under the current administration, American foreign policy in Central America is less doctrinaire than in the past. The desperate urgency felt by those of us who taught Rigoberta Menchú's testimonial in the mid and late 1980s has been slightly reduced, yet the issues Menchú's story raise continue to be vital, not only for Guatemalans or on college campuses, but for the increasingly dynamic, complex, and tense relationships between cultures and peoples worldwide.

In exploring these relationships in the classroom, contributors to this volume are on the cutting edge of new, more meaningful pedagogical approaches that connect students to an increasingly global understanding of themselves and others. Many of these approaches have been inspired by the pedagogical praxis of the Brazilian educator Paulo Freire, and thus are part of the emerging critical teaching movement whose best known thinkers include Henry Giroux, Ira Shorr, Bob Peterson, Bill Bigelow, Linda Christiansen, Peter McLaren,

Patrick Shannon, Mark Hurlburt, Lil Brannon, and C. H. Knoblauch. As it translates Freirian teaching to North American contexts, *Teaching and Testimony* takes testimonial narrative in general and Rigoberta Menchú's story in particular as starting points for problem-posing learning. Indeed, this book identifies testimonial narrative as central to the creation of an engaged cultural studies approach for North American students.

Reading these chapters it becomes evident how much those of us already putting together testimony with teaching can learn from one another. Because Menchú's book has achieved broad recognition and its publication has been a remarkable success—surpassing 100,000 volumes—there are many teachers now using Menchú's story who will be intensely interested in what they will find in *Teaching and Testimony*. At the same time there are many more teachers directly and loosely involved with cultural studies or critical pedagogy movements who will find *Teaching and Testimony* immediately relevant to their approach and concerns. Moreover, *Teaching and Testimony* should appeal to a wide variety of teachers who are not necessarily yet familiar with Rigoberta Menchú or self-consciously defining themselves as critical pedagogists, but who are eager for innovative and effective ideas for the classroom.

It is the hope of myself and Steve Benz that *Teaching and Testimony* will also increase interest in Menchú's story. In the broader scheme of things, *I, Rigoberta Menchú* remains a marginal text in school curriculums and classroom reading lists. Many of our fellow teachers who might find her testimonial relevant to their students and discipline remain unfamiliar with the work and approaches to teaching it. (It is still difficult for public school teachers to fund the purchase of classroom sets of *I, Rigoberta Menchú*, or any other single text for the matter—no matter how much needed to supplement nationally produced textbooks.) Curriculum can become calcified, administrators may attempt to keep controversy out of classrooms, teachers may be uncertain about dealing with depictions of violence. Yet *Teaching and Testimony* demonstrates the relevance and effectiveness of Menchú's testimony for teaching and learning across a great variety of levels and disciplines.

Testimony is an encompassing term that reaches back to the communal, even tribal, honor for the spoken word. Giving testimony is central activity in various legal, historical, literary, psychoanalytic, ethnographic, and religious practices. Marking any expression as "testimony" stresses its truth content, the accuracy of its rendition of something experienced or witnessed. In the legal sense testimony involves providing evidence in a formal investigation of an event or events in the past. As an act of memory situated in time testimony is vital to our knowledge of history; it stresses the personal as reflective of a larger collective. When previously excluded voices are heard testimony can dislocate established frameworks and shift paradigms. Peter Nabokov's *Native American Testimony: A Chronicle of Indian-White Relations from Prophecy to the Present* (1991), for example, could be seen as the eruption of previously marginalized testimony into the documentation of formal history. Testimony may serve as an expression of loss and a ritual of mourning. Simultaneously, as a communicative act testimony aspires to human continuity, the establishment of justice, and the making of the future. Indeed, the very activity of testifying turns victims into survivors, witnesses into agents of change. Teaching testimony brings this transformational potential into the classroom. It stresses the power of language to recreate past experiences, foster new understanding, and enlarge the circle of witnesses.

While in the broadest sense any form of literature, biography, or history could be recognized as a form of testimony, *Teaching and Testimony* uses the term to focus on the introduction into the classroom of previously excluded voices. In Latin American studies *testimonio* has received a good deal of critical examination and come to mean specifically a longer oral narrative connected to a collective historical experience of oppression, marginalization, or struggle created by an individual who, because of her or his own circumstance, must collaborate with a second person for transcription and editing (see Beverley, Shea, Sklodowska, Sommers, and Yúdice). *I, Rigoberta Menchú* is such a testimonio. While *Teaching and Testimony* collects stories of the classroom encounter with the testimony of Rigoberta Menchú, there are, of course, many other testimonial and testimonial-like narratives that focus on the experience of oppressed or marginalized people and that are important for North American students to read and discuss. Testimonial narrative as a genre, as a form of narrative, and as a subject of classroom attention has only begun to be explored.

We should recognize that testimonials have played a role in the classroom well before *I, Rigoberta Menchú* became available in the late 1980s. Narratives of survivors of the Jewish holocaust such as those of Anne Frank, Elie Wiesel, Primo Levi, and others have led to powerful learning experiences. (In their recent book *Testimony: Crises of Witnessing In Literature, Psychoanalysis, and History* Shoshana Felman and Dori Laub [1992] focus on holocaust testimony and describe their own experiences teaching it at Yale.) Testimonial is an important narrative form for learning across the curriculum. Ethnographic testimonials such as Studs Terkel's *Working* or Oscar Lewis's *Children of Sanchez* have been used effectively by teachers in many different fields of study. African American and Native American traditions, in which testimonial-like narratives are prominent, from the slave accounts to *The Autobiography of Malcolm X* and *Monster*, from *Life Among the Piutes* to *Black Elk Speaks* and *Lakota Woman*, are increasingly recognized and taught.

Throughout this volume the contributors to *Teaching and Testimony* refer to many testimonials they are already teaching along with *I, Rigoberta Menchú*: David Blot also uses *Don't Be Afraid Gringo*, the story of an Honduran peasant woman; Teresa Longo includes *Let Me Speak*, the testimony of a Bolivian mine worker in her course; Teresa Longo and Tace Hedrick both have their students read Elena Poniatowska's *Massacre in Mexico*; Jonnie Guerra and Sharon Ahern

Fechter use Harriet Jacob's *Incidents in the Life of a Slave Girl*; Janet Varner Gunn compares Menchú's testimonial and Anne Dillard's memoir, *An American Childhood*. June Kuzmeskus and Meri-Jane Rochelson organize their teaching around testimonial narrative.

An awareness that the most disempowered can speak out and be heard gives students hope that their voice, too, might be valuable. The more informal oral language of testimonials may be closer to a student's home language than works found in standard school textbooks or anthologies. As published validations of the lives and experiences of people that might otherwise be unknown, testimonials send the message to students that all lives are important, that their own experiences may be worthy of serious attention and academic analysis. Teachers who work with testimonial find that testimonials not only bring new perspectives to the classroom but they enable students' own writing. The collective authorship of many testimonial narratives invites students to consider collaboration in writing, and the genre can offer a model for seeking out stories worth listening to and recording. Students may be stimulated to take part in the making and dissemination of testimonials themselves, a project richly explored in this volume by Meri-Jane Rochelson and David Blot. The "real world" context of testimonials gives them a vitality in the learning process, catalyzing examinations of the relationships between classrooms and "the world outside." While focusing on the testimonial of Rigoberta Menchú, *Teaching and Testimony* nonetheless breaks ground for books and articles yet to be written on the teaching possibilities of other testimonial works and testimonial narrative more generally.

While teachers are likely to find chapters in *Teaching and Testimony* that are written out of situations and settings similar to their own, one of the great strengths of this book is the opportunity it provides for us to learn from different disciplines, approaches, and pedagogical situations. *Teaching and Testimony* invites all of us to become more interdisciplinary in our own classrooms and more conscious of the overall educational system and the specific locations in which we work. Reflecting on our own disciplines and practice is a primary purpose of this book. While *Teaching and Testimony* is closely unified in its focus on the teaching of Rigoberta Menchú's particular story, it brings together teachers from a wide diversity of situations for interactive and mutually supportive learning.

As it traverses these levels and disciplines, *Teaching and Testimony* organizes thinking about pedagogy in a way that is particularly sensitive to purpose and context. Since almost all the chapters are stories of teachers and students, they are full of intriguing turns and surprises. Those few chapters that are not classroom narratives are, we feel, particularly important to the intentions of the volume and are certain to hold the reader's attention as well as provide trenchant analysis of crucial issues.

For North American students and teachers, learning about other locations can be disturbing, even threatening. This is the theme that my coeditor Stephen Benz takes up in the second chapter of the introduction. By identifying preparatory and concluding activities for readings of Menchú's testimonial, Benz indicates the need to teach carefully and reflect critically about the crossing of cultures entailed in teaching *I, Rigoberta Menchú*. This theme animates all subsequent chapters.

A starting point for teachers intending to use *I, Rigoberta Menchú* is greater knowledge about Menchú's life and the debate her work has aroused; the first section, "Controversial Figure," addresses these issues. In his chapter, "From Peasant to National Symbol" the Guatemalan novelist Arturo Arias describes Menchú's emergence as a public figure, informing us about how her testimony was transcribed and filling us in on the subsequent events that led to the Nobel Prize. While Menchú was attaining public stature in Guatemala and around the world, her testimonial simultaneously became a center of contention in America's academic "culture wars." The next chapter responds to Menchú's vilification by Dinesh D'Souza's *Illiberal Education*. By revealing political bias and the factual incorrectness in D'Souza's account, Gene Bell-Villada, professor of Spanish at Williams College, turns the tables on those that charge the academy with "political correctness."

The ensuing group of chapters enrich our understanding of the Guatemalan and Latin American context with a specific view to facilitating the teaching of *I, Rigoberta Menchú*. This section, "Teaching the Latin American Context," provides a variety of approaches to thinking about the culture, politics, literature, and language of the region. In the first chapter Mary Louise Pratt describes how she immerses her students in the social and political situation in Guatemala while simultaneously cultivating an understanding of the testimonial as both a political and personal document. Inserting Menchú's text in the humanities curriculum at Stanford was perceived by the media as an assault on the Western Canon, yet Pratt's account of the way she makes the work meaningful to her Stanford students underscores the educational value of bringing previously marginal voices to the center of attention. Pratt's chapter is followed up by another by Gene Bell-Villada, outlining his approach to appropriate Latin American background materials—particularly the film featuring Menchú, *When the Mountains Tremble*. Bell-Villada also describes how he addresses students' preconceived notions about Latin American history, indigenous cultures, and social issues such as feminism. In the third chapter of this section, "The Testimonial of Rigoberta Menchú in a Native Tradition," Luis Arata helps teachers understand specifically how Menchú's testimony expresses a continuity of Mayan beliefs and traditions. While students sometimes react negatively to the adoption of Western practices by the Quiché, Arata describes the fluidity and flexibility of Mayan thought. In essence his chapter demands that Western readers recognize the biases of their cultural frame and invites a reversal of critical gaze. The understanding of cultural difference is further complicated by William Westerman's consideration of the diametrically opposed functions of violence in different social classes in Guatemala. Bringing together the disciplines of folklife and peace studies Westerman examines the conflicting roles of military violence and community self-defense in Guatemala with his students at Villanova University. After exploring historical, cultural, and social contexts for Rigoberta Menchú's testimony the next chapter describes the possibility of reading Menchú's story against a background provided by Central American literary works. Teaching at a private high school in Nebraska Judith Peterson has formulated an interactive curriculum made up of works excluded from even the most current multicultural textbooks. An argument by Sharon Ahern Fechter for the inclusion of Rigoberta Menchú's testimony into Spanish language learning is the last chapter in this section. Fechter proposes that while the testimony can be used for traditional syntactical and grammatical study, more significant is the possibility that its incorporation into the context of second language acquisition can facilitate crosscultural understanding.

After situating Menchú's testimonial in a Spanish American context *Teaching and Testimony* explores what happens when Menchú's story and middle-class Euro-American students come together. In the classrooms described in these chapters there is a complex interplay of openness and denial, sympathy and resistance, activism and alienation. Working with small-town students in Massachusetts, June Kuzmeskus describes an inspiring high school classroom that weaves together testimonial narrative and students' writing. Becoming conscious of their own identity by examining others, Kuzmeskus's students engage in a problem-posing form of learning tied to their responsibilities as democratic citizens. Across the country in a small liberal arts college in Oregon Patricia Varas and Catherine Collins facilitate a similar process in their freshman humanities course as they utilize *I, Rigoberta Menchú* to help students understand differing world views. While both of these chapters are hopeful about the way students can learn and grow, they also hint at some of the deeper difficulties that confront us in attempting to understand the implications of a third-world story for first-world readers. In her chapter, "Having to Read a Book about Oppression" Robin Jones shares her finding that relatively privileged students at the University of Colorado don't automatically love the work. Instead their expectations for entertaining reading appear to be disappointed by a "depressing story." Distanced by Menchú's difference, Jones's students relate to the testimonial, when they can, on an intellectual rather than empathic level. Working with students at the University of Iowa, Steve Mathews explores a similar network of problems. Mathews believes that rhetoric about American multiculturalism has created barriers to understanding international exploitation and the need for international alliances. Stacey Schlau's students at a Catholic university in Pennsylvania react to Rigoberta Menchú's testimony with denial, finding it overwhelming, "too much blood and gore, too much rhetoric and politics, too much indigenous culture." By faulting the older generation of the Quiché for teaching the young about their oppressive circumstances her students blame the victims and fail to recognize Maya resistance strategies. Readers of *Teaching and Testimony* will discover that these difficulties, rather than defeating teaching, serve to engage, even energize it.

Indeed, as these teachers and others throughout *Teaching and Testimony* describe bringing together Euro-American students and Menchú's testimony, certain problematics are increasingly clarified and addressed. Teachers find that many of their students are disconnected from the testimonial's graphic descriptions of violence. Already desensitized by violence in popular entertainment, Jones speculates that her students may be unable to distinguish real from fictive suffering. Conversely Schlau and others argue that the violence described in the text is overwhelming, leaving students feeling powerless. Mathews believes that his students are conditioned to understand the representation of violence as classical tragedy—intended to release pity and fear—rather than as part of a particular historical circumstance that can and must be connected to our own. In teaching testimony at Yale Shoshana Felman found that the crisis her students experienced was productive (1992, 53); the contributors to *Teaching and Testimony* would tend to agree. As they explore representations of violence and the reactions of their students, these teachers find ways to overcome empathetic failures. Thus, rather than *I, Rigoberta Menchú* having a numbing or dehumanizing effect, over and over, the evidence collected here suggests that careful teaching of the work serves to resensitize, to have a profoundly humanizing effect on American young people.

While the presence of violence in the testimony may at first distance Euro-American readers, the issue of Christianity initially and problematically invites them in. Menchú's Christian activism seeks affiliation across boundaries of nation and culture, yet Christian students struggle over whether or not to identify their beliefs with those of Menchú, some opting to see her version of liberation theology as apostate, others recognizing it as a rediscovery of true faith. For those with an understanding of culture as a clean and neat category, or with a recognition of the nefarious role of religion in the conquest, Menchú's Christianity presents a puzzle—in the hands of a Guatemalan Indian the Bible has become a weapon in a life and death struggle for her own way of life. These complex problems of religious identification and its classroom significance continue to be explored in subsequent chapters as well (see also Hedrick, Goldrich, and Willinsky).

In marked contrast to teachers of traditional Euro-American students, the authors included in the next section, "Rigoberta Menchú and Minority/Nontraditional Students," find that their students are more readily able to identify with Menchú's story. Teaching English in a second-language classroom to Latino students from the Caribbean and Central America, David Blot finds that reading Menchú's testimony at the Bronx Community College encourages his students to value themselves and openly share about their own lives. He finds that Menchú's testimonial affirms his students' experience and empowers their writing. Working with court-mandated, minority teenagers in inner-city Minneapolis, Angela Moroukian believes that her students sympathize with Menchú because they have a personal understanding that ill treatment need not be deserved. Alienated—and excluded—from traditional schooling Moroukian's students open up when they are given choice and authority. Like the teenagers June Kuzmenkus teaches, Moroukian's students hunger for an opportunity to make an impact and to influence an adult world that seems to discount them. Many teachers in *Teaching and Testimony* discover an affirmative power in working with testimonial narrative, yet as these chapters demonstrate the effect is contextually and pedagogically sensitive, tied, in part, to the social location of the classroom.

While we need to recognize testimony as a valid form in its own right—one that like the novel entails enormous variety—the study of testimony as a genre soon engages questions of form and voice, of representation and verisimilitude, and of production and reception. Testimonial narration presents an individual who speaks for others, offering a specific version of "the truth," and, presumably, an experience or perspective that is otherwise not being heard. Since Menchú herself did not read or write at the time her testimony was recorded, she depended on Elisabeth Burgos to organize and edit her story (though as Arturo Arias points out Menchú did have a final opportunity to review the manuscript as it was read aloud to her before publication). Readers of *I, Rigoberta Menchú* depend on Ann Wright's translation from Spanish. Menchú tells us that what she experienced really happened and asserts that her personal story is representative of other native and poor Guatemalans. (Based on what all of the contributors to *Teaching and Testimony* believe—many of them experts in the region—her claims are both fully believable and well documented, but, especially in the classroom, no truth is holy; students ought to be encouraged to explore the validity of Menchú's claims.) Testimonials, like other texts, are published and circulate in particular kinds of marketplaces. When and if they enter a classroom, it is usually because they are chosen by specific teachers for certain reasons. Classrooms and curricula exist within established institutional and pedagogical frameworks. All of these factors exert an influence on the way that a testimonial, or any other text, will be understood. Moreover, the very act of identifying a text or voice as speaking from an oppressed or marginal position shapes the way readers understand its meaning. As we have seen, the readiness of the reader to attend to a testimonial influences what they bring away from it.

Thus understanding testimonial narrative may need to engage emerging critiques of anthropology and ethnography (such as James Clifford's [1986] *Writing Culture*), the postcolonial analysis of subjectivity (see Gyatri Spivak's chapter, "Can the Subaltern Speak"), the possibility of intellectual/subaltern alliances (Beverley, "From Margin to Center"), reader response, poststructuralist and deconstructionist theory, and so on. All of these approaches can help us become sharper thinkers about testimonial narrative; at the same time, I believe, theory should help us understand ourselves and the process of communication so that we become better able to hear what others are saying, to identify difference and find common ground, and to act more wisely on behalf of peace and justice.

While many of the chapters in *Teaching and Testimony* engage with the problematics of the testimonial form, the chapters in the next section, "Testimonial Constructions," make this issue central. The section begins with the wonderful "Testimonial Dictionary" produced by a collective of graduate students and their professor at the University of Wisconsin. Rather as Roland Barthes analyzes Balzac's "Sarrasine" in *S/Z* (1974), so the Wisconsin collective deconstructs their own teaching of Menchú's testimonial. They identify coded terminology and examine the power relationships inherent in testimonial creation, its classroom study, and linguistic and cultural translation. Tracing similar themes, Tace Hedrick finds that her nontraditional students in central Pennsylvania arrive in class with preconceived notions about literature that block their identification with the text. Though recognizing the defamiliarizing power of testimonial, Hedrick is intrigued by the possibilities for feminist teaching with Rigoberta Menchú; her students are able, ultimately, to connect Menchú's story to their own oppression as women. (For those interested in explicitly feminist approaches see also Schlau, Jones, and Fechter and Guerra). Clyde Moneyhun uses Menchú's testimony to teach critical thinking to his Freshman Composition students at the University of Arizona. Urging them not to accept the testimonial at face value, Moneyhun challenges them to question their initial reaction and think carefully about the creation and purposes of testimonial narrative. In the last chapter in this section Meri-Jane Rochelson describes the way she organizes an entire course around testimony and oral history. Putting into action a plan that several other contributors to *Teaching and Testimony* suggest, Rochelson has her multi-ethnic class of honors students at Florida International University work with individuals in their community to produce testimonial narratives. Conscious of some of the complex questions of voice and appropriation, Rochelson's students found themselves entering into collaborations that deeply engaged them in the activity of witnessing.

In many of the chapters in *Teaching and Testimony* Rigoberta Menchú's testimonial is linked with other related works for certain specific reasons: to facilitate students' exploration of Latin American context, of other contemporary experiences of oppression, of the expression of hitherto marginal voices, and so on. As the contributors demonstrate, establishing these kind of linkages forges interactive and engaging curricula. The chapters in the next section of *Teaching and Testimony*, "Comparative Strategies" focus directly and in inno-

vative ways on the possibilities for comparative teaching of testimony. At
Mount Vernon College, a women's university in Washington, D.C., Sharon
Fechter and Jonnie Guerra team teach an interdisciplinary course on women's
lives. In this class their students develop an extensive comparison between *I,
Rigoberta Menchú* and a nineteenth-century slave narrative by Harriet Ann
Jacobs, *Incidents in the Life of a Slave Girl*. Although Fechter and Guerra recognize significant difference between the two works and contexts, by bringing
them together they facilitate their students' learning about important issues
including the history of the testimonial form, the ongoing nature of violence
and servitude, the mistreatment and social control of women, and strategies
women have used to fight for themselves. If the texts taught with *I, Rigoberta
Menchú* tend to foreground the experience of other minority peoples, Janet
Varner Gunn's activity of comparison is particularly interesting as her students
at Hobart and William-Smith juxtapose Menchú's story with Annie Dillard's
autobiography, *An American Childhood*. This comparison allows them to consider the difference between the "autobiography of nostalgia"—which individ-
uates the narrator's past—and the collective narration and community experience that characterize testimonial. In her effort to integrate the theme of social
justice into an otherwise traditional high school curriculum in a homogeneous
suburban community in Michigan, Geraldine Rodriguez inserts several sections of *I, Rigoberta Menchú* into her course. Her students compared Menchú's
testimonial with both *To Kill A Mockingbird* and *A Connecticut Yankee in King
Arthur's Court*. Rodriquez's approach shows the power of even subtle curriculum modification, as her students not only learn about Menchú but are subsequently able to make a serious and meaningful reading of Twain's comic novel.
As with other students described in *Teaching and Testimony*, Rodriguez's high
school sophomores' encounter with Menchú's story initiates reflection on their
role in a democratic society.

The teaching of testimony not only generates self-reflection on the part of
students, it fosters it among teachers as well. An interplay between pedagogical
experimentation, personal growth, and professional commitment is thema-
tized in virtually every chapter in *Teaching and Testimony*. The last grouping of
chapters foregrounds the activity of "Reflective Teaching" and views it from a
variety of perspectives. For more than ten years Dan Goldrich has taught a
remarkably engaging large section political science class (175 students) on
Central America at the University of Oregon. The first chapter of the section
describes the way that Goldrich's course incorporates a wide variety of personal
testimony from Central America, including not only Menchú's written testimony but her speaking presence as well. Goldrich's reflection on his teaching
is tied to his efforts to address the personal and emotional impact of Central
American testimony on his own life. As with other contributors, the encounter
with testimony seems a crucial part of enriching the commitment to peace and
justice for the teacher as well as the student. The next chapter by Teresa Longo

is actually a teacher's diary written as she reflects on her students and herself as they read Rigoberta Menchú's testimony and move forward in their course on Latin American Cultural History at William and Mary College. Longo's journal indicates the spillovers in teaching Menchú's story, the ways that reading the testimonial effect student understanding of the rest of the curriculum, the possibility of weaving the issues one cares about in teaching into one's own intellectual and scholarly life. Next we have included a selection from a computer conference of my own students, aspiring secondary English teachers at Western Michigan University, as they discuss the topic of teaching *I, Rigoberta Menchú* in their future classrooms. Though these students express a variety of viewpoints, their reflections remind us both of how we evolve as teachers and of the learning that can be generated by authentic dialogue with peers and colleagues.

The final chapter in *Teaching and Testimony* pulls together a number of strands in earlier chapters. Like Edward Said, John Willinsky is interested in the way that the understanding of cultural others is shaped by the long history of European colonial domination. While Dinesh D'Souza would appear to posit an essential cultural difference between Mayan Indian and Westerner, Menchú, Willinsky argues, has a more complex vision of culture. She simultaneously defends against the anthropological—or educational—passion for appropriation (via her secrecy) and strategically utilizes transcultural forms (e.g., her Catholicism). Willinsky is concerned, as other contributors to *Teaching and Testimony*, that a facile treatment of cultural otherness may maintain a colonizing relationship rather than developing common cause in securing dignity and human rights. Thus his analysis draws on Rigoberta Menchú's testimony to reflect on a central problem for contemporary multicultural pedagogy.

Indeed *Teaching and Testimony* provides an important starting point for thinking about the multicultural movement and efforts to diversify teaching and learning. In schools and universities across the country there is a good deal of talk about multiculturalism but insufficient reflection about how to do it well. Consequently one of the crucial contributions of this book is the presentation of classroom narratives of critical and effective multicultural teaching. From these narratives there emerge three guiding principles.

First, these chapters assert that at the center of multicultural learning must be respect for the words and experience of others, expressed and interpreted as much as possible in and on their own terms. Although no testimony offers a transparent truth, these chapters stress the importance of listening to the located, present-oriented voices of real people. Such voices are seen to play a role in creating culture through a dynamic, interactive, and communicative process. Multicultural teaching must not be a form of tourism that looks only at superficialities of culture to ultimately reinforce distinctions between "us" and "them." In this sense the integration of testimony into teaching eschews canonical or folkloric repetitions of fixed "tradition" in favor of creative, conscious, constructivist, and even "postmodern" positioning within and against established social, cultural, and political boundaries. To link "teaching" and "testimony" is to call for richer, more dynamic, and more empowering forms of "cultural literacy" than are dreamed of in E. D. Hirsch's philosophy. Emerging from urgent historical circumstances testimonial knowledge is created in a collaborative act of performance and transcription that challenges orthodox cultural authority.

Second, just as a meaningful approach to cultural border crossing involves attention to the voice of others, throughout *Teaching and Testimony* it is evident that the views and experiences of students themselves must also be highly regarded. There is a persistent effort on the part of teachers in this book to meet their students where they live. In North America this may mean that teachers need to begin by challenging (imperial) cultural privileges that insulate some students from even recognizing that any vision or experience other than their own exists. For other teachers it may mean the acknowledgment of the struggles of their students and an effort to connect them to the struggles of others. Developing pedagogy from their students' perspective and becoming learners themselves in the classroom, the contributors to *Teaching and Testimony* engage in the reformulation of authority through a classroom ethic of voice and participation. What is at stake in the multicultural pedagogy put forward by *Teaching and Testimony* is the fostering of critical and engaged democratic citizens affirming the voices of others and their own.

Third, the chapters in *Teaching and Testimony* demonstrate that meaningful multicultural teaching cannot be confined by established academic disciplines or learning frameworks. The contributors have developed approaches that facilitate student understanding not only within disciplines but simultaneously across and against them. Multicultural teaching must incorporate a style of pedagogy that crosses educational boundaries, integrating historical, political, anthropological, sociological, and textual studies. Moreover, the knowledge explored through teaching testimonials is as dynamic and diverse as the contexts in which they are taught. Given their urgency and historical specificity testimonials resist canons and canonization, and they differ substantially from rarefied textbooks. The contributors to *Teaching and Testimony* offer evidence that pedagogies for multicultural study must consciously and courageously interrupt narrowly framed learning and fixed ways of knowing in an effort to empower the marginalized and change the future.

As this volume puts forward a rich tradition of teaching developed in the early 1990s, it is also relevant to ask about the future, about where we go from here. Followers of multicultural, cultural studies, and critical pedagogy approaches have so far principally directed their energies to a determined effort to democratize society through transformations of the educational system. *Teaching and Testimony* documents at the classroom level the partial success of this effort. At the same time such successes are recognized and celebrated, how-

ever, by returning once again to the voice of Rigoberta Menchú we can complicate and enrich our vision of social and educational change.

It would clearly be wrong to equate her testimonial with a narrow or traditional individual biography; *Me llamo Rigoberta Menchú y asi me nació la consciencia* (*consciencia* meaning both "conscious" and "conscience") can and
should be read as the story of an exemplary and revolutionary process of self
and community education. Menchú describes a people under harsh oppression
educating themselves outside of an internally colonizing school system as they
participate in a daily struggle to maintain their lives and identity. In *Pedagogy
of the Oppressed* Paulo Freire describes the importance for oppressed peoples
of escaping "the duality in which *to be* is *to be like*, and to be like is to be like the
oppressor" (1992, 33). The Menchú family attempts to circumvent this duality
by refusing to send their children to the national school where they would lose
their Indian culture and become "ladinoized." As a girl Rigoberta Menchú
learns about history through the daily practice of Quiché customs, through
birth ceremonies where infants are told of the suffering that the people have
experienced, and marriage ceremonies where the drinking of Coca-Cola is
examined as a threat to Quiché culture. The process of learning is organized
around the "scattered centers" of diverse communities where women and families play a central role. Rigoberta's mother travels to villages where she doesn't
speak the language, but is able to communicate with the women as she participates with them in daily tasks. When one of the government soldiers is captured, it is the women of the village who, by telling stories of their own experience, manage to reeducate him. Rigoberta's father's efforts to secure land rights
for the people of his village lead repressive authorities to imprison him, but the
prison itself—outside the control of the Guatemalan national educational system—ironically becomes a crucial place for the Quiché to learn about the
broader agenda of the resistance movement, the relationship of the peasants'
struggle for land in the countryside with the workers' struggle for rights in the
city. (Barbara Harlow has examined jails themselves as important places for
education in resistance movements.) Thus, the struggle described in *I,
Rigoberta Menchú* is not simply along ethnic divisions but involves identification in concentric circles with family, village, Guatemalan native peoples of different languages, and with the poor and working classes. The resistance to
exploitation and oppression described in the testimony necessarily involves
change through contact with the *ladino* world. Nonetheless, the Quiché incorporate Western practices strategically, making them part of the dynamic development and expression of a living Mayan culture.

In attempting to examine the significance of the Mayan experience of revolutionary educational praxis for North American students and teachers, we
should begin by recognizing that even in predominately literate, "information
age" cultures, schooling may involve an assault on home language, family life,
and culture. The remarkable educational experiences described in Rigoberta

Menchú's testimonial are not based on preset or nationally administered content standards or behavioral objectives, but emerge from home and work life. Rather than adjusting individuals to fit into already given roles and relationships (what we might call vocational or family life education), the Quiché liberation struggle transforms and democratizes the categories themselves to better serve peoples' needs. It behooves critical educators to turn attention toward transformative pedagogies that can be integrated into sites and institutions beyond school buildings as well as across the disciplines. They might want to complicate their stance on the home schooling movement. Or, for example, Menchú's testimonial might suggest that in the effort to broaden the scope of transformative teaching we not forget the jails and prisons and their relationship to maintaining the social order. With America rapidly locking up more and more minorities and the poor—rather than addressing fundamental issues of economic inequality, racism, drug dependency and violence—it becomes increasingly important to listen to and learn from those voices who speak of gaining political understanding in prison, to examine other testimonials such as those by Malcolm X, Eldridge Cleaver, George Jackson, Angela Davis, Mary Crow Dog, Leonard Peltier, Luis Rodriquez, and Kody Scott. Like her fellow enemies of the state, Rigoberta Menchú calls on us to remember the powerful and precious connection between justice and peace.

As "scattered centers" themselves of counterhegemonic pedagogy the contributors to *Teaching and Testimony* have already made significant contributions to rethinking classrooms, schools, and society. Their efforts constitute resistance to prepackaged curriculum, imposed national standards, established lists or supposedly comprehensive encyclopedias of cultural knowledge. Following Rigoberta Menchú they have challenged the artificial divisions established by national borders, resisted a totalizing global modernity, connected cultural knowledge to international economic and political systems of exploitation, and established links between their students and, in Fanon's phrase, "the wretched of the earth." The ongoing challenge, like that faced by the Guatemalan resistance movement, is to convert oppressive educational forms into liberatory ones, to integrate learning and living within and beyond the classroom, and to elaborate the strategic alliances that can create a united front for the development of more democratic forms for social, cultural, economic, and political life.

2

CULTURE SHOCK AND
I, RIGOBERTA MENCHÚ

STEPHEN BENZ

Because *I, Rigoberta Menchú: An Indian Woman in Guatemala* seems such a simple text, two problems immediately arise when the book is put on a course syllabus. First, some students dismiss Menchú's story as insignificant and/or crude, even going so far as to argue that the Guatemalan should not have been awarded a Nobel Peace Prize for simply telling her story into a tape recorder. Second, because the narrative appears to be so straightforward, unadorned, and understated, its readers tend to rely on certain assumptions about Latin Americans and Native Americans. For teachers, those assumptions may be based on experience and study, but for students more often than not the assumptions are usually derived from preconceived stereotypes—myths about the indigenous Central Americans that have been perpetuated for generations. Without careful contextual preparation, many students, relying on these misconceptions, start down a misguided path with the text, using it simply to confirm what they had already believed about "Indians." While *I, Rigoberta Menchú* is a profound and moving text that has been central to some remarkable classroom successes, it is necessary to recognize that certain problems are also inherent in its inclusion on course syllabi (I am speaking here of my experiences in a typical humanities class in a U.S. liberal arts college), problems that can easily turn the teacher's enthusiasm into a disappointing classroom experience. Teachers must be prepared to understand that without some background, some context for approaching Menchú's narrative, many students, resorting to their preconceived notions of "primitive Indians," will simply dismiss the text or greatly misunderstand it.

One purpose of this volume is to address both the successes and the problems that teachers have experienced in teaching this challenging text. In the chapters that follow, teachers from fields as diverse as political science, freshman composition, Spanish, humanities, women's studies, sociology, and education discuss not only the benefits but also the frustrations inherent in teaching Menchú's testimonial.

My own experience in dealing with these frustrations has been that *I, Rigoberta Menchú* is better taught with some preparatory activities and discussions. My literary training, heavily biased towards New Criticsim, imbued me with the attitude that texts should be approached without contexts. The author's life, the historical period to which a work belongs, and prior critical receptions are regarded, at least initially, as irrelevant. Usually, when I assign a text for a class—a novel, for example—I have students read the entire work before we discuss it or before I provide any background. The idea, of course, is for students to experience the text without all the "clutter" that might predetermine their response. But such an approach simply does not work as well with *I, Rigoberta Menchú*. This text, it would seem, requires careful preparation and some sort of strategy that will insure that students have a meaningful encounter with it.

When I was an undergraduate, I was fortunate to participate in a semester abroad program in Central America. After years of taking students to Latin America, the program's leader, Ronald Frase, had learned that the experience of visiting poor countries for the first time could prove depressing—even nightmarish—for many U.S. students. Some, overwhelmed by it all, responded by denying what they experienced—blaming the victims for their poverty, for example. Others sought to "hide out," to insulate themselves by withdrawing into whatever miniature replica of gringo life they could find or create (going to American movies, McDonald's, and the Holiday Inn, for example). Still others were virtually debilitated by the experience and found it impossible to process what they had witnessed. In an attempt to forestall this reluctance to risk learning about others and themselves, Dr. Frase built into the program "briefing" and "debriefing" sessions that prepared students for the overwhelming nature of a lengthy trip to the third world and helped them to deal with the inevitable culture shock during and after the experience. It seems to me that this same approach would prove useful with *I, Rigoberta Menchú*. So profound, so disturbing, so confusing is the encounter with her narrative, students often need some sort of briefing and debriefing before and after reading the text. Without this preparation, some students experience the classroom equivalent of culture shock and end up rejecting the significance of their encounter with Menchú's story. From my perspective, addressing this rejection is particularly important because my students attend a multicultural college in a multicultural city; if students can learn to cope with culture shock in their encounter with a text, if they can remain open to learning about others, they will perhaps have a better chance of succeeding as they begin to learn about the various cultures and peoples that they must live and work with.

BRIEFING

One thing I've learned is to allow several weeks on the syllabus for *I, Rigoberta Menchú*. A superficial classroom experience, as much as anything else, can contribute to a debilitating reaction to the book. I start by asking what students know about Guatemala or Central America in general (shockingly little) and about the Maya. Most students have had some cursory overview of ancient Maya civilization in a World History course. Mostly they remember that the Maya built pyramids and disappeared mysteriously (it seems high school textbooks have been slow to incorporate the newest information about the Maya civilization). In short, it appears that the majority of students have adopted a standardized view of the Maya, a view that comes out of colonialist rhetoric and serves the purposes of the invaders, who wish to be seen as restoring and improving a decadent civilization. To counter this received view, the first thing I want to dispel is this "Unsolved Mysteries" notion of the Maya. We discuss the chronology of Maya history and some possible explanations for the collapse of classic Maya civilization (see Stuart et al. [1993] for a basic overview of the theories). The main point is that the people who were living in Guatemala when the Spanish arrived and who are still living there today are the descendents of the ancient Maya, and the culture they practice today is substantially similar to the sophisticated culture of "classic" Maya civilization. In other words, we must dispense with the standard view that contemporary Maya culture is primitive (one of the preconceived notions that students have of indigenous peoples).

One approach is to discuss Maya art, both classic and contemporary. Borrowing from Menchú's account of Quiché ceremonies in which the whole community gathers to discuss some object (like a Coca-Cola bottle!), I have students sit in a circle and examine photos of Maya art, a painted bowl, for example, a carved stela, or a wall covered with pictographs (some fine examples are available in Schele and Freidel [1990], including my favorite, "The Maya Cosmos," an intricate painting on a tripod plate; also see the February 1995 issue of *National Geographic*). Even a brief examination of the mathematics, the writing, and the cosmogony of the Maya reveals the sophistication of the culture (Schele and Freidel also provide an excellent discussion of the Maya world view). Next, we read some of the stories in the *Popol Vuh*, particularly its account of creation (Tedlock's [1985] translation is the best and includes excellent pictures). Finally, I bring in items from contemporary Guatemala for discussion: some weavings (photos of weavings can be found in Vecchiato [1989]) and other objects of folk art (photos of Guatemalan folk art can be found in Panyella [1981]). The point of all this is to provide a tangible encounter with Guatemalan culture; after such an encounter it should be impossible to dismiss the people who produce such objects as primitive or unintelligent. And most students do appreciate the sophistication of Maya culture after this brief investigation; some, however, are puzzled by the very different world view of the Maya, and a few are openly hostile to any culture that is "pagan" and "non-Christian." To address this issue, we talk about the influence of North American missionaries on the Maya. I hand out an article about the growth of Evangelical

Protestantism in Guatemala (from Norman Lewis [1988]) and we discuss some of the cultural issues connected with this influx of missionaries.

Another activity that helps prepare students for reading *I, Rigoberta Menchú* involves examining photographs of Guatemala. I use my own slides, but with some investigation an instructor can put together a good album from published sources. The most important source in this regard is Jean Marie Simon's (1987) *Guatemala: Eternal Spring, Eternal Tyranny,* which captures both the beauty and the violence of contemporary Guatemala. Photos, particularly Simon's, help establish the veracity of Menchú's text: having seen for themselves, hostile students—or those predisposed to rejectng whatever an illiterate Indian women might say—have a harder time denying the "unbelievable" stories that Menchú recounts.

It will probably prove necessary to cover some history in the briefing sessions. The best summary of Guatemala's history from the Conquest until the early 1980s is Jim Handy's *Gift of the Devil* (1984). I like to supplement information derived from Handy with documents from different historical periods, such as the letters of Pedro de Alvarado, conquistador of Guatemala, written during his military expedition to the Guatemalan highlands in the 1500s. For more contemporary history, the teacher needs to include some information on the CIA-backed coup of 1954. Though Menchú does not refer to this event, it is the crucial historical prelude to the civil war, the military oppression, and the activism that are central to her story.

We can begin by noting that Guatemala was once a very progressive country, indeed the most progressive in the Americas. After a student-worker revolt overthrew a corrupt dictatorship in 1944, free elections brought a man named Juan José Arévalo to the presidency of Guatemala (Arévalo wrote a book called *The Shark and the Sardines,* which is worth reading—in fact it is justly famous in all of Latin America). Under Arévalo's leadership, the Guatemalan government pursued an aggressive social program that extended the privilege of education, promoted health and welfare, and—most crucially—set about to redress the inequities of land tenure. Needless to say, land owners were not pleased, especially the largest land owner of all—the United Fruit Company. In the early 1950s, Arévalo's successor, Jacobo Arbenz, continued the reforms and extended the land redistribution programs, which by this time included small takeovers of unused United Fruit property. Conveniently for United Fruit, two of its former lawyers, the Dulles brothers, now ran the U.S. State Department and the CIA. By 1954, alleging communist infiltration in Guatemala's government, the CIA launched a covert invasion that toppled the Arbenz government and put an end to the reforms. The resulting vacuum of civilian leadership left the military in control of the government—a control that they have yet to yield—and brought a cold war mentality to Guatemala's internal affairs. The country has never recovered from the CIA's tinkering. Teachers can learn more about the invasion from Schlesinger and Kinzer's (1983) *Bitter Fruit* and from

Immerman's (1982) *The CIA in Guatemala*. With a little searching, it is also possible to find some of the propaganda produced by the CIA prior to the invasion. Magazines such as *Time* and *Harper's* sent reporters to Guatemala—at United Fruit Company expense—to "see for themselves" the extent of communist influence in the country. The articles are instructive not only for their bearing on Menchú's life, but also as an illustration of the extent to which the United States media has been easily duped and manipulated by the "military-industrial complex." An overview of this history is necessary for U.S. students so that they may situate themselves in relation to Menchú's story. In other words, they need to understand that what they will be reading about is closely connected to U.S. foreign policy in the cold war period. It is crucial that students recognize the connection—more real than they initially think or are willing to admit—between their lives and the lives of indigenous Guatemalans.

DEBRIEFING

After three or four briefing sessions, we move on to the text itself. For two weeks, we discuss whatever the students select from their reading: customs, ceremonies, religion, politics, violence, and education are consistently among the most popular topics; these issues are discussed at length elsewhere in this volume.

When it comes time for the "debriefing" sessions, I again bring in objects for our discussion circle (when we come back to the circle a second time, students recognize its origin in the Quiché customs that Menchú describes). We start with another book of photos, one I bought in Guatemala while I was teaching at the national university. This book, produced for tourists, shows nothing but lovely landscapes and smiling people—an obvious contrast to Simon's photos and Menchú's testimony. I let students make what they will of the slick production. Some students are angry that such a deceptive book is even produced. Someone usually notices that the photographs have English captions and that the book is obviously directed toward foreign visitors. One student compared it to the kind of propaganda given to tourists in the Soviet Union—a bald attempt to dupe tourists and convince them that all is wonderful in Guatemala. To reinforce the point, we study some tourist brochures.[1] The slogan of these brochures—"Guatemala: Friendly and Colorful"—further disturbs students. I then point out that the brochures seem to succeed in getting their message across, since more than 125,000 U.S. tourists visit Guatemala each year, and the travel articles written for publications such as *Condé Nast Traveler* blithely ignore the political situation in Guatemala.

Continuing our circle discussion, we next examine materials produced by the United States goverment and distributed in Guatemala (these I gathered during my visits to Guatemala; teachers may also extract statements from State Department reports, which are quoted in Simon's (1987) *Guatemala: Eternal Spring, Eternal Tyranny*). One document, a briefing for embassy personnel, provides information on setting up a home in Guatemala. Personnel are informed that "Most domestic employees speak only rudimentary Spanish and are uneducated and relatively untrained. Good cooks are hard to find, and it is preferable to seek a servant who has worked for other Americans and has references. Laundresses, nursemaids, and general cleaning maids are available but inexperienced; reliable ones are becoming scarce." Such statements, read in conjunction with Menchú's chapter on working as a maid in the capital, reveal how much closer the United States citizen is to the wealthy ladino families of Guatemala than to maids such as Rigoberta; after reading the testimony, that proximity proves rather discomfiting.

Despite a teacher's best efforts, there remain students who cannot shake their deeply rooted antipathy for "those people like Rigoberta." Some will argue that she is "whining" too much. Some say that she doesn't know what she's talking about. Some say that she didn't deserve the Nobel Peace Prize. It is at this point that I introduce the phenomenon of "Rigoberta Jokes." These jokes, which have circulated among Guatemala's ladinos since the awarding of the Nobel Prize, reveal the animosity, the racism, and the sexism of those who cannot tolerate the idea of an indigenous person speaking for herself and her people. So nasty, so incriminating are the jokes, even hostile students find it difficult to align themselves with Rigoberta's detractors.[2]

To address the claims of those who feel that Menchú "didn't do anything to deserve a Nobel Prize," I give my own "testimony." I spent two years (1988–90) teaching at the Universidad de San Carlos, Guatemala's national university. During that time, Menchú's book and other printed material about her organization were unavailable on campus or anywhere in Guatemala. Regarded as subversive material, it was essentially banned in the country. Few students, most of whom were ladino, studied Maya languages; and those students who were indigenous tended to avoid appearing so, that is, they dressed like ladinos and acted like ladinos. In 1993, a few months after Menchú was awarded the Peace Prize, I went back to Guatemala for a week and was stunned by the transformation. *Me llamo Rigoberta Menchú* was available in the campus bookstore, along with another book by Menchú and the CUC, *Trenzando el futuro*. Several classes were using the books for course texts. Language courses in Quiché and other indigenous languages were filled with ladino students interested in their "roots." A newspaper had started publication in Mayan languages (one issue that I show to my classes has a picture of the Rodney King beating on the front page), and indigenous students were wearing their traditional outfits to class. These changes, I was told, were directly the result of the Peace Prize and the tremendous international reputation that Menchú had earned. Much like Martin Luther King or Nelson Mandela, she had succeeded in winning attention for the cause of her people, and her courageousness in speaking out and returning often to Guatemala for marches and protests was evidence of her strength as a leader. She had done what few people could do: thrust into the crucible, she had responded to the challenge and risen up against overwhelming forces. Based on what I have witnessed, I tell the class, I cannot accept anyone denying her accomplishments.

But since some people insist on doubting the reliability of Menchú's narrative, it may prove necessary to bring in supporting evidence. Amnesty International reports (excerpted in Simon's book) include testimonies more shocking than Menchú's. Robert Carmack's (1988) *Harvest of Violence* collects testimony and analysis by North American anthropologists who have witnessed massacres in the highlands. Victor Montejo's (1987) *Testimony: Death of a Guatemalan Village* provides another first-hand account of a massacre. There is, indeed, no shortage of supporting evidence.

Two films help provide a capstone experience to a unit on Rigoberta Menchú. The first, a documentary entitled *When the Mountains Tremble*, features Menchú herself and gives students a chance to see and hear her. The second, a feature film called *El Norte*, tells the story of two young Guatemalan immigrants to the United States. This film is especially important because it brings the Guatemalan tragedy home to our country and shows the two cultures in direct conflict, literally rather than metaphorically in our backyard. (Other films that work well in a unit on Menchú are listed in appendix 2).

The four or five weeks that this approach requires may seem like too much time to spend on *I, Rigoberta Menchú*. There are, however, serious—if unexpected—dangers that sometimes result from a superficial or curtailed treatment of the book. An occasional sidetrip into the third world can be more harmful than productive. International travel provides an analogy. In our time, tourism has become extraordinarily easy. One can now go anywhere in the world quickly, efficiently, and more or less comfortably. This ease has opened up the third world for first-world tourists, who are now to be found in what were once remote and inaccessible places. It would seem likely under these conditions that first-world travelers would learn what native and indigenous peoples are "really" like, that our knowledge and tolerance of others would increase in accordance with our ability to drop in on those "others." But, in fact, something quite different has happened. Because international tourism tends to be superficial, designed more for the comfort of the tourist than for crosscultural understanding and genuine encounter, it has in most cases reinforced stereotypes and confirmed the first-world tourists' preconceived expectations about the third world.

Guatemala provides a good example. Chichicastenango, a traditional market village in the highlands of El Quiché has in the last thirty years or so become a favorite of tourists looking for local color and bargains. Two first-class hotels have been built to cater to tourist needs. Visitors clad in bermuda shorts roam the village on market days, buying handicrafts and filming the "picturesque" market activities and religious rituals of the Quiché. But all the tourists really see is what they have been led to expect. They confirm their stereotypes of Indians: they see pagan rites, superstition, poverty, pretty costumes. After a day in town, they return to the capital or the resorts on Lake Atitlan feeling that they have experienced Quiché culture, when of course they have done nothing of the kind.

Reading *I, Rigoberta Menchú* poses similar problems. If the reader is merely a tourist, dropping in on the Quiché to confirm expectations, then the encounter has little depth to it. The student soon forgets the book, may not even finish it, and what he or she remembers is merely a very generalized notion of what Indians are "supposed to be like." Naturally, as teachers we want to be more than mere tour guides. We want the encounter to be significant for our students. But unless we prepare our students for their journey with Rigoberta and then help them come to grips with what they have learned, her story will become just another bauble bought along the way, a decontextualized souvenir, useless except as a conversation piece.

NOTES

1. Brochures are available free of charge from the Guatemala Tourist Commission, Suite 510, 299 Alhambra Circle, Coral Gables, FL.

2. The following examples typify the jokes circulating around Guatemala City in the early 1990s:

¿Por qué verdaderamente ganó Rigoberta el premio Nobel?—Porque ya es una indita muy desenvuelta. Why did Rigoberta really win the Nobel Prize? Because she's a little Indian who's very articulate/unwrapped. (A play on the word *desenvuelta*; in Guatemala, Indian women are often called *envueltas* because they wear their skirts wrapped around the body.)

Rigoberta llego al aeropuerto de Noruega para asistir la entrega del premio Nobel, y el guardia le toco la bolsa de su blusa y le dijo, ¿Qué lleva allí? Ella le dijo "Misiles.": El guardia inmediatamente llama a todos los policias, y llegan todos corriendo con sus pistolas, cuando le preguntan de nuevo, ¿Qué lleva allí? Dice Rigoberta: Mis hiles, mis tijeres, me aguje. When Rigoberta arrived at the airport in Norway for the Nobel award ceremony, the guard asked what she had in her blouse and she said "missles." He immediately called all the other guards who came running. Then they asked her again and she said, "My threads, my scissors, my needles." (Plays on Indian mispronunciation of the Spanish word for threads; suggests she is suspected everywhere of being a terrorist.)

Dicen que Mattel va a hacer una muñeca de Rigoberta, ahora que ganó el Premio Nobel. La Barbie y Ken son muy felices porque ya van a tener una sirvienta They say that Mattel is going to make a Rigoberta doll, now that she has won the Nobel Prize. Barbie and Ken are very happy because now they will have a maid.

CONTROVERSIAL FIGURE

3

FROM PEASANT
TO NATIONAL SYMBOL

ARTURO ARIAS

In this chapter we will problematize the role Rigoberta Menchú has played inside Guatemala as a political actor, and the transition of her political image in the eyes of both the Maya and ladino population. Nowadays both sectors generically perceive her—for good or ill—as a living icon who represents emblematically both Guatemalan nationalism and Mayan identity in the eyes of the outside world. However, this has not always been the case. This circumstance emerged as part of the political process that Guatemala as a whole lived during these years.

In order to analyze this process, we will trace her development as an internationally known Mayan leader in order to explore the symbolic role she played within Guatemalan society. However, in order to make this analysis comprehensible, we will first summarize the nature of oppression and resistance in this Central American nation.

Guatemala, the largest and richest country in Central America, borders the southernmost Mexican state of Chiapas on the West, the Yucatán Peninsula to the North, El Salvador and Honduras to the East, and has the Pacific Ocean to its South. Approximately the size of the states of Ohio or Tennessee, it has a population of about 10 million people, half of which are Mayan. Most Mayans live in the central and western highlands of the country, named the Sierra Madre as in neighboring Mexico. The Sierra Madre is the southern continuation of the Rocky Mountains and gives Guatemala its mountainous landscape.

The Spaniards conquered Guatemala in the early sixteenth century, burning and looting Mayan cities as well as executing its entire elite class. In one of history's first holocausts, it is estimated that as many as 2.5 million Mayans might have died in the fifty years following the Conquest. Since then, Mayans have been enslaved, oppressed, and discriminated. Independence from Spain in the early nineteenth century did not improve their lot. Mayans were forced to work against their will in the coffee plantations and treated as subhumans.

As a result of this history of exploitation, oppression, and racism, Mayans began to organize themselves in the 1960s in order to struggle for their civil and human rights. This long struggle led to the formation of an organization called the Committee for Peasant Unity (CUC in Spanish) in 1973. Vicente Menchú, Rigoberta's father and an activist of Catholic Action, was one of its founding members. Given the oppressive nature of Guatemala's military dictatorship, CUC and analogous organizations had to operate underground. Eventually, the army's systematic destruction of Mayan villages led to a widespread insurrection in the Guatemalan highlands that lasted from 1979 to 1982. The insurrection was brutally suppressed by the army with the destruction of more than 450 Mayan villages, over 100,000 deaths, and more than a million refugees. Rigoberta Menchú survived by fleeing to neighboring Mexico, and first told her story at the peak of the genocide against her people, when some experts wondered if Mayan culture would ever be able to recover from what seemed a fatal blow against it.

RIGOBERTA AND THE *POPOL VUH*

A great polemic exists to this day concerning the authorship of the *Popol Vuh*, the sacred book of the Mayan peoples. Some critics argue that it was even written by Spanish friars in order to indoctrinate recalcitrant Mayan peoples. Nevertheless, one thing stands out about its composition: After the holocaust of the Spanish conquest, when the Mayans' particular way of life had come to an abrupt and nightmarish end, there was a need to record their history, in order to register who they were, where they had come from and what they had been about as a people, in order to leave behind traces of their passage on this Earth. The sense of sorrow, the sense of possible extermination, yet the need to affirm themselves and their identity, became the dominant sources behind the writing of the *Popol Vuh*.

Following perhaps unconsciously this narrative model and motivation, Rigoberta Menchú records her story—transcribed by Elisabeth Burgos-Debray—when, once again, Mayans have just suffered a new holocaust, are contemplating the possibility of extinction, and feel a need to justify who they are, what their actions were about, and why they chose the path they did.

The *Popol Vuh* tells how people were created from a mix of yellow and white corn, which explains why agriculture has a sacred character. Corn, the center of belief, is a sign of group identity—that which defines it as an ethnic identity and a cultural universe. Corn has a "mythic" value, not a commercial one. "Corn" is also an emblem for the totality of the Mayan community. Individual kernels of corn are of no consequence as such. In analogous fashion, Rigoberta Menchú does not see herself as an individual in the traditional modern Western sense, but as an emblem, an icon of her community. She, too, is "corn," rather than an individualized kernel without mythic value. This apparently simple explanation helps explain the sense that Rigoberta Menchú has of telling not her personal story, but the story of her people.

When the traditional system is destroyed by the Highlands insurrection of 1979–82, a new aesthetics of identity becomes necessary. Therefore, Rigoberta Menchú visualizes herself as a shamanistic storyteller explaining the Maya world: their nature, their costumes, their beliefs. In so doing, it will also explain and justify the political path that led to armed insurrection in the Guatemalan highlands.

RIGOBERTA THE UNKNOWN

When Rigoberta Menchú was forced to flee Guatemala and was exiled to Mexico City, she was virtually unknown in her own country or even among the majority of the Mayan peoples. Nationally, the name of Vicente Menchú—her father—had gained symbolic notoriety after the destruction of the Spanish Embassy by the Guatemalan army on 31 January 1980, where Menchú and twenty-seven others protesting human-rights violations in the Ixil area of the country were burned to death by the Guatemalan army along with the ambassadorial staff. A year later, an organization called "'Vicente Menchú' Christian Revolutionaries" was created. It soon became part of the 31 January Popular Front, an umbrella group that included the Committee for Peasant Unity (CUC) of which Vicente Menchú had been a founder, labor groups, and other popular organizations representing different segments of Guatemalan society. However, starting in the summer of 1981, most of these organizations were crushed in an urban military offensive whose purpose was to destroy what the military government considered the rearguard of a revolutionary movement and its safe-houses in the city. By the end of 1983 there was no trace left of the 31 January Popular Front, and of the organizations that composed it the only one that survives to this day is the CUC.

Rigoberta Menchú's public recognition as of the end of 1981 was that of being the daughter of a well-known Mayan grassroots activist and a martyr of the Spanish Embassy. This knowledge, however, was limited to the members of the opposition movement to the government. Vicente Menchú himself had not been a national public figure, and for mainstream Guatemalans he was simply "another Indian" burned to death in the Spanish embassy tragedy. Rigoberta Menchú was herself a member of the CUC and worked on its behalf in Mexico City. In its desire to gain international recognition, the Guatemalan opposition to the military dictatorship launched a media campaign during the course of 1981 in which various representatives of different organizations now residing in Mexico toured both the United States and Europe in order to alert the world to the ruthlessness and viciousness of the Guatemalan army.

It was during this tour that Rigoberta Menchú began to be noticed as a particularly articulate spokesperson for the movement. Arturo Taracena, the Guatemalan representative of the movement in France, noticed her capabilities and encouraged Elisabeth Burgos's interest in exploring further the nature of Mayan society and what was befalling them as a result of the army's policies. As a result, he arranged for a meeting between Rigoberta Menchú and Elisabeth Burgos. As Alice Brittin indicates, both actors had to be pushed into the project.[1] Rigoberta Menchú was not fully conscious of the importance of producing such a testimonial but was urged to do so by both Taracena and the leadership of the CUC. On the other hand, Burgos had no expertise on Guatemala but she was an ethnologist very well connected to publishing houses through her ex-husband Régis Debray. Eventually the decision to tape Rigoberta Menchú's story was made, a process that proceeded during the first weeks of 1982 at Burgos's house.

Subsequently, Burgos and Taracena in Paris, as well as members of CUC's leadership in Mexico, including Menchú herself, were responsible for editing the book. Rigoberta Menchú has told Alice Brittin that at the time reading Spanish for her was still difficult, so that other people had to read to her virtually the entire manuscript. Both she and the others deleted "things that spilled out of my mouth and it was necessary to take them out."[2] Brittin (1993) goes on to observe that

> The intervention of Solidarity organizations, Arturo Taracena and the CUC in the compilation of *Me llamo Rigoberta Menchú* confirms the obvious political bias of this testimonio and explains, in part, the politically charged level of discourse prevalent throughout the text. . . . However, as Rigoberta admits, what most inspired her to make public her story was the opportunity to share the "memory" of her life in hopes that it would not be forgotten like so many others. (15)

The edited manuscript was presented by Burgos to the Casa de las Américas Contest, where it won the award as best testimonial narrative for 1983. That award marked the beginning of Rigoberta Menchú's international notoriety, yet she still remained basically unknown in her country of origin. For that to change, the gradual opening in Guatemalan politics that began in 1986 would be necessary.

RIGOBERTA'S SLOW ENTRANCE INTO GUATEMALAN CONSCIOUSNESS

The small political opening that began in Guatemala in 1986 allowed for the first time a freer circulation of Rigoberta Menchú's book within the country.[3] The opening also enabled many members of the democratic left who were not linked directly to armed struggle to return to the country and begin to participate in its political affairs. Most of those who returned at this time from within this sector were "ladino," non-Mayan Guatemalans. However, they had lived in Mexico for close to seven years and their ethnic consciousness had been raised during the hard years in exile where most of them personally met Rigoberta Menchú, as well as other Mayan leaders such as Pablo Ceto, Antonio Calel, Francisca Alvarez, or Domingo Hernández Ixcoy.[4]

In many instances, these political activists were the first ones to start speaking publicly about Rigoberta Menchú herself as well as of Mayan rights, and began to open up a debate inside the country that had remained bottled up during the years of the insurrection in the highlands. Sensitized to some degree to the more open attitude toward native peoples that existed within progressive circles in Mexico City as well as in the United States and Europe, many of these activists were appalled to hear the distinctive language still used in Guatemala to address Mayans. It was, even to someone only partially sensitized, a grossly discriminatory, racist, and offensive language which connoted quite explicitly the semifeudal mentality that was very much dominant among the great majority of ladinos of all walks of life and which institutionalized racism to a level seldom seen in contemporary times except in other clearly biased societies such as South Africa.

It was this gross bias and outright racism that concerned many of the returnees, and led to a rise in all kinds of public activities around the problematics of ethnicity. Many of the returnees formed new Non-Governmental Organizations (NGOs) or else grouped themselves in centers for social research, and out of these new institutions they began a vigorous campaign to air in public the issues of ethnicity and racism. For the most part, in those years (1986–90) these issues came linked to both human rights issues and broader political issues such as democratization, the opening of the political system, and peace negotiations with the insurgents. Yet, the issue of ethnicity was dealt with in specific terms within that larger framework.[5]

Coinciding with those concerns was the interest that international anthropologists and social scientists had in the ethnic issue. Furthermore, the gradual return to the country of Mayan cadres who had done university work in the United States and Europe during the years of the conflict contributed to a broadening awareness of ethnic issues (García-Ruiz 1992).

In the first case, many anthropologists were concerned with the areas where they had done field work in the 1970s and with the fate of some of their informers. During the insurrectional years many of them formed part of a loose network called Guatemalan Scholars Network (GSN) and regularly presented papers dealing with Mayan issues and concerns at meetings such as the American Anthropology Association (AAA) and the Latin American Studies Association (LASA). In these forums, they met the Mayan leaders in exile, including Rigoberta Menchú, whose book most of them had read as soon as it came out since the solidarity network in both the United States and Europe made sure that it came to their attention. They themselves returned to the country as soon as it became viable and went back to their field work with a more politicized consciousness. As such, they themselves became channels for communication between the outside world and the Mayan communities, and in many cases they informed the communities about Rigoberta Menchú's book and her own rising international fame (Carmack 1988).

On the other hand, Mayan scholars who had spent the insurrectional years abroad were for the most part "etnicistas";[6] that is, they opposed the alliance between Mayans and poor ladinos under the mainly ladino leadership of Guatemala's revolutionary organizations, favored a more separatist agenda for the Mayan peoples and, in many instances, had class differences with the majority of Mayans that had joined either CUC or revolutionary organizations. For the most part, they were themselves members of the Mayan elite and had a visceral dislike for many of the Marxist ideas espoused by more revolutionary Mayans. Nonetheless, these Mayans were highly educated, had Ph.D.s in some instances, were well connected with funding sources and academic centers in both the United States or Europe, and were also determined to open up spaces for their own agendas within Guatemalan society. For this group, Rigoberta Menchú was not a natural ally, given her own class origins, her membership in the CUC, and her alleged links with the Guerrilla Army of the Poor (EGP). Yet this same sector recognized the symbolic status that Rigoberta Menchú had achieved internationally and felt that, despite their own personal distaste, she could very well become a useful icon for articulating Mayan demands in opposition to ladino society within the recently opening constitutional spaces.[7]

Finally, the revolutionary organizations themselves, grouped around the Guatemalan National Revolutionary Unity (URNG) championed her cause as a means of validating their own agenda and demands at a time when they had suffered major military setbacks and were being hardpressed to negotiate with the Guatemalan military from a position of weakness. Therefore, their own clandestine agents inside Guatemala exalted the figure of Rigoberta Menchú in order to further awareness of their own demands within certain sectors of Guatemalan society. From abroad, Menchú herself encouraged these activities.

As a result, by 1986 there was a confluence of factors not the least of which was Menchú's energy, intelligence, and dedication, which all contributed to make known the name of Rigoberta Menchú within Guatemala.

RIGOBERTA FINALLY RETURNS TO GUATEMALA

After her name had begun to spread and conditions in the country were deemed safe enough, Rigoberta Menchú ventured back into Guatemala. At that point, it was the military that possibly had the greatest hand in transforming Rigoberta Menchú, still a relatively obscure figure for the majority of Guatemalans inside the country, though already well known by both left- and right-wing political sectors (the so-called political class), into a nationally known heroine.

In an attempt to prove to the world that Guatemala was now a democracy, President Vinicio Cerezo had been courting exiled leaders and personalities to return to the country. The son of President Cerezo personally invited Rigoberta Menchú to return to the country in 1986. Then, in March of 1988, the Guatemalan Ambassador in Switzerland, José Luis Chea, invited the RUOG delegation attending the U.N. Geneva meetings that spring to return to their country.

RUOG was a civilian, international diplomatic branch whose acronym stood for Unitary Representation of the Guatemalan Opposition. It was founded by prominent Guatemalans in exile at the height of the massacres committed against the Mayan population and mainly operated out of New York City. It had been in existence since 1982 and its primary function was United Nations lobbying work. Rigoberta Menchú had been invited to be part of RUOG from its inception and as their representative had participated every year at the spring meetings in Geneva, Switzerland, where the U.N. Sub-Committee for Ethnic Issues met.

Rigoberta Menchú flew into Guatemala on 18 April 1988 as part of a RUOG delegation that included three other prominent figures from exile.[8] Given the nature of the Guatemalan military as well as the fact that all members of RUOG were accused of being members of the revolutionary armed opposition, the URNG, an international delegation was formed to escort RUOG, thus offering some degree of protection to its members. Included in the delegation were members of the European Parliament, German Congress, Mexican Parliament, the Catholic Church, and human rights organizations. The delegation also included aides of several U.S. Congressmen. The purpose of the trip was to meet with Guatemala's National Reconciliation Commission and in the words of Rigoberta Menchú, "to observe if indeed there is a political opening in the country."[9]

Divided by contradictions between its diplomatic efforts and an internal hardline policy still dictated by its military, the Guatemalan government accused the members of this delegation of being subversives. They were required to apply for political amnesty or would be subject to arrest or denied entry to the country. No one complied with this dictate.

The day of their scheduled arrival, the Guatemalan government sealed off the airport and surrounded it with hundreds of armed security forces. Local press trying to enter the airport grounds to cover the event were attacked by secret service agents who destroyed their equipment.[10] As a result, some 200 people who had assembled to welcome RUOG members were not able to get inside the airport. However, the attitude of the security forces so outraged the press and media that it turned the event into a front-page news item where all members of the delegation were uniformly portrayed in a positive light.

Shortly after their arrival at La Aurora airport on a Mexicana flight originating from Costa Rica, Rigoberta Menchú and Dr. Rolando Castillo Montalvo were seized by government agents, arrested, and charged with "attacks against the internal security of the state."

Their arrest lasted only a few hours and turned into a carnivalesque fiasco that further undermined the credibility of the government and created an instant national reputation for Rigoberta Menchú. They were taken to the Supreme Court building in the Civic Center, followed by a parade of sympathizers and well wishers trailing the grotesque display of police force. Once inside the Supreme Court, after some bureaucratic maneuvering, Judge Oscar Sagastume declared that he was releasing Menchú and Montalvo for "lack of proof."[11]

While the ordeal lasted, thousands of university students and members of the Mutual Support Group (GAM, a group that organizes the relatives of those who have "disappeared") marched through the streets of Guatemala City to the Supreme Court, carrying banners and singing. After Rigoberta Menchú and Castillo Montalvo were released, they were hailed as heroes (right in the middle of the Civic Center) and then followed by the demonstrators to El Dorado Hotel where the RUOG delegation and the international observers were staying. There an informal meeting took place.

The arrest and subsequent release of the RUOG members made front-page news in the Guatemalan press for several consecutive days, provoking a nationwide debate. The spectacular show of force at the airport, followed by the complete backdown of the government, was widely depicted as an embarrassment for the government. Simultaneously, and for the first time, Rigoberta Menchú's face appeared not only in all newspapers, but on television as well. Her name became for the first time a household name among average Guatemalans, and copies of her book began to circulate more freely from hand to hand. After this event, Rigoberta Menchú remained constantly in the public eye and in the center of Guatemala's national consciousness.

THE PATH TOWARD THE NOBEL

Three weeks after the incidents described in the previous section, a coup attempt took place in Guatemala. Among the elements cited by the coup plotters as triggering their intentions was the government's capitulation to the RUOG delegation. In political terms, the failed coup attempt had consequences for the democratic opening in the country. For Rigoberta Menchú, however, the coup created an opening to assert the agenda of the CUC and the resistance movement. To ordinary Guatemalans, the fact that her presence in the country was perceived by the hard-line sector of the army as threatening enough for a coup attempt gave her a measure of authority. From that moment on, Rigoberta Menchú remained prominent in the pages of local newspapers as well as on television screens. If anything, these events established a context to recognize her as a symbol of broader oppression and resistance. Her dignity in confronting Judge Sagastume demonstrated her moral fiber, which impressed many Guatemalans, including progressive and middle-of-the-road ladino sectors that would otherwise behave, unconsciously, in racist ways.

From this moment on, the terms of the national discourse began to change. Rigoberta Menchú stopped being a *revolutionary* (a word that carried a positive connotation for the Guatemalan progressive sector) or a *subversive* (a word that carried a negative connotation for the Guatemalan right) and became a symbolic representation of the aggrieved, the bereft, the orphaned, those who had put their life on the line and had lost everything except their dignity and their will to continue the struggle. For progressive ladinos she became a symbol of democracy and freedom of expression. Rigoberta Menchú united peoples of the Guatemalan racial divide on this issue, as well as different social sectors within both ethnic groups. Rigoberta Menchú had become a living icon capable of playing a significant role in an effort to create a meaningful democracy in Guatemala. By 1990, many progressive ladinos were finally buying and reading Rigoberta Menchú's book, though the text never became a bestseller outside the university campuses.[12]

This "new look" was already evident in Rigoberta Menchú's next major visit to the country, the second week of October 1991, to celebrate the Second Continental Meeting that commemorated 500 years of indigenous popular resistance.[13]

As the first international forum of representatives from indigenous and popular movement groups from throughout the hemisphere, the conference was a historic achievement. It was held at the fairgrounds just outside Quezaltenango, Guatemala's second-largest city and the largest urban center in the northwestern highlands. Given the international context of the event, the Serrano government did not interfere with its developments and even tried to gain diplomatic credibility by presenting an image of welcome and tranquility. Indigenous groups took advantage of this stance to make it the most public display ever of their cause within Guatemala's borders. Michael Willis (1991) described its public impact as follows:

> After an inaugural event and press conference at the Ritz Hotel in Guatemala City, the delegates and guests left for Xela (Quezaltenango) in a caravan of vehicles which were decorated with streamers and banners. Each bus was a moving billboard that stated demands of indigenous Guatemalans such as "Stop the displacement of Indians from our lands of origin."
>
> The buses with their colorful decorations grabbed attention as they passed pedestrians and vehicles. Yet, people were cautious about their signs of support. Waving and applause came only in areas where

little traffic was passing. On the highway to Xela and in town the visible presence of military or other security forces was minimal.[14]

In that context, all Guatemalan indigenous organizations participated in huge numbers alongside international delegations. It was the first time that groups of a broad ideological range, from "indigenistas" to neo-Marxists closely allied to the URNG, participated jointly in an indigenous event.[15] On 12 October, Majawil Q'ij organized a march as the closing event of the conference.[16] More than 25,000 people joined the march. It became one of the largest indigenous marches in Guatemalan history. It was also Rigoberta Menchú's first march in Guatemalan territory since 1980 and the very first in which the respect and affection of the masses of Mayan peoples for Rigoberta Menchú became palpably evident. Michael Willis describes it as follows:

> For the people of Guatemala, the return of exiled indigenous leader Rigoberta Menchú was a highlight of the week. Two previous attempts to return for visits, in 1988 and 1989, had been cut short by government intervention and death threats. This visit was Rigoberta Menchú's triumphal return. Throughout the week she was accompanied by Danielle Mitterrand, the wife of the president of France, and an entourage of reporters. Guatemalan press accounts of the conference featured photographs of Menchú. All the news media carried interviews with her in which she spoke candidly about the impunity of human rights violators in Guatemala, the negotiations between the government and guerrillas, and the demands of indigenous peoples in Guatemala and the Americas. The evening after the October 12 march, Guatemalan television carried a 15-minute interview with her. Over Menchú's voice the camera showed the thousands of Mayans marching through the streets of Xela and under the shadow of the volcano on the way to the fairground.[17]

As the article by Willis goes on to mention, throughout the march indigenous women brought their small children to Rigoberta Menchú to receive her blessing. That gesture, more than anything, signified the degree of recognition that Rigoberta Menchú had finally achieved among her own people and the fact that she was finally being seen as an icon, as a symbolic representative of all Mayan peoples over political or ideological differences. This perception was later confirmed by another well-known Mayan leader, Gloria Tujab.[18] At this stage, Rigoberta Menchú had achieved such a degree of recognition that even groups that opposed her particular position on ethnic issues felt compelled to support her when the Continental Campaign announced that she was being nominated for the Nobel Peace Prize. Moreover, her political clout was manifested when even ladino politicians went out of their way to get their pictures taken with the person they themselves had reviled as a "subversive."

THE NOBEL PEACE PRIZE AWARDED TO RIGOBERTA

When Rigoberta Menchú returned to Guatemala in July 1992, she was already an official Nobel Peace Prize candidate and a well-established national celebrity. The moment she arrived at Guatemala City's Aurora International Airport she was greeted by cheers and applause from hundreds of Guatemalans who had crowded the airport awaiting her arrival. Susan Poff, who accompanied Rigoberta Menchú on this trip, described the scene: "Members of the press besieged her in their eagerness to speak with her. Outside the airport, a large crowd waited to welcome her; people pressed in on all sides to exchange a few words, give her flowers or shake her hand."[19]

Her public reception during this trip indicated that a symbolic mantle now covered Rigoberta Menchú. Her growing international recognition gave her the power to publicly articulate critical perspectives on the rights of the indigenous population, the continuing violation of human rights in the country, the lack of social or economic justice, and the need for a new consciousness to confront the nation's crises, without being harmed or silenced and while being treated as an honored dignitary for verbalizing such views.

Rigoberta Menchú used this power—both the symbolic and the real—as a means not only of redesigning her own identity so as to appear more and more the Mayan leader as opposed to the "radical, leftist" popular one that had mainly defined her identity of ten years before, but also as a means of redefining the indigenous movement as a whole. As Susanne Jonas points out:

> This issue—a continuing discussion of "new ways of being Indian"— takes on added significance in the context of the 1992 "500th Anniversary" of the Spanish Conquest. . . . In the words of CUC activist Rigoberta Menchú, 1992 could be the occasion for a genuine encounter among all of the cultures of Latin America (certainly Guatemala), "a moment of self-discovery, in which we all listen to each other." (1991, 239)

Rigoberta Menchú had become a de facto spokesperson for all Mayan peoples because she could speak out and utter a discourse in which most Mayans recognized themselves, yet could not express for fear of reprisals. In such a role, she could unify the Mayan peoples, whose positions about what needed to be done to further their own cause remained plural and contradictory. In voicing their support for her Nobel candidacy, representatives of different Mayan groups declared: "Her voice is the symbol of the struggle of our Mayan people of Guatemala for peace and development. . . . Her work has shown the way to

restoring the dignity of our peoples and the remembrance of our history. . . .
Rigoberta Menchú's struggle is an expression of the resistance of all Mayans,
and is a contribution to the construction of a new society in which neither Mayans nor any other peoples will be marginalized or neglected."[20]

At this point in time, only extreme right elements dared attack her, accusing her of "living a life of luxury with intellectual Marxist Europeans" or of
"being utilized by all those señores who hate Guatemala and have harmed her
so much."[21] However, on the whole, the tide had changed even among mainstream ladinos in expressing pride in the international achievement of a com-
patriot.

Rigoberta Menchú left the country on 16 July after a meeting with various
indigenous organizations in Chimaltenango organized by Rosalina Tuyuc of
CONAVIGUA (the National Coordination of Widows),[22] promising to return
for the celebration of the 500th year of indigenous resistance to Western occupation of the Americas. This date would mark the beginning of the commemoration of the International Year of Indigenous Peoples.

As a result, Rigoberta Menchú was in Guatemala when the announcement
of her being awarded the Nobel Peace Prize was made on 15 October 1992.
When the news of her victory hit the airwaves, the bells of all the Catholic
churches in the Highlands began to ring, as well as those of the popular neighborhoods in Guatemala City. A demonstration took place the next day in Guatemala City to celebrate her victory.

The government responded with equanimity in public and President Serrano even praised her and sent his congratulations. However, it was privately
shocked by the political implications of the award as it had never believed that
a Guatemalan indigenous woman could actually win such a coveted prize. They
were not prepared for such a turn of events.[23] Only the Foreign Affairs Minister,
Gonzalo Menéndez Park, was undiplomatic enough to verbalize what many
inside the government felt in private: that the prize was undeserved because
Rigoberta Menchú was a subversive element. Menéndez's remarks so infuriated
public opinion however, swollen by nationalist and patriotic pride, that he was
forced to resign within a short period.

Rigoberta Menchú's award singlehandedly changed the configuration of
Guatemalan politics. If repressive elements of the apparatus of state were winning the upper hand up until the Nobel Peace Prize announcement, from that
point on momentum began to build in favor of progressive and popular forces.
Other factors, such as Helen Mack's winning the Right Livelihood Award—the
alternative Nobel Prize—at about the same time for her struggle to bring to justice her sister's assassins, and Serrano's own missteps, would contribute to this
momentum. However, the turning point was without question Rigoberta
Menchú's Nobel Prize victory, and it was read as such by the great majority of
Guatemalans who now unquestioningly recognized her as a national leader and
the Mayan peoples' most charismatic leader. As Susan Berger points out:

Political configurations were also shaken by the recent awarding of the Nobel Peace Prize to Rigoberta Menchú Tum. While some members of the government were quick to congratulate Menchú, others were obviously frightened by the significance of the event. For the first time, indigenous Guatemalans—more than 55 percent of the population—had an internationally respected leader who could use her prominence to fight for political recognition for the indigenous majority. Indicative of the seriousness of this challenge, after Menchú's award, political violence against popular sectors increased in the form of threats against union and human rights activists, as well as disappearances and assassinations.[24]

Because of this, the ladino "political class" (professional political sector) virtually ignored the Nobel ceremony, excepting the National Unity of the Center (UCN) that published a newspaper ad congratulating Rigoberta Menchú for her award. Whereas President Serrano's comments were muted, he did add that "Guatemalans were sick and tired of being accused of violating human rights."[25]

RIGOBERTA IN THE MIDST OF THE SERRANO CRISIS

After the Nobel Prize ceremonies in Oslo, Norway, Rigoberta Menchú settled back in Mexico City. However, she wanted to get the Vicente Menchú Foundation off the ground as soon as possible, and to capitalize on the aura of the award by forging ahead with Mayan unity. First, she lead a powerful display of power: a world council of native peoples against racism. This World Summit of Native Peoples took place between 24 May and 28 May in Chimaltenango. The idea was to come up with a manifesto that would be then presented to the United Nations in order to declare not only a year but an entire decade in commemoration of indigenous peoples.[26] Other demands included a U.N. High Commissioner for Indigenous Peoples and a Universal Declaration of Indigenous Rights.[27]

However, the World Summit, which proceeded without any incidents, was clearly overshadowed by President Serrano's self-generated coup launched in the early morning hours of 25 May. Rigoberta Menchú stayed in Chimaltenango until the end of the Summit, but upon its closure she headed immediately for Guatemala City. Once in the capital, she immediately led the popular sectors in their public demands for a return to a constitutional regime. She also led marches through the streets of the capital against censorship, against the coup.[28]

Rigoberta Menchú and other members of the popular sectors had at first demanded the resignation of the entire Congress and the creation of a new Constituent Assembly that would write a new constitution for the country.[29]

However, when it became evident that their demands could not carry the day, they joined other sectors of Guatemalan society in signing the petition that called for the resignation of the president and vice president, of the Executive Committee of Congress, and the arrest and prosecution of corrupt officials.[30]

Recognized as both a popular and a Mayan leader, she was also invited to join the ad hoc commission that grouped sectors from all walks of Guatemalan society, including for the first time members of Guatemala's elite who ran the Chamber of Industry and Commerce (CACIF).[31] Susan Berger (1993) observes that "In fact, even Rigoberta Menchú was asked to participate in the negotiations, though she ultimately walked out, claiming that representatives were not interested in her real participation but hoped to use her presence to legitimize the process."[32]

However, something followed which was unprecedented in Guatemala. After walking out from any compromise that might allow President Serrano to save face, Rigoberta Menchú and other popular sectors actually collaborated, however guardedly, with members of CACIF if not with the political class. The ad hoc commission that brought them together was labeled the National Instance for Consensus (INC). It was this body that eventually selected for Congress the candidates who would replace Jorge Serrano as president: Arturo Herbruger, president of the Supreme Electoral Court (TSE) and Ramiro de León Carpio, Human Rights Ombudsman, who was eventually chosen by Congress on the evening of 5 June.

Rigoberta Menchú had, as a result, a voice and a vote in selecting the man who would run the affairs of the nation and attempt to settle the constitutional crisis. This crisis marked the first time Rigoberta Menchú had actually exercised a national leadership role within Guatemala's borders, and it earned her the recognition of all sectors of Guatemalan society including CACIF, which had labeled her a "subversive element" only months before. No one could deny Rigoberta Menchú's cleverness or political ability at this point.

In fact, on 4 June, when INC was meeting to propose to Congress a successor to President Serrano after the latter had resigned and his vice president, Gustavo Espina, had been prevented from illegally taking office, it was Dionisio Gutiérrez, a businessman and a member of CACIF, who threw into the pool the name of Rigoberta Menchú.[33] His proposal was not entirely wholehearted, and it was a way of paying her a backhanded compliment for having joined them the previous day in signing the compromise petition. However, the enormity of actually having a member of CACIF propose her for president of the Republic, even if only as a symbolic gesture, cannot be overlooked. Rigoberta Menchú had indeed become a living icon representing emblematically both Guatemalan nationalism and Mayan identity in the eyes of her compatriots. At the grassroots level, the cry of excitement was even more audible. Various enthusiastic supporters confirmed both publicly and privately that "Rigoberta es presidenciable" (Rigoberta is presidential timber).

QUO VADIS RIGOBERTA?

It is evident in tracing the political development of Rigoberta Menchú as a Guatemalan leader that a new, indigenous opposition is emerging in Guatemala that is increasingly using its political clout in order to press for its own particular demands. The Highlands insurrection of 1979–82 paved the way for both Vicente and Rigoberta Menchú and probably neither of them would have emerged as leaders without it. Nonetheless, Rigoberta Menchú's role as a living icon and a spokesperson for all Mayan peoples has succeeded where the Highlands insurrection did not: it has given a voice within the nation to the Mayans; it has given new hope, new means of political enfranchisement, and a new pride. All of this has facilitated the merging of disparate Mayan groups within one unified political identity and has brought them into a new political coalition.

The emerging Mayan coalition represents an interesting historical convergence. Some of these groups have emerged as autonomous nationalist movements divorced from the revolutionary process. Others have emerged in the shadows of the URNG and have often been accused of being part of its base of support. Yet they all share in common the platform of seeking a distinct Mayan identity, a "new way of being indigenous" that they all associate with the achievements of Rigoberta Menchú. All these movements trail in her wake, bask in her achievements, and recognize her as their de facto leader even though she holds no political positions independent of the National Directorate of the CUC. Each of these groups is working in its own way to expand the existing political space by attacking the most repressive institutions of the Guatemalan army.

As Victor Perera points out,[34] the new Mayan opposition made its influence felt in the low turnout for a referendum called by President de León Carpio on 30 January 1994. The Mayans called for nonparticipation because the referendum did not address issues embodied in Mayan demands: the abolition of civil-defense patrols; the end of forced military recruitment; the appointment of an independent truth commission to investigate human-rights violations and agrarian reform and other economic incentives for Guatemala's indigenous majority. Only 18 percent of eligible voters turned out to vote on the referendum.

It is a fact, therefore, that Rigoberta Menchú is already playing a significant political role within Guatemala's borders. She has always understood that her power is not personal nor individualistic but collective and symbolic. It comes from what she represents for Guatemalans: the embodiment of an otherworldly, ethical, and moral authority in her quest for the redemption of her peoples and the continuation of the cause initiated by her father. It also comes from her personal ability to understand that the only way now left for Guatemalan peoples as a whole is to seek each other and deepen, despite all its contradictions and stumbling blocks, the democratic path in the process of pressuring from below a racist state apparatus and political class that will only be dismantled gradually.

In her development from international symbol of oppression and racism in the eighties to concrete political actor within Guatemala's own borders in the nineties, Rigoberta Menchú has succeeded in recasting a new identity over the ruins and fragments of other times, identities, and spaces.[35] Rigoberta Menchú's memory was transposed onto the testimonial narrative as a strategy of resistance and this project has succeeded in recasting her as a public figure, in inserting her within Guatemala's national historical continuum. This is where she finds herself now. Mayan resistance is alive and has been revitalized with Rigoberta Menchú's experience. She has undergone a transition in which she emerged from the peripheral silence to which all Mayans are condemned by virtue of racism, and has become a national leader and internationally recognized personality. This transition gives her the power to reclaim Mayan identity as a tool to restructure both Mayan society and the nation as a whole. As Antonella Fabri affirms, "a new speaking subject is engendered as a gendered, ethnic and subordinated body that can function as a civilian of the new society."[36] Menchú's book is a different system of knowledge from the one traditionally imposed by Guatemala's ruling elite. For symbolic and ethical reasons, the majority of Guatemalans now identify themselves with the system of knowledge articulated by her discourse, rather than with the one articulated by its national elites. As a result, Rigoberta Menchú's voice marks the coming of a new epoch in which Mayans and other marginalized Guatemalans repossess the conscience of past traumas in order to forge ahead with a new dynamism and new strategies of action.

It only remains to be seen how much farther she can go, in her compelling and urgent quest to alter forever the Guatemalan political and ethnic landscape, as the country emerges from the debris of civil war and the ashes of personal pain and suffering. It remains to be seen how well she can keep up the acrobatic act of being simultaneously a messianic leader and a practical politician forced to compromise and develop a knack for everyday political pragmatism. Through her commitment and integrity Rigoberta Menchú has emerged as a national leader, and the great majority of Guatemalan peoples have begun to follow her and can actually visualize the ultimate revelation: a Mayan woman at the helm of the nation.

NOTES

1. Alice Brittin. "Close Encounters of the Third World Kind: Rigoberta Menchú and Elisabeth Burgos's *Me llamo Rigoberta Menchú* (1993, unpublished, 10).

2. Ibid., 11–12.

3. It must be noted that Rigoberta's book was sold only in a couple of bookstores in the country, and in very limited quantities. Most of the copies that circulated prior to the Nobel Prize were passed around hand to hand and were read almost exclusively by the political class.

4. All these Mayans had been founders or leaders of CUC and had been members of the Guatemalan Patriotic Unity Committee (CGUP) formed in Mexico in 1982. This committee, modeled along the lines of El Salvador's FDR, included many ladino personalities among its members.

5. Personal testimony of Luis Alberto Padilla. Padilla had been president of the Guatemalan Commission for Human Rights in Mexico during his exile in that country. Upon his return, he founded the Guatemalan Association for the United Nations (AGNU). Under this mantle was created the Institute for International Relations and Peace Research. This institute organized the first conference ever held on Ethnic Issues inside Guatemala in August 1988.

6. As an organized movement, this position had not been significant prior to 1982. However, the segregationist and separatist ideas of indigenous struggle, achieved the mobilization of some sectors, basing that mobilization on hatred of ladinos, a racist response by some Mayans to the system's racism. This attitude grew by leaps and bounds when many Mayan communities correctly blamed the EGP and its ladino leadership for the army's offensive that destroyed over 450 villages in 1982. The EGP's armed units withdrew to the safety of the jungle, thus abandoning the exposed highland villages to their fate.

7. Gloria Tujab. Personal communication (summer 1992).

8. The other three were labor lawyers, Frank LaRue and Marta Gloria de Torres, and the ex-dean of the School of Medicine of the University of San Carlos, Dr. Rolando Castillo Montalvo.

9. *Report on Guatemala* 9, 3 (summer 1988):2.

10. The government later claimed that the purpose of this show of force was to protect the exiles against threats by groups of the extreme right. See *Report on Guatemala* 9, 3 (summer 1988).

11. Rigoberta Menchú was accused of belonging to a fictitious guerrilla organization called the Committee for Campesino Action.

12. Personal communication from Sagrario Castellanos, Guatemalan cultural critic (2–19–94).

13. As they themselves defined it, "popular" referred to sectors such as workers, peasants, women, shantytown dwellers, etc., who had been marginalized and oppressed by the same forces responsible for five centuries of indigenous suffering and who also had a significant history of organized resistance. See *Report on Guatemala* 12, 4 (winter 1991):2.

14. Ibid.

15. Among the Guatemalan indigenous groups participating in the event were CUC, the National Coordination of Widows (CONAVIGUA), the National Council of

the Displaced (CONDEG), Majawil Q'ij, Jun Ajpu, Communities of Peoples in Resistance (CPR), and the Peasant Committee of the Highlands (CCDA). See *Report on Guatemala* 12, 4 (winter 1991).

16. Majawil Q'ij is the coordinating body for Guatemalan indigenous organizations involved in the popular movement. Founded in July 1990, it consists primarily of nine peasant, human-rights, and indigenous-rights groups. The name means "New Dawn" in the Mam language.

17. *Report on Guatemala* 12, 4 (winter 1991).

18. Personal communication (summer 1992).

19. Susan Poff. "Rigoberta Menchú Visits Guatemala." In *Report on Guatemala* 13, 3 (fall 1992):11.

20. Ibid.

21. Ibid.

22. *Crónica* 6, 256 (18 December 1992):17.

23. Ibid., 16.

24. Susan Berger. "Guatemala: Coup and Countercoup." *NACLA Report on the Americas* 27, 1 (July/August 1993):4–5.

25. *La Jornada*. Mexico City (11 December 1992):46.

26. *Crónica* 276 (21 May 1993):31.

27. *Crónica* 278 (4 June 1993):48.

28. Ibid., p. 15.

29. Ibid.

30. Ibid., p. 17.

31. The next day, the Constitutional Court made the final arrangements for Serrano's departure, and Rigoberta Menchú found herself in the National Palace sharing the spotlight with the Guatemalan political class. However, when it was rumored that the army endorsed their position, Rigoberta Menchú chose to abandon the palace rather than give the impression that she shared the same position as the army or that she accepted their endorsement of the proceedings.

32. Berger, *Report on the Americas* 27, 1 (July/August 1993):6.

33. *Crónica* 279 (11 June 1993):30.

34. Victor Perera, "The Mayans: A New Force in Guatemalan Politics." *Los Angeles Times* (6 February 1994):M1.

35. Whether this is actually possible is a problem raised by Antonella Fabri. See "Memories of Violence, Monuments of History." Paper presented at the AAA Meeting, 2–7 December 1992, in San Francisco, 8.

36. Antonella Fabri, "The Silences and Discourses of Bodies: Women, Medicine and Violence in Guatemala." Read at the AAA Annual Meeting. Chicago, 1991.

4

WHY DINESH D'SOUZA
HAS IT IN FOR
RIGOBERTA MENCHÚ

GENE H. BELL-VILLADA

The 1992 Nobel Prize for Peace went to Rigoberta Menchú, at the time a thirty-three-year-old Guatemalan Indian activist. The award was well deserved on collective, historical, and personal grounds. Clearly timed to coincide with the Columbus quincentennial, the prize is perhaps the first such instance of a major deliberative body, with almost universal prestige, officially granting recognition to the legitimate aspirations of the Native American peoples. More specifically, the Nobel Committee acknowledged the courageous and tragic political struggles of Rigoberta and her kin, as told by the young woman in her oral autobiography, *I, Rigoberta Menchú: An Indian Woman in Guatemala* (1984).

The book is a highly poetic evocation of the way of life of the Quiché-Mayan Indians, a very moving recollection of their battles against rich white land owners and the brutal military, and a horrifying eyewitness account of the murderous repression that the Guatemalan army has inflicted on the mostly peaceful resistance of Rigoberta and her fellow activists. A kind of "underground classic," it is a compelling political autobiography in the tradition of those of Frederick Douglass and Malcolm X.

Rigoberta's Nobel Prize may make possible an opening for the struggles in her country, as happened in the case of Bishop Tutu in South Africa. Conditions in the two nations have in fact been comparable. The award also furnishes Rigoberta some means of protection against her local enemies, the Guatemalan generals who, on the day the prize was announced in October 1992, attempted to defame her publicly by calling her a "terrorist," attributing "thousands of deaths" to her, and accusing her of staying in "five-star hotels." The Nobel Peace Prize, moreover, helps counteract another, long-standing defamatory campaign of Rigoberta's most vocal and obsessive U.S. foe, the conservative publicist Dinesh D'Souza.

On 3 October 1991, D'Souza gave two lectures at Williams College, one in the afternoon and one in the evening, for a fee of $5,000. He began each talk by holding up and waving a copy of *I, Rigoberta Menchú* (shades of Joe McCarthy at Wheeling, West Virginia), and then proceeded to trash the book, citing it as an instance of the politically motivated low-grade reading being done in "multiculturalist" courses. Oozing sarcasm, D'Souza intoned a mock litany roughly based on this passage from his (1991) national bestseller, *Illiberal Education*: "Rigoberta is a 'person of color,' and thus a victim of racism. She is a woman, and thus a victim of sexism. She lives in South America, which is a victim of European and North American imperialism. If this were not enough, she is an Indian, victimized by latino culture within Latin America."[1] For the new right, of course, *victim* has become a quickie term of contempt, so long as one refers to the victims of Western expansion. On the other hand, D'Souza and his coreligionists tend to pose as suffering victims of campus leftism.

Throughout D'Souza's two talks he struck a tone that pervades *Illiberal Education*—the reasonable, rational centrist, concerned with holding the fort against extremists of every kind. Neither from his lecture nor his book would one guess that he had been editor in chief of the scurrilous *Dartmouth Review*, or that his first published volume (1984), grandiosely titled *Falwell: Before the Millennium*, is a fulsomely flattering biography of the notorious right-wing televangelist. (A sample quotation: "Listening to Falwell speak, one gets a sense that something is right about America." In a curious twist, Falwell's liberal and leftist opponents are made to come off as fanatics, the preacher himself as moderate and enlightened; similarly, in D'Souza's recounting of the Scopes trial of 1929, the secularists are portrayed as unsavory villains and the fundamentalists as victims.)[2] Indeed, about the only time D'Souza bared his fangs at Williams was in animadverting to the Guatemalan. Later in his chat, for instance, when mentioning Menchú's attendance at a political conference in France, D'Souza described it with a look of glee on his face as "Rigoberta vacationing in Paris."

The third chapter of *Illiberal Education* bears the breezy title "Travels with Rigoberta." The three pages actually focusing on Menchú constitute a nasty attack on her life story and also a formidable compendium of distortion and falsehood. A close look at those passages will help account for the extraordinary bloodlust that this earnest, poverty-stricken, yet much-admired Guatemalan Indian woman seems to bring out in D'Souza, the upper-class, professionally smooth, financially successful Indian of Portuguese descent from a onetime overseas outpost of Europe.

The distortions begin when D'Souza distorts the most elementary, neutral facts about Rigoberta's book: "Rigoberta does not write: rather her views are transcribed and translated by the French feminist writer Elisabeth Burgos-Debray" (1991, 71). Why "translated"? The original interviews, after all, were conducted in Spanish, whereas the subsequent translation into English is by Ann Wright. Moreover, the transcriber, Ms. Burgos-Debray, is not French but

Venezuelan, albeit she is married to the socialist activist and government func-
tionary Régis Debray, whom D'Souza in his talk casually referred to as "the
French communist."

A bit further down, D'Souza coyly notes: "Burgos-Debray met Rigoberta
in Paris, where presumably very few of the Third World's poor travel" (72).
D'Souza could have found in Burgos-Debray's own introduction the fact that
"Early in January 1982, Rigoberta Menchú was invited to Europe by a number
of solidarity groups as a representative of the 31 January Popular Front"
(Menchú 1984, xiv).[3] An invitation to such an event usually means that one's
travel expenses are fully paid (as were D'Souza's to Williams College). D'Souza's
innuendo that Rigoberta's poverty might be fraudulent comes across as a cheap
shot. In fact there are hundreds of thousands of poor immigrants from the third
world in Paris, many of them political refugees, as Rigoberta was at the time.

Getting into the text itself, D'Souza comments: "Much of the book simply
details the mundane: 'Rigoberta's Tenth Birthday,' 'Rigoberta Decides to Learn
Spanish,' and 'Rigoberta Talks About Her Father' are typical chapter titles"
(1991, 71). In reality the first two, as D'Souza cites them, are just half of those
titles, subtitles even. In full, they read, "Life in the Altiplano. Rigoberta's Tenth
Birthday," and "Farewell to the Community: Rigoberta Decides to Learn Spanish." Hence the complete chapter titles indicate that an entire way of life, and
Rigoberta's relationship thereto, are being jointly presented. Similarly,
"Rigoberta Talks About Her Father" is a kind of postmortem eulogy immediately following a chapter in which Mr. Menchú is murdered by the armed forces.

D'Souza complains, "It is not always easy to follow this narrative because
it is lavishly sprinkled with Latino and Indian phrases" (71). A casual inspec-
tion of the text shows at most a couple of those foreign words (not "phrases")
per page. Some are familiar culinary items (tortillas); most are used repeatedly
in sufficiently clear contexts (compañeros); others denote local crops, artifacts,
or concepts that have no equivalents in English. To help the non-Guatemalan
reader, there is a four-page glossary in the back of the book. And then there is
that adjective *Latino*, which D'Souza brandishes once again, saying, "She rebels
against Europeanized Latino culture" (71). Actually the term *Latino* never
appears in Menchú's book. The term employed by her, and by Guatemalans
generally, is *ladino*. Had a more diligent D'Souza turned to the glossary, he
would have found this definition for ladino: "Any Guatemalan—whatever his
economic position—who rejects, either individually or through his cultural
heritage, Indian values of Mayan origin. It also implies mixed blood" (Menchú
1984, 249).

Hence, while D'Souza seems to think that Rigoberta's "ladinos" are Europeans, they are, more precisely, Guatemalan mixed breeds who dislike everything Indian and who "wannabe" white.

"Europeanized . . . culture" is not an issue in Rigoberta's narrative. Hers is
a very local revolt against the arbitrary power of the rural land owners and the

urban rich who mistreated her and her family. Moreover, she and her cohorts are avowed Christians, which is about as "Europeanized" as one can get! And though she often speaks with understandable suspicion of Guatemala's ladinos, toward the end of the book she admits to the existence of sympathetic ladinos who will side with native people's struggles—much as Malcolm X, Dick Gregory, and other African American activists have granted that there are politically dependable whites. *I, Rigoberta Menchú* is not an ethnic separatist's tract.

These distortions appear within a mere dozen or so lines of D'Souza's text. They are just the beginning, however. His second paragraph on Rigoberta states, "her parents are killed for unspecified reasons in a bloody massacre reportedly carried out by the Guatemalan army" (1991, 71). Once again D'Souza gets his facts wrong. Rigoberta's father and mother died in two separate incidents rather than in a single "bloody massacre." As Menchú's chapter 25 reveals, Vicente Menchú was not killed for unspecified reasons but for his active involvement in the peasants' occupation of the Spanish Embassy in 1980; the Guatemalan authorities' response was to burn the building to the ground, resulting in the deaths of everyone inside. As D'Souza presents it, the action was "reportedly carried out" by the military, but the adverb is false: at the time of the episode it was public knowledge that the Guatemalan authorities were considered responsible. As for Rigoberta's mother, she was kidnapped by government troops, who, after torturing and raping her, tied her to a tree and stood guard as she died of exposure, then left her body to be devoured by wild animals.

In a passage often quoted by reviewers, D'Souza says of Rigoberta, "She becomes first a feminist, then a socialist, then a Marxist" (71). All these characterizations are wide of the mark. Throughout her book Rigoberta finds much to defend in certain traditional women's roles in Mayan culture (having lots of children, for example). And though she criticizes machismo and suggests ways of combating "this sickness [that is] part of society," she rejects the idea of a separate organization for women, which she finds a "paternalistic" solution that "would be feeding machismo" (Menchú 1984, 222). Nowhere in the text will readers find the word *feminist*; modern-day, Western gender concepts are scarcely present in Menchú's reflections.

D'Souza notes further that "there is even a chapter titled 'Rigoberta Renounces Marriage and Motherhood.'" D'Souza's flippant tone suggests blitheness and bravado on Menchú's part. The truth is that the pages where she ponders this decision are a melancholy and even agonizing chapter in which she praises family life, expresses a yearning for conjugal companionship and children, and wistfully recalls a young man she once loved. Rigoberta is painfully aware of the bleak realities in her country, however, and she puts forth with simple eloquence her reasons for remaining celibate: "because I don't want to be a widow, or a tortured mother" (225).

Regarding Rigoberta's becoming a "socialist" and "a Marxist," she never defines herself as such. In reality she is a Christian activist who describes the mission of her religious brethren as "creat[ing] the kingdom of God on Earth among our brothers." Long passages tell of her community's study of the Bible, a book she characterizes as "our main weapon" (134). In the concluding chapter, Rigoberta mentions a debate with a Marxist *compañera* who criticized her for being Christian, to which Menchú replies: "The whole truth [is not found] in Marxism." Speaking in the name of spiritual values, Rigoberta declares: "No one can take my Christian faith away from me" (246). Despite this evidence to the contrary, D'Souza latches onto Rigoberta's "discoursing on 'bourgeois youths'" as proof of her Marxism. He appears ignorant of the fact that the word *bourgeois*, like other cognates from the Romance languages (*burgués* in Spanish, *borghese* in Italian), simply denotes the "middle classes," the existence of which is a social fact independent of the speaker's ideology. In conjunction with his innuendo about Rigoberta's jet-setting to Paris, D'Souza remarks: "Nor does [her] Marxist vocabulary sound typical of a Guatemalan peasant." One wonders, how many has he met? As I observed in "Two Americas, Two World Views, and a Widening Gap (Bell-Villada 1982), Marxist idiom is fairly commonplace throughout Latin America, where it thrives as a kind of "counterculture," even among non-Marxists.[4] Latin American journalists, teachers, writers, community activists, and religious people routinely make use of Marxian concepts in their analyses and public statements. In this respect, then, Rigoberta's "Marxist vocabulary" is a norm and not the exception among political commentators south of Texas. D'Souza appears snobbishly to overlook that a Guatemalan peasant woman might routinely use Marxist terms.

The larger question raised by D'Souza and his defenders, however, is a set of "unresolved doubts about the place being given [to Rigoberta's book] in the new multicultural canon," as C. Vann Woodward puts it.[5] (I will not quote D'Souza's more mean-spirited statements here.) The issue as commonly posed is not as simple as it seems. First, no educator of any repute has called for abandoning Plato, Shakespeare, or Marx in preference to Menchú—this is a fantasy of the new right. Rigoberta's story is, rather, an instance of the subgenre of political testimony (of which the narratives of Frederick Douglass and Malcolm X are prime examples from the United States).

In Latin America such testimonials exist in the thousands. Among them Menchú's is one of the best, and happens to be readily accessible to U.S. students. (D'Souza all but claims that *I, Rigoberta Menchú* is a low-quality book, a judgment he makes on exclusively ideological, not literary or cultural grounds.) Other, more established testimonial works include the conservatively correct *Hunger of Memory* by Richard Rodriguez, Orwell's nonfictional writings (his chapter "Shooting an Elephant," his memoirs *The Road to Wigan Pier,* and *Homage to Catalonia*), or, from more distant eras, Walt Whitman's Civil War prose, the many religious confessions from St. Augustine on, and in some measure the prophetic books of the Bible.[6] These titles appear on many college reading lists yet elicit no snarls from officialdom's self-appointed watchdogs.

But getting back to my own question: Why does D'Souza have it in for Menchú? Why does he join the Guatemalan generals in assaulting her with every weapon available? Part of the answer, I venture to infer from his own statements, is that at the time D'Souza wrote *Illiberal Education* he had scarcely sampled *I, Rigoberta Menchú.* (Perhaps he has since.) There appears no other way to account for his errors concerning the simplest data in the book. And so, apparently not having reconnoitered the territory, he resorts instead to carpet bombing. Summing up his nonanalysis of Rigoberta's memoir, D'Souza asks: "Whom does she represent?" He answers that ". . . she embodies a projection of Marxist and Leninist views onto South American culture" (1991, 72). There is indeed a projection, but of a different sort. Given D'Souza's ignorance of a text he nonetheless savages, we can turn his conclusions around and assert that his view of Rigoberta Menchú is itself a projection—the new right's wildest and most ignorant fantasies projected onto a person of whom they know nothing and who embodies everything they love to hate. It is possible to construe D'Souza's intimations of academic fraud regarding *I, Rogoberta* as projections of his own intellectual fraud—the projection of a projection, so to speak.

One wonders: If D'Souza can be so irresponsible in his research of a work that he singles out for attack, then how reliable is he on the hundreds of items he cites in the forty-four pages of endnotes in *Illiberal Education?* D'Souza was in his mid- to late twenties when he was "researching" and writing this opus. How many scholars of that age have had the background and the time to read and digest so much material? How much is his charlatanism in treating *I, Rigoberta Menchú* the rule and not the exception? We do know that the shoddy scholarship in *Illiberal Education* is more than textual. Jon Wiener (1992) has done some fact checking and found out that D'Souza simply invented entire interviews, fiercely distorted others, and greatly exaggerated an ambiguous and relatively minor racial controversy at Harvard.[7] Similarly, the D'Souza version of recent curricular changes at Stanford "turns out to be seriously inaccurate," as C. Vann Woodward notes.[8] *Illiberal Education* can be seen as a compendium of falsifications in fancy academic dress.

And yet this mock-scholarly scam became a bestseller, received high initial praise from outstanding liberals like Woodward and whilom Marxists like Eugene Genovese, and made its slippery scribe rich and famous. It stands as a perfect symbol of "intellectual" life under Reaganism, the spectacle of this scantily researched screed, built on unread books and outright untruths, enjoying a triumph of the right-wing will and thrusting its false problems into the cultural arena.

NOTES

1. Dinesh D'Souza, *Illiberal Education: The Politics of Race and Sex on Campus* (New York: Random House, 1991), 72.

2. Dinesh D'Souza, *Falwell: Before the Millennium, A Critical Biography* (Chicago: Regnery Gateway, 1984), 205.

3. Rigoberta Menchú, *I, Rigoberta Menchú: An Indian Woman in Guatemala*, ed. Elisabeth Burgos-Debray, trans. Ann Wright (London: Verso, 1984).

4. Gene H. Bell-Villada, "Two Americas, Two World Views, and a Widening Gap." *Monthly Review* 34, 5 (October 1982):37–43.

5. C. Vann Woodward, "Letter to the Editor." *New York Review of Books* 26 (September 1991):76.

6. On the matter of the autobiographical and confessional mode in literature, see Northrop Frye, *Anatomy of Criticism* (New York: Atheneum, 1968), 307–8.

7. Jon Wiener, "What Happened at Harvard." In *Beyond PC: Toward a Politics of Understanding*. Ed. Patricia Aufderheide (Saint Paul, Minn.: Graywolf, 1992), 97–106.

8. C. Vann Woodward, "Freedom and Universities." In Aufderheide, *Beyond PC*, 34.

TEACHING THE
LATIN AMERICAN CONTEXT

5

ME LLAMO RIGOBERTA MENCHÚ
Autoethnography and the Recoding of Citizenship

MARY LOUISE PRATT

Among many startling events in the history of what has come to be called the "culture wars" in the North American academy, I still remember vividly a call I received from a fact checker from *Fortune* magazine. In connection with an article they were running, he asked, could I confirm whether we were still teaching *I, Rigoberta Menchú* in the first year culture course at Stanford? (Yes, we were, I replied, in one of the eight tracks in the course.) What did students think of it? (In the end-of-year survey, I told him, of everything read over the year, students chose it most often as the book that had the greatest impact on them.) Could I confirm that Elisabeth Burgos-Debray was the wife of the revolutionary Régis Debray? (I could not.) Did I honestly think that this was a great book? (Yes, I said, it is a great book.) All of this was asked in a tone of sneering incredulity that made clear there was nothing neutral about this fact checker's commitment to factuality. I was not surprised during my next plane trip to pick up *Fortune* and find yet another watered-down excerpt of D'Souza's mindless attack on the Menchú-Debray book. Some version of it had been marketed to every major magazine in the country that month.

The brouhaha confirmed to me the appropriateness of the term I had come to use as a point of entry in teaching this remarkable book: *force*. Think, I would tell the students the week it was assigned, about what gives this book its force. How does it mobilize your mind and your imagination? How does it force you to think and know things you would not otherwise think or know? Take notes about where you find yourself resisting its force, where it forces you into rejection or denial. *Force* seemed to me a term that might generate a viable poetics of the testimonio, one not at odds with its political compromise and activist imperative.

In what follows, I aim to outline the four readings of the Menchú-Debray book that I present to my classes, but I would first like to suggest some of the contextual grounding I believe is necessary to the effective reception and teaching of this powerful text. First, language: It is inevitable that in North America the testimonio coproduced by Rigoberta Menchú and Elisabeth Burgos-Debray will be taught more frequently in English translation than in the Spanish original. The English translation, by Ann Wright, is very good, but readers and teachers still need to know that the book reads rather differently in Spanish than in English. Among other things, the Spanish version retains more of an oral quality and the markedness of Menchú's Spanish as that of a nonnative speaker. If a class includes students who are native speakers of Spanish, it is a good idea to ask them to read parts of the book in both languages and report on their perceptions. Perhaps the sharpest and most revealing contrast is in the title and presentation of the book in the two languages. English language readers, for whom the book is titled *I, Rigoberta Menchú: An Indian Woman in Guatemala,* need to know that in Spanish the book is *Me llamo Rigoberta Menchú y asi me nacio la conciencia* (My name is Rigoberta Menchú, and this is how my consciousness was born). It is worth discussing in class the ideological import of the English title, which uses a stereotyping gesture to subsume Menchú into a category she is supposed to exemplify or typify. This gesture may have something to do with the way attacks on the book (from both right and left) have focused on the issue of Menchú's supposed failure to "typify" her culture. The cover illustrations repeat the contrast. The Spanish edition (Mexico: Siglo XXI, 1985, 1988) has a full-face, black and white photo of Menchú herself, looking out and smiling, her rebozo folded on top of her head in everyday fashion; the English translation bears a color photograph of a crowd of Guatemalan indigenous women in a religious procession, their heads and shoulders reverentially bowed and covered by their rebozos, and—most telling of all—their backs to the camera. A small, full-faced, black and white photo of Menchú appears in the upper-left-hand corner beside the title. A comparison of the two covers gives a valuable lesson in the politics of translation and the perils of the transcultural (transnational, translingual) discursive field that Menchú and Burgos-Debray collaboratively entered.

After many years of teaching *I, Rigoberta Menchú* in both English translation and the Spanish original, I have found it particularly essential to contextualize the book in two ways: (a) historically, in relation to both the long- and short-term histories of what is now Guatemala; and (b) generically, in relation to the testimonio as genre and as intervention in the print genre system. Both kinds of contextualization make it more possible for students to situate and respond to the textbook in ways that neither neutralize its demand for action and activism on the part of metropolitan readers nor leave them in a paralysis of generalized angst.

HISTORICAL CONTEXT

To teachers needing historical knowledge pertinent to Menchú's testimonio, among sources in English I strongly recommend Suzanne Jonas's book *The
Battle for Guatemala* (1991). The historical remarks given here are largely sum-
marized from Jonas's book, and are intended to give an idea of the kinds of specifics we can and should be presenting in our classrooms. It is important that
North American students not simply subsume this book, and other Latin
American texts that make their way northward, into generalized stereotypes
about violence, irrationality, and authoritarianism in Latin America. Such texts
must be used rather to catapult students past these stereotypes by providing
more textured interpretive strategies.

Prior to the European invasion of the Americas, the Maya peoples of
Mesoamerica were organized into what Jonas describes as "complex, stratified,
protoclass societies" (13) whose prosperity contrasts horribly with the severe
poverty Maya populations endure today. The idea of "primitive" cannot be
accurately applied to pre-Columbian Maya societies—they were not less
sophisticated or complex than European societies of the time, though they were
very different and were evolving along different lines.

At least two-thirds of the Maya population died in the first hundred years
following the Spanish invasion, a history of which Menchú is very aware. In the
book, her grandparents are invoked repeatedly as the mouthpieces of the pre-
Columbian past:

> Then the grandparents tell us many things they've been witness to,
> things that must be passed on by their children. They are witnesses
> that our ancestors were not sinners, they did not kill. They apply past
> experience to the present. They say: "Today human life is not
> respected. . . . Our forefathers told us that our old people used to live
> until they were a hundred and twenty-five, now we die at forty or
> thirty. You younger people must ask yourselves why this is so."
> (Menchú 1984, 68)

Spanish colonialism introduced many of the basic coordinates of contemporary Guatemalan society. Land was appropriated from indigenous communities, concentrated in the hands of Spanish land owners, and worked by inden-
tured, forced, or enslaved indigenous workers—the fruits of whose labor
accumulated, as it does today, in the hands of the small landowning elite. As
Menchú is acutely aware, the most dramatic and intolerable conditions of contemporary Guatemala society—a hugely unequal division of labor and a hugely
unequal distribution of wealth—were laid down in the sixteenth century. As
the history of slavery in the United States also shows, such drastic inequalities
are maintained only through intense, systematic violence and terror and

intense social and ideological manipulation. White supremacy has been the key in legitimating both the inequalities and the violence within humanist ideology. Less well acknowledged, as Jonas observes, is the role played by rape as a form of systematic violence, both physical and epistemic, and as the source of a mixed-race population that, in Guatemala, forms the basis of the ladino class (Jonas 1991, 16).

In the centuries following the European conquest, indigenous populations in Mesoamerica, as in many parts of the Americas, found ways to survive the European conqest in significant numbers and to secure economic and territorial footholds on the margins of the colonial system, notably by retreating to agriculturally undesirable areas like the highlands where Menchú's life begins. Continuous struggle, negotiation, and compromise with the colonial system became part of life, "resistant adaptation" to colonial rule (Stern 1987). As Menchú's account attests on every page, postconquest indigenous cultures tended to evolve around the ideas of resistance and survival, around an often fierce commitment to maintaining and developing indigenous ways of life as a means of guaranteeing a degree of autonomy and community. Resistance and survival become fundamental axes of culture, consciousness, and identity. In the face of genocidal conditions, there is nothing sentimental about this commitment to culture. It is often synonymous with the very will to survive; the alternative to the struggle for land and culture is not simply assimilating to the dominant society. More likely it is isolation, destitutution, despair, and death. Menchú's testimonio attests to the way resistance and survival can become a central axis of existence for indigenous groups; a path towards autonomy in a world with no good choices; a focus for the very meaning of life; and, insofar as it could be achieved, a source of strength and pride in the face of intense prejudice and hostility. It is important to underscore that, as Menchú's text amply demonstrates, cultural survival does not imply retaining traditional ways of life frozen in time but implies being *in possession of* a degree of collective freedom, autonomy, and identity. Menchú deliberately speaks in her testimonio from a position of *proprietorship* over herself, her culture, and her history. One of the ways she signals her cultural and existential self-possession is by repeated allusions to the secrets she chooses not to reveal.

While many of the conditions Menchú describes have roots in the pre-Columbian and colonial eras, her account reflects a more recent historical narrative that begins in the 1870s and 1880s when coffee replaced cochineal dye as the main export crop of what had for fifty years been the Republic of Guatemala. The national economy was quickly transformed and rural society was essentially reorganized in the servce of this new cash crop. By 1880 coffee accounted for 92 percent of Guatemala's foreign exchange earnings, and by 1900 Guatemala was importing food staples for the first time in its history (Jonas 1991, 18). The consequences for the Guatemala's indigenous population were dire. The coffee boom created a demand for more agricultural land, which was satisfied by round after round of land grabs from indigenous subsistence communities and the church. As the boom increased the size of the wealthy class, pressure on Indian lands increased. So did pressure on the indigenous labor force. Coffee cultivation, as Menchú reviews for her readers in vivid detail (Menchú 1984, chapter 6), is labor intensive. The coffee boom resulted in "labor grabs" as devastating as the land grabs, and the national government became increasingly involved in efforts to force indigenous inhabitants into the kind of exploitation Menchú describes in such detail (chapters 4, 6, and 7). In 1934, for example, in response to the Depression, the Guatemalan government passed a "vagrancy" law requiring all landless peasants to work at least 150 days per year for either the *fincas* or the state (Jonas 1991, 18). This law, intended to further undermine the autonomy of indigenous communities, became the basis for the agonizing highland-to-coast migration system that structured Menchú's early life. That same year the Labor Department was made an adjunct of the National Police (18). Legal configurations such as this underlie Menchú's important observation that, as an Indian and a peasant, one literally *has no recourse* within offical structures. It is important for students to reflect on the implications of social arrangements that leave groups with no possibility for redress.

United States corporations had large scale economic interests in the Guatemalan finca system—indeed the United Fruit Company held a monopoly on fruit exports (mainly bananas) and also owned Guatemala's railways and its electric company. The legendary dictator Jorge Ubico, in office from 1931–44 began his career working for the Rockefeller Foundation, and his repressive policies catered to U.S. corporate interests. In 1944 reaction to Ubico finally coalesced in an uprising of small merchants, students, and largely urban workers. Ubico was overthrown and Guatemala entered a decade of democratic reform. Labor laws were revised in favor of workers rights, and the vote was extended to all citizens (but see Menchú's account of voting, 1984, 26). In 1952, under a newly elected socialist president, Jacobo Arbenz, a dramatic land reform was declared in which all idle land over 220 acres was to be expropriated and redistributed to landless peasants, who would pay for it over time. The United Fruit Company alone stood to lose 400,000 acres. In two years, over a million acres of land were redistributed to some 100,000 families like Menchú's. Menchú's father's political activism dates from this period, when he was an Arbenz supporter, and her account alludes to his efforts to make a land claim.

President Arbenz's government became one of the earliest victims of U.S. cold war policy in Latin America. In 1954 he was brought down by an invasion organized by the United States, led by a Guatemalan general trained at Fort Leavenworth, and supported by CIA air cover (readers will recognize here the model for the Bay of Pigs invasion nearly a decade later). In a now familiar gesture, Henry Cabot Lodge, then head of the UN Security Council, thwarted UN intervention by calling the conflict a "civil war." In the months following the coup, the new dictatorship embarked on a campaign of terror intended to erad-icate the socialist movement in the country. Suspected Arbenz sympathizers, including Menchú's father, were hunted down (with the help of lists of "com-munists" provided to the U.S. embassy) (Jonas 1991, 32). Eight thousand peas-ants were murdered and another nine thousand people subjected to imprison-ment and torture. "My father," says Menchú, "has very black memories of those days. He says many, many of our people died, and we only escaped because of our own quick wits" (Menchú 1984, 26).

In the 1960s and 70s, under authoritarian rule, large-scale commercial agriculture entered another period of expansion in Guatemala, triggering yet another round of land grabs from peasants. This is the period in which Menchú's own life story begins, with her parents setting up a homestead in yet another new place, which they will eventually have to defend from ladino encroachment, and compelled to support themselves by migrating to the fin-cas. By the mid-1960s, records Jonas, only 10 percent of rural families could live off the land. Obviously Menchú and her family were not among these, though such self-sufficiency remained the goal toward which they constantly strived. Menchú's narrative registers the deterioriating conditions for labor in this period, culminating for her in the needless death of her baby brother.

Socialist and democratic aspirations did not disappear with the overthrow of Arbenz, however. At the same time it was intensifying exploitation of rural land and labor, the Guatemalan regime was facing left-wing guerrilla move-ments that, based on the model of the Cuban revolution, were forming in many parts of Latin America. Though they made little contact with the indigenous population, by the 1960s these movements in Guatemala were perceived as con-stituting a genuine threat. The regime's response was a campaign of state terror. From the mid-1960s on, death squads became a fact of life in Guatemala. People disappeared by the hundreds at the hands of a secret paramilitary force called "la Mano Blanca" (the White Hand), tortured corpses turned up in public places to intensify fear. In 1967 the eminent poet Otto Rene Castillo was tortured for four days before being burned alive, echoing Menchú's account of the fate of her brother over a decade later. In an equally dramatic episode in 1968, the national beauty queen, Miss Guatemala, fell under government suspicion for her leftist sympathies. She was arrested, stabbed, tortured, raped, poisoned, and her naked corpse left out for the vultures (readers will be reminded of Menchú's account of her mother's death). Such episodes exemplify the calculatedly sym-bolic use of violence that typified what came to be called the "counterinsurgency state" in Latin America (see Fagen 1992). The participation of the United States in shoring up the Guatemalan regime remained constant. Using tactics later deployed in Vietnam, the U.S. undertook to "transform the Guatemalan army into an effective modern counterinsurgency force" (Jonas, 70) and to create what came to be a model for the counterinsurgency state, characterized by institutionalized violence and the absence of consensual politics. Guatemala was regarded as a "laboratory" for the fight against communism in the third world. There was thus nothing random or "underdeveloped' about the military institutions and strategies Menchú and her fellow villagers confronted in the 1970s. These were part of a highly orchestrated global strategy.

Though the guerrilla movements of the 1960s were not effective in mobilizing indigenous populations and rural peasantries, increased exploitation and repression eventually were. Earnings for agricultural workers in Guatemala declined 50 percent in the 1970s. The pattern of forced labor migration to which Menchú and her family—and the vast majority of the rural population—were condemned created the conditions for a range of organized movements against the system. Menchú narrates how migration to the fincas brought into contact groups unaware of each others' existence and their shared socioeconomic plight. The years 1976 to 1978 saw the rise of the organization joined by Menchú herself in 1979, the CUC: Comite de Unidad Campesina (Committee of Peasant Unity) (Menchú 1984, 161). Other powerful oppositional social movements—some political, some religious, some armed, some not—coalesced around the same time. This large-scale organized rural uprising is the setting for Menchú's emergence as a leader and a militant. Her account registers some of the pivotal events of this period: the massacre of 100 indigenous peasants at Panzós in 1978 (160) and the occupation of the Spanish embassy in which her father was burned to death in early 1980.

By the late 1970s and early 1980s, the Guatemalan state faced what had become a large-scale indigenous uprising. Moreover, it faced a new development that appeared capable of bringing down the whole landowning system: coalitions of indigenous and ladino peasantries (see Menchú 1984, 118). Never before had peasant organizations overcome the gulf of racism and mutual hatred that had divided indigenes from ladinos. These divisions had always worked in the interests of the landed elites (not the least because indigenous communities often saw the ladino peasants who continuously encroached on their land as their primary enemy, rather than the large land owners). The huge strike coordinated by the CUC in February of 1980, which mobilized some 75,000 workers (see Menchú 1984, chapter 32) dramatized the extent of the new threat. The state's response, once again, was a relentless campaign of terror.[1] The years from 1980 to 1983, when some of the most dramatic events of Menchú's narrative take place, were a period of total war on the part of the Guatemalan government against the indigenous population. At least one hundred thousand people, the vast majority indigenous peasants, were killed in those horrendous years. In the face of organized uprisings against the exploitive rural regime, the government and the military adopted the specific goal of eradicating indigenous social and economic structures. As Menchú describes (160), in a gesture that reflects both the cynicism and the paranoia of the regime, as well as its racism, indigenous ways of life were simply equated with communism

and subversion. The primary weapons deployed against them were village massacres (as Menchú's account attests) and forced displacement of populations
into Vietnam style "model villages." Over a million people were displaced either
into such villages or into refugee camps across the border in Mexico. United
States influence remained constant. One of the main architects of this genocidal campaign, General Augusto Rios Montt, seized the presidency in a coup
in 1982. Before entering the service of his country, Rios Montt had been a
department head at the Interamerican Defense College in Washington D.C.

   It is in the context of this campaign of combined ethno- and geno-cide that
Menchú traveled to a conference of exiled indigenous leaders in Europe and
conducted the interviews that became her testimonio. Before turning to the testimonio, a couple of general reflections are in order. In establishing the historical context for reading *I, Rigoberta Menchú*, I have found it valuable to establish both the long and short views. On the one hand, that is, students should
be able to see Menchú's story as the contemporary continuation of the invasion, conquest, and resistance set in motion in 1492. At the same time, it must
be located in the specific dynamics of cold war politics in this hemisphere, and
particularly in relation to the rise of socialist and guerrilla movements, on the
one hand, and, on the other, the United States' decision in the late 1950s to create strong militaries in Latin America to fight communism. The nightmarish
spectacles of violence that form some of the most unforgettable chapters in the
book must be traced both to the Spanish inquisition and to contemporary tech-
nologies of torture and fear deployed in many parts of Latin America since the
late 1960s. It is also important, in my view, to encourage reflection on the realities of militant resistance such as that Menchú describes. The course her community, and so many others, embarked on must be understood as a desperate
one chosen in the absence of all other recourse. It is a choice made out of a sense
of having nothing left to lose and nothing worthwhile to look forward to, for
oneself or one's descendants. In her speeches in North America Menchú often
reminds her audiences that they have very little idea what it is like to live with
no viable choices in virtually any sphere of life. It is important for students to
engage with such experiential realities and the specific social and governmental
structures that create them.

I, RIGOBERTA MENCHÚ AND THE TESTIMONIO

As other writers in this volume discuss, the testimonio arose as a form during
the period of intellectual and artistic experimentation following the Cuban
revolution, when means were sought to integrate all sectors of the new society
into print culture medium that had formerly been virtually monopolized by
the educated elite. Testimonio emerges in the context of an imperative to rene-
gotiate relations between intellectuals and grassroots constituencies in the
domain of print culture. From this perspective, perhaps its most salient feature

is its *collaborative* mode of production. Testimonios are produced through voluntary collaboration between a metropolitan intellectal and a subaltern or grassroots individual. The two subjects are linked by shared commitments to social justice and the radical transformation of capitalist society. Despite their solidarity, their collaboration is nearly always an exercise in cross-class, cross-cultural, and often cross-race interaction involving mutual dependency, accountability, and risk. Burgos-Debray's introduction to *I, Rigoberta Menchú* provides an excellent opportunity to discuss these complexities. Many readers, including myself, find this introduction infuriating and offensive. Burgos-Debray represents her relation with Menchú in sentimental and paternalist terms that imply the very attitudes of racial and class superiority Menchú is combatting, both in Guatemala and among metropolitan readers. In my classes I have often expressed surprise that these embarrassing pages have not been removed or replaced, given the way they contradict the project of the book. Menchú, I was sure, would want them left out. But last year a student in one seminar offered a different analysis.[2] If she were Menchú, she argued, she would insist the introduction remain there unrevised, so that readers could see clearly the attitudes she was up against, even among her most enlightened sympathizers, and the risks she was taking by entering into the testimonio relationship. From that perspective, the most effective act of self-criticism on Burgos-Debray's part would be to leave the text as is and available for comment. I wholeheartedly agree with this insight, and now teach the introduction in these terms.

The coproducers of testimonios are usually understood to share at least one objective: educating metropolitan reading publics and inciting them to meaningful action. Testimonios seek to correct what is often called the "sanctioned ignorance" of metropolitans, an ignorance produced by the cooptation of the media, by ideological mystifications, systematic information gaps, by psychic displacement, alienation, denial, and self-interest, and by the generalized diffuseness that characterizes power in the metropolis. The assumption is that educated metropolitans, as committed as they might be to values of justice and democracy, must be compelled to become aware of the realities of grassroots life and struggle and take responsibility. The testimonio thus unabashedly assumes the form of what Michel Foucault called a "discourse of truth and falsehood" and usually consists predominantly of *experiential narrative.*

When I teach Rigoberta Menchú's testimonio I like to propose four readings of the text, each of which foregrounds different parts of the book.

Reading 1. Political Autobiography. This might fairly be called the "preferred reading" of the book, signaled in the original Spanish title by the words *y asi me nacio la conciencia* ("and thus was my consciousness born"). This reading foregrounds the linear narrative of maturation, emplotted in terms of key turning points in Menchú's development as an adult, a resistant subject, an activist, and a leader. Her early work on the finca introduces her to the realities of ruthless exploitation; her little brother's death triggers "rage and hate." Her visit to the city creates a consciousness of national reality while her experience as a maid rules out assimilation. The militarization of her village life, particularly the horrific death of her friend Doña Petrona (152) clarifies the life-and-death nature of the struggle and her commitment. Entering political organizing at the national level represents a new phase, and a transition out of a struggle conceived in terms of the Indian/ladino opposition ("For me it was unbelievable to walk with a ladino," 168). This is also the beginning of Menchú's formation as a leader, marked by her decision to avoid motherhood. The political autobiography ends with her decision to go into exile, a decision that led directly to the production of the testimonio.

It is interesting, when doing this reading, to distinguish between Menchú's coming to consciousness and that of the reader. For most readers, the turning point in terms of consciousness raising is the chilling description in chapter 24 of the torture and death of her brother,[3] followed in chapter 27 by that of her mother. It seems clear that Menchú and Debray intended these accounts to have an intense impact on the reader. But in Menchú's coming to consciousness, the critical juncture is her experience as a maid in the city.[4] It is here she comes into contact with the larger social structure that has been determining her life and struggles from afar ("that was when I discovered the truth in what my grandmother used to say: that with rich people even their plates shine," 94). The experience also demonstrates to her that modernization is not the answer. Its contradictions surface with a new directness as Menchú finds herself living in the midst of plenty and excess, but confines herself to scarcity and deprivation: the family dog eats better than she does. She sees the imperative to learn Spanish and begins the process of doing so. Working independently as an adult outside her family structure (her father comes to her for money, 96), she begins to envision her own life and construct her own critique based on her own gendered experience of the social and racial hierarchy ("we had very little, but I had never suffered like I suffered in the house of those rich people," 99). Refusing abuse and ultimately quitting the job are among her first independent acts in confronting the system. "I will never forget this part of my life," she tells herself (101).

One source of the book's force as political biography is the specificity and concreteness with which Menchú describes the practices that constitute injustice, inequality, and exloitation. This practice too seems particularly strategic in relation to her anticipated audience. In the chapter just discussed, the incident of the Christmas Eve tamal, first left for her on the stove by her employer, then taken away for a late-arriving guest, is one such instance. Another is the detailed description of coffee harvesting;

> Coffee is picked from the branch, but sometimes when it was ripe and
> fell off the branch, we'd have to collect it up off the ground. It's more

difficult to pick up than to pick from the branch. Sometimes we have to move the bushes to get at the coffee. We have to pick the nearest beans very carefully—bean by bean—because if we break a branch we have to pay for it out of our wages. It's worse when the coffee bushes are young. The branches are more valuable than on the old bushes. (35)

Unlike many materialist analyses, Menchú gives as much weight to psychic suffering as to physical, making existential well being a sine qua non of the struggle for justice, and epistemic violence—heartless words, racist epithets, shunning—a torment no less unbearable than hunger or physical abuse. These things too acquire an intense concreteness and specificity in Menchú's account. The effect, and I expect the intent, is to get Westerners "out of their heads," to force an engagement with what abstractions like justice and injustice mean at the level of lived experience—an engagement that does not spontaneously occur from a position of privilege. There is no ambiguity in Menchú's account about what is wanted.

The strategic insistence on concreteness and specificity culminates for readers in the dramatic accounts of the torture and deaths of her brother and mother. In teaching these overwhelming chapters, it is important, in my view, to underscore the intentionality with which they are constructed to break through the disengagement and indifference of an audience far from the situation. When I teach these passages, I teach them as dramatizations of runaway state power that, as Menchú observes, subjects both those who are tortured and those who torture. Without detracting from the extraordinary force of those scenes it is possible to launch from them a discussion of how states subject and how state power is written on the body in the reader's home society as well.

Reading 2. Autoethnography. Another dimension of Menchú's consciousness-raising project involves the conveying of a world view and a way of life. I use the term *autoethnographic* (see Pratt 1992, 1994) to refer to any attempt on the part of a marginal or subordinated group to represent itself and its lifeways to the center or dominant group, usually through a partial appropriation (transculturation) of the dominant group's own idioms. Autoethnographic texts will often appropriate and adapt Western discourses of "manners and customs," for example, to construct representations intended to correct distortions or affirm alternative values. Because they are contestatory in this way, autoethnographic texts cannot be made sense of as "authentic" expressions of an "other" culture, but as interventions the "others" make in the repertoire by which they are represented by the "selves."

The autoethnographic reading of *I, Rigoberta Menchú* foregrounds sections describing life in the *altiplano,* clustered at three points: chapters 2 and 3; 8 through 12; and 27 through 30. In these chapters one finds experiential narrative interspersed with a generalizing descriptive discourse. ("We have ten

sacred days, as our ancestors have always had. These ten days have their
nahual," 18). It was undoubtedly a deliberate editorial decision to group these
chapters and intersperse them with the political narrative. Among other things,
the autoethnographic chapters evoke what the resistance movements are fighting for: not, for instance, modernization or Western-style prosperity or simply
"a bigger piece of the pie," as some readers might assume, but a cosmos, the
possibility of an alternative way of living. As the book recapitulates the back-
and-forth rhythm of home-to-finca labor migration, the altiplano gets defined
as the space of culture, while coast and city embody purely utilitarian values of
exploitation. Though an anthropologist would surely regard Menchú's
accounts of life on the finca or her time as a maid as rich in ethnographic material, Menchú clearly distinguishes her culture from these realities: culture is
that which defines her and to which she is committed; for obvious reasons,
Menchú chooses not to present herself as defined by, nor committed to, her
place in the national class system and its structures of exploitation. Her autoethnography is highly partial in nature. Over and over she affirms the superiority of communal subsistence lifeways over the possessive individualism of the
West (see reading 3 below). In relation to finca society and the city, Menchú is
fruitfully read as an ethnographer, that is, someone observing from the outside.

   In the space of the altiplano, Menchú undertakes to construct a meaningful cosmos. She underscores the fact that her culture is an ancient one, as
indeed it is. In our freshman culture course we teach *I, Rigoberta Menchú* alongside the ancient Mayan mythic text, the *Popol Vuh,* with which it resonates at
many points.[5] For example, Menchú describes the ceremony held when a child
is forty days old, in which the child is told it is "made of maize, because his
mother ate it while he was forming in her stomach." This ceremony echoes the
Maya creation myth narrated in the *Popol Vuh,* according to which the fourth
attempt to create the human race succeeds by creating men of maize. The
instructions to the child that it must "live as his 'grandparents' have lived,"and
that "the sun is the father and our mother is the moon" are also echoed in the
Popol Vuh, and attest to the continuities between contemporary Maya culture
and its pre-Columbian roots. Similarly, the eight-day ceremony involves incorporating a child into the world by placing the newborn in a bed whose four corners are marked with candles "to represent the four corners of the house"
(Menchú 1984, 11). In classical Mayan cosmography, it is the world itself that
is mapped as a four-cornered space whose center is marked by the intersection
of its diagonals. Renato Rosaldo (in a personal conversation) argues that
Menchú's description of the nightmarish nocturnal truck ride down to the fincas echoes the account in the *Popol Vuh* of the protagonists' voyage through the
underworld. The nahual, of course, is an ancient tradition whose mythic significance is also dramatized in the *Popol Vuh.*

   In discussing the autoethnographic project in Menchú's testimonio, I have
found it useful to make comparisons with the conventions of standard ethnog-

raphy as it is used to describe indigenous and tribal cultures. In a number of key ways, Menchú's account intersects with or reproduces metropolitan ethnographic norms. She focuses a lot on myth and ritual and describes them in an objectivist, formulaic way. She values her culture's archaism and otherness to modernity, and shares the ethnographer's anguish at its vulnerability and loss. Her often idealistic evocations of altiplano village life seem to reproduce the ethnographic ideal of the isolated, self-sufficient closed corporate community that can be studied as a cultural whole. She shares the assumption implicit in traditional ethnography—that traditional subsistence cultures are to be envied for their integration with nature, their material and spiritual balance, their lack of alienation. She insists on secularity and relativism: "We Indians have more contact with nature. That's why they call us polytheistic. But we're not polytheistic . . . or if we are, it's good, because it's our culture" (59).

At the same time, Menchú's autoethnographic discourse employs a number of strategies to counteract exoticization and objectification. For instance, while valuing her culture's archaism and its pre-Columbian roots, she also values (and foregrounds) its resistance, its acquired anti-Westernism. The ceremonies she describes, far from being "pure" enactments of Maya tradition, are full of anticolonial, anti-Western proscriptions that have been incorporated into the ritual: so much for the "untouched" ideal. The generalized description of customs or rituals is readily interspersed with narratives that particularize, or even contradict the formulae. Chapter 12 takes this form, for instance. In the account of a wedding in chapter 10, the detailed formulaic description is counterposed to the anecdotal narrative of her sister's marriage: "In my sister's case, after the second ritual we all had to go down to the finca . . . so it was five months later that we celebrated the third ritual" (70) Not only does the ceremony deviate from the formula, as ceremonies nearly always do, but the marriage itself does not work out. "My sister's problem was that she went to live in another community with another language and different customs" (74). So much for the idea of a unified Maya world. And who expects rituals to work out the way they are supposed to?

Autoethnography can often be read even more radically, as parodying ethnographic norms and tropes. I often suggest such a reading of Menchú's description of her home village in chapter 1: "The village is called Chimel. I was born there. Where I live is practically a paradise, the country is so beautiful. There are no big roads, and no cars. Only people can reach it."[2] Almost inevitably the description invokes the anthropological trope of the isolated village where, from time immemorial, an ancient culture has been living out its ways undisturbed, in harmony with the land, rooted in the particularity of place under the watchful eyes of the ancestors. What a rude shock, then, when the next paragraph begins: "My parents moved there in 1960 and began cultivating the land. No one had lived up there before because it's so mountainous. But they settled there and were determined not to leave no matter how hard the life was. . . . Now it's a village with five or six caballerias of cultivated land" (2). Menchú's "ancestral village" barely predates her birth and has no history within her culture or any other; the site is not inviting or ideal but harsh, a last resort. Between the anthropological trope and Menchú's reality is the history of modernization and greed. Yet the account is not a negative one. On the contrary, the ancestral village trope is substituted by another to which Westerners will also respond: the founding of the city, the escape from defeat and oppression into what will become the new kingdom. The village expands over Menchú's lifetime: capitalism does not have a monopoly on progress (or anything else) in the originary world she evokes.

Briefly, *Reading 3* analyzes *I, Rigoberta Menchú* as a project in *intercultural mediation*, and focuses on the myriad mechanisms Menchú uses to establish correspondences and differences between Maya and Western ways of life and systems of knowledge. Her broad and creative uses of comparisons, contrasts, parallelisms, and parody demonstrate the possibility of being partisan and grounded without necessarily being ethnocentric. This reading also attends to Menchú's representations of the process of cultural contact and transculturation, and the kind of agency available to members of minority cultures contending with continual encroachment from dominant institutions. Menchú's pragmatic attitude to Catholicism comes up here, as well as her remarks on schooling and immunization. Of particular interest is Menchú's presentation of herself as a subject constituted by multiple knowledges, whose commitment to a particular cultural tradition does not cut her off from any form of knowledge or learning, or from exercising choices her home culture does not include. In these respects, Menchú exemplifies a figure I have come to call the "vernacular intellectual."

Reading 4 returns to the narrative unfolding of the text, but reads it this time not as political autobiography but as a story of love and loss. Beginning with the traumatic experience of being lost alone in the mountains when she was seven years old (chapter 5), and ending with her lone journey into exile, Menchú's narrative recounts a life of tremendous suffering and grief. In between is loss after loss of nearly everyone dear to her—despite her heroic labor on behalf of her community. The end of the book leaves open the question of how a person survives such accumulated losses.

Though not the preferred reading of the Menchú-Debray book, I believe this tragic structure accounts for a good deal of its force, especially for readers familiar with the experience of deep personal loss. Here too, the pact with the reader seems to be one of sharing. Menchú will take the reader with her down a road of suffering, struggle, and grief; the reader contracts to go, on the assumption that there is something important to be learned from the process.

This narrative of love and loss intersects in an interesting way with the political autobiography. Maturation seems to be encoded in Menchú's narrative in terms of isolation and solitude, not increasing connectedness or the achievement of one's place in a community. The highly symbolic childhood episode when she is lost alone in the mountains is designated as the first time she "really felt grown up" (28). Her entry into adulthood is marked not by marriage and the founding of a household but by separation and virtual exile as a maid in the city. Her work as an organizer is described not in terms of the experience of collectivity but in terms of lonely treks from village to village and the effort to relate to those different from herself. The consolidation of her identity as a leader is marked by the decision not to marry or have children. Her exile directly follows this logic of separation.

Ten years after the appearance of her *testimonio*, Rigoberta Menchú gave a speech to a predominantly student audience at the university where I teach. There were three points she seemed particularly eager to get across to her public, and all seem pertinent to the teaching of her *testimonio*. First, she said it was important—and very difficult—for privileged first-world people to comprehend what it is like to live without choice. "When I was small I could not choose," she said, "to feel hunger today but not tomorrow. I cannot choose whether to feel grief today but not tomorrow." Second, Menchú argued that it was essential—and difficult—for students to recognize the distinction between knowing something because one had experienced it, and knowing something because one has learned about it. People who know things by learning about them, she argued, must develop respect for those who know those things from having lived through them. *Respect* was the operative term. The academy, in truth, does not distinguish between knowing by learning about and knowing by experiencing or, if it does, it does so by privileging the former and not the latter. Yet, from Menchú's point of view, this epistemological distinction is absolutely fundamental, and the hierarchy of value runs the other way. The reading of her testimony that follows is one based on humility, among those whom privilege has protected from the suffering she recounts, and respect for those who endure it and find the strength to struggle for change. Teaching the book provides an ideal opportunity to explore the construction of academic knowledge and the motives for the academy's extraordinary means of discrediting experiential knowledge. Finally, there was the issue of responsibility. The people in the centers of power must, Menchú stressed, begin to take responsibility for the role of their societies and their governments in producing conditions the rest of the world must endure. Her call was not for North Americans to change Guatemala—"We can do that," she said—but for them to do something about North America. This, when the hour closes, is the message I try to leave with the classes I teach.

NOTES

1. The Carter administration cut off aid to Guatemala on the basis of its abysmal human rights record. As elsewhere in Latin America, this policy had a moderating effect

on repression. Elections were even held in 1978, though none of the viable candidates represented real change. The results were interesting. Though voting was required by law, two-thirds of the electorate abstained, and 20 percent of the ballots that were cast were spoiled (Jonas 1991, 122). President Lucas García was elected by a mere 15 percent of the voters, but the election, tragically, was recognized by the international community anyway.

2. I thank Davina Chen, doctoral student in the program in Modern Thought and Literature at Stanford, for this insight.

3. I thank Renato Rosaldo for sharing this reflection with me, and for many other insights that have come from our conversations about Rigoberta Menchú.

4. There are several widely differing English translations of the *Popol Vuh.*

6

CREATING A CONTEXT
FOR RIGOBERTA MENCHÚ

GENE H. BELL-VILLADA

I teach a yearly course at Williams College called "Latin American Civilization." The group of twenty to thirty students, mostly freshmen and sophomores, tends to be self-selected. That is, they gravitate toward the course out of some varyingly defined interest in its contents, and they come fairly open to the troubling issues commonly associated with the region's politics and culture.

Since 1989, the concluding title on the class reading list has been *Me llamo Rigoberta Menchú.* . . . The first few years I simply had the students read the book for a specific question on the final examination, with minimal in-class prepping on my part. My hunch was that the sheer eloquence of Rigoberta's powerful account, coupled with her own qualities of strength, courage, and down-to-earth humanity (and further helped by Elisabeth Burgos-Debray's excellent job of editing), would by themselves do the job of reaching her American undergraduate readers.

I was not disappointed. About the only complaints I received were of the "Oh no! Not another book!" kind. Indeed, to a degree that was quite moving, the students *liked* the book and admired its protagonist. In an instance I have not forgotten, a male student who struck me as comfortably straightlaced and middle-of-the-road began his exam essay by saying, "Rigoberta es una mujer increíble" (Rigoberta is an incredible woman). As a separate assignment, then, Rigoberta's life story pretty much stands on its own, and I recommend this approach as eminently doable.

The students, it bears noting, do not read Rigoberta innocently. In 1990 the excellent documentary *When the Mountains Tremble,* which features a twenty-three-year-old Rigoberta as narrator and interviewee, became available on video (at a whopping $280 purchase price). The class views the film concurrently with their reading assignment, and of course seeing and hearing Rigoberta on the big screen adds vividly to their book knowledge. Moreover, the larger context artfully portrayed in the movie—the savage military repression; the complicity of the landlords, the Church hierarchy, and the U.S. government; the shallowness and falsehood of the white oligarchy's little rituals; and the opposition struggles being waged by labor unions, liberation theologians, and Mayan guerrillas—lends a gripping "you-are-there" supplement to Rigoberta's printed pages and our class discussions.

In addition, the students have been building up some background. By the last weeks of the course they have read the more pertinent doctrinal chapters of Sarmiento's *Facundo*, followed by some critiques of his nineteenth-century Europhile, racist view of native peoples, as found in classic essays by Martí ("Nuestra América") and Fernández Retamar (*Calibán*), and also in José Vasconcelos's confused, counterracist, yet highly influential tract, "La raza cósmica." They have seen *Blood of the Condor*, Javier Sanjinés's very beautiful feature film about the conflicts between Western and Aymará cultures in Bolivia. They have learned something about the Mexican Revolution and its importance in first recognizing the most elementary rights of indigenous peoples, institutions, and values. Finally, they have written a seven-page paper comparing Rómulo Gallegos's *Doña Bárbara* and Alejo Carpentier's *The Lost Steps*, two well-known novels that represent, respectively, the mutually irreconcilable "Sarmiento" and "Martí" schools of thought in Latin America.

Hence they approach Rigoberta's exemplary story with some notion of debates such as "What is 'culture'?" or "What is 'civilization'?" and particularly, "What is to be the place of the indigenous in a 'modernized' Latin America?" In a continent where there are republics with majority Indian populations and a history of Indian revolts, where *mestizaje* plays a key role in providing social mobility but also fosters divisions among native ethnics, and where politicians assume stances ranging from sincere concern to hypocritical opportunism to racist contempt, Rigoberta Menchú is one of the latest if more outstanding instances in a complex totality, a broad picture that the students have been piecing together over the previous months.

Two other long-standing issues surround Menchú's book. The first is that of land tenure. During the first week the students have learned the meaning and implications of the word *latifundio*; the matter of inequitable land ownership in Latin America, with its deformed agricultural system and its routine large-scale abuse of nonwhite peasants, has been thereby raised for further discussion. With this knowledge, the students are prepared to "read" the privations endured by the Menchú family not simply as a moral clash between villains and their victims, but as a *sociopolitical* problem that generates endless class warfare, from above as well as from below. In this regard, mention is made at some point (sometimes with helpful seconding by a well-informed student of economics) of the major land reforms that were undertaken in Japan, South Korea, and Taiwan in the 1940s and 1950s, serving to instance the thesis that true economic development cannot take place unless a country's "land question" is resolved and the nation thence becomes self-sufficient in food output and distribution.[1]

The fact of the CIA-directed overthrow of reformist President Jacobo Arbenz is also indispensable information for discussing Menchú's text. Though in her book she makes no mention of the United States, the U.S. intervention of 1954 is forcefully dramatized in *When the Mountains Tremble*, with some vintage newsreel footage included—yet another useful aspect of that movie. Even a rudimentary acquaintance with those events is necessary for the students to understand the murderousness and impunity with which the Guatemalan military has ruled that country to this day, despite the recent shadow play of civilian government and elections in which all twelve candidates were conservatives.[2]

This cumulative learning had, thus far, sufficed in enabling my students to situate *Me llamo Rigoberta Menchú*, and indeed it still could. By the late 1980s, however, Rigoberta had begun to emerge as a presence on the first-world scene, through efforts not her own but of admirers and detractors. In 1989 her book (in English translation) became optional reading in the controversial "Cultures, Ideas, and Values" course at Stanford University. The inclusion prompted in turn the mendacious and mean-spirited attack on her in Dinesh D'Souza's best-seller *Illiberal Education* (1991). His misrepresentations were then uncritically repeated by C. Vann Woodward in *The New York Review of Books*. (A letter to the editor by me led to a retraction from Woodward, who, in his reply, admitted to not having read Rigoberta's book at the time he was writing his essay.)[3]

Meanwhile, shortly before the Columbus Quincentennial year, Rigoberta was attracting considerable attention for her labors on behalf of all new-world indigenous, and of course her 1992 Nobel Prize for Peace thrust her into the international arena and granted her a moral stature comparable to that of other nonviolent activists like Martin Luther King and Desmond Tutu. By 1993, over 100,000 copies of *I, Rigoberta Menchú* had been sold in the United States. As of this writing, Rigoberta's latest work is as an unofficial mediator between guerrillas and government in the 1994 rebellion of Mayan Indians in Chiapas, Mexico.

Given this qualitative change in Rigoberta's public standing, a fuller, more concrete and immediately relevant context, I realized, had become necessary for presenting (and now, discussing) Rigoberta's book. In the interests of balance and of casting a useful glance at her ideological opponents, I started to include handouts by two conservatives: the three pages of *Illiberal Education* in which D'Souza blasts *I, Rigoberta Menchú*,[4] and the essay "Questions of Conquest" by Mario Vargas Llosa.[5] Both were assigned to be read after Menchú.

The D'Souza excerpt serves to demonstrate the degree to which Rigoberta has evolved into a symbol and a target in the U.S. curricular wars. Because D'Souza had spoken at Williams College, our home institution, in 1991, there remained some memory still of his slippery, less than forthright style of argument. (Some of his talk-show appearances, I gather, may be available on video.) For all his suave righteousness, however, D'Souza's attack on Rigoberta is so wondrously ignorant and inaccurate that many class members are soon seeing through his game and catching on to his falsehoods. Twenty minutes with D'Souza's three pages are enough to reduce his credibility to zero.

Vargas Llosa's piece is a more serious matter. Written by the renowned Peruvian novelist on the eve of the Quincentennial, "Questions of Conquest" is a subtle, intelligent, often anguished look at the ongoing legacy of Spanish invasion and takeover. As is only to be expected, the essay reflects the author's own conservative preoccupations with the twin evils of "totalitarianism" and "fanaticism," a theme that has held center stage both in his novels since *The War of the End of the World* and in his concurrent political crusades (the latter of which culminated in his failed bid for the Peruvian presidency in 1990). Vargas Llosa, let it be said, expresses eloquent admiration for the advances that had been made by the Incan Empire, "a civilization that had reached a high level of social, military, agricultural, and handicraft development that in many ways Spain had not reached."

Yet why, according to Vargas Llosa, were the Spaniards able to defeat and destroy this high culture? His tendentious explanation is not unfamiliar: because of "the vertical and totalitarian structure" of Incan society, in which "the individual had no importance" (Llosa 1990, 49). Moreover, Vargas Llosa raises the stakes by finally asserting that, in the balance, the Conquest was an improvement over those "antlike societies" of yore, inasmuch as it "would give way to the creation of the individual as the sovereign source of values by which society would be judged" (51).

As a prime instance for his marginally positive "take" on the Conquest, Vargas Llosa cites none less than Fray Bartolomé Las Casas, whose heroic labors on behalf of the indigenous victims, the novelist observes, "could not have been possible among . . . the pre-Hispanic cultures." Hence, the invading Spaniards, by tolerating Las Casas, also brought "freedom," the force driving what was to become "the most powerful civilization in the world" (51). And while deploring the ever-continuing massacres of Indians then and now, Vargas Llosa concludes, "If forced to choose between the preservation of Indian cultures and their complete assimilation, with great sadness I would choose modernization, because . . . the first priority is . . . to fight hunger and misery" (52–53).

His greater sensitivity, compassion, and intellectual richness notwithstanding, Vargas Llosa's meditations are almost as deceptive as D'Souza's verbal gunslinging. First, there is something twisted and repugnant about his invoking Las Casas in possible *defense* of a war of genocide that was opposed by Las Casas himself. The argument is specious as well; it smacks of those sophistries, still trotted out by apologists for the Vietnam War, to the effect that the U.S. napalmings, carpet bombings, and defoliation were ultimately moral because U.S. antiwar protestors had the right to demonstrate against those actions—and indeed that the war was being fought precisely to defend the right to protest![6]

Vargas Llosa ignores the fact, moreover, that Las Casas was no mere "individual," no ordinary subject of the Spanish Crown, but a prominent man of the cloth, a member of Spain's spiritual élite and conquering priesthood—a Dominican friar and, later, Bishop of Chiapas—who thus operated under the protection of the Roman Catholic Church (if often in conflict with its higher prelates). It does not diminish Las Casas's moral stature to observe that his freedoms were not so much "individual" as *institutional* in origin. What would have been the fate—we may speculate—of a humble artisan, or of an ex-Jewish *converso*, who took it upon himself to criticize the entire project of Conquest and Christianization? Incidentally, even Hitler's Germany allowed churchmen to speak out against the Nazi régime's euthanasia programs, and it took their protests seriously.[7]

But getting back to Rigoberta: Vargas Llosa, we have seen, argues that assimilation and "modernization" of the indigenous will put an end to their "hunger and misery." Menchú's story dramatically gives the lie to Vargas Llosa's rosy conclusions and shows that, if anything, the Guatemalan version of Westernization has led to increased poverty for its Indian population as well as a military repression surpassing that in Fascist Italy and Franco's Spain. The greed of Guatemala's white land owners and officer corps continues unabated, and the Menchú family is but one of the countless victims of a free-trade utopia as envisioned by Friedrich von Hayek, Milton Friedman, and Mario Vargas Llosa. "Questions of Conquest" is among the Peruvian novelist's less innovative works of fiction.

Besides this "dialogue of texts" with her conservative coevals, two larger issues further frame our class discussion of Rigoberta: the Catholic Church and the struggles of women. The initial paper written by the students was a brief survey of Imperial Spain's Counter-Reformation crusade and neo-Scholastic culture, followed by a closer look at the great and endlessly fascinating Sor Juana Inés de la Cruz, notably the ways in which she coped, both as nun and as frustrated scientist, with her colonial society's restrictions. The students thus have some nodding acquaintance with the contradictory character of Latin American Catholicism: a dead weight yet also a possible haven for study, the spiritual arm of the oppressor yet also a sometime refuge for the oppressed (a matter raised with some cogency in chapter 5 of Octavio Paz's *The Labyrinth of Solitude*, which we read early on in the course).

Rigoberta, as we know, frankly describes herself as a Christian, and reading and study of the Bible figures prominently in her account of her coreligionists' regular activities. She specifically represents "the Church of the poor" (234–35), a subject dealt with toward the end of the important chapter 32, where she refers to the nuns and priests who are working, against inhuman odds, for justice in Guatemala.[8] In order to place Rigoberta's beliefs in context, I furnish the students an introductory sketch of what "liberation theology" is, starting with the 1968 Medellín Conference and on through such elementary facts as the *comunidades de base* and the involvement of church people in the Nicaraguan and Salvadoran revolutionary movements. The *Encyclopedia Britannica* has an adequate brief entry on liberation theology in its "Micropaedia" section, and in addition Jorge Castañeda, in his recent, highly acclaimed book *Utopia Unarmed*, gives us some informative, richly textured pages on the phenomenon of the ecclesial base communities.[9]

Last but not least there is the fact of Rigoberta as a woman—how that condition shapes her life, and how she in turn shapes her view of womanhood. Before we plunge into her book I explain to the class that "feminism" in Latin America is a completely different phenomenon from what it is in the United States, and that in some ways the word *feminist* may not be fully accurate. In this regard I furnish another handout, "América Latina: La mujer en lucha," by the Mexican sociologist Sara Sefchovich, a three-page essay that succinctly summarizes the Latin American "difference."[10] On a continent where lack of food, jobs, sanitation, and instruction are shared more or less equally by both genders, and in which the victims of military repression, torture, and murder are not exclusively of one sex or another, the battle for women's rights—Sefchovich notes—is not against men but rather is part of the larger battle for social justice.

In late-twentieth-century United States, by contrast, social struggles generally take on the form of single-issue, special-interest-group politics—labor unions here, environmentalists there, African Americans in this corner, other ethnics in that. Among the diverse components of this "pluralist" setup is a distinctively American brand of feminist "separatism" that is well-nigh inconceivable south of Texas. (I have met Latina women who frankly admit to feeling a certain resentment and even contempt for the exclusively gender-based approach of some U.S. feminists.) It is worth noting that the most widely recognized women's group in Latin America—the Argentine "Madres de la Plaza de Mayo"—builds on the traditions of motherhood and stresses not women-specific rights but a *connectedness* with their male and female kin, not gender separation but human solidarity (a noun that has largely vanished from the U.S political lexicon, except when speaking of Poland). Again, Castañeda's wide-ranging book provides a fine introduction to the "Madres" and other such groups (226–29).

Rigoberta in this regard represents, once again, a fundamental drift in Latin American culture. Despite D'Souza's glib labeling of her as a "feminist," she actually champions the right of indigenous women to bear many children and defends numerous other traditional female practices as legitimate aspects of the Mayan people's way of life. And while she sees *machismo* as a disease, she strenuously rejects as self-defeating any idea of creating a separate women's organization, calls instead for a broader-based solidarity in which "we [men and women] must fight as equals."

These overlapping contexts help place Rigoberta Menchú within the past and present history of Latin America. Her several identities as Guatemalan peasant, indigenous Mayan, Latin American woman, Christian revolutionary, and committed activist all serve to sum up and personify many of the larger questions that typify five centuries of Latin American oppression. In addition, by encountering her as the narrator of *When the Mountains Tremble* and as the direct or indirect target of conservatives both in the United States and Peru, American undergraduates are afforded the opportunity to "experience" Rigoberta, more variously and vibrantly, outside the pages of her own book. Still, as I noted above, Rigoberta's account is sufficiently plain speaking and powerful to be dealt with in a separate examination question or in an ordinary student book report. Even a class that is not necessarily about Latin America—courses, say, in women's studies, or on indigenous peoples or autobiography—would benefit from including her on their reading lists. *Me llamo Rigoberta Menchú* (along with its foreign translations) has become a kind of "underground" classic for our time.

NOTES

1. In this regard, see the article on "Land Reform" by Peter Frost in the *Encyclopedia of Japan*, and also Ezra Vogel, *The Four Little Dragons: The Spread of Industrialization in East Asia* (Cambridge, Mass.: Harvard University Press, 1991), 19, 50, and 87. On Taiwan, see Thomas B. Gold, *State and Society in the Taiwan Miracle* (Armonk, N.Y.: M. E. Sharpe, 1986), 65 and 67; and John C. H. Fei, Gustav Ranis, and Shirley W. Y. Kuo, *Growth with Equity: The Taiwan Case* (New York: Oxford University Press, 1979), 38–50. I am grateful to Professors Peter Frost and George Crane, of Williams College, for these references.

2. For a full account of the events of the 1950s, see Stephen Schlesinger and Stephen Kinzer, *Bitter Fruit: The Untold Story of the American Coup in Guatemala* (Garden City, N.Y.: Doubleday, 1982). Shorter summaries can be found in David Horowitz, *The Free World Colossus: A Critique of American Foreign Policy in the Cold War* (New York: Hill and Wang, 1965); John Gerassi, *The Great Fear in Latin America* (New York: Macmillan, 1965); or Eduardo Galeano, *Open Veins of Latin America* (New York: Monthly Review Press, 1973). For an overview of the present situation, see Tom Barry, *Guatemala: A Country Guide* (Albuquerque: The Inter-Hemispheric Education Resource Center, 1989).

3. C. Vann Woodward's article was in the 18 July 1991 issue. My letter to the editor appeared 26 September 1991.

4. Dinesh D'Souza, *Illiberal Education: The Politics of Race and Sex on Campus* (New York: Random House, 1992), 71–73.

5. Mario Vargas Llosa, "Questions of Conquest" in *Harper's Magazine*, December 1990, 45–54. Page references to this article will be cited within the body of the text. An anthologized version of the piece, in John King, ed., *On Modern Latin American Fiction*

(New York: Farrar, Straus and Giroux, 1989), 1–17, leaves out some important polemical material.

6. I deal with this pattern in my own novel, *The Carlos Chadwick Mystery: A Novel of College Life and Political Terror* (Albuquerque: Amador Publishers, 1990).

7. See Arno Mayer, *Why Did the Heavens Not Darken?* (New York: Pantheon Books, 1990), 383–84.

8. *I, Rigoberta Menchú: An Indian Woman in Guatemala.* Edited and introduced by Elisabeth Burgos-Debray. Translated by Ann Wright (New York: Verso Books, 1984).

9. Jorge Castañeda, *Utopia Unarmed: The Latin American Left after the Cold War* (New York: Knopf, 1993), 205–7, and 210–16.

10. Sara Sefchovich, "América Latina: La mujer en lucha." In *Perspectivas*, ed. Mary Ellen Kiddle and Brenda Wegmann, 3rd ed. only (New York: Holt, Rinehart and Winston, 1983), 79–81.

7

THE TESTIMONIAL OF RIGOBERTA MENCHÚ IN A NATIVE TRADITION

LUIS O. ARATA

When I taught for the first time a graduate course on pre-Columbian America, I chose to include *I, Rigoberta Menchú* among the required readings on the Maya, along with the *Popol Vuh*. The intended purpose was to give my students a clear sense that Maya culture still lives on and that, as far as the Maya are concerned, the past illuminates the present.

An extraordinary aspect of the ancient Maya civilization is its resiliency. Deeply seated traditions live on among the contemporary Maya, altered to some degree but still aligned with the spirit that brought them about. This is particularly true for the traditions described in the testimonial *I, Rigoberta Menchú*. A retracing of the ancient Maya roots of her beliefs shows that the resilience of these traditions is not accidental but is ingrained in a self-sustaining way, like the image of a tree, for example, is preserved in its seed.

As we explore relations between past and present, it is important to keep in mind that Rigoberta Menchú was not necessarily aware of the historical details of these traditions. She insists that traditions are observed because they come down from the ancestors, and the Maya are taught to always follow the lessons of the elders. The traditions are followed more out of reverence than necessity. It is part of a way of life. For us, outsiders to the Maya culture, it helps to have a sense of historical perspective when reading Menchú's testimonial to appreciate the profound Maya reverence for the past as well as their flexibility when forced to change. This sense of tradition coupled with the capacity to assimilate change is a key to Maya endurance against overwhelming odds such as the Spanish conquest of five centuries ago and the recent atrocities depicted in Menchú's harrowing testimony. What follows are the principal links to the Maya past found in Menchú's testimony. They provide students with a context needed to better appreciate Menchú's point of view. The bibliography lists the principal books used in connection with a first comprehensive look at the Maya.

THE NAHUAL

Menchú indicates that one of her basic beliefs is the notion of the nahual (Menchú 1984, 20). The very concept of nahual has an extensive history. The term itself is not Maya but Mexica, brought into Maya territory by the Aztecs. In the Aztec language Nahuatl, the term *naualli* (Miller and Taube 1993, 122) refers to the animal counterpart of persons. The person is born with such a relationship to a nahual. As Menchú indicates, the nahual refers to the double of a living being. For people, the nahual is often an animal, and it links the person to nature. The relation of the nahual works both ways. Every animal has a human counterpart also. To hurt an animal is to hurt its counterpart and vice versa.

The notion of nahual appears in the *Popol Vuh,* which is the most important ancient alphabetic Maya text that has survived. The *Popol Vuh* tells that the first four humans were able to transform themselves into their animal counterparts. This feat was possible subsequently only by sorcerers and other powerful persons.

The Aztecs also believed in the *tonal* or *tonalli* (1993, 172). This is the personality or spirit companion of a person, different from the nahual, and is strictly determined by the day of birth. But the Maya seem to have only one ancient term to describe both the tonal and the nahual. Menchú, as well, indicates that the nahual is determined by the calendar (Menchú 1984, 18), which is contrary to Aztec tradition. This single Maya concept is the *uay* or *way.* Nikolai Grube wrote: "*Way* means 'nagual'" in all lowland languages, and "animal transformation." Grube indicates that various Mayas in Quintana Roo told him of a sorcerer who can transform himself into a cat or a spider monkey. "They called the animals in which the sorcerer transformed himself *u way,* 'his nagual'" (cited in Coe 1992, 256–57). A glyph for this term has been found. It is the glyph of the *ahau,* meaning lord, but with half of the face covered by a jaguar skin (257). Actually, a common way to refer to a sorcerer or prophet of Yucatan, any person who has power beyond human means, is "balam" or jaguar (Ximénez 1965, 94). The jaguar is the most important animal alter ego. Not only does it form part of the *uay* sign, but its skin was widely used for book covers, as if it could also be the alter ego of the words contained in them. In Yucatan emerged a series of alphabetic books probably based on more ancient hieroglyphic texts. They became known as the books of *Chilan Balam* or books of the jaguar prophet. According to Diego de Landa's *Relación de las cosas de Yucatán,* the "chilan" was a priest who relayed the answers of the gods (Tozzer 1941, 43). The books of *Chilan Balam* are indeed books of prophesies. Their generic title suggests a rich play of meanings, because not only do they seem to have been composed by the mythical jaguar priest, a person whose nahual was the jaguar, but also we can imagine that such books were bound in jaguar skin like the ancient codices. The books that contained the answers of the gods within jaguar skin were like prophets. The phrase *Chilan Balam* can designate the writer of the prophesies, the reader who interprets them, or the book where they are contained.

This fluidity of meaning, not unlike the metamorphosis of a person into a nahual—or in less concrete terms, the relation of the spirit to its nahual—is a basic concept of Rigoberta Menchú's testimony. It is such fluidity that allowed the Maya to assimilate Spanish concepts without giving up their own, especially in matters of religion. Menchú (1984) explains the process of assimilation this way:

By accepting the Catholic religion, we didn't accept a condition, or abandon our culture. It was more like another way of expressing ourselves. If everyone believes in this medium, it's just another medium of expression. It's like expressing ourselves through a tree, for example; we believe that a tree has its image, its representation, its nahual, to channel our feelings to the one God. (80)

The flexibility of expression is a crucial aspect of Maya resiliency. The ability to adapt without giving up what is most important provides a continuity through change. The designs of a *huipil,* for instance, are an image of the ancestors (81). Similarly, the ancient hieroglyphic writing not only expressed a content, but also embodied it visually, like a huipil does. This redundancy of expression makes the system stronger. When the Spanish missionaries burnt the ancient hieroglyphic Maya books because they saw in them the work of the devil, the Maya were able to switch to the medium introduced by the Spanish, the alphabet, and express themselves through it. The same happened with language, as Menchú indicates:

Since the priests don't know our language and they say the prayers in Spanish, our job is to memorize the prayers, and the chants. But we didn't understand exactly what it meant, it was just a channel for our self-expression. It's very important for us, but we don't understand it. (81)

In Guatemala alone, there are over twenty Maya languages spoken. Menchú first learned Quiché, then Cakchiquel, Tzutuhil, and Mam (161). Finally she decided to learn Spanish, because she realized that it was the one language that permeated all Maya groups (162). This relativity of language, this notion that language itself is not a transparent thing but just another instrument of expression, is perhaps one of the most basic and ancient Maya characteristics. It may well be the root of their extraordinary expressive flexibility.

THE CALENDAR

According to Menchú, the Maya days that determine the nahual amount to a total of ten (18). In this set or week of ten sacred days we have an instance of an acculturation that merged two entirely separate systems into a single one. The original Maya calendar had weeks of twenty days rather than ten. These twenty days were combined with thirteen numbers to form a ritual 260-day calendar widely used throughout Mesoamerica (Miller and Taube 1993, 48). It was from this calendar that a newborn's spiritual makeup was established based on the birth date. The number would determine the strength of the day's figure. Among the present Maya there are many groups that still follow this ancient calendar. Barbara Tedlock (1992) in *Time and the Highland Maya* gives a detailed account of this practice.

Menchú, like many contemporary Maya, observes a modified calendar. The emergence of the ten-day week reflects a transformation of the counting methods to match the decimal system introduced by the Spanish. The ancient Maya used a vigesimal counting system, and the number of days matched the base of this system. Both were twenty. Then the Spanish introduced a base-ten system of counting. In time, some Maya modified the number of days of their week to match the base-ten counting, which became prevalent. However, they did not go so far as to adopt entirely the seven-day week of the Spanish. The ten-day week shows the trace of the ancient Maya notion that the number of days in a week was the same as the basis of their counting system.

THE ANCESTORS

Worship of the ancestors is a Maya cornerstone. In the *Popol Vuh*, the mythical grandparents Xpiyacoc and Xmucane have a central role in modeling life and making it come about. The grandparents are the asexual or mother-father aspect of the Makers. They are the diviners, the daykeepers. They are also called "midwife and matchmaker" since their function is precisely to mediate conception as well as birth. Although the Makers in their parental aspect engender life, it is the asexual grandparents who hold the wisdom to mediate conception and make it come about.

During the fourth and final process of creation described in the *Popol Vuh*, Xpiyacoc is the one who grinds the maize nine times to fashion the first four successful human beings. These perfect humans immediately praised their grandfather and grandmother: "thanks to you we've been formed, we've come to be made and modeled" (*Popol Vuh*, 166). Part of the initial perfection of the first four humans was that they were also mother-fathers, asexual like the grandparents. This perfection was taken away when the Makers realized they needed to scale back a little their creation. They created wives, and the first humans became fathers, which made them quite happy, but it also removed them from the realm of the grandparents.

Barbara Tedlock notes that the Maya of Momostenango believe in a trinity of sorts, comprising the gods, the world, and the ancestors (1992, 41). The gods are mostly the ones of Christianity. They took the place of the engendering aspect of the Maya Makers. The world comprises all that is human and earthly. And the ancestors are like the ones of the *Popol Vuh*. Menchú's testimony shows this similar division into three realms of what is most sacred, retaining, unchanged, the concept of ancestors. She invokes Heart of Sky, one of the Makers of the *Popol Vuh*, in the same breath as God: "The Bible says that there is one God and we too have one God: the sun, the heart of the sky" (Menchú 1984, xviii). She has moved away from the ancient Maya pantheon of Makers, but this was possible because in principle all the Makers are aspects of one creative spirit that can manifest itself in different ways depending on the occasion. So the adoption of a single Christian God is compatible with ancient Maya beliefs.

Whereas the flexibility of expressive means embodied in the notion of the uay or nahual gives the Maya their ability to adapt to new mediums, it is their worship of ancestors that gives them the backbone of permanence. For the Maya, the departed ancestors are an ever present force, source of legitimacy and tradition. The ancestors are omnipresent as well. Their image appears in a huipil, in the newborn, in the words of books, in the teachings of oral tradition. Menchú stresses repeatedly that all she knows comes from the Maya ancestors. This knowledge is not to be questioned and must be accepted as truth: "if an elderly person tells us this, then it must be true" (123).

Ancestral wisdom extends to details of dressing: "anyone who doesn't dress as our grandfathers, our ancestors, dressed, is on the road to ruin" (37). The huipil a woman wears links her to the ancestors. Even the way Maya sit is significant: "Indians think it is dreadful to sit on chairs," indicates Menchú. She indicates that especially the woman must sit on the ground, on woven mats, "because the woman is the mother of the home and the earth is the mother of the whole world" (73). The mat was a fundamental symbol of authority among the Maya, equivalent to a throne but with an earthly connotation. The kingly title *Ahpop* used by Maya rulers means literally "he of the mat." The title *Popol Vuh* given to the Maya book of creation, means "book of the mat," or book used by council members who sat on mats. By metonymy, the mat represents such council of rulers. The terms *Popol* and *pop* are considered equivalent. And in typical Maya fashion, *pop*, the term for "mat," has yet another dimension of meaning. It is the name of the first month of the Maya solar calendar of 365 days. The act of sitting on a mat introduces as well a new month, since the last day of a month is designated by the seating of the following month using a glyph that is the same as the seating of a ruler (Harris and Stearns 1992, 19).

"Nearly everything we do today is based on what our ancestors did," explains Menchú (1984, 17). She indicates that the main purpose of elected leaders is to embody all the values handed down from the ancestors: "every-thing that is done today, is done in memory of those who have passed on" (17). This is why the traditions expressed in Menchú's testimony are profoundly steeped in ancient ways.

SOWING

The rituals of birth and baptism described by Menchú are grounded in rich tra-ditions. One of these customs is that of the bundle. Menchú indicates that when a baby is born, "he's given a little bag with garlic, a bit of lime, salt, and tobacco in it, to hang round his neck" (12). She indicates that the function of the bag is to ward off evil things in life. This little red bundle recalls the ancient sacred bundles that had a deeper ritual meaning (Miller and Taube 1993, 47). A sacred bundle is "a sort of cloth-wrapped ark with mysterious contents" (*Popol Vuh,* 329). In the *Popol Vuh,* Balam Quitze, one of the first four humans, handed over to his successors one such small bundle as a sign of his being. It was called the "bundle of flames." The bundle was not to be unwrapped. Its contents were never seen, but the bundle was precious to those who remained: "it was a memorial to their fathers" (*Popol Vuh,* 198). From then on, the bundle became an object for remembering the ancestors. Some bundles probably contained bits of ancestral remains.

In Menchú's testimony, the bundle retains a ritual value. But now the con-tent is known, and they are things from the earth rather than ancestral objects. A slight shift seems to have taken place in the direction of celebrating the earth, which is another basic spiritual element in her testimony and certainly among the Maya, past and present.

Menchú gives testimony of the Maya reverence for the earth and their deep understanding of natural balances: "We must only harm the earth when we are in need. . . . This is why, before we sow our maize, we have to ask the earth's per-mission" (Menchú 1984, 56). The Maya of British Honduras held a similar con-cept when it came to fishing. Part of their fishing ritual involved a prayer: "O God, holy water, I am going to molest your heart, I am going to dirty you on account of your animals" (Tozzer 1941, 156). The earth is perceived as a living organism. Planting and fishing can disrupt it, but a display of reverence could maintain it in proper balance and yield a good harvest.

Prayer precedes sowing. Menchú indicates that prayers are offered to the earth, the moon, the sun, the animals and the water, because they join with the seed to provide food. Then all make promises not to waste food (Menchú 1984, 53). This respect for the environment as the provider of life permeates Maya beliefs.

It is not surprising then that many of the ancient Maya deities were asso-ciated with natural elements. Two important agricultural gods have been iden-tified: the maize deity Yum Kaax, nicknamed God E in the Schellhas nomenclature, and Chac, the god of rain, known as God B (Miller and Taube 1993, 146). The deity for the sun seems to be God G, Kinich Ahau, or "sun-faced lord." But the Maya had a rather fluid conception of deities and were not bound to a specific set of canonical, identifiable gods. The *Popol Vuh*, for instance, offers a different range of identifications. The sun and the moon are the Hero Twins, Hunahpu and Xbalanque, after they ascended into the skies following their victory over the dark lords of the underworld who were preventing the coming of the first dawn (*Popol Vuh*, 159–60). Menchú identifies the sun with Heart of Sky or the father, and the moon with the mother (Menchú 1984, 13). In the *Popol Vuh*, Heart of Sky is one of the Makers who presided over the entire sky-earth before the sun was created. This deity divided itself into two, Heart of Sky and Heart of Earth, when the earth was created.

The fluidity embedded in Maya cosmogony has allowed many Maya to adopt Christian symbols without giving up their own. Menchú's testimony stresses that there is no difference between the Christian God and Heart of Sky because she was taught that all Maya deities are different manifestations of one central spirit. Her view does not contradict the cosmology of the *Popol Vuh* and other ancient sources. However, there is an important difference: the Makers in Maya traditions always held council and discussed how to go about making things. They proceeded by trial and error. The ancient Maya did not have a god that acted alone, who never made mistakes. According to the *Popol Vuh*, the first moment of creation happened when all the Makers "agreed with each other, they joined their words, their thoughts" (*Popol Vuh*, 73). The ancient Maya never conceived of a Maker alone. Creation was a sort of festive occasion.

The *Popol Vuh* tells that in the fourth attempt, the Makers finally got the right ingredients to fashion the first successful human beings. Neither mud nor wood did the job. The ingredient that worked in the end was maize. In a similar vein, Menchú indicates that a newborn is told that he was made of maize because "his mother ate it while he was forming in her stomach" (Menchú 1984, 13).

Among the Maya, the birth of a child is compared to the sprouting of seed. Likewise, death produces a scattering of new seed. There is no rebirth, reincarnation, or life after death, as much as there is a sense of regeneration to perpetuate the spirit of the ancestors. "The child will multiply our race, he will replace all those who have died," tells Menchú. "From this moment, he takes on this responsibility, and is told to live as his 'grandparents' have lived" (13). This is precisely the spirit of the *Popol Vuh*, where the rhythms of the sowing and harvesting of corn, the flow of the seasons coupled with the motions of the sun and the moon, already prefigure human destiny.

HARMONY

When reaching into the past to explore Menchú's testimony, it is important that students understand the reason for this incursion into ancient Maya ways. In the final lines of her testimony, Menchú sounds a cautionary note: "I'm still keeping my Indian identity a secret. I'm still keeping secret what I think no-one should know. Not even anthropologists or intellectuals, no matter how many books they have, can find out all our secrets" (247). Her statement seems to go against the grain of any historical exploration. But it is in this conflict of interests that lies one of the most valuable lessons of her testimony. Knowledge, per se, is of little value. Knowledge gains value depending on how it is used. Once the facts of ancient Maya traditions are connected with Menchú's testimony, it is essential that students ponder about her insistence that no matter how much factual information we have, something will always remain out of our grasp. For Menchú, Maya traditions are something alive, but for us they have no experiential content. This is a fundamental difference. Maya traditions will remain at the level of devalued curiosities, unless we can draw connections into our own separate traditions and let Menchú's testimony resonate in our own world. Her secrets will remain meaningless until we can understand how to express our beliefs through a tree, as she puts it.

The question of language serves to better understand the difference between knowledge and experience. When reading Menchú's testimony, students must keep in mind that it is the edited account of a long interview conducted by Elisabeth Burgos-Debray. This in itself is a problem, since what we read is not entirely of Menchú's making. When it comes to the question of why Menchú learned Spanish, the different perspectives of Burgos-Debray and Menchú become striking. The editor indicates that Menchú learned Spanish, the "language of the oppressors in order to use it against them" (Menchú 1984, xii). Burgos-Debray put Menchú's act in strictly political terms: "Spanish was a language which was forced upon her, but it has become a weapon in her struggle."

Menchú sees the issue of language from an entirely different perspective. In Guatemala alone, twenty-two Maya languages are spoken. Menchú grew up speaking Quiché. Then she studied three other Maya languages along with Spanish. "Since Spanish was a language which united us, why learn all the twenty-two languages of Guatemala? It wasn't possible, and anyway this wasn't the moment to do it.... I learned Spanish out of necessity" (162). Menchú repeated the same act taken over five centuries earlier by Maya scribes. When Spanish missionaries saw in hieroglyphic writing the hand of the devil and they proceeded to systematically destroy all Maya hieroglyphic texts, scribes learned to use the Spanish alphabet and began to transcribe their traditions to this safer medium. For instance, this is how the *Popol Vuh* survived. The book itself indicates its sources are ancient texts (*Popol Vuh*, 27, 71, 219). For the scribes, the Spanish alphabet was another medium in which to express their beliefs still using their native languages. For Menchú, Spanish is the language that will allow her to communicate with those outside the world of Quiché. For her, Spanish is just another medium, and a very practical one. What is fundamental, however, is that she can use it to express her beliefs and to communicate. Her choice was practical and based on a flexibility which is eminently Maya.

When exploring Menchú's testimony in a native tradition, it is important to maintain a sense of respect. There is a difference that cannot be undone. Her deepest secrets are not a way of knowledge. They are not secrets at all. They are a way of life. Perhaps the most basic lesson of her testimony is that we must respect difference. We can have diversity in harmony. It is a treasure chest of richness.

8

OFFICIAL VIOLENCE
AND FOLK VIOLENCE
Approaching
I, Rigoberta Menchú
from the Perspectives of
Folklife and Peace Studies

WILLIAM WESTERMAN

I, Rigoberta Menchú is autobiography, the story of one woman, but it is also the story of a family, a village, a people, and ultimately the human struggle for justice. Personally I have been privileged to encounter Rigoberta Menchú from a variety of angles. As a teacher and reader I have been fortunate to read her words and learn some of her story. Closer to my heart, as an activist, I consider myself lucky to have heard her voice in person, listening to her public appeals for justice to a North American audience as well as to, in a more relaxed moment, some ribald jokes she shared among fellow refugees.

If my own personal approach is divided between scholar and activist, I am also fortunate to work in not one but two fields, each of which is itself interdisciplinary. I have taught selections from her book in a department of Folklore and Folklife, in a course entitled "Folklore, Politics, and Ideology," and in a department of Peace and Justice, in an introductory course to that field. Each of those two fields continues to define itself, to borrow from other fields, and to approach our world from vantage points that other fields do not, and each gives us special insight into the relevance of the Quiché struggle for human rights to our own quest to understand and create a better world. The approach

For helpful readings of an earlier draft of this chapter, I thank, in addition to the editors of this volume, Elizabeth Morgan and Prolung Ngin for their helpful comments. I would also like to thank Dorothy Noyes for encouraging me to write on this topic from the outset.

of peace studies corresponds with that of folklife studies, as both begin from the perspectives of those who speak and are often not heard, those who tell their stories of injustice and oppression from firsthand experience.

One theme in Menchú's testimony of concern to both fields is the articulation of different forms of violence in the war of the Guatemalan military against the Guatemalan people. We can define violence as the use of force to cause harm, damage, destruction, or even death. In Menchú's text we can distinguish two kinds of violence: "official" violence and "folk" violence. These correspond to distinctions between, for example, official religion and folk religion, as Don Yoder has outlined (1974, 74, 76, 80), or between official elite culture and folk culture. If we apply such a concept, it becomes clear that there are vast differences in the use and execution of official violence and folk violence, that is, the violent forces of states and other formal institutions used against the people as opposed to those used by the people in their own defense.

The violence of the rich, the army, and the government consists of invasion and atrocity, not to mention economic deprivation and the use of professional soldiers and technology, while the violence of the people consists of self-defense, home-made weaponry and a home-grown strategy. I have attempted to teach this book in two courses not only to develop an awareness of oppression against indigenous nations, especially in Guatemala, and against women, but also to raise awareness of the meanings and varieties of violence in the contemporary world. Students, particularly those who have grown up in the United States and those who come from middle- or upper-class backgrounds, tend to conflate different kinds of violence into the same animal, or they privilege the violence associated with legal authority over other forms, blurring distinctions between the violence of people under attack, such as the Quichés, and the violence of those in power, such as the army. If we want them to question critically the ideas they hear from official or media sources, explaining and articulating the varieties in human violence can be a useful first step.

Violence against indigenous people has been a way of life since the European invasion, and that can be an important lesson for students. For an understanding of how European domination has manifested itself it is necessary to examine all the component parts of indigenous *campesino* folklife: land, settlement, and housing patterns, local and family economics, work patterns, foodways, and religion and belief, particularly where syncretistic beliefs are involved. European colonial powers established official religions, notably Roman Catholicism, official languages, mostly Spanish, Portugese, and English, and official systems of economics, namely feudalism, capitalism, and private property. All these systems, imposed upon, within, and alongside the indigenous (and in the case of African Americans, imported) culture of farming and working people, dramatically affected and even devastated traditional ways of life, systems of belief, and many forms of art and culture. Even the style of fighting and attacking, the very style of violence itself, bore the mark of the invaders. The colonial armies, the state, and the organized church intervened in virtually all aspects of traditional folklife in the native nations they invaded. Indigenous life was changed by force. Religion, language, and land ownership were and remain central areas of conflict, and those conflicts were never contested fairly; Europeans never regarded the Native Americans as equals, and had little or no respect for their traditional practices and beliefs.[1] Thus the overt goal of European invaders was to change forcibly the folklife of the indigenous inhabitants of the region. With the power—and what they felt was legitimacy—of the state and the official church behind their guns, their blades, their fires, and their dogs, they carried out an orchestrated campaign to destroy native cultures, which lasted hundreds of years.

It is not then an exaggeration to characterize the last five hundred years as an invasion and occupation of native lands. The violence that accompanied and indeed accomplished this invasion was by definition "official"; church sponsored or state sponsored or both, it was carried out with a fervor legitimated by the motivating inspirations of God and country.[2] In contemporary Guatemala, as Menchú details for us, the military conducts an "anticommunist" campaign designed to maintain the economic status quo of the government, and the ladino land owners engage in every form of tactic to ensure the continuation and development of exploitation through a finca plantation system. One of the achievements of Menchú's testimony is that she spells out how this economic system neither is inevitable nor has evolved naturally. It is the result of planning, invasion, and violent domination by the state in an attempt (with mixed success) to destroy the traditional folklife of the Mayans. Their way of life has survived, but only in the face of the unrelenting violence of the state. As she says, "But we have hidden our identity because we needed to resist, we wanted to protect what governments have wanted to take away from us. They have tried to take our things away and impose others on us, be it through religion, through dividing up the land, through schools, through books, through radios, through all things modern. . . . we know that they are weapons they use to take away what is ours" (Menchú 1984, 170–71).

Menchú depicts the severity of official violence in the horrendous passages describing the murders of her brother, father, mother, and Doña Petrona Chona. The objectives of the army in the murders were twofold. First, they intended to kill those who opposed the government. And second, they needed to communicate to the survivors the seriousness of their threat, and the unimaginable pain of the torture and mutilation as a deterrent. The horror of the killing alone is not enough; the agents of the state must amplify this horror to convey their full intent to the people.

And so the murders of Rigoberta's family—and thousands of others—are brutally stylized. Killing with impunity by maintaining a fiction of legitimacy, a state can kill with an illusion of humaneness (as in U.S. capital punishment) or can intensify the punishment by terrifying the survivors. The Guatemalan government and military have consistently chosen mutilation and the most sacrilegious forms of murder precisely to break the living. Like the Nazi concentration camps, like the atomic bomb, the war against the indigenous campesinos is a final solution, designed to exterminate and devastate, either physically, culturally, or spiritually, an entire race of people. Only a state could have such weapons and such perverse creativity at their disposal, and only a state could get away with murder on such a large and indiscriminate scale, by legitimating acceptable murder and torture. Given the expense of weaponry, only a state could wield all the sophisticated technology necessary for a war of psychological debilitation.

An examination of this weaponry of official violence also leads us to an important distinction between these different types of force. While there might be some disagreement among folklorists, it is fairly safe to generalize that the standards and materials of production for folk art forms, whether verbal or material arts, are often developed within the community in which they are used. That is not to say that a rejection of outside technology is a requisite for something to be considered folklife, but that the standards of appropriateness, the aesthetics, the proper usages, and the practices are developed within the same community. A folk artist is likely to adapt outside materials to suit community or individual purposes, rather than follow directions or orders from above.

The weaponry of the Guatemalan military is imported, and it incorporates all sorts of technology with which the campesinos are unfamiliar. The soldiers have to learn from their officers (and from U.S., Taiwanese, and Israeli advisors) how to use these weapons and how to develop strategies for counterinsurgency.[3] In contrast, the campesinos have to develop their own weapons, or steal the weapons from the army. They also decide things more democratically, after discussion, rather than rely on a more hierarchical system of following orders. The difference is almost analogous to that between an academically trained painter, learning technique from a teacher in an art school with purchased materials, and one who works in a community having learned technique from traditional cultural elders and undertaking a radically different decision-making process, one based on native standards and tastes and sometimes using natural materials. Even the contrast in Menchú's descriptions of how the parties plan their actions—the campesinos discuss the situation among themselves, while the Indian soldiers must follow orders from their officers under fear of prosecution if not death—demonstrates this difference between a top-down (or originating from external sources) official style, and a community-based folk style, where decisions more democratically rely on input from the participants themselves.

Official violence, targeting the poor and the indigenous, does not occur in a historical or social vacuum, although North Americans tend to view it that way. Nor are violent incidents isolated. Violence pervades all of Guatemalan society, not in an abstract way, but concretely in all sectors of life. Official violence is interconnected. Single events are frequently part of larger campaigns of repression, or they can be connected loosely in an atmosphere in which certain behaviors are encouraged, permitted, or at the very least likely to flare up. Such acts are part of a system of structural violence, acts against individuals and communities when the roots of the problem lie in structural tensions and problems (that is social, political, economic) in the larger society. The violence is systemic, and we must remember who controls the system.

Not all violence in Central America, as some have noted, is part of that system, but all violent acts need to be placed in social and historical context if we are to understand them. So suggested Ignacio Martín-Baró, one of the six Salvadoran Jesuits assassinated in 1989, in an important essay on the impact of violence written a year before his death, but not published in English until 1991. He described the idea of structural violence, noting that the "high level of violent coercion [was] required to maintain social hierarchies in the situation of structural injustice characterizing Central America. . . . In other words, the violence is an attempt to safeguard the social interests of the dominant classes" (Martín-Baró 1991, 341), though not all violence is structurally part of a class struggle. Acts of war and repression in particular are part of this social struggle of the dominant classes to protect their interests. In context, however, the commission of violent acts—even those not associated with war and political repression—reveals much of the underlying structure of a society at all levels, large and small. "The violence of parents against their children, for instance, reflects not only internal family conflicts but also the characteristics of a culture which has placed the destiny of its children almost totally in the hands of their progenitors" (342).

With great clarity, Martín-Baró describes what I have been calling "official violence":

> Repressive violence targets the civilian population, not the enemy army,[4] and its objective is to achieve, by violent coercion, the political control not achieved through persuasion or social consensus. . . . Certainly, the cruelty to victims observed in certain assaults or the treatment of the civilian population in certain military operations often derive from the characteristics of their authors more than from any objective requirement of the actions themselves. However, what characterizes the predominant forms of violent actions at the present time in Central America is their depersonalization, and even their professionalization: assaults, bombings, kidnappings and torture are carried out with the same technocratic dispassion with which a watch is repaired or a chicken is cooked. (337)

This is to my mind the very opposite of the violence to which Menchú's village must resort. Furthermore, the idea of professionalism is also the very antithesis of the self-defense of the villagers; killing is the profession of the army because only the dominant classes can afford to pay others to commit their violent actions for them.

Could we suggest that official violence serves to maintain the status quo, the existing oppressive social structure, while folk violence either serves to subvert that order or exists outside the system of social domination? Perhaps—although there are some forms of violence, such as domestic abuse, that uphold the oppressive domination of women while sharing some characteristics of folk violence, such as the use of available materials and the apparent origins within the community (family, neighborhood) structure. But again, the aim is not to classify all incidents of violence into one box or another but to provide a model for understanding the characteristics of violent acts as a way to reveal to students (which we all are) the underlying power structures of society.

Violence is not random, though individual violent acts may seem to be. Viewed from a distance—and not necessarily a disinterested one—they form patterns, patterns which may be mere shadows of the actual structure and its reinforcement. Each grisly murder in Rigoberta Menchú's experience, each threatening message from the army and death squads, each death she witnesses from starvation, disease, and malnutrition, each army massacre in a village, is a representative example of what has taken place in many villages, across El Quiché and across all Guatemala (and indeed, across Central America). Rape by government forces is one of the most frightening acts and symbols, perpetuating the oppression of individuals, all women and children, and all native campesinos. Every such act of official violence—concrete or symbolic—reveals, as part of a larger structure, a social hierarchy that oppresses entire classes of people.

Ironically (and yet, on the army's part, intentionally), many of the individuals who perpetuate that larger system of oppression through violent acts are Indian campesinos themselves, like the two captured in her village, who are coerced into taking the actions they take and who are kept from seeing that larger pattern of oppression by being indoctrinated with a demonizing, genocidal ideology (Menchú 1984, 148). Upon capturing these soldiers, the villagers engage them in discussions in the hopes of getting the men to recognize the larger context of their violent actions (125, 148–49): "We made him see that it wasn't the soldiers who were guilty but the rich who don't risk their lives" (138).

We cannot restrict ourselves to the analysis of violent *acts*. A full discussion of violence in this book must also include the topic of institutionalized violence, though it is more often implicit in Menchú's work, whereas in analyses from the perspective of liberation theology it is more explicit. Menchú does recognize, however, that perhaps the most insidious and continual form of violence against the Native Peoples in Guatemala is economic, that is, the control of land, resources, and production by the ruling oligarchy that guarantees starvation, malnutrition, poor sanitation, and disease among the campesinos. As the German theologian Dorothee Sölle has written, "Each day there are fifteen thousand casualties in the war of the rich against the poor" (1983, 3). If ever one kind of violence was by definition official, it is institutionalized violence, because only the people in positions of power are those with access to social and economic control and decision making. The poverty and oppressive working conditions that Menchú outlines are indeed signs of this economic violence.

The term *institutionalized violence* dates back at least as far as 1968, and the conference of Latin American bishops in Medellín, Colombia. Work already undertaken by clergy and lay people throughout Latin America in the 1960s identified the nature of these injustices. One group of Brazilian priests, for example, wrote, "We feel we have right and a duty to condemn unfair wages, exploitation, and starvation tactics as clear indications of sin and evil" (quoted in Gutiérrez 1973, 109). The Peruvian theologian Gustavo Gutiérrez, active in the drafting of the Bishop's letter, wrote that such institutionalized violence "is responsible for the death of thousands of innocent victims" (108).

In fact, as Menchú describes the division of communal lands by the Guatemalan government (e.g., 1984, 158), we can see the clear links between economic domination and the destruction of the community supports that keep people united against their common enemies of death and the military. We can also see the conflicts between the communal way of life of the Mayans and the Euro-American concepts of individualism and private property, which literally divide up Menchú's community. This conflict mirrors the other conflicts that the Latin American liberation theologians write about, between socialism and communal ownership on the one hand and capitalism and private property on the other. But in both cases, private property—historically a result of theft and sociologically the destruction of thousands of years of traditional folklife—is a very real form of injustice and violence.

Ultimately it is this debate, on the extent to which economic injustice is in fact a form of violence, that has led many theologians (and others) to question the meaning of nonviolence and to ask if it is not better to pick up a gun to end the grave violence sooner, rather than act nonviolently, thus allowing the current violent system to claim more victims during the lengthy and complicated process of liberation. Just as the revolutionary priest Camilo Torres took up a rifle in 1973, so does Rigoberta Menchú's younger sister, when she joins the guerrillas (243). One can argue they were joining the just war to end the larger system of violence that remains predominant.

Though in United States society it may be difficult to communicate to affluent students how economic inequality can indeed be a form of violence, Menchú's story usefully details how the military leaders and economic oligarchy must resort to physical violence to uphold their murderous economic system. Thus, in teaching her work in the North American classroom, we can illustrate the links between economic, institutionalized violence and the more direct physical form with which U.S. students would be more familiar. Yet it is not only intentional killing that provides this link. The descriptions of her

young brothers' deaths—Felipe from insecticide intoxication and Nicolás from
malnutrition (38)—are among the most gripping instances in her book of the
direct relationship between economic injustice and callous physical murder.
When Rigoberta's friend dies also from insecticide poisoning at the finca (87–
89), she questions who is responsible. The people who sprayed the crops are
directly responsible, but who hired them? And why did they spray when workers were in the field?

I, Rigoberta Menchú is as much a statement on the resilience of traditional
life as it is a condemnation of state-sponsored oppression and racism. The two
themes are intertwined throughout.

> When children reach ten years old, their parents and the village
> leaders . . . remind them that our ancestors were dishonoured by the
> White Man, by colonialisation. But they don't tell them the way that
> it's written down in books. . . . No, they learn it through oral recom-
> mendations, the way it has been handed down through the genera-
> tions. They are told that the Spaniards dishonoured our ancestors'
> finest sons, and the most humble of them. And it is to honour these
> humble people that we must keep our secrets. And no one except we
> Indians must know. (13)

> Again this is all bound up with our commitment to maintain our cus-
> toms and pass on the secrets of our ancestors. . . . Nearly everything
> we do today is based on what our ancestors did. This is the main pur-
> pose of our elected leader—to embody all the values handed down
> from our ancestors. . . . Everything that is done today, is done in
> memory of those who have passed on. (17)

Without the resistance, without the secrecy, the culture would have died long
ago. It has survived not because of some mystical or historical accident, but
because those who practiced it made the conscious choice to keep much of it
hidden from the Euro-American view, and to combine that with a refusal to
submit totally to European domination. Those aspects of the Euro-American
cultures the indigenous Guatemalans have adopted (as in Menchú's case, Catholic Action) have been used in conjunction with, not instead of, native beliefs
and practices.

Showing to students that this is an oral, agricultural, traditional Native
American culture is only part of the teacher's task. The fact that the culture has
been guarded like riches from outside invaders, and the historical fact that such
protection has required conscious action and struggle, is another significant
part. The means of self-defense, whether newly invented or passed down orally,
are part of the traditional culture, since such defense has become such an
important part of the way of life for the past five hundred years.

What typifies the violence that Menchú and her people use? As she says, "We didn't like violence but if it was the only way of saving our lives, we would use it with justice" (146). In the moving episodes (chapters 17–19) of the army invasions on her communities, describing two separate captures of individual government soldiers, Menchú speaks of some of their methods of defense, what in English is termed "people's weapons" (*armas del pueblo* in Spanish, which encompasses the double meaning of the Spanish word *pueblo* as both "people" and "village"). The materials they use are literally what they have around, including household tools, axes, machetes, and even hoes. They also use materials from the natural world as weapons of defense: stones, lime, chile, and salt, devising ways through practice to make these effective in harassing and disarming the invaders. And they invent and create their own more complicated weapons and traps, including adapting the catapults they use to scare birds from the maize fields and developing their own forms of Molotov cocktails. Even the traps and techniques for escape and survival they develop from their knowledge of the materials in their natural environment. But ultimately the weapon of struggle is not merely physical, but spiritual. "Our main weapon," Menchú states, "is the Bible" (130), but of course the spirituality is not only Christian but traditional Mayan as well.

Her justification for self-defense comes from the Bible, but here too it is interwoven with an appreciation of her own culture: "Many relationships in the Bible are like those we have with our ancestors, our ancestors whose lives were very much like our own. The important thing for us is that we started to identify that reality with our own. . . . We tried to relate [the Biblical stories] to our Indian culture" (131). Recognizing that through both Indian and Christian traditions they had the moral justification to defend themselves, they began to fashion their own forms of resistance. She concludes, "We even got the idea of using our own everyday weapons, as the only solution left open to us" (132).

All these are in direct response to their "constant fear of the enemy, with its more and more modern machines [and] modern weapons" (142). The responsive and reactive nature, the mere fact that these are acts of resistance, in some way already sets them apart. The campesinos are not upholding an unjust social order, they are trying to wrest control of that order away from those who use their economic and military power against the people. But as the weight of the state and the economic power lie behind the violence of the government, such actions of resistance must take on different forms, even when and if the same weapons are available (from different sources).

It is the organic process of using these weapons and learning to use them that differentiates the people's response from the government's oppression. "We knew how to throw stones, we knew how to throw salt in someone's face— how to do it effectively. . . . We've often used lime. Lime is very fine and you have to aim it in a certain way for it to go into someone's eyes. We learned to do it through practice; we practiced taking aim and watching where the enemy is. You can blind a policeman by throwing lime in his face. And with stones for instance, you have to throw it at the enemy's head, at his face. . . . These things we're practicing the whole time in the village. And if we're stuck in our homes, we can resort to throwing hot water at them. . . . We need to be on the constant lookout for new techniques" (129–30).

Defense of the communities becomes an important arena of conflict, and safe communication a necessity of survival. The use of lookouts, signals, and warnings, decoys and traps are early means of resistance against army invasions, and all are secretive, even one could say folkloric, means of defense. The signals of self-defense (128) become the folklore of the resistance. The people use the weapons they have, including machetes and tools, and devise traps of their own making. For this protection, they utilize as well their "friends from the natural world . . . the plants, the trees, and the mountains" (128). And when there was no instruction, no word of mouth on how to make a weapon or devise some form of protection, the villagers would invent something for themselves.

An encouraging thing about these communities is their inclusive vision of the larger Indian-ladino conflict. Recognizing that they are defending themselves, other villages, and Indian culture in general, they see themselves as protecting not only their own immediate interests but those of their fellow citizens. Both times a soldier is captured, an important part of their work involves attempts, through oral means, to convert the soldier to their side, to show him how he is carrying out a war against his own people. If successful, this ideological victory could affect the soldiers' actions after they return to their unit; thus in most cases, a soldier returning from having been captured by guerrillas or campesinos would be killed by his military unit. But this ideological struggle is a cultural one, pitting the Indians against the ladinos, and offering to welcome any indigenous soldier back into the ranks of the people, that is, into a larger version of their community.

Ultimately, elsewhere in the mountains, defensive acts of resistance by civilians lead some to join the armed guerrilla movement. Guerrilla warfare is almost by definition a form of folk war. It is unorthodox, carried out surreptitiously, and uses nonconventional, invented means. It also relies on matériel that is either stolen or otherwise purchased or acquired illegally. The uniforms, when they exist, are most often stolen, but often there are no uniforms. Sometimes the combatants wear whatever dark civilian clothes they have, and they have even been known to wear plaid and other nonstandard colors and patterns in Central America. They also darn their own torn clothing. So much of the materials used by guerrilla armies is makeshift, as opposed to the formally outfitted and funded official armies. As with the defense of the village, the combatants in the mountains make use of all they know, including their cultural background, and derive and implement their methods within the community.

Guerrillas are also, in the Guatemalan and Salvadoran examples of the 1970s and 1980s, fighting for liberation as opposed to oppression. Consequently they do not resort to the tactics of the government forces (rape and torture being the two most prominent excessive forms of state terror). They do not invade but hide themsevles away in the mountains. They have relied on their own signals, systems of communication, mass media, and of course, music. In short, they have had to fend for themselves, develop their own physical means of fighting and their own intelligence networks and ideological and communicative strategies. Above all, their goal is not to maintain the social order but to change it and recreate a new, more just order.

This official/folk dichotomy is at best a heuristic model, and no more. I don't intend to set up a model of violence in order to have students classify which is "official" and which is "folk." The value in this model for me is that it ascribes power and responsibility to particular groups and individuals and establishes that all parties in the conflict are not operating from similar positions within the historical context. The mere fact that official violence has the weight of the state behind it (e.g., conventional war, armed forces used to control the populace, the death penalty, low-intensity conflict) is enough to merit such a distinction; even if students want to condemn all acts of violence outright, it is helpful in a political analysis to distinguish between state-sponsored violence and more independent acts. Official violence typically rests comfortably within the economic, political, and social order (indeed, it upholds that order), it is part of the overall social power structure, and it utilizes modern weapons and technology, most of which are imported from specialized manufacturers. Folk violence, on the other hand, utilizes homemade weaponry or materials from the natural environment, fashioned by the very community (pueblo) that will use them. In the case of Guatemala, such violence is part of a larger resistance movement against a social order that kills and oppresses, and therefore the existing violence is used in what many have safely called a "just war." Insofar as the objects of the violence are private or government property, and attempts are made to minimize cruelty (such as releasing the captured soldiers unharmed), the folk violence in this case is comparatively muted, though it is certainly possible to think of other examples elsewhere in the world where such violent resistance may be more severe.

I'd like to report that my experiments with this text were completely successful, that I presented these distinctions with great clarity and that my students grasped the material and began to question all forms of violence around them. In fact, I was hampered by, among other things, my inexperience, and I hope next time to be able to provide clearer paths for approaching the material. Few students felt outraged and appalled by the human rights violations, and few felt the urgency I did when I first heard Menchú's story (although, interestingly, I first heard her story orally, from her lips). Factors other than inexperience undoubtedly contributed to my shortcomings in treating the material as well. For example, though her Nobel Peace Prize was announced a few weeks after we had covered her book in class, so scant was the reporting that few students knew when they returned from fall break that she had won the award. Part of the problem in breaking through has to do with getting students to think about the level of repression and the state of human rights in the world, when many of them have never looked at that closely before. Both Peace Studies and Folklife Studies require us to examine some of the most basic ideological underpinnings of our lives; her book is a shock especially to those who have never before considered these issues of violence and repression (one wonders what most U.S. immigration judges would make of it, while they were denying 99 percent of Guatemalan political asylum claims).

I also suspect that sometimes the level of official violence in the book is too strong for some students to bear. I did have the experience for example of students' confusing the murder of her mother with that of her father. In addition, since the book deals with a very different culture, even the geography and language can be unfamiliar; some students mixed up the name of the author with the name of her people, and were even confused as to Rigoberta's gender. Perhaps these problems all arise from an unwillingness to read the material.

That unwillingness to read brings up an important point that as a folklorist I not only cannot ignore here, but do not overlook in my course. This is essentially an oral text, a testimonio, not a written work of literature. All oral texts lose something on the page. Even if the content by and large is preserved in writing, much of the meaning and the experience will be lost, in part by the transition from oral to written form, and in part by the intervention of one or more editors. Such oral features as style, gesture, intonation, and the spatial and temporal contexts of narration can bear on the force and meaning of the narrative. The present generation of students in the United States is particularly focused on aural and visual media and seems to consistently respond more enthusiastically to guest lecturers and films. The fact that students have to *read* Rigoberta Menchú's story starts them (and her) at a disadvantage (though I confess I haven't used the film in which Menchú appears).

I bring this up because as a folklorist, one trained in working with live people and oral materials, I am especially aware of what is irrevocably lost in a book such as this. As much as I admire Elisabeth Burgos-Debray's mission in bringing Menchú's story to the world,[5] I must also point out here, as I do in my classes, the little acts of "violence" she has committed in bringing this story to the page. Menchú speaks in her second language[6] but her story has been edited and, worse, rearranged from her own organization of the material in her telling, apparently to a form more comfortable for Euro-American audiences. Burgos-Debray admits to developing a chronological outline at the beginning of her interviews with Menchú to guide the discussions. Menchú initially follows this chronology, then begins to digress in her own way. Yet, Burgos-Debray notes that, in the editing process, she reorganized Menchú's testimony: "I followed my original chronological outline, even though our conversations had not done so, so as to make the text more accessible to the reader" (xx).

As I tell my students, I am of two minds about this. Obviously, anything to help the message get across with all the power and immediacy it has for the teller has to be for the better. And yet, I ask myself, Why is it that indigenous, non-Western texts must always be reshaped to make them more accessible to Westerners, when one could argue that it is Westerners who could benefit from the knowledge that there are other ways of ordering the world and configuring experience and information that are equally valid? The irony is that it is not in silencing Menchú but in providing an outlet for her voice that this intervention occurs. Folklorists know that each culture, each community arranges its land, its homes, its furnishings differently—which probably most people would readily accept—and we also recognize that each of us arranges our words and narratives differently. If there is something to be learned from the criticism of this book it may be that an editor's well-meaning (and perhaps beneficial in some important ways) paternalism can perpetuate a form of official—albeit subtle—violence: the Native American notion of narrative being dominated by the Euro-American.

I believe this is one of the most important books of our time and worthwhile reading for all college students. However, not only the book itself but also the methods used in editing the book show that none of us are free from the violent legacy of the cultural invasion of this hemisphere, that even well-intentioned acts of love can have harmful consequences. Even more important, this book shows us that cultural violence works on many different levels, that it can be murderous against people and destructive of landscapes or that it can subtly change the words and texts of the most profound speakers for peace. The book is about voice and culture, about the struggle for human rights within a cultural tradition, about the conflict between a traditional culture and economic and military forces that are not only cruel but blind to what and whom they destroy. For me the value in teaching the book is in its depiction of the nature of official violence and unofficial resistance and in, more importantly—given the audience in the North American classroom—the variety, worth, and dignity of human existence in all its forms. The fact that many U.S. students cannot identify where Guatemala is or who the Quiché people are, while they support a government that has traditionally funded, armed, and aided precisely those who have done so much to eradicate Mayan culture and its citizens, should not be overlooked. If any book can begin to liberate the oppressors, this is it.

NOTES

1. Many students, if not unaware of this, are not yet ready to accept it.

2. In the peace studies class I had also assigned the first volume of Eduardo Galeano's *Memory of Fire* trilogy, and my discussion of these books led one student to ask

me in front of the class—remarkably, to my mind—"Do you love Indians or something? I mean, you're always talking about Indians, like you're Joe Indian." I was stunned.

3. This does not preclude the existence of customs and practices developed by soldiers themselves—that is, their own folk traditions—but the main point remains that the Guatemalan army is outfitted and supplied by the government of Guatemala and other outside governments as well.

4. Although I would certainly classify army vs. army violence as official.

5. And I am by no means alone in the field of folklore in this regard (see Whisnant 1987).

6. But since I have been guilty of doing interviews in second languages, I have little to argue with here.

9

LITERATURE FROM
THE LAND BETWEEN
A High School Unit on
Central American Literature

JUDITH E. PETERSEN

The descent was slow, slow the arriving at the maize-
field. From one side to the other, one side to the other
of the zigzag track. They never stopped. They hurried
along, one side to the other. So they wouldn't feel the
weight that was growing heavier and heavier. The
weight on their backs, and the other one. The one
burning in their insides like an incandescent gas. The
one they could sense somewhere in the irregular band
of shade that the trees threw on the dry grass. The
three of them terror-struck, the weight of their children on their backs. Feliciana thought she was going
crazy. She was barefoot, but her feet had ceased to
exist for her. Her face swollen from being unable to
cry, my God, from being unable to cry. Side to side
down the hill.

—*Arturo Arias, "Woman in the Middle,"*
in Paschke and Volpendesta 1988, 103

I teach in a Jesuit high school where we are often reminded that peace without
justice is meaningless. One element of our mission is to make students aware
of their world and the injustices in it. Partly because of this mandate, I helped
to develop a comparative literature course that examines works from the South
Pacific, the Caribbean, Latin America, Asia, and Africa. A section of the Latin
American unit focuses on Central America, including Rigoberta Menchú.

When we began developing the course, I was struck by the lack of modern
and contemporary material offered in anthologies from the focus areas. We

know so little about "developing" countries partly because the literature is unavailable to us. In my home, Omaha, Nebraska, I cannot find college classes in literature from Latin America, undergraduate or graduate. What I know is self-taught by finding books about literary history and by researching and reading. Even the latest high school anthologies ignore Central America. For example, Prentice-Hall's *World Masterpieces* (1991), a tome of 1,420 pages, has no Central American literature. Neither does *Other Voices, Other Vistas*, ed. Barbara H. Solomon (1992), nor McDougal, Littell's *Multicultural Perspectives* (1993), nor Houghton Mifflin's *Themes in World Literature* (1989), nor National Textbook Company's *World Literature* (1992). In fairness, most of these volumes do include Mexican and South American authors. However, I believe Central America's voices are different from either their neighbors to the north or the south. I wonder if this is merely ignorance or if it is purposeful. Is what we know controlled by our government so that Oliver North becomes a hero and the Iran-Contra Affair a minor distraction on the evening news?

Unfortunately, if we intend to provide our students with some knowledge of Central American literature, we must search it out for ourselves. As teachers we must do the best we can to provide an accurate view without the guidance of textbook publishers. Although I am not an expert, I hope to provide at least an introduction for my students, something to ignite their thinking. I have discovered a couple of short story anthologies and a handful of other sources from which I developed the unit on Central America at Creighton Preparatory School. They are *The Faber Book of Contemporary Latin American Short Stories* (edited by Nick Caistor, Faber and Faber, 1989) and *Clamor of Innocence: Stories from Central America* (edited by Barbara Paschke and David Volpendesta, City Lights Books, San Francisco, 1988). I have also used writings from *Granta: A Paperback Magazine of New Writing* (most specifically no. 36, summer 1991) and *I, Rigoberta Menchú*. The Central American unit lasts for two to three weeks and includes the following:

Delfina Collado's "Katok" (Costa Rica)

Salarrué's (Salazar Arrué) "We Bad" (El Salvador)

Arturo Arias "Woman in the Middle" (Guatemala)

Rigoberta Menchú's *I, Rigoberta Menchú* (Guatemala)
an excerpt—nonfiction

Sergio Ramírez' "Center Fielder" (Nicaragua)

Sergio Ramírez' "Election Night in Nicaragua"
(Nicaragua)—nonfiction

The last four selections, Arias, Menchú and the two Ramírez pieces, are used as contrasts. By comparing fiction with nonfiction, each can enrich the other, filling in gaps, verifying different perspectives. In our reading of Central American Literature, there is a shifting of ground, a fighting of shadows, a fear of the known and unknown. This literature brings an immediacy to the distant news stories we read and witness on TV, and when my students want to know why it is so violent, we look at the recent history of the area. Literature records the pain, the fears, and the anguish of the people, personalizing the news stories. Overall, my students and I are dismayed by the violence and uncertainties of life that are portrayed.

I begin the unit with Delfina Collado's "Katok." This is a retelling of the European invasion of Costa Rica. Collado describes an edenic environment before contact. "They danced and sang while they burned incense to their plumed gods and to their drowsing sorcerers, always by the shore of the emerald lake, full of secrets and interwoven with fragrances" (Paschke and Volpendesta 1988, 63). Collado describes a peaceful people living in harmony with the earth. However, warning signs had been seen and rumors had been heard of approaching men with "corn-colored" hair. Katok, a wise and well-loved chief, advocated giving their treasures to the invaders in return for peace. The Europeans demanded allegiance to their king and god; refusal brought death. Katok protested: "Sovereign Christian, hard of heart and deaf of spirit. You destroy our gods and our past. You take away our lands and our heritage, our wives and our daughters" (66). Katok's defiance brings him death, yet his death apotheosizes him into a new god "of peace and love." One of my students, Jason Velinsky, reacts to this quotation saying, "This was a very meaningful statement because it described how the strangers ignored their Christianity and basic human love for the greed that overwhelmed them."

I am not sure if in Costa Rican mythology there is a Katok, nor do I know if he existed in history. Nonetheless, we can examine his story as an apt allegory of the beginnings of New Spain in Central America. It is true this story has an obvious slant in favor of the indigenous people.They possess all positive virtues; the Europeans only the negative. However, I believe that it is important for students to see "history" through the eyes of the "underdog," the "vanquished." In this view does Katok represent an ongoing indigenous resistance to assimilation? Can students connect the story to struggles in the present such as the Zapatista uprising in Chiapas?

"We Bad" by El Salvador's Salarrué illustrates the effect of random, senseless violence on both the victim and the "criminal." Set across the Salvadoran border in Honduras, the wild environment harbors lawless men ready to attack the weak:

> But Honduras is deep in the Chamelecón. Honduras is deep in the silence of its rough, cruel mountains; Honduras is deep in the mystery of its terrible snakes, wildcats, insects, men. . . . Human law does not reach to the Chamelecón; justice does not extend that far. In that

region, as in primitive times, it is up to men to be good- or bad-
hearted, to be cruel or magnanimous, to kill or to spare according to
their own free will. Clearly the right belongs to the strong. (Paschke
and Volpendesta 1988, 69)

One is struck immediately by the contrast with Collado's idealized description of Costa Rica and Salarrué's Chamelecón. Collado's description of Costa
Rica is fantastic, dreamlike, surreal occurring at the point of European contact.
In contrast, centuries later, the wild, still untamed Honduran land has become
sullied by invaders. This is untamed, "savage" territory. We are told it was this
way in "primitive" times (Katok's?). Laws depend on the goodness of the people.
     Goyo Cuestas and his son travel through the Chamelecón to Honduras
hoping to sell their phonograph. But there are evils, snakes, the cold, mud, and
bandits. As Goyo and his youngster become food for vultures, armadillos, and
trees, the bandits play with their stolen phonograph and "laughed, like children
from an alien planet." Later upon hearing the beauty of the music and realizing
the magnitude of their sin of murder, they know themselves: "'We bad.' And the
thieves of things and of lives cried, like children from an alien planet" (Paschke
and Volpendesta 1988, 70).
     Although this is a story about senseless killing, hope is found in the beauty
and power of the music. The bandits too are victims of a lawless, untamed
world. Goodness is "alien." But there is a seed; a hope for tomorrow in the recognition and contrition of the bandits. Student Clark Long personalizes this
seed of hope in his response to the story, "There have been many times when I
have done something wrong and didn't care about the consequences while I
was doing it, but after it was over realized that what I did was, in fact, the wrong
thing to do."
     In "The Woman in the Middle," the Guatemalan writer, Arturo Arias, uses
short, choppy sentences that sound like gunfire bursting around the women.
The structure and the profusion of pronouns leaves the reader confused and
breathless. Mystery and an unnamed fear follow and surround the three
women on their dangerous journey. Unexplained passages repeat like flashes of
memory, visions of violence: "Like a bloody bird," "Moving within an aura,"
"She chewed dust," "Gigantic black dogs, their fangs thirsting for meat,"
"Magdalena just lying there in the gully," "The dry earth, no corn grew" (Paschke and Volpendesta 1988, 103–7). As these phrases repeat, sometimes with
subtle variations, they swirl like the feeling of panic that the women experience
as they attempt to escape, with their babies on their backs, from the gunshots
and the soldiers. Never are we told whose soldiers they are, why the village has
been destroyed, how Magdalena has died, or ultimately what happens to the
three women. Instead we are left with their palpable fear. We experience,
momentarily, the chaotic and violent universe of the Guatemalan peasant, a
world that does not have justifiable reasons for the upheaval and destruction.

One of my students, Todd Bonkiewicz, states, "Arturo Arias's story concerns the horrors of war: the confusion, the blood, the agony, the insanity, and the misery of losing loved ones."

The chaotic fear Arias captures is given a name and a face as my students read an excerpt from *I, Rigoberta Menchú*—chapter 7: "Death of Her Little Brother in the Finca, Difficulty of Communicating with Other Indians." We now realize that the depiction of violence in "The Woman in the Middle" is not merely fantasy, a Central American Stephen King, but a reflection of reality, a reality that occurs all too often. As with Arias's story, we meet Guatemalan peasants who are at the mercy of more powerful people, the ladinos. The fincas (plantations) are owned and run by ladinos who exploit the peasants by perpetuating their ignorance and dependency. The Indians live in shelters with four or five hundred others of different languages and ethnicities. Lacking the money to pay for medication, Rigoberta and her mother must watch Rigoberta's brother die of malnutrition. They lose their jobs because they take a day to bury and mourn for him. Rigoberta and her mother are kept separate from others in her family and village by those in power, and thus they are unable to unite and gain control of their own destiny. Student Stephen Schima writes, "Rigoberta Menchú's story strings together generally simple sentences with fluid colloquial language. The 'matter of fact' manner in which the atrocities of life on a finca are told creates a tone of despair. The whole passage is written as a diary and is, in actuality, nonfiction. The fact that it is nonfiction makes the whole experience more compelling." To my students this callousness and cruelty seems unbelievable, as though it belongs to an ancient time. Human life is expendable. Grief for the loss of a baby takes too much time away from work. Yet, these are events within the lifetime of my teenage students.

In both Guatemalan pieces, we see peasants, often women, pitted against more powerful, nameless enemies. Their lack of a common language, the lack of human recognition demonstrates the Guatemalan peasants' political impotence. As a class we empathize with the powerless, and we are angry at those who take advantage of the less fortunate. We are amazed at the peasants' ability to survive the injustices they are forced to experience. Yet, we know that we see ourselves and our own society in the plight of the Guatemalan Indians. When students become smug that these things happen in third-world countries and not ours, it is time to look at ourselves. I invite students to compare the powerless Guatemalans and America's minorities, homeless, and poor. In doing so, we realize our similarities. When asked to compare the two Guatemalan pieces, students focused on the injustices they found in both. One student, Trevor Herron, comments:

> Both are written about the injustices of Guatemala from a native Guatemalan's perspective. They are both very powerful stories that reveal tragic problems in our world. They hit you in your heart, and make

you take some time out to try to think and feel what the natives of
Guatemala think and feel. . . . The most important similarity between
the two stories is how powerfully disturbing they are. They let nothing go unnoticed, and they pummel you with their message of problems of their country. They just touch your heart and keep on tugging
on it until you want to do something about the problem.

Students are surprised by the atrocities and conditions presented in these
pieces. Some of the students are moved by the fictional portrayals, while others
need the explicit reality of nonfiction. Few are unmoved.

"The Center Fielder" by the Nicaraguan Sergio Ramírez is another one of
my students' favorite stories. In this story, there is a prisoner, "Snake" Parrales,
who at one time was an excellent baseball player. He, like many of my students,
fantasizes about catching the winning catch, winning the game. He also fantasizes about going back for a high fly, up over the fence to freedom. We learn that
Parrales's crime is that his son had been seen with two men, one of whom was
probably an American, said to have ammunition. Parrales's son "disappeared,"
and we discover, had been killed. We are never told what government is in control of Nicaragua in the course of the story, nor are we even sure Parrales's crime
is terrible. Instead, we come to sympathize with him, the fate of his son, and his
eventual end. We sense that he is representative of many who spoke out or acted
against those who were in power. Ramírez hints that such power is fleeting:
"The air conditioner had recently been fitted into the wall and fresh plaster was
still visible" (Paschke and Volpendesta 1988, 145). The material reforms of a
new regime may disappear as easily as Parrales's son. I often worry that it is difficult for my students in Nebraska to understand that speaking out against
those in power can be fatal. However, Jason Knag writes, "We often turn our
heads and pretend not to see the suffering or not to hear the cries for help from
our Latin American neighbors. We must learn to stand up against the pain and
suffering inflicted by corrupt governments in our world."

After reading Sergio Ramírez's "Center Fielder," my students are surprised
to learn that Ramírez was vice president of the Sandinista party in Daniel
Ortega's government. This fictional story captures their attention; his themes
are punctuated by a nonfictional piece, his article, "Election Night in Nicaragua" (Granta: A Paperback Magazine of New Writing, no. 36 [summer 1991]).
In this article, he discusses the elections of February 1990. We hear Ramírez's
passionate hopes for his country, the programs they envision for the poor, the
educational programs for the peasants, and the free elections that Ortega's government advocated. We imagine his disappointment when we consider the
election was lost to Chamorro in 1990. Ramírez's view point is one we in the
States do not often receive; here, we are taught to question the motives of the
Sandinistas, fearing their "communist" leanings. Articles like this remind us
that the situation in Central America is not that simplistic. As one of my students, Jack McGill, says,

How often have I seen newspaper headlines about war in Nicaragua? For as long as I can remember, the newspapers have been full of news of hostilities. I don't think I actually read many of the reports. Many of the terms and names were unfamiliar to me: Contras, Sandinistas, Ortega, and Chamorro. . . . So essentially, I knew that there was war in Nicaragua, but I found this war confusing and very distant. Reading "Election Night in Nicaragua" changed that. . . . I think it's dangerous to take anything said about Nicaragua on face value. You always have to see what side the statement comes from. I wanted to be careful not to believe everything Ramírez said. I can't be sure he's telling the whole truth. He may have tried to, but he may have failed unintentionally. Also, reading this will probably make me believe less of what I read in the paper. When I see stories about Nicaragua, I will remember Ramírez's thoughts and feelings.

By looking at other cultures in their social, historical, and political complexity, we can learn much about ourselves and our relationship to events in lands not so far away. I would be thrilled to know that by reading this literature my students have been moved to help eliminate the injustices in Central America, to begin to question some of the news reports and propaganda, to realize that there is more than the simplistic (or slanted) explanations our government and media provide for us. I know this is a big order, but my own students have convinced me it is not impossible to fill. Student Ryan Bodner illustrates the global aspect of the literature when he writes about the conclusion of Salarrué's "We Bad": "Anybody would have felt this way. No matter who they were, they'd realize they did wrong. It's the feeling of guilt. Everybody feels guilt. Africans, Canadians, Asians—they all can have felt guilt. Africans don't feel one way and Canadians another. Human beings all experience the same feelings."

My most cherished hope is that all of us become more compassionate for the less fortunate globally and here in the United States, in the inner cities, on the reservations, in Omaha, and in our school. It is all too easy for us to condemn ladinos hundreds of miles away. It is more difficult to recognize and condemn what we do to each other. Perhaps Rigoberta's gift is to remind us that we can all be compañeros, struggling together to create a more just world.

10

THE TESTIMONY OF RIGOBERTA MENCHÚ IN THE FOREIGN LANGUAGE CURRICULUM

SHARON AHERN FECHTER

Many scholarly works have been devoted to Menchú's work in terms of its content and value as testimonio. Teachers and scholars have also begun to publish their own testimony on the incorporation of *Me llamo Rigoberta Menchú y así me nació la conciencia* into the liberal arts curriculum (e.g., Gunn, Guerra, and Fechter). While many college and university teachers have incorporated Rigoberta's work, in whole or in part, into general education and women's studies offerings, little attention has been focused on the use of the testimony itself as a tool for language learning. In fact, Rigoberta Menchú's testimony in the original Spanish, *Me llamo Rigoberta Menchú y así me nació la conciencia,* provides a powerful language learning medium at both the high-intermediate and advanced levels of instruction in the undergraduate Spanish curriculum or at the advanced placement level within the secondary school curriculum. The testimony is both content rich and linguisitically accessible to the language student at these levels of proficiency. This chapter will offer a theoretical basis as well as concrete suggestions for incorporating the testimony into the language classroom.

RIGOBERTA'S TESTIMONY WITHIN THE CONTENT-BASED CURRICULUM

As the concept of interdisciplinarity has gained importance nationally in terms of the undergraduate curriculum in general, so too has the dedication to a communicatively based foreign language curriculum. At the same time, there has been an increasing number of content-specific course offerings in foreign languages. Content-Based Instruction, in fact, serves the goals of communicative competence and interdisciplinarity at the same time.

Content-Based Instruction (CBI) is one among several communicative approaches to language learning and teaching. The substantial and ever-increasing body of literature treating this kind of instruction in the second-language classroom provides the theoretical underpinning for the incorporation of testimony such as Menchú's into the skills-based foreign language curriculum.

Leaver and Stryker (1989) define Content-Based Instruction as an approach in which language proficiency is achieved by shifting the focus of the course from the learning of the language per se to the learning of the subject matter. They have characterized the content-based curriculum as one that is based on disciplinary subject matter and utilizes authentic materials as a medium of instruction at the same time that it promotes the learning of new information along with the acquisition of language skills. Mohan (1986) asserts that such instruction focuses on preparing the learner for chosen communicative environments. These then become authentic, rather than artificially imposed, arenas for communication. Brinton (1989) define Content-Based Instruction simply as the integration of specific content with the goals of language teaching. The specific goal of CBI, in their view, is to eliminate the artificial separation between language instruction and other subject matter. Giauque (1987) makes a clear distinction between teaching content in a foreign language skills course, such as advanced composition and conversation, and teaching language for specific purposes, whose purpose is primarily technical or vocational. It is within the former paradigm, that is, teaching academic content in a language skills class, that the use of *Me llamo Rigoberta y así me nació la conciencia* is described below.

CBI is not necessarily radically different from traditional foreign language methodologies. Foreign language educators involved in content-based instruction know that they can utilize the methodologies of the traditional language classroom and effectively apply them in the CBI curriculum. The content-based classroom, while being interdisciplinary in its approach, is also well grounded in the communicative methodologies of the foreign language classroom. Thus, a course incorporating Menchú's testimony could focus on Rigoberta's message concerning the situation in Guatemala from the perspective of political science. Similarly, her text, particularly the first chapters, might be considered from the point of view of cultural anthropology. Finally, the student of literature might approach the work as an example of the emerging genre of testimonio. The authentic material would be the testimony itself and, as students gained greater insight into the content from any one of a variety of interdisciplinary perspectives, all of their second-language skills would be called into use.

We know from Stephen Krashen's (1988) work in second language acquisition that success in learning a language is a function of student motivation and self-confidence. The Spanish class that is constructed on a content-based model can increase student motivation to learn the language by providing a "practical" reason for doing so. Self-confidence is enhanced because the students' background knowledge and interest in the content area can be activated and easily brought to bear on the language learning situation. Students bring their disciplinary training (as well as biases) to the reading and interpretation of Rigoberta's testimony. The language classroom, particularly at the advanced level, then becomes a model of and a forum for reasoned interdisciplinary exchange—and this occurs in the target language. Students acquire not only language skills but disciplinary content as well. Reminding students in the traditional undergraduate environment that Rigoberta herself was about the same age as many of them are when she learned Spanish eases students' approach to the linguistic challenges that the work presents. Intermediate students are particularly heartened by this fact, and students in my classes approached the reading with greater enthusiasm because of it. One intermediate anthology even suggests that the instructor point out errors that might indicate that Spanish is not Rigoberta's native language (Labarca and Pfaff 1991). Discussing Rigoberta's motivation for learning Spanish by clarifying the urgency of her need to communicate also helps students to define and refine their own motivation in learning the language and reading the testimony. Most students in my courses immediately identified with this need and related it to personal experiences of not being able to understand or be understood.

Researchers agree that the content or theme-based course is most appropriate and effective at the high-intermediate or advanced levels of proficiency. Many cite the third year at the university level or perhaps the Advanced Placement courses at the secondary level as the ideal (Giauque 1987; Benouis 1986; Rivers 1985). This is due to the fact that learning at the beginning levels is primarily lexical. Although students can assimilate a content-based lexicon at this level, a higher degree of proficiency is required to effectively communicate the ideas inherent in such a course. Carney (1986) asserts that "The depth of grammar and structure needed in a commercial course and the demands of textual analysis to be done . . . preclude a satisfactory offering at the beginning and intermediate levels. Such attempts quickly boil down to no more than samplings, and they interfere with the essential exposure to grammar and culture that must be given on lower levels" (45). While Rigoberta's testimony in its entirety might be ideally suited to the third-year university level, significant portions of the work are, in fact, accessible, both linguistically and contextually, to the high-intermediate student of Spanish. I have had greatest success at this level with the first few chapters describing family life and village customs. The later content regarding the repression and torture has proven to be very difficult at this level. Intermediate anthologies (*Convocación de palabras*, Heinle and Heinle; *Lecturas Sociopolíticas*, Harcourt, Brace and Jovanavich) have begun to incorporate segments of women's testimonio, both Rigoberta's and

Domitila's, and provide annotations and marginal translations of particularly challenging lexical or grammatical structures.

The first few chapters of Menchú's (1992) testimony, specifically chapter 1, "La familia," can be successfully adapted and used at the intermediate level. These chapters contain a wealth of material that can be viewed from the perspective of cultural anthropology or comparative cultures. The material fosters an appreciation of diversity and promotes a crosscultural understanding of family and family values. Among the grammatical structures that could be highlighted in conjunction with the consideration of the content of these chapters are verb tenses—present, imperfect, preterite—and the contrast of preterite and imperfect. Students in my classes were readily able to identify the instances of preterite and imperfect and to restate the narration using the same structures. The language functions to be considered include narrating in the present and the past, comparing, and describing in the present and the past.

Advanced classes might view the work in its entirety in its consideration of testimonio as a literary genre. The testimony of Domitila provides a useful adjunct resource. Such an approach requires higher language proficiency level at the same time that it calls upon higher level thinking skills more appropriate to the advanced level. Students at this level are also more likely to have specific training in literature and literary genres as well as to have better developed analytical and critical thinking skills—all skills promoted by language study. The consideration of the testimony in terms of its sociopolitical content requires a higher level of proficiency as well as a greater degree of sophistication and training in other liberal arts disciplines. Certainly, the consideration of the testimony in its entirety calls for a greater academic as well as cognitive/intellectual preparedness on the part of the student. Structures incorporated at this level include complex orations, subjunctives, compound tenses, and patterns of subordination. The language functions that might be highlighted at this level include persuading, and explaining.

SYLLABUS DEVELOPMENT—
THE INCORPORATION OF THE TESTIMONY

The development of a syllabus for any content-based course is based on an analysis of individual students' needs. This is particularly true in the case of Menchú's testimony, where the accessibility of the material, in terms of the content itself (perhaps to an even greater degree than the linguistic challenges it might present) could prove to be problematic. The syllabus for this kind of offering would incorporate the components of the general communicative syllabus as elaborated by Yalden (1983). Specific details and methodologies employed in teaching Menchú's testimony in such a way as to incorporate these elements would naturally differ as the level of language proficiency differed. Some of the components Yalden cites and the ways in which these might apply in the development of a communicative syllabus in a content-based Spanish course that utilizes Rigoberta's testimony are cited below.

Learners need to have a clear understanding of the purposes for which they are studying the language. Students would understand that their reading, discussion, and interpretation of Menchú's testimony would be intended to further their knowledge of the specific disciplinary focus of the content-based course. As noted above, this disciplinary focus could be one of several corresponding to the academic majors and interests of the students registered in the class.

Student readers of Menchú's testimony in Spanish would recognize not only that the immediate setting in which they would be using the language would be primarily academic, but also that their knowledge of Spanish and of Rigoberta's work would be of great importance in the world outside the classroom. The syllabus would further clarify the communicative events and situations in which the students would participate; that is, *how* they would be asked to communicate about Menchú's testimony. This is accomplished by means of a detailed description of the language tasks and activities, both within and outside the language classroom, which the students are required to undertake. For example, students in my classes were asked to react in their language journals to the readings in Spanish and understood from the first that keeping a language journal was a standard task. Students also need to understand the language functions and notions involved in these events. For example, a knowledge of registers of speech is extremely important if a student interviews a native informant regarding the situation in Guatemala. Specific discourse and rhetorical skills involved in the language class naturally vary from task to task and and from level to level.

Finally, the grammatical and lexical content needed to perform the communicative tasks required at each level need to be identified. Rigoberta's prose is fairly straightforward—simple declarative sentences abound and the compound, complex, and compound/complex orations are fairly accessible. Nevertheless, there is significant use of some complex grammatical structures, including perfect tenses and subjunctive forms, and substantial portions of the text in Spanish would be most appropriately used at the advanced level. High-intermediate students of Spanish, whose lexicon would be somewhat limited, might need to work with excerpts from an annotated edition, such as that provided in intermediate readers. More advanced students of Spanish should be able to use the original version. As in every communicatively based second language classroom whatever the proficiency level might be, the emphasis in using Rigoberta's testimony, in terms of language skills, remains on general competence and fluency in understanding and discussing the work.

Most content-based foreign language courses systematically incorporate structure and many actually treat it as an integral part of the course, though it may be "hidden" in the content. Grammar at this level is best incorporated as a function of the students' need to communicate the content under consideration. The structure then becomes a direct outgrowth of the content and is therefore always presented in context. The numerous structural forms and paradigms found in Rigoberta's testimony allow for the successful integration of the work into the foreign language curriculum at more than one level of instruction.

The rationale, methodology, and goals of the content-based second language course are shared with the students in the syllabus itself so that they not only understand *what* they will be doing, but also *why* they will be doing it.

Foreign language educators would undoubtedly agree on the importance of using authentic materials, the "cultural touchstones" (Carney 1986) that promote language learning. By incorporating a multimedia approach in conjunction with the use of Rigoberta's testimony as authentic input, it becomes more likely that the specific needs of all types of language learners will be met. It is useful to supplement the reading of Rigoberta's testimony with other types of materials that bear directly on the situation in Guatemala, that perhaps illustrate the universality of Rigoberta's message in Central and South America, or that view her work as representative of a larger body of literature. The selection and use of adjunct resources would depend, naturally, on the themes selected for inclusion in the content-based offering as well as on the proficiency level of the classroom. Appropriate adjunct materials that have proved helpful when used in conjunction with Rigoberta's testimony appear at the end of this chapter.

ACTIVITIES AND ASSESSMENT

The materials selected for input in the language classroom are ideally linked to the design of activities, assignments, and assessments. In *Language and Content,* Mohan (1986) classifies activities in the content-based foreign language classroom in two categories that respond to particular types of input. They can be either expository (including readings, presentations, and class discussions) or experiential. Experiential activities might include role playing, workshops, simulations, field trips, demonstrations, interactions with native speakers, and structured or unstructured LEAs (Learning Experience Activities). In order to incorporate the experiential component into a language class using Rigoberta's testimony, students can be provided with a variety of opportunities for "field" work from which to choose. In many areas, advanced students in particular might have access to a local Latin immigrant community where they could interact by means of interviews with native informants and perhaps "give back" through volunteer efforts—tutoring, translating, and the like. They can also be asked to investigate or choose to participate in the activities of such groups as the Vicente Menchú Foundation or Amnesty International. One of my advanced students, who was particularly moved by the power of Rigoberta's testimony, developed this initial experiential task into an internship with

CARECEN, a local organization dedicated to helping Central American refugees. Students and teachers at colleges, universities, and secondary schools located in large urban areas can also take advantage of local events. Menchú herself lectures widely in the United States and these events afford an excellent opportunity for Spanish students to improve their listening skills while simultaneously enhancing their knowledge and understanding of Rigoberta's testimony, both oral and written. Menchú's spoken language, like the written compilation, is extremely accessible to students of Spanish, particularly at the advanced level. Journals in which students react in Spanish to their reading of the testimony or report on the adjunct extracurricular activity provoked by the reading of the testimony can be employed in either the expository or experiential mode at either the high-intermediate of advanced level. Journals are a particularly useful vehicle for students to communicate some of the emotion that the testimony can evoke. One of my students was particularly shaken by the descriptions of the torture. I would not have been aware of the depth of her feeling had it not been for the journal.

Whatever the classification of activity types, it is important that there be a variety of activities to appeal to all kinds of learners, that all language skills be incorporated into this variety, and that activities correspond closely to the content-based input. Although the primary focus might be composition and conversation in the advanced level in particular, listening and reading skills can be developed simultaneously.

Teachers of traditional composition and conversation classes at the advanced level recognize the need for specialized grading techniques in this type of class. This is especially true in the content-based course where the instructor is assessing not only language skills, but also the assimilation of disciplinary subject matter. As varied as are the forms of input and activities in such an offering, so too are the forms of assessment. Assessments are best if they correspond closely to the kinds of activities in which students engaged as they were studying the testimony and learning the language skills necessary to communicate effectively about the content of the testimony.

TEACHING RIGOBERTA'S TESTIMONY

I have employed several teaching methodologies that have proven to be very effective in my content-based classes incorporating Menchú's testimony. Cooperative learning strategies allow for the most open and effective exchange of disciplinary perspective among the students as they interpret the work. Circular or seminar seating further facilitates this exchange. I make a conscious effort to limit lecture to the minimum so that Rigoberta's voice, both in terms of the language she uses and the message she is trying to communicate, can be "heard" unmediated. I also allow time for informal discussion provoked by formal presentations that highlight themes and issues raised in the work or that provide useful background information. Finally, I try to afford students ample opportunity for independent work so that they may consider the testimony in-depth from their unique disciplinary perspective.

Professionals engaged in curriculum development in general are well aware of the importance of infusing diversity into the curriculum at all levels and across disciplines. This is especially true in the language classroom where issues of race, gender, and ethnicity arise naturally from the study of the target language and culture. Rigoberta's testimony provides an excellent vehicle for incorporating these issues into the foreign language skills-based curriculum.

RELATED RESOURCES FOR SPANISH LANGUAGE INSTRUCTION

Poetry: Menchú, Rigoberta. "Patria abnegada" and "Mi tierra," in *El clamor de la tierra* (Menchú 1993). These poems are very useful as a counterpoint to the straight-forward prose of the testimony. They communicate Rigoberta's longing for her lost land and her journey into exile.

Novel: Allende, Isabel. *Casa de los espíritus* (Allende 1982). The repression in Chile as depicted in the novel can serve as a "fictional" account of the kind of repression and torture Rigoberta describes in the novel.

Short Story: Valenzuela, Luisa. "Los censores" (Valenzuela 1992). This short story shows political repression and its effects from the "other" side.

Women's Testimonio: Barrios de Chungara, Domitila. *Si me permiten hablar . . . Testi-monios de Domitila, una mujer de las minas de Bolivia* (1982) Domitila's testi-mony provides a nice counterpoint to Rigoberta's and can evoke interesting comparisons. It also serves to point to the universality of Rigoberta's struggle.

Political documents: Manifestos of the the *Comité de Unidad Campesina* (CUC) and the *Comité Nacional de Unidad Sindical* (CNUS) appended to the Siglo Veintiuno Editores edition of *Me llamo Rigoberta Menchú y así me nació la conciencia.* These are particularly useful in the content-based class that is focused on the political aspects of the testimony.

Film is also an important media; for specific suggestions see appendix 2.

RIGOBERTA MENCHÚ
AND WHITE, MIDDLE-CLASS
STUDENTS

11

WRITING THEIR WAY TO COMPASSIONATE CITIZENSHIP
Rigoberta Menchú and Activating High School Learners

JUNE KUZMESKUS

I work in a heterogeneously grouped secondary school, where students elect all their English classes, each one based on themes that the teachers (who design all their own courses) perceive to be of value and interest to students at the various grades. Pioneer Valley Regional School draws students from four small, sleepy western Massachusetts towns. One of them is home to Northfield Mount Hermon School, the faculty of which sends some of its children to Pioneer for grades seven and eight, but by far, most of our students come from blue- to no-collar families and live on small farms, in remote houses hidden in the hills, or in the centers of towns identified by little more than a town hall, a church, and a library. Years ago, descendants of Polish immigrants were the dominant group here. While that is no longer the case, nearly all residents of the school district are European-Americans.

In my school, I'm considered "the writing teacher" because students' own writing is foregrounded in my classes, with literature in the background, used mainly as inspiration and models for the development of the students' own voices. Although I will describe units in two of my classes ("Reflections" in the tenth grade and "Writing for Self-Expression" in the twelfth grade), student interest in elements of *I, Rigoberta Menchú* has created a place for it in another class ("The Art of Research" in the eleventh grade). In this chapter, I will explain why I selected *I, Rigoberta Menchú* as reading for my students, how I have used the book and the initial effects it has had on students at my school. I say "initial" because I just began using the book last semester after attending the workshop "Teaching Rigoberta Menchú's Testimonial" at the fall 1993 NCTE conference in Pittsburgh. That workshop helped me conceptualize previously missing connections between Menchú's testimony and the other works my students read and, more importantly, between her story and the overarching goals of my teaching.

As varied as my classes are, I choose all readings for two consistent reasons. The first is to raise students' awareness of the human cost of racial and ethnic injustices typically glossed over in their history classes or on the news. In my room, I hope to inspire them to anger and compassion, while, at the same time, focus their attention on the motivations and personal characteristics of leaders and potential role models like Harriet Jacobs, Elie Wiesel, and Rigoberta Menchú. We learn about what made them survive and, ultimately, defeat their oppressors. I want my students to experience the value of testimony and the transformative power of developing voice. Thus, my second reason gets at the students' own development as motivated, thoughtful writers. I know many of my students struggle with problems that limit their effectiveness as students and truly mar their lives. They confront problems they feel they can't speak of, that compel them, they think, to suffer silently. The courses I teach provide a forum and an academic validation for consideration of a range of expression—painful as well as joyful. Within this approach, testimonial literature has value for my students far beyond the classroom. It provides a much needed signal not to give up on themselves or on others. It inspires them to reach out and speak for themselves, to generalize from their own experience. Using testimonial as a model teaches students first to name their hardship, to contextualize it, and then to reach out through their writing to activate themselves and others. In this way, my students begin to reduce their isolation and harness the power inherent in the commonalities and compassion to be found both among their classmates and in the world beyond the school doors.

In my tenth grade class, called "Reflections," students write from and about their experiences and read autobiographies. My twelfth grade class, "Writing for Self-Expression" (described in more detail below) features writing and reading of short stories, poetry, essays, memoirs, and personal narratives. In addition, we read two or three novels. In the tenth grade class, students typically read *Incidents in the Life of a Slave Girl, Night, I Know Why the Caged Bird Sings, Woman Warrior*, Tillie Olson's *Yonnondio*, Russell Baker's *Growing Up*, Annie Dillard, and some excerpts from *All I Need to Know I Learned in Kindergarten*. I have chosen these works for a variety of reasons: they are fine pieces of writing and they are accessible reading for nearly all tenth graders; they reflect a mixture of gender and ethnicity; they reflect conditions I want students to consider; even after multiple readings, they powerfully "speak" to me and to most students who have read them.

Everything we read becomes a starting point for student writing. Since I want students to relate directly to their reading, they keep reader response journals in which they quote and respond to passages that stand out for them. I ask them to note what the central characters learn, what they want, what they are challenged by, how they react to those challenges, who/what supports them, who/what challenges them, and what makes them different from many of those who surround them. These same questions are used in many of my responses to the students' individual pieces of reflective writing, both for the purpose of content development and to encourage students to take a step back for a clearer view of their own situation

Because our main focus is the students' own writing, we limit class discussion of the books to once a week. Students begin sharing responses to the week's reading in small groups. Each group eventually processes an overriding statement about something members found to be significant, generally in response to a guiding question that requires students to focus on conditions and personal characteristics of the people or characters involved. Students keep notes of the discussions along with their reading journal entries. Instead of a "facts test," when we complete a book, students select material from class discussion, class notes, and journal responses for a brief essay (analysis or focused response) or saturation paper (adopting the persona of one of the people or characters in the book and reconstructing or creating a situation in his or her voice, from his or her point of view). The possibilities for these reading-related writings, given as a "take home" test/project over a weekend, are many and as varied as the students in the class. One student might analyze the theme of powerlessness of children, as portrayed in *I Know Why the Caged Bird Sings*, comparing Maya's trials with those of children more and more commonly in the news, or in our school itself. Another student might "become" Harriet Jacobs's son, from *Incidents in the Life of a Slave Girl* (Jacobs 1987), writing a letter to his mother in which he complains that he cannot understand how freedom can be more precious to her than he, her child. Then the student "becomes" Harriet writing her reply. After one or two such projects, students begin garnering ideas for such writings early in the books that follow, both during the semester and in succeeding classes. Taken in its entirety, this process of reading, response, small group discussion, and independent writing allows students to truly make their own meaning of the texts.

Thus, the authors we read provide role models for courage in the midst of life's challenges, as well as valuable models of writing. I want students to know that there is a "tradition" of literature that people have created to give voice to individual and collective experience. The tradition we explore gives trouble and sorrow a means of expression that is not self-indulgent or self-destructive. Together, we find that one step in the process of growing, healing, and preventing further suffering is to put it into words and bring those words to others.

While I'm sure all my students know that slavery existed in "the Old South," there are certain responses I read over and over when students read *Incidents in the Life of a Slave Girl*: "How could anyone actually own a person?" "How can you at one moment buy and beat someone like a beast and another moment have sex with someone who could be their sister?" "How can slaves believe in the same god as the slaveowners? If I were a slave, I couldn't believe in a god that would approve of slavery." "If I had been alive then, I would have done all I could to help free slaves, and I never would have owned any."

But as we read on, students realize that such inhumanity was not limited to bygone centuries. Before students read *Night*, they are familiar with the fact that during World War II, Nazis rounded up Jews and sent them to concentration camps. Some students even know what they did to them there, but reading *Night* affects all students, no matter what degree of familiarity they claim in similar ways: "This is the ultimate cruelty and for what reason? No reason justifies the way the Jews were destroyed." "If I were a Jew at that time, I couldn't believe in a god that would let such crimes happen to my people. At least Elie, unlike Linda, recognizes the same thing." "No one can convince me that trainloads of people were destroyed without villagers knowing what was happening." "Why didn't the Jews escape when they figured out what was going on?" "I never could have followed orders to do those things."

In their journals, students express outrage and an inability to understand a set of standards that accepted the cruelty captured on the pages of these books. In each case, students declare varying degrees of resistance to such systems that they would exercise. Easy to say, so many years after the fact, and this comfortable escape has always left me unsatisfied. The common assumption that they would be better belies the reality of chapters of the Ku Klux Klan and other white supremacist groups in our back yards. Such an attitude ignores the existence of an inequitable system of which we are all a part today that continues to blame its victims for problems beyond their ability to control.

This dissatisfaction and the desire to challenge my students' sense of entitlement led me to consider including *I, Rigoberta Menchú* in the list of readings in my class. What Menchú writes about has gone on in the lifetime of my students and in many ways continues into the present. There is no easy stance to be taken in response to her story, unless one ignores it. And, just as important, there are powerful connections between the experience of slavery and the Nazi holocaust and the experience of Guatemalan Indians. They may involve different places, different faces, but the vital struggle for self and community has essential similarities. Reading *I, Rigoberta Menchú* allows my students to feel all the more strongly that they can and must take action. Perhaps unlike with slavery and Nazi holocaust, *I, Rigoberta Menchú* invites them to be part of a solution, if not in Guatemala, then somewhere, now and in the rest of their lives.

Before we read the book, I took an inventory of what students knew about Guatemala and Latin America. Though most of them can place a few countries on a map, they know very little about the region, except for a few stray names and phrases, like "Castro," "illegal immigrants," and that everyone there speaks Spanish. For most students, a map unit in a seventh grade social studies class, "World Cultures," is their only other academic experience with Latin America. In fact, none of my tenth grade students knew that there were any people in Latin America before the Spaniards came. When I asked about some of the Columbus controversy they'd heard about in 1992, one student commented that he thought "all that was just about Indians in this country."

Initially, we approached *I, Rigoberta Menchú* just as we had the other books. The early chapters of the book distanced some students, as they were put off by values and beliefs they had difficulty reconciling with their own judgments and experiences. They questioned what some considered an ill-conceived faith in the oppressor's religion and a backward adherence to sex role expectations. Both of these qualities seemed antithetical to someone they had heard me describe as a "freedom fighter." Several students, referring to a similar difficulty in understanding why slaves, as portrayed in *Incidents in the Life of a Slave Girl*, so faithfully worshiped the "white God of the slave owners," wondered the same about Menchú. One young woman complained that Menchú accepts the very sex role expectations so often decried in school and community activities designed to promote sex equity. Because I had read Menchú's story purely to learn about that which I did not know, I was surprised at this criticism. I asked that they read to understand what makes her the way she is, the importance those beliefs and practices have to Menchú's life and survival, as well as definers of her culture. I can't ask them not to judge, since that's ultimately what I want them to do, but I do want them to attempt to enter and understand the Quiché people's situation before rendering an easy, "politically correct" dismissal of their complexity.

As we continued reading the testimonial, I asked students to use a three-column chart they would keep in their journals to help map their way through (1) the values and practices of Menchú's life, (2) the incidents that occurred to create, alter, and/or destroy them, and (3) their effects on those values and practices. We used the first column to note the basic assumptions of her life and identity. I suggested to my class that one way to better understand Menchú's reality was to adopt those assumptions without judging them based on their own world view, at least while they were reading, responding and taking notes for this chart. I explained that this approach would help them more fully understand her testimony with an open mind. "Otherwise," I said, "you are assuming that anyone different from you is somehow lesser or less smart than you." Most students kept the charts, which provided a concrete aid for observation, as well. It soon became clear that while conditions might have changed many traditional Mayan practices, they only increased the Quiché's hold on their values and beliefs. This, my students unabashedly admired.

Through their reading, the students did begin to get a grasp on a sort of sketchy time line of Latin American "development" and an awareness that different racial and ethnic groups live there. They began to connect this history to themselves. One student noted, "The white people treated them just like we did the Indians in this country." His comment raised for me the issue of "white guilt" that may arise in class and that I have seen coloring many of the students' responses. In a school composed of nearly all white students, a reading list rich in works by people of color inevitably raises the question, "How much of their more oppressed condition is my fault?" Although I do feel there is some burden of guilt to be borne, since European Americans continue to derive privilege from a racist past and present, I respond in a variety of ways. My principal message is that while many injustices have been and are now committed by whites upon people of color and by one ethnic group against another, the students are only responsible insofar as they are able to make a change for the better but, nonetheless, do nothing. I recognize that it is difficult to always "do the right thing," especially considering the complexity of responsibility for acts over which none of us have clear, direct control. I view it as part of my responsibility as a teacher to suggest becoming informed about voting patterns and campaign focuses of legislators, becoming informed about operational practices of businesses and products, supporting where their values are best represented and withholding support from where they are not. In our area, a local "alternative press" paper provides annotated lists of voting records of our local and national legislators, and I have photocopied and explained how to read it. Many bookstores have consumer guides that address these concerns with some accuracy; I show students some that I have purchased over the years. It is not my intention to make students feel guilty or overwhelmed by injustices past and present, but rather to build a greater awareness of both the effects of injustice and the tools by which they might address injustice in a positive way.

Closer to home, in our classsroom, we have discussed, practiced, and supported students' efforts to interrupt racist and sexist behaviors and remarks in their homes and among friends. This "lesson" arose from one student's admission of listening in helpless, frustrated silence to her grandfather's racist remarks year after year. Another student sympathized, saying that while he is not homophobic, his friends are and often embarrass him with their ignorant and cruel remarks. Because he has so few friends, he said openly, he didn't feel he could afford to lose them by challenging them. We finished the class with a session in role playing. I played the racist grandfather, the young woman played herself, and we conducted a discussion in which she confronted my racist remarks, trying a variety of approaches suggested by the other students until she was satisfied with her response. (Recently, she approached me to say she had confronted her grandfather with little success, but she felt that it was a start. "At least he now knows I disagree with him, even though he's sure I'm wrong.")

We spent three weeks reading *I, Rigoberta Menchú*, and during that time, the students asked more questions in their journals about politics, agriculture, economy, history, and geography than I could answer. Following their desire to know more, we decided to enter into a research unit. Though we were taking a tangent away from my prior intentions, we, nonetheless, set aside two weeks and moved into the library. It was time to find some answers.

Before we went, I asked students to reread their journals and list topics of particular interest to focus their study. Some students worked alone, some together. Many students looked for information about geography, agriculture, and politics. Others focused on some particular element of indigenous culture, like art or food. One student wanted to find out all she could about Menchú herself. One politically astute student wanted to learn more about women's resistance movements in Latin America. Two students wanted to find out more about political prisoners, whom they had previously thought of as limited to POW/MIAs in Viet Nam. Students reported findings during two class periods. In the course of our research we discovered—with the exception of information on geography, agriculture, and familiar, U.S.-centered perspectives on politics—how little our traditional high school library could help us uncover on many of these topics. The only dependable, informative source we had at hand, in many cases, was *I, Rigoberta Menchú*, itself. This suggests to me that more resource material, and perhaps of a different kind, is needed if students are to pursue their interest in Latin American studies, the connections between Central American people and their own lives, or other issues this book has introduced to them.

At our school, all courses are just one semester long, and our two weeks of research brought us to the end of the fall 1993 semester. Since students can choose all their English classes, I have agreed to tailor my eleventh grade "The Art of Research" so that my students can continue their study next year. Where in the past, "The Art of Research" has integrated the study of issues of equity and the environment into activities that build students' research and writing skills, this more specific focus will be a more relevant, student-centered opportunity to learn and practice the same skills, the principal difference being that the students have delineated the focus of the subject matter in advance. I believe that this kind of teaching puts the legitimate intellectual and ethical interests of the students first, and though it requires flexibility from the teacher, when done well, it can make school learning truly meaningful. Seventeen of the twenty students have already signed up.

As part of the exploration stimulated by the NCTE panel, I also tried using *I, Rigoberta Menchú* in my twelfth grade class, "Writing for Self-Expression." Although Menchú's book is nonfiction, I used it at the end of a unit on the novel, as the works that preceded it, *Animal Dreams* (Barbara Kingsolver), *Love in the Time of Cholera* (Gabriel Garcia Marquez) and *Eva Luna* (Isabel Allende) just begged for Menchú's story to follow and give added perspective to the artistic and intellectual landscape they had created. The political conditions that Hallie, in *Animal Dreams*, relates lurk everywhere in the other two works. In addition to the novels and Menchú's first chapter and last four chapters, we viewed the movies "Romero" (dir. John Duigan) and "Salvador" (dir. Oliver Stone). The combination of fact and fiction was powerful. As in the other class, students were surprisingly engaged as their curiosity about the "side issues" and the hints of the travesties going on in the novels came to life in the films and Menchú's book.

In this class, students also used journals, but as they are two years older, these students weren't satisfied with simply writing and learning more. With the tenth graders, I had asked, "Now that you know about it, what do you want to do with this knowledge?" The twelfth graders didn't need me to lead them. Instead they turned to me and to each other and asked, "What can we do about it?"

I was impressed that they found they could do several things, both individually and collectively. Some of the students were already active student leaders who have been less than satisfied with the conventional role that student council relegates them to. Others are students whose skepticism about groups and school itself has kept them from previous involvement in school activities. One of the twelfth graders is doing an independent study on political prisoners and has begun organizing a chapter of Amnesty International at our school. At my suggestion, she has gathered a core group of students from various grades to build continuity into an effort she won't be here to see fully organized. Despite the generally defeated apathy that surrounds us, several recent graduates have pursued study and work in the fields of environment, education, and social justice. Much, if not all of the awareness of the importance of these endeavors was introduced in school. Previously such graduates, supported by one or two teachers but in all other ways isolated, went off to get involved with "things that matter." In this complacent, rural community, the current level of interest and desire for involvement in global issues at our school is especially significant. Even if the involvement in Amnesty International (or any other long-term result of the study of testimonial literature) is limited to letter writing and fund raising, students will have participated in something together that impacts others beyond the school.

I have used *Night, I Know Why the Caged Bird Sings, The Autobiography of Malcolm X, Black Boy*, and so many other nonfiction works and asked, "Now that you know about it, what do you want to do with this knowledge?" I have asked this question after reading and a video explaining the current California grape boycott, after discussions about hate crimes reported in our local paper, after workshops intended to raise awareness of harassment and discrimination. It is a question that seems to be central to my teaching. A few students have responded with interest and activism. The difference between the effect of all my previous efforts and what took place with the reading of *I, Rigoberta Menchú* is summed up by one student's comment on the course evaluation from last semester's twelfth grade class. In answer to the question, "What aspect of this course will be most likely to remain with you for some time into your future?" he wrote,

As I get ready to leave this school, I can't say any one thing we did in this class stays with me more than others, but I look back and see how it all adds up for me. I took your class in tenth grade and we read *Malcolm X* and *Night*, my eyes got opened because they were real nightmares that no one paid attention to until it was too late. I started feeling guilty even though I hadn't done those things, because people like me had done them. Last year, I had you again and we watched something about how pesticides are killing grape pickers' kids. It's the first time I ever cried in school, but it was okay because everyone else was too. I stopped eating grapes, mom stopped buying them because they just sat in the fridge, . . . but it really made me think about all our intentions and how they don't mean much—how powerless we are. Then you gave us those chapters by Rigoberta. Thinking about what she did makes me unable to say that good intentions don't mean anything. I now see that good intentions aren't enough, but good intentions combined with good actions are the best things each of us can do. I'll never be like Rigoberta, but I know I won't look the other way and think who cares? Ever again.

12

THE FRESHMAN EXPERIENCE AT WILLAMETTE UNIVERSITY
Teaching and Learning with Rigoberta Menchú

CATHERINE ANN COLLINS

AND PATRICIA VARAS

> The coffee beans they slave to pick every day for practically no pay results in my favorite cup of coffee in the morning. And the capitalist system that has resulted in the economic progress of my nation and culture has ruined their culture. Do I have a right to enjoy my lifestyle while Rigoberta's people suffer? It seems self-centered and heartless for me to do so.
>
> —*Willamette freshman student*

Teaching students to trust and respect themselves and others, to be humane beings committed to social action is a challenging and often uplifting experience. This task is what twenty-four faculty members at Willamette University, a small liberal arts college in Salem, Oregon, set out to do every year with a freshman class of 400, in a core freshman course, World Views, which is designed as a required introduction to the general education curriculum. The course has subsequently emerged as a defining component of the Willamette experience, touted to prospective students and granting institutions. In addition to providing a common academic experience for incoming students, the

The authors want to acknowledge the assistance of the faculty who shared assignments, pedagogical strategies, and samples of student work: Maria Blanco-Arnejo, Virginia Bothun, Cesie Delve Scheuermann, David Douglass, Ellen Eisenberg, David Goodney, Mark Janeba, Susan Kephart, and Lane McGaughy. A special thank you to all of the students and peer tutors who have participated in the World Views program.

World Views course has a campuswide impact, enhancing faculty collaboration, teaching, and learning.

For three years, Willamette students and faculty involved in the World Views course overwhelmingly supported the inclusion of *I, Rigoberta Menchú* as a required text. Faculty perceived it as a key text, and it enjoyed high popularity among the students. In this chapter we have gathered samples of student and faculty comments to illustrate the failures and successes we encountered in teaching Rigoberta's testimony. Finally, we include some samples of our study guides and essay questions that may be of interest to other teachers or programs considering the adoption of *I, Rigoberta Menchú* in their curriculum. We have attempted to be as candid as possible; although we strongly endorse the inclusion of this text in our freshman program, we acknowledge the difficulties it poses as well.

As a faculty we have high expectations for how World Views will shape the intellectual life of our students. As is the case in most freshman core courses, we want our students to develop critical thinking and reading abilities; to learn to express their ideas orally and in writing in a way that reflects solid analytic skills while demonstrating a personal investment in the ideas; to be reflexive about their own assumptions and patterns for structuring the world by recognizing the linguistic, social, political, economic, and religiously constructed nature of our reality; to listen attentively to other voices whether in class discussions, mass lectures, or the art and artifacts of other cultures; and to foster active rather than passive learning by disabusing our students of automatically accepting the authoritative voice. Thus, a significant purpose of the course is to foster the kind of liberal arts academic community where interpersonal connections naturally form around shared academic concerns.

One of the rewards of teaching in the freshman World Views course comes in watching the students becoming more critical readers and thinkers, willing to challenge biased/accepted information. Whether traditional mental frameworks will hold or be changed is less important than learning to think critically and discovering the ability to question. We want students to learn to identify unquestioned assumptions about other people in their own reasoning. For one student this meant realizing that she had never questioned her negative characterization of "guerrillas." The combination of reading *I, Rigoberta Menchú* and viewing the film *When the Mountains Tremble* challenged her conventional wisdom:

> I just realized after seeing this movie that almost everything I've read/ heard about guerrillas before was really negative—that is, they were painted as terrible, violent people without morals, who would rape and kill anyone that passed them. But, after seeing the film and reading Rigoberta Menchú, I realized that the picture of what they were from her point of view, was very different than what they were from

the media's. So I don't know if they were romanticized or not because this is the first time that I've seen them in a more positive light.

A number of students found Rigoberta's implied belief in communism difficult to accept. For students who are products of forty years of cold-war rhetoric, this became a stumbling block to their acceptance of the Quiché rebellion. One student writes, "Rigoberta Menchú seems to be attacking the capitalist system, denouncing unequal distribution of wealth and the ownership of the land. Is she, and her Indian movement, communist?" In class discussion he was not the only student to believe that if Rigoberta sympathized with the communists her arguments could no longer be accepted as credible. For these students, the hold of conventional world views was hard to break. They found it difficult to question their own world view because they tried to keep discussions apolitical, thus their initial admiration for Rigoberta and sympathy for her people quickly turned to disdain.

In many cases, however, we see students more willing to acknowledge that critical thinking entails learning to recognize the assumptions behind our judgments, assessing the sufficiency of proof, and questioning the logic of particular causal links within arguments. Students were surprised, and even outraged, at the United States' intervention record in Guatemala. To prepare students for the text, many classes discussed the overthrow of Jacobo Arbenz, orchestrated by the CIA, which shaped Guatemala's current political crisis. Rigoberta's testimony politically challenges the U.S. impulse to intervene in the affairs of other countries, an impulse that for many students is an ideological given in their world view. Rigoberta was a valuable lesson for one student who discovered how important context becomes when we judge another's actions. Initially unwilling to see why violence might be a fitting response to repression, the text and discussion led her to conclude: "I have learned that the first step in understanding ourselves is to recognize our environment and the influences it has on us. . . . I have gained a great respect for Rigoberta and her fighting people, not only for their courage and persistence, but for their ability to analyze their situation and alter the environment in which they live." At the same time one young man, who had initially resisted a series of texts addressing power differences and repressive responses by those with power, reevaluated the issue after class discussion of Rigoberta. Interested in how the African Americans have been treated in this country, he saw a parallel between this response to power and what occurs in Latin America. He wrote in his journal:

It appears that when a power structure is losing control it turns to unjust military or police action. Like a vice grip, the authorities tighten up the situation, control it, and even turn on the people to prove their superiority. The problem is, they are viewed as the "good guys" because they are keeping law (though inhumane) and order (though unequal), and they are protecting "national security" (though the people are less secure).

Such a case seems to exist in America as well. The police in ghetto areas do not seek to eliminate the problem, but rather contain it. They don't protect the people in the ghetto, they protect those outside the ghetto. Because there is such an escalation of crime, the police possess more freedom to take violent action.

That a student feels comfortable admitting his naiveté and going on to try to work through comparisons of U.S. actions and motivations in Latin America with conditions in his own locality suggests to us that the student has gone beyond learning about results and begun to question what underlies such actions. Equally rewarding is the shift from arguing that Latin Americans should "just change their world view" when it leads to situations North Americans see as problematic, to the recognition that "it is very hard for me to break out of my vision of Latin America."

Learning to be reflective about one's own ideas starts with recognizing how controlling a world view can be. One student finds it hard to deal with what she perceives to be a characteristic of Rigoberta's community—the unwillingness to change a way of life that encourages poverty and to adopt a lifestyle that is less oppressive: "they are resigned to 'work, poverty, and suffering' because that's how their ancestors lived. I never thought anyone would want this kind of life. However, that's my world view. Because in our society your ancestors want you to do better than they." Part of the lesson of *I, Rigoberta Menchú* is recognizing that we must examine the basis for our own judgments. A young man writes, "It's interesting that later on when Rigoberta was a maid in the ladino house, she said how much of a mess it was. The rich are usually just as messy, they just have other people to clean up after them. But it's our world view, I think, to judge people's clothing and hygiene when they are poor and think of them as less." And one student's final essay reflects how she has begun to question the "correctness" of her own world view. Writing about cultures she previously knew nothing about she concludes: "I have learned that some of their practices which would have seemed stupid to me are indeed logical to those who create and follow them."

Over the course of the semester, many students develop an appreciation for examining their own world view. "One can't really expect to get along with others or fully understand or accept others until they examine their own way of looking at things. Everything we do is colored by our own world view—how we were raised as well as our own experiences—and we all need to recognize this or we go through life expecting others to live "up" to our expectations." Early in the semester students seem to resist the possibility of multiple truths, assume the alien world view is inferior, and often fail to apply the lessons of world views to their own thinking, speaking, and treatment of class members during discussions. Rigoberta is a vital element of World Views that sensitizes students to the consequences of colliding world views when those in power do not appreciate the voice of the other. One student returned after Christmas break to share the fact that she had reread Rigoberta, slowly this time, and had given the book to a friend and a parent because she thought they really needed to read about "what's really happening in Guatemala that we don't ever hear about." Another student evaluates the group discussion by writing, "It helped me define my beliefs by forcing me to explain and justify them."

Having explained how Rigoberta helps us to achieve broad intellectual goals for the World Views course, the next section of the paper suggests how Rigoberta's testimony has been employed in our program. Following a brief discussion of how Rigoberta supported units on issues of class, gender, and religious syncretism, the focus will be Rigoberta as the centerpiece for a unit on human rights.

ALTERNATIVE APPROACHES TO TEACHING *RIGOBERTA*

Each year the course is reorganized into new pairings of texts. During the first year, *Rigoberta* was paired with Isabel Allende's *The House of the Spirits* in a loosely defined unit on issues of class, gender, and repression. Faculty asked students to consider questions such as the following in their essays:

1. Are both *The House of the Spirits* and *I, Rigoberta Menchú* feminist texts? Consider the way that they portray their major female characters as leaders (e.g. Clara, Alba, Blanca, Rigoberta)

2. Write an essay in which you consider the theme of storytelling as protest. How can the act of telling a story assert authority, reconstruct reality, or militate against the way things are now? How does storytelling differ from other forms of protest? Support and illustrate your thesis with material from *House of the Spirits* and *I, Rigoberta Menchú.*

During the second year of the Latin American theme, *I, Rigoberta Menchú* was paired with David Carrasco's *Religions of Mesoamerica* to develop an awareness of religious syncretism and liberation theology. It was then followed by a series of articles raising the question of Latin American identity, asking the student to think about how contemporary Latin America is tied to her past. The articles included Julio Cortázar's short story "The Night Face Up" to draw attention to the difficulty of oppression in the colonial past and in the present; an excerpt from Columbus's diaries and a selection by Sepúlveda to consider how cultural values and patterns color one's interpretation of what constitutes rationality and civilization; and, finally, "Critique of the Pyramid," in *The Other Mexico*, by Octavio Paz to explore the juxtaposition of modern Mexico with her traditions in order to challenge the identity crisis of contemporary Mexico.

Student papers and discussion questions explored the concept of "otherness" for indigenous and for the mestizo who denied his/her indigenous forebears. They also questioned the historic, psychic, and cultural reality addressed by Paz in "Critique of the Pyramid," together with issues of religious syncretism and liberation theology. These themes led to student essays such as the following:

1. Both *Religions of Mesoamerica* and *I, Rigoberta Menchú* deal with issues of difference. Write an essay in which you consider the nature of difference and the possibilities for its treatment. How is treatment of difference an ethical act? What principles should guide us when we confront difference in others, and where do these principles come from?

2. According to *Religions of Mesoamerica,* various forms of sacrifice, including self-sacrifice, played an important role in many Latin American cultures. In some ways the treatment of indigenous peoples described in *I, Rigoberta Menchú* can be considered sacrifice. Exploitation, persecution, and systematic violence seldom happen by accident; rather, they perform a function within the dominant culture. Write an essay in which you consider the concept of sacrifice. What is the definitive character of sacrifice? What role does consent play? What of ritual? Is there a morality or ethic to sacrifice, and, if so, how does it apply to Latin America?

3. Part of the tragedy of the Quiché Indians of Guatemala, as described by Rigoberta, is that they have been radically displaced not only geographically but also culturally. In Carrasco's terms, the Quichés no longer have the freedom they once held to engage in their rituals of world making, world renewing, and world centering. Write an essay in which you examine the relationship between ritual and cultural identity. How is this relationship played out in terms of personal happiness, success, and growth? What is the role of secrecy and disclosure in these rituals?

During the third year *I, Rigoberta Menchú,* the centerpiece in a unit on human rights, was paired with one of the first testimonials written by the Cuban Miguel Barnet, *The Autobiography of a Runaway Slave,* and a series of supplementary articles.

The most powerful discussions of this pairing centered on inhumane treatment. One student writes: "I don't understand what could possess someone, a man, to beat a woman. I suppose if you don't think of [them] as equal, or even human, more like an animal, then somehow they would feel justified. I can't even imagine beating or harming in any way an animal or person. Now this is where my own world view . . . figures into my attitude, right?"

Another woman was most troubled by Rigoberta's description of her mother's torture and death: "That filled me with such anger. I really love my mom and that just made me think of how I'd feel if that happened to my mom.... All I really want to know now is what can we do? Realistically? I want to do something, but what?"

Feeling the need to do something, to resolve the problem, is echoed across the sections. For the first two years faculty felt overwhelmed by the depression that settled over their classes. A professor comments "they [the students] are questioning now their own responsibility as Americans for what is happening in the world," and "some of the discussions were geared toward real solutions. Several students said they cannot go back to their regular lives, they feel compelled to act, to help the situation in Central America." For many of our students Rigoberta is the first text they've read that reveals U.S. interests in Latin America. They are frustrated because of their ignorance and because they discover that traditional sources of information—school, family discussions, mainstream media—have not made them aware of the problems faced by the indigenous people of Latin America or of our own government's motivation for involvement in Latin America. "I'm getting so sick of the phrase 'protecting U.S. (or American) interests.' My interests are in people and whether they live or die—not whether some company gets rich by exploiting people and paying them $.50 a day."

In including *I, Rigoberta Menchú* and *When the Mountains Tremble* in the course, one potential danger is that for some students the "reality" becomes that all Latin America is violent: "Mass dead bodies strewn about, dead people on the street, and military personnel with guns everywhere. It is so awful. It is so different than the life I have.... Never in a million years do I worry about being murdered. It's so different there. How do we begin to understand the unbelievable [things] that happen in those countries?" Violence is thought to be unique to poor countries, endlessly they are "glad to live here in the U.S.A." What happens at home becomes less important, violence is less pervasive than down South.

If students leave their reading of *I, Rigoberta* and the unit on human rights feeling that the situation in Latin America is hopeless, it is because their doubts and hesitations about the legitimacy of Rigoberta's testimony set the tone for questioning the validity of the oral narrative chosen by Rigoberta and Burgos-Debray. The paradox is obvious: a folktale can be whimsical, a testimony must be "truthful"; every statement must be verifiable, memory must not be distorted. Thus, to be able to develop a more fruitful discussion it is necessary to present an analysis of testimony as a form of acquiring knowledge that should not be undermined by misconceptions and prejudices.

Nevertheless, *I, Rigoberta* was the best received of the texts during the third year. A faculty member reports, "they [the students] were eager to discuss this text." All of the faculty proposed the text be retained; 87 percent of the students found it very helpful, 10 percent were neutral, and only 3 percent found it was not a helpful text for the unit. This eagerness is part of a course development that had as the center of discussion the evolution of, specifically, a Maya world view, and generally, a Latin American one. Also, in previous years, when *I, Rigoberta* was the only piece of testimonial literature read, students discovered what they saw as inconsistencies in the text and consequently dismissed the discussion of torture and intolerance of Rigoberta's people as a biased, and therefore inaccurate, representation of affairs in Guatemala. Where in previous years the syntax mistakes and repetitions made *I, Rigoberta* less credible for some students, the students of the third year may have believed Rigoberta's arguments precisely because of such "flaws":

> I think that if you compare Rigoberta's story to that of *Autobiography of a Runaway Slave,* Rigoberta Menchú is more believable. Not that I didn't believe Esteban's story, but Rigoberta's editor didn't edit to the extent that Esteban's did. Elisabeth Burgos-Debray allowed Rigoberta Menchú to tell her story. She left in sentence mistakes, and there is a lot of repetition. . . . I think this really is in Rigoberta's voice because of the repetitiveness, awkward sentences, and the way it skips around not really chronologically. I get a sense of who Rigoberta is. This doesn't seem like just a story, but a person's real life and culture.

The importance of experience gave Rigoberta's voice an immediacy that could not be conveyed by any other text. After all, as a student confesses, "I just have to force myself to trust the editor." The students' ambiguity toward the authority of orality challenges the role of the editor/compiler. If someone takes over your story it must become his/her story. Authorship and ownership of discourse are so embedded in our culture that the students are at odds in accepting the editor as a facilitator for the otherwise voiceless narrator. The difficulty in accepting the editor may hinder the complicity that must develop between the narrator and interlocutor/reader.

Rigoberta's authority was supported by a lecture given by Marta Torres, an exiled Guatemalan labor lawyer who has worked closely with Rigoberta Menchú. Her lecture was a testimony of her life, which, as she told us, is representative of Guatemalans' lives. The impact on the students of meeting a sufferer and fighter of repression, a woman who as a student wrote "looked very much like a mother," led to a major interpretative leap:

> We were no longer dealing with something fictional or that happened in the past. This was all real, and it is happening right now as I write this journal. Marta's simple dialogue and soft-spoken voice seemed symbolic to me, like she represented the small voice of the indigenous people of Guatemala asking for help to overcome the powerful government.

Students seem to consider visible experience more powerful than the written word. The violence that they read about seems somewhat unimaginable. Students constantly claim they try to put themselves in Rigoberta's place to see what it is like to be Rigoberta, but find that it is impossible. Some students try thinking of their own families while reading Rigoberta, they experience a real "eagerness" to identify with her, but they only have to turn the page and look around them to realize how foreign her testimony is. Experience means reality, concreteness, truth. During her lecture Torres showed a short video, filmed clandestinely by anonymous youth, in which torture and beatings were depicted graphically. After its showing, the 400-member audience was completely silent, there was no doubt that everyone was deeply moved and appalled by the violence perpetrated.

A similar reaction took place when students viewed the documentary *When the Mountains Tremble.* Of all the senses, the students feel that the visual one is less susceptible to being tricked. In this way Torres's lecture and the documentary are eye openers. John Berger points out in *Ways of Seeing* that, "seeing comes before words" (Berger 1972, 8). At the same time, however, this preference should not be dismissed as intellectually/ideologically naive, because there is an element of volition/choice among the students to see and acknowledge what they are seeing: "we only see what we look at. To look is an act of choice" (8). Thus, viewing the film *When the Mountains Tremble* led one student to see human rights violations motivated by economic interests. Although this is clearly a part of Rigoberta's explanation, the film made this a much more significant "cause" of the repression. Another student wrote:

There is a strong economic motive for the repression of the Indians. The Spanish-speaking city dwellers can steal the lands from under the Indians because they don't speak Spanish and can use that land to get rich quick. . . . The U.S. gives money to Guatemala to help fight off communism. This is to protect our interests. The government uses this economic aid to pay for military equipment so that it can oppress more people and make more money.

What is significant about this response, typical of the attitude of the class after reading Rigoberta's account and viewing the film, is that similar claims earlier in the semester about U.S. economic interests motivating or facilitating destructive practices (e.g., destruction of the rainforest) were vigorously denied or accepted as a sad, but necessary, price to pay for progress. The documentary film, being more readily experienced, prompted a deeper level of awareness among the students.

We encourage students to question the assumption that written/objective discourses are the only valid means of knowing, that they alone embody "truth." Discussing two vital concepts—oral versus written history and the idea of the "other"—encourages our students to construct Rigoberta's reality and question what they "traditionally" learn through the media and high school textbooks. Throughout the semester students deconstruct written history, learning to question "objective" conventional belief. For example, they are continually asked to consider oral narrative—folktales, personal experience, and testimony—as a means of learning about realities foreign to our own.

A second key issue throughout the semester is a discussion of the notion of the "other." Reading an excerpt of Columbus's diaries and Bernal Díaz's *The Conquest of New Spain*, the students explore the concepts of savage-barbarian-children-Indians-New World-discovered vis-à-vis civilized-educated-European-Old World-discoverer. Once this world view is established as fictional rather than factual, the "other" can be more fully addressed. Some students, after the lesson of the human rights unit, saw an uneasy balance between the "interests" behind human rights violations and the importance of information in creating tolerance:

When one is limited by their world view they are unable to see people as people and then as individuals, they cannot really treat them fairly or humanely. It is only when one looks beyond another's working utility and quits seeing them as just another number, that it becomes impossible to treat them badly, because they become a person with feelings and a family who they care about enough to become a slave for them. We saw this happen in Rigoberta Menchú, when the Indians captured a soldier and talked to him . . . they forced him, through education, to see them as people, people like him, who deserved rights.

Gender difference is another form of otherness that needs to be explored in reading Rigoberta's text. We have found this to be one of the most difficult issues for students to appreciate. While racism is "obviously wrong," male students, especially, feel threatened by discussions of sexism. Because women's experience is quite different from men's, some students devalue their testimonies. A male student asked in class "why are we reading about women?" Many male students find it hard to accept the validity of separating experience by gender, perhaps because doing so exposes their privilege. Human beings suffer, that is the main line; that women might suffer more strikes them as an exaggeration. At the same time, however, when facts are presented to them (i.e. women in developing countries encounter double tasks at home and in the fields), male students attribute women's experience to "choice"; marriage, having children, being overworked or unemployed all may be viewed as a simple matter of decision making.

These two topics—objectivity and "other"—raise problems that inevitably reflect on the students' reading and understanding of *I, Rigoberta Menchú*. The idea that change from the West is unavoidable and, therefore, natives, women, and minorities "better catch up" undermines the students' appreciation of Rigoberta's ties to her Maya ways. As a student says, "cultural differences made it difficult to completely empathize with the plight of the Quiché. For instance, their Indian secrets and ways of life, like maize, which they protect so much are rather unreal to me." Paradoxically, Rigoberta's ability to live in the city and to use a Westernized political discourse make the students forget that she is a Quiché Indian, further detracting from their ability to accept the "other." Furthermore, the fact that she is a woman mingling in a public space believed to be reserved for men, demonstrates to the students the uniqueness of Rigoberta's experience. This statement echoes D'Souza's contention that Rigoberta is not representative of Latin American peasants, but "embodies a projection of Marxist and feminist views onto South American Indian culture" (D'Souza 1991, 72). D'Souza seems to be underestimating Rigoberta's suffering and actions, and to be anticipating in his judgment what only history will be able to tell/define for us, "immortality," "greatness," and "usefulness":

> Rigoberta's claim to eminence is that, as a consummate victim, she is completely identified with the main currents of history. Undergraduates do not read about Rigoberta because she has written a great immortal book, or performed a great deed, or invented something useful. (72)

D'Souza's underestimation of Rigoberta's experience places her as a victim while Rigoberta's perception of herself is that of a member of a community marked by suffering and struggle. The need to victimize Rigoberta is D'Souza's way of undermining her experience; the "other" loses any possibility of dialoguing or sharing his/her experience since there is no common ground for discussion. The "other" is a "consummate victim" with whom he can not identify.

Difficult as it is, the students are challenged to revise their notions of truth. What "la vida real" (real life) as Barnet calls it, is for a Guatemalan Indian peasant in the mountains is not necessarily what textbooks and the media have portrayed. A student concludes his essay:

> Although it may sound a little funny, the truth is not always the most important part of testimony. Some testimonies intend to alert the reader to a particular situation and to increase support, and while they are helpful and inspirational for some people, their goals are not always met with more skeptical readers. However, the most important factors, that cannot be disputed for any testimony, are the opinions and views of the informer. This is not only important in that it informs the reader about the particular individual giving the testi-

mony, but it is also most likely representative of a more commonly held world view.

A sympathetic reading of testimony should obviously not be taken for granted, however. If we refuse to acknowledge the many traps and obstacles that may hinder the reception of the narrator's story we will keep having many "betrayed" readers, who, believing that experience validates the truthfulness of testimony, demand that everything said must have been experienced by the narrator. A colleague writes: "As I recall my students were shocked and truly affected by Rigoberta's 'story'. The students wanted to believe her literally, rather than metaphorically; if something was not literally true it tended to discredit her." One student argued in an essay titled "Testimony or Propaganda?" against accepting Rigoberta's story as the "truth" because "she is distorting the facts" and because she is "biased." Another wrote, "leaving out certain things from your testimony is wrong because you should convey the facts as best as you know. You are not supposed to tell selected facts to make your side sound better. You are supposed to relate the truth and then let the reader form his own opinion." Even though this student feels her "cause is a noble one," because he lacks full information he distrusts her. Demanding "trustworthy" information, facts become the key issue to this student's support or rejection of Rigoberta's testimony. Many students, accustomed to Western narratives, are still in search of an authoritarian, first-person hero/heroine who controls the narrative and talks directly to the reader. If that hero/heroine isn't present, they can feel betrayed.

For those students who feel "betrayed" we can say by reading their journals, essays, and following their discussions that their reading of *I, Rigoberta* has not developed the necessary relationship to testimony as a discourse that (1) moves the reader toward change; (2) gives voice to the voiceless, especially women; and (3) questions "not only Western versions of what is true, but even Western notions of truth" (Gugelberger and Kearney 1991, 9). They have difficulty casting Rigoberta as voiceless, perceiving her instead as an extraordinary being, witnessing her suffering and award of the Nobel Peace Prize. In so casting Rigoberta, our students reflect what is part and parcel of our Western value system, namely a preference for highlighting individual effort and the concept of hero/heroine. The collective voice of the testimony, again, is undermined by Western notions of truth and objectivity.

Students need to read testimony as a "practice, a part of the struggle for hegemony" (Yúdice 1991, 29) in order to understand the direct link between telling the story and making it, realizing the political strategies implied in this effort. In his paper a student argues, "Rigoberta Menchú gives her testimony with the goal of informing more people about a situation that is forced into secrecy. However, much of Menchú's testimony is false according to the government of Guatemala." The student points out that the events in the narrative are verifiable, and that because of her political goals Rigoberta must tell the truth: "Menchú's goals are to bring many different people together. She attempts to unite Native Indians, poor ladinos, and people who can sympathize [sic] from outside Guatemala. Therefore, it would not be wise to have conflicting information and she has no choice but to resort only to the truth."

I, Rigoberta Menchú is not included in the syllabus merely for covering areas usually under-represented in the canon (i.e., indigenous, female, repression), but because reading a testimony is an act, a ceremony (Yúdice 1991, 90) that calls us as readers to question not only our political system but our world view. A colleague writes: "at a very personal level, some students also learned that in comparison their lives are incredibly easy, and they understand now how materialistic and empty their way of life may become. . . . Along with Rigoberta's, the consciousness of my students were born." After reading the testimonial, one student's journal critiques our choice of texts for the human rights unit, arguing we see only the point of view of people like Rigoberta or the slave Esteban; we don't, he argues, see the world view of those in power:

> World views helps us see the "real world," not the viewpoint we previously had. . . . This is a liberal course. That seems appropriate because liberalism means "change," and the intent of the course is to change, or modify, our world views. The problem is, we don't get a complete picture of Latin American culture if we target certain groups. I feel that there is a whole other story, or world view, that we skipped over during the course. Also, being politically correct is certainly not enhancing our world view.

The course has failed for this student because at its conclusion he still assumes that the goal was to create politically correct, (politically) liberal automatons. Undoubtedly he is not alone in this judgment. We need to discover a way to make it clear that to examine one's world view is neither to prescribe an alternative perspective that should go unquestioned nor to proscribe anyone's perspective.

For those students who perceive that reading *I, Rigoberta* is an exciting and enlightening opportunity, the text is not to be studied as a representative work of "all the Indians of the American continent" but as a text that speaks "for all those who wish to change their situation." By internalizing differences, the student discovers a creative way of getting close to Rigoberta even though cultural and class differences remain. Rigoberta's "silences" were interpreted in the following way by a student: "Rigoberta sees all of these things [Maya religious practices] as very important to her. I somewhat empathize with this because in my Church, we do some things that others don't understand which we don't consider as much secret, as we do sacred. They're very important to us and we don't want 'just anyone' to know about them—especially if they are not willing to learn the basic things."

We must accept as a conclusion that there is no homogenous response to Rigoberta's testimony among students. Their opinions vary greatly and are all directly linked to two main constructs of their U.S. world view: their notions of the "other," including gender, and of the validity of oral narrative or accounts. To read *I, Rigoberta* requires more than having reached a certain political level that is developed through knowledge of historical facts. The students have to challenge the formal system that has evidently "lied" to them, while at the same time accepting that "truth" is an interpretative act that is built through many kinds of actions, and is not a fact that will be learned in books. Truth as shown in *I, Rigoberta Menchú* is not a monopoly owned by the powerful, but a way of life that the voiceless are able to share through testimony. When a student is compelled to act, even in a romanticized and somewhat confused way, we are particularly aware of the connection they made with Rigoberta's testimony:

> In class when Greg started to argue that the slavery, early in the U.S. history, was so sinister that no other treatment could possibly come close, I had, in my mind, agreed with him. . . . After getting through a substantial portion of the book, I began to realize, that in certain ways, they were worse off than the slaves. . . . I began to realize all this, and tried (still trying) really hard to acknowledge the fact that it still goes on today. During class and while reading the book I get all emotional, but as soon as I'm back into my world again, I tend to forget what is happening. This really is frustrating, because I want to help them. I keep thinking, "if only there was a way I could help." But in my heart I know that there is little I can do. . . . I cannot let them down [parents] by going to risk my life for people I haven't known anything about. If it was for my people, though, I would not hesitate a second. . . . Actually, I get confused around this area. I probably tend to contradict myself because of my conflicting views.

In conclusion, students consistently credit Rigoberta's testimony with enhancing their critical, reflective thinking because the text forces them to examine their own judgments and to question the assumptions of their own world views. Because the immediacy of Rigoberta's experience does not allow the students to divorce themselves from what they are learning, in reading *I, Rigoberta*, students gain an appreciation for other voices that are seldom heard. As hard as it may be for all of us, students and teachers, we learn in a wrenching way to read, discuss, and write as active participants instead of as passive vessels.

In the midst of these successes, frustrations nonetheless arise. Having been raised in a culture that places so much emphasis on factual, "objective" knowledge—largely controlled by the media and an ideology reflective of values such as Manifest Destiny—our students must struggle with the uncomfortable truth of their personal and cultural biases. Disbelief in the reality of what is happening south of the border results from feelings of betrayal and isolation from authority. To be able to cope with these feelings students project their uncertainties on the "other." If the authoritative voices of their own culture have lied to them, why believe in someone who is so foreign to their own world view? Thus, students rationalize the inevitability of U.S. involvement in Central America. This rationalization is tinged with a pessimism that does not cease to surprise us; corruption, the clash of cultures, progress, the need to protect ourselves from evil forces, and the need to protect our economy are all cited as more than sufficient reasons for rejecting what seems to us obvious—U.S. complicity. Recognition of this complicity has not, however, resulted in a simplified agenda of political correctness as some students perceive it.

For some students, accepting the legitimacy of another world view remains difficult. Some students prefer to deal with their feelings of impotence through word taunting, they still feel the need to define the "other" as an enemy, a "communist," fearing that failing to do so will undermine their own value system; while others wallow in their helplessness unable to discover what they can do in response to Rigoberta's call.

With Rigoberta's testimony we do learn much about the Guatemalan people and their history, about Rigoberta and her suffering, but what interests us most as teachers is the way that the book touches the humanity of everyone who reads it. The value and appreciation of the text stems from the perennial questions it raises about others and ourselves. The urgency of the questions raised by Rigoberta's testimony are acknowledged in the overwhelming and consistent support for its inclusion in the World Views syllabus. Responding to the Rigoberta text, one student writes:

> Before this class, many students I have talked to never knew this sort of condition existed for the indigenous person of Latin America. The stories of beatings and killings were something that was supposed to have only happened in the past and not in present day society. It is still happening now, however, and many students have become aware of these situations . . . this understanding that is gained about the world around us is an important part of development for students.

The student's statement brings us back to the crux of the matter: we are not only pursuing intellectual development in World Views, we want to foster moral, humane beings conscious of their own values, but equally committed to an active role in society. World Views succeeds when students realize their potential to interpret and change their world.

13

HAVING TO READ A BOOK ABOUT OPPRESSION
Encountering Rigoberta Menchú's Testimony in Boulder, Colorado

ROBIN JONES

There's an old joke about a minister who preaches eloquently from the pulpit about the joys of children but yells bloody murder when he finds a few kids carving their initials in the fresh cement outside the church. The minister prefers his children in the abstract, not in the concrete. This is rather like the situation I encountered when I first taught *I, Rigoberta Menchú* in a course on women writers in the summer semester of 1993 at the University of Colorado at Boulder. My most carefully laid plans and minutely organized lectures met the concrete reality of students and their own interests and needs. The result was not a failure or a disappointment but is interesting in demonstrating various reactions that teachers might expect in teaching this testimonial.

In teaching Menchú in Oregon, Allen Carey-Webb recounts that his "students were immediately sympathetic to the story and were anxious to know more, to involve themselves" (1991, 44). My students began by distrusting the text and the teller, disliking the information, being bored, depressed, and in general having a negative reaction and attitude to the work. Bear in mind, Boulder, Colorado, has a reputation for being the politically correct capital of the nation (at least in its own mind) and these students may have just been acting out their own version of backlash, something I see a lot in teaching women's literature or "ethnic" literature. Taking that attitude into account, this paper will sketch out my ideal as complicated by the real, and will discuss some possible teaching resources and suggestions.

As far as I know, I was the first person in the English department to teach this work (others now include it in women's literature and modern/contemporary literature) though I had seen it taught in the Religious Studies department in a course on colonialism and I believe it was also taught in an anthropology course. My experience in working with this text began as a project of my own concerning political violence against women. I wrote a paper about the violence in Menchú's work and how violence alters/affects identity and power relations. I was excited to apply my ideas about the violence in this work to the classroom, because I was concerned: how does one teach horror? How does one discuss the unspeakable acts of torture and murder, starvation and suffering? How does one not trivialize betrayal, rape, and execution in the relatively safe and mundane setting of the classroom? This was to be my personal challenge in teaching this work.

These questions are ones I also ask when I teach works of the Holocaust in my Jewish American literature class, and the class usually spends one classroom period trying to understand the dilemma in which we find ourselves, discussing objectively and rationally that which is often known as one of the most unnatural, illegitimate, and foul murders of a people. I mention my own discomfort at requiring students to write papers that will be graded on syntax and grammar, giving grades on tests about this subject. What an odd situation, for a student to boast: "Yeah, I aced the Holocaust." To repeat: how do we teach the literature of atrocity, especially those works immediately relevant to our own time, without turning them into some learning exercise that takes away from the human power and dignity of the voices and stories of the text? How do we keep these works from becoming "just texts" instead of the real experiences of real people?[1]

I've found in my Jewish American literature class that by constantly pointing out the distance between the text and reader, the knowledge needed to understand the work and the knowledge lacking, then some sense of perspective is achieved that situates reader and text/event in relation to each other. This is what I had hoped to do with Rigoberta Menchú's testimonial, achieve a certain foundation of knowledge from which we would examine the work and our own reaction from a variety of perspectives dealing with gender, ethnicity, politics, violence, and voice. My foundation for this work depended upon themes set up within the syllabus.

In this class were twenty-five students, four from the Women's Studies program with which this course was cross listed. All the students were in their early twenties, if not younger, all were white, and at least half of them appeared to be fairly well off financially. The class, which met every day for an hour and a half for five weeks, was based on the theme "Gender/Genre Border/Boundary." Each week we read a specific work (or works) to understand genre and discussed the various borders or boundaries established by language, experience, culture, politics, and so on. The genres were essay, autobiography, poetry, short story, and novel. We began with essays by Virginia Woolf ("A Room of One's Own"), Gloria Anzaldua ("Speaking in Tongues: A Letter to Third World Women Writers"), and Audre Lorde ("The Uses of Anger: Women Responding to Racism").[2]

These initial works established the importance of place, voice, power, language, ethnicity, gender, and class in understanding women's experience in general and women's writing in particular. Though the class was resistant to what they felt were "angry women writers" ("Why are they so angry? *I* didn't oppress any-body"), we established an understanding of the difficulty many women face to write and publish, the assets of understanding language through new experiences, and the effects of economics, power, and personal identity in writing. All our discussions were based on and developed from the rhetorical strategies of the essay.

Because these works seemed so personal to the class, I was glad that I had chosen the second week to do autobiography, a genre complicated and enriched by women's experience and by the testimonial genre. I had hoped once we had identified the genre(s) of Menchú's work we could discuss how these various aspects represented different voices within the narration: the personal voice of Menchú, the collective voice of the community, the voice that symbolizes a political imperative of social change. Many readers may already be familiar with the genre critiques of Menchú's work, indeed most work on Menchú has by necessity discussed and positioned genre before moving to the contents of the work. I recommend the study of genre now in order to understand the information Menchú offers readers and how that information might be considered through differing genres (as autobiography, ethnography, testimonial, or even bildungsroman as Doris Sommers suggests [1991b, 41]). Because so much work is already available, I will here only briefly discuss some of the ideas I introduced, which the class used to explore Menchú's work.

The class had read the first half of the book over the weekend and I began with an introductory lecture wherein I explained categories with which we might understand the work. I first discussed the work as autobiography and outlined some traditional subsets of this genre: apologies, exploration, exemplars, and simple recordings of one's life. I then noted how women's autobiography might contain issues about women's health, the family, gender inequities, aspects not always found in men's works and that might suggest new paradigms of autobiographical definition. I further argued that autobiography was part of a process of creating a subject through writing and is thus very important to women's experience.

I moved next to the genre of ethnography, and noted some of its characteristics such as the process of separating a community into various categories in order to study separately domestic issues, religion, or economics. The choices made in these studies raise then the problematics of authority and authorship that have been part of current debates in the anthropological field. What does the ethnographer feel is important to study, how does she or he understand this subject or gather information, and who then is the author of this work: the ethnographer or the subjects studied or who relate information?

This of course leads to the question of identity and appropriation (Gayatri Spivak's essay "Can the Subaltern Speak?" is helpful here).[3]

Finally I moved to the genre of testimonial. I had wanted to introduce some varying definitions of testimony so that students could locate these differences within the text and speculate as to why they might exist. One of my own understandings of the testimonial genre rests on the positioning of the narrative subject as individual, voice of the community, public voice of political and moral conscience. I wanted students to follow Menchú's negotiations of identity and with language in articulating her position. I hoped they would pay particular attention to the developing sense of consciousness raised in the narration. I began by introducing theories of Laura P. Rice-Sayre who identifies testimony as a "doubling of . . . oral history into a public plea," (1986, 49),and Barbara Harlow who notes that

> Crucial to the testimonio is the antiauthoritarian relationship between the narrator and the compiler . . . of the narrator-protagonist's account of the events to which she or he bears witness. This counter hegemonic relationship in turn implicates the reader, both in the events and in their retelling. (1987, 11)

Both Rice-Sayre and Harlow point out issues that my own class identified, that Menchú's work takes on more than one form in that it is a history of her self, her people, and her growing political consciousness, the latter giving voice to a sense of political imperative and call for action. Also the whole question of authorship and mediation is a topic I will address more fully.

Nancy Saporta Sternbach notes shared traits in "women's discourse and testimonial literature": the use of oral history as narrative, female sexual slavery as a motivating force in these narratives, and the equating of the personal with the political (1991, 92–93). Her ideas prove useful in looking at a history of women's writing though it seemingly depends on a feminist outlook that might not necessarily include ethnicity. This subject is dealt with further by George Yúdice who suggests that the testimony's "personal story is a shared one with the community to which the testimonialista belongs. The speaker does not speak for or represent a community but rather performs an act of identity-formation which is simultaneously personal and collective" (1991, 15). Yúdice adds that "testimonial writing is first and foremost an act, a tactic by means of which people engage in the process of self-constitution and survival" (19), an idea that reaffirms the position of women writing themselves into subjecthood.

John Beverley most materially defines the testimonial as

> novel or novella-length narrative in book or pamphlet form, told in the first person by a narrator who is also the real protagonist or witness of the events she or he recounts. . . . Since, in many cases, the

narrator is someone who is either functionally illiterate or, if literate, not a professional writer, the production of a testimonio often involves the tape recording and then the transcription and editing of an oral account by an interlocutor who is an intellectual, journalist, or writer. . . . The nature of the intervention of this editorial function is one of the more hotly debated theoretical points in the discussion of this genre. (1993, 71)

Truer words were never spoken. My lead-in lecture on genre produced not the detail-plotting exercises of negotiation and voice change that I had scheduled and looked forward to but a summary dismissal by the class of the text's very relevance since its authenticity was in question. Because the book was spoken by Menchú, taped, transcribed and edited by Burgos-Debray, and then translated by Wright, students resisted the entirety as a "reliable text." My explanations of postmodern problematics of authorship and authority were met by stony hostility and some amazing logic: "She didn't really write this, so why did she get the Nobel Prize?" The class resisted the testimonial factor of the book because it lacked authority, the ethnographic concept of the book because it was too full of conflicting and unnecessary detail, and the autobiographical aspect of the work because Menchú's life was unfamiliar and had no real relevance to their own lives. I am of course paraphrasing class discussions and after-class office hours visits into generalizing statements that hardly reflect the complexities of the classes' reactions.

In retrospect, this opening attitude was not surprising because I had the first week cautioned students to be "skeptical of the spectacle"—to be aware that Woolf's writing did not represent all women's experiences, as neither did Anzaldua's or Lorde's. From this position of skepticism, the class set out to deconstruct Menchú's book by pointing out places of inadequate detail and meaning. I suppose in some ways it was a dream come true, to have a class full of critically thinking and inquiring students, but I wasn't prepared for this kind of criticism. The work to me had taken on sacred dimensions and had become untouchable. The students were quite right to decenter my authority to deal with the text and their own agenda. But this agenda, as well as my own, needed some mediation.

Marc Zimmerman had noted in his essay "Testimonio in Guatemala: Payeras, Rigoberta, and Beyond" that there is indeed a problem with representation in this work, that there are doubts about the details of this work, some distortions, "ambiguity, half-truth, and outright error" (1991, 31). Zimmerman lists many of the sources that influence these doubts and to which the Boulder students also alluded: Menchú's own fear in revealing too much, Burgos-Debray's editing, Menchú's politics, perceptions, and linguistic abilities. Yet he feels all these issues have "failed to shake its foundations; the atrocities, the losses . . ." (32) just as Doris Sommer sees in Menchú's silences and gaps not an inadequacy of narration but a distancing device that points out the "insufficiency" of readers regarding Menchú's own knowledge and community (Sommer 1991b, 32). Beverley further adds that

> the complicity a testimonio establishes with its readers involves their identification by engaging their standards of ethics and justice in a speech-act situation that requires responses—with a cause normally distant, not to say alien, from their immediate experience (1993, 78).

This was the first task then for me, to work with student responses and habits of identification to understand their reading(s) of the work. That first day, after my opening lecture and their first response, we began to note our own differences and sources of knowledge about this kind of reportage and voice. We discovered that the students were not used to what George Yúdice calls the "voiceless" speaking (1991, 15). They wanted a more familiar voice of authority, a mediating presence. Beverley points out that the testimonio gives voice to "the child, the 'native', the woman, the insane, the criminal, the worker..." (1993, 71), which while debatable does demonstrate the opposite positions readers may take, as adults, elites, neglecting experiences of gender, objective, citizens with voting and economic power. Certainly these were the positions my students seemed to take up, well-educated people who felt they had no experiences to compare with Menchú's. One of the basic positions students articulated was that they felt they had no right to read the story, it was so different from their experience. Hence "no right" translated into "no interest" in reading the work. In the future such essentialist and experiential requirements might be countered by having students read bell hooks's essay "Essentialism and Experience" in *American Literary History* (spring 1991), which is in response to Diane Fuss's work *Essentially Speaking*.

Another response was for students to read into the work their own agenda. One student writing assignment is to prepare a "first thought" where an assertion about the story is made and proved. One such response was that the work "suggests ecofeminist ideologies and provides alternatives to environmental degradation." The student supported this assertion continuing: "The agricultural and economic activities of the cultures in the mountains were sustainable and bioregional," and that "women in the native cultures were not oppressed by men from their own culture, but the native women suffered violent oppression from the male dominated finca system," hence

> sustainability is the leading answer to the world's ecological crisis. Organizing women to fight the capitalistic system and install feminist ideologies is in the spirit of radical feminism. Ecofeminism ties environmental problems to the fight against male dominated oppressive societies.... The loss of Indian sustainable cultures has forced the

Indians into the capitalistic system. The capitalistic system destroys the environment, while the solution to the problems capitalism has created lies within the sustainable practices of the Indian culture.

Working through this response proved valuable in establishing what the reader was looking for—environmental issues—and avoiding—ethnicity and gender. While I am pleased with this response in the width of thought I was still puzzled that the human element was neglected and the ecological concerns (and these are very important concerns) inserted instead. Discussing this response with the student increased both our experiences with the work and I will add a component of this issue to the class the next time I teach the work.

In order for students to understand and perhaps trust the testimonial text a little more, while still retaining a critical attitude, I would recommend an exercise where the students themselves produce testimonials within the class or their own community to analyze and understand the process of soliciting, gathering, and editing information from another person. Such an experience might then turn their attention to what Beverley calls "the particular nature of the 'truth effect' of the testimonio" (1992, no. 3, 82), the events of the text itself. The discussions of genre are important, but unless we apply these to the content of the work, I find them distracting and distancing.

In dealing with the ethnographic details of the text, it is helpful to perhaps organize discussion around several key points of cultural history (for example marriage customs, religious practices) and then question our own cultural standards of importance, to determine which information we are interested in pursuing, what bores us, and why. This was certainly my own problem in first reading the book, in that I found myself skipping over some sections and paying more attention to others. My class read the entire book. I wonder if other teachers assign sections and which sections these might be. One student wrote in their class evaluation simply "I had trouble getting through Menchú." A different organization for reading the material might be helpful, though that organization would have to be held up to examination along with the text.

In discussing specific issues such as birth, marriage, or death, we can become aware of the changes that may have occurred within the Indian culture as a result of colonialism, religion, and economics; we can note voice changes in the narration, and what specifically precedes and follows such issues—what point Menchú (and admittedly Burgos-Debray) might be making with the insertion of the subject at that particular time. "Details" then take on another meaning when examined in light of the text as a whole.

Another point to raise to students is how we regard history as that which is dead and past and how Menchú reclaims ethnography in defiance of its tendency to record the lives of those soon to be assimilated (or extinct).[4] George Yúdice comments that "testimonial writing also emphasizes a rereading of a culture as lived history" (1991, 26). "Lived history" emphasizes the immediacy and vibrancy of a culture, one that may be struggling to survive but which is indeed very much alive. Menchú's customs are not just exotic rites and rituals collected by ethnographers (and upon which students might be tested), they are the repeated actions that maintain her community. Her "ethnographic" tendencies reiterate that hers is a culture that is most present, not extinct. As Doris Sommers points out:

> The phenomenon of a collective subject of the testimonial is, then, hardly the result of personal style on the part of the writer who testifies. It is the translation of a hegemonic autobiographical prose into a colonized language that does not equate identity with individuality. It is thus a reminder that life continues at the margins of Western discourse, and continues to disturb and challenge it. (1991b, 39)

Some students admit they like to read about "other cultures that aren't mine." I suggest such statements display a need to exoticize an "other" and position oneself as the "norm." I recommend they interrogate their own culture and behavior (and some students have never thought about themselves having a culture) to see how similar or different some experiences are. This may lead to a discussion concerning the need to create difference and what might be the consequences of creating difference.

Another issue rose when students acknowledged a distance from the text because of Menchú herself. One student acknowledged in the final evaluation at the end of the semester: "I didn't like Menchú—I'm not sure why, somehow her point of meaning is confused for me." Perhaps one of the problems students had in identifying with Menchú, besides the obvious of class, gender, and ethnicity, is that Menchú herself at times stands apart from her community and is "other." Doris Sommers points out that Menchú "resists identification with other women" as well as identification with "European(ized) (sic) readers" (1991b, 40). This appears to be true; other women in Menchú's work are either already dead or have no voice on which Menchú reports at length.

This distrust was acted out by students stating they were unable to trust the narration through what they felt was Menchú's hypocrisy. I find a similar situation when I teach Thoreau's Walden. Students are disgusted that a man who preaches independence still sends his laundry home to his mother (I suppose this hits pretty close to home for a lot of them). A specific example of this is when students complained that Menchú said she was a Christian yet she would criticize the church. This resistance can be dealt with by analyzing the rhetoric of her politics which use allegory from religious tracts, and by understanding the colonial history of missionary activities. But that this issue comes up in such a way exposes once again an attitude that prepares the students to be ready to resist the class: the backlash against multiculturalism and "political correctness."[5]

I had given the class Dinesh D'Souza's (1991) essay "The Politics of Force-Fed Multiculturalism," where he identifies Menchú as "a mouthpiece for a sophisticated Western critique of society, all the more useful because it issues from a seemingly authentic peasant source" and as a victim of "quadruple oppression." I had hoped the class would note the rhetorical inadequacies of D'Souza's own argument, the generalizations and misreadings that confuse his own meaning. They were however, quite relieved to read him, they seemed reaffirmed in their arguments against Menchú's work through his essay. Unless I went line by line through the essay (and I was tempted) to point out the same problems in his work of which they accused Menchú, there seemed not a lot I could do. The atmosphere in the class was becoming "me against them," by the end of the second day I was overtly pushing the book and they were assuming the glazed faces of rejection and discomfort. My need for them to appreciate the book was overpowering their inability to please me and still voice their own objections. We had been discussing these issues in class, one on one and in small groups of four or five. We were all tired and tense. I will mention here that I wasn't fearful of silencing them, they had already been vocal with problems they found with the first genre. Part of their discomfort appeared to arise from their awareness of how much I cared about the book and their reluctance to disappoint me (which could be wishful thinking on my part).

Luckily on Wednesday I was silenced by turning the class over to a student presentation. Each week, a group of students was to prepare a presentation that depended upon the themes "gender/genre" or "borders/boundaries." The Menchú group presentation seemingly, and I'm not sure consciously, tried to work with both themes, by focusing on one aspect of the work and what it represented. The group presentations have always been highlights in class, in that the students are in charge. They research, plan, and orchestrate the classroom activities for the day, challenged by me to teach a class the "way they would have preferred to learn themselves." Various presentations in previous years have included role playing, in-class writing of a group poem, a dramatic presentation of a scene, game shows, interviews of authors/characters, art work, and music. My role is to participate as any other member of the class and to record discussions and ideas. This group excelled in its format, being innovative and specifically trying to understand in depth the importance of one particular aspect of the work: food.

Before class began, the group members had set up an ornate table with cloth and candles, croissants and other pastries, orange juice, and coffee. Nearby was a small, bare table with styrofoam containers of coffee and doughnuts. As class members entered, we were assigned one of three roles: ladinos, overseers, peasants (I was a peasant). This latter group (the largest) was seated on the floor and handed one corn tortilla each. Ladinos sat at the best table, overseers with the doughnuts. As the class sat (or squatted), the group read passages from Menchú's work: Menchú as a maid in the city; the soldiers coming to take the food the village has been growing; Menchú asking other Indians what they eat, while banana trees provide shade for coffee bushes but the hungry people are not allowed to pick the fruit. After each scene was read, the class was to jot down their reaction (though I had noted in my remarks to the group afterward that this seemed insufficient unless countered with the position of that person as ladino, overseer, or peasant—if we were to role play we should go all the way). The point of the presentation was to demonstrate levels of power structures through accessibility to food, which to dieting Americans is sometimes a new and startling concept. The passages demonstrated the various boundaries/borders that influence gender, class, and ethnic identity. I found the presentation helpful in clarifying social orientations and power but was surprised by the class reaction. The four students who posed as ladinos confessed they couldn't eat their food, which was very appetizing—they felt too self-conscious and uncomfortable. The class spent much time analyzing this factor and ignored the discomfort of the peasants on the floor (the advantage of role playing is that the peasants were busy participating in the class discussion but not in their roles). This sympathy seemed strangely misplaced—to question how and why the "powerful" felt toward those with less power—and it was the powerful here who directed the discussion. When I directed attention to this phenomena, the students quickly severed the hypothetical link with the text and assured me they felt uncomfortable not as ladinos but as fellow students. In other words, the transfer had failed and the students had seen this "skit" not in light of the work but from their own experiences.

The food angle was not unexpected. The previous week we had discussed in some detail Virginia Woolf's *A Room of One's Own*, particularly the scenes where the narrator dines, first sumptuously at a literary luncheon, then more stringently at a woman's college. The domestic detail of food pointing out class/gender discrepancies seemed useful and appropriate to the class, and I was pleased they continued with this theme (as they did throughout the semester). What was unexpected was the ability of the students to empathize with the text and then just as quickly remove themselves from it. Intellectually I believe they were "getting" Menchú's work, but emotionally, consciously, they were rejecting it.

On Thursday we moved to a discussion of the violence in the work (students had by now finished reading the entire book). When I first decided to teach Rigoberta Menchú's testimonial, one of my major concerns was how to deal with the graphic violence and horror reported by Menchú. Her brother is burned to death in front of the family, she must gather up the pieces of her friend who has been hacked and butchered to death, her mother's body is exposed to the elements after rape and torture. How could I "teach" these events to students without trivializing the inhumanity of such actions or Menchú's own reactions? How could I develop an awareness of my students' understanding of such a personal and painful work? I had prepared (gleaned from my earlier paper) a critical understanding of the violence as based on Elaine Scarry's *The Body in Pain,* as well as Foucault's *Discipline and Punish.* In my opening lecture for this day I discussed two particular scenes, the death of Menchú's brother and the dismemberment of her friend Petrona Chona. I noted the issues of ethnicity and gender that were specific targets of violence as well as the political renaming that made such physical acts possible. The theory once again seemed acceptable to the students, but their own reactions to the text startled me: what I had feared would repulse them seemed to have little effect. Of course I am addressing the generation that grew up with slasher movies, Freddy Krueger, and the Terminator, but I had expected some problems. The main reaction to the violence was that Menchú was being "too graphic." If she wanted to arouse sympathy she should have "softened" the images. In other words, she should have retold the story in a gentler fashion so the reader could stay within the story. Students did not feel horrified as much as manipulated, as if this was indeed a slasher movie, not a real account of the death of a family member.

One student announced that she felt Menchú had "whined too much," written about only the "bad stuff." When, she asked, was Menchú going to show what she intended to do about all this? Considering that "all this" included generations of colonialism, technology unavailable to Menchú and her community, and systems of power and powerlessness difficult to comprehend, I'm not sure if my response was adequate: "Isn't this book 'doing something'? What is this book, other than some sort of action, some sort of revelation and truth from which to learn and work?" The next time I will ask students to consider what actions Menchú could be taking in addition to her testimonial. I see now the power of literacy appears banal to many students (perhaps because they feel disempowered in their own writing in classrooms). At this point, I could have gone back to the essays to remind them of the history of women *not* writing, so they would be aware of that difference.

The final day I had arranged to show the film "Sun, Moon, and Feather" from Spiderwoman Theater. Disappointed as I was by the reaction of the class to the reading (which now at least was half in favor of the book and half disapproving), I had thought to cancel the film and continue discussion. However the film was too good to pass up—an important connection to United States culture in demonstrating women's voices, experiences, genres, and acculturation. It is also wonderful to watch—provocative, entertaining, and enlightening. Spiderwoman Theater is a New York based group, three of its members being the sisters Muriel Miguel, Gloria Miguel, and Lisa Mayo. The sisters' film problematizes the authority of autobiography in demonstrating how identity is collectively created, constantly in flux, frequently mistaken, and often an act of performance.[6] The same issues of oppression, authority, and creativity discussed in genre aspects of Menchú's work can also be found in "Sun, Moon, and Feather," and the ability of students to make the connections is a positive and helpful step in understanding women's writing/art and the experiences of people of color.

The film addresses stereotypes of Native Americans, media representations of women and ethnicity, and blends a diversity of media perspectives (documentary, home films, movie clips, animation). The film opens with the three sisters telling their own versions of growing up in a brownstone apartment in New York. Each has a different perspective, and the overlaying voices and pictures confuse which story is the accurate one, subverting the notion of only one authenticity of narration. They demonstrate their own cultural construction by playing "Cowboy and Indian," acting out a Jeannette MacDonald and Nelson Eddy love scene ("Indian Love Song"), thus skewing both ethnic identity and gender roles ("I get to be Jeannette this time." "Alright, but then I get to be Nelson Eddy."). The lighter touches of this film make it endearing to students even while they are confused by its pastiche of style and story (I recommend they see it at least twice).

I had planned to end the week on autobiography with this film, not only because of the ties to Menchú's work, and because of its destabilizing of the issue of the "I" in autobiography, but also because I thought after the final horrific scene in Menchú's book I would need to distract the students from so much pain. I felt students would be numb and depressed and would need another forum in which to readjust themselves and their feelings. I knew they would be depressed, yet I was still surprised and frustrated when they themselves admitted this.

It seems that the events of the book had not depressed them so much as having to read a book about oppression. Their question "Are all the works going to be this depressing?" seemed to divert attention away from the texts and to their need to be entertained. I wonder whether this question is raised in classes (perhaps an "American Masterpieces" course) not specifically addressing issues of gender and ethnicity. Do students respond this way to *The Scarlet Letter*, *Moby Dick*, *Huck Finn?* Certainly there are depressing elements about these more canonical works also, but I find there is an expectant hostility to women's works and "ethnic" works regarding the revelation of oppression (the same revelation I felt Hawthorne, Melville, and Twain were addressing, though on different subjects).

I suggest that when students describe a work as "too depressing," this statement be interrogated to find out which element of the story they find most depressing. I suspect that what is really at stake is the student's reaction to being decentered as a subject and feeling disempowered by the strength of an unfamiliar life experience. The feeling of being destabilized can be depressing, and perhaps this is what these students experience along with being overwhelmed by the horror of Menchú's work.

A similar reaction occurs during Holocaust Week on the CU campus: students and colleagues avoid the event because it is "too depressing." When commemoration and learning are avoided for this reason, it may be time to question the experience and meaning of "depressing."

Overall, student evaluations at the end of the semester were positive to the course in general and to its themes. One person wrote: "This class has taught me to read everything that I can get my hands on. I can only broaden my intellect by taking in a great deal of perspectives. I am more motivated to read and learn." This same student also suggested, however, that while "Menchú and (Toni Morrison's) *Beloved* were excellent texts . . . summer is too short for two depressing novels." Genre issues aside, this seemed reflective of the general attitude of the class—that there was a quota for "depressing literature," and that we had overstepped it.

If this is the worst criticism of the course and of the time spent on Menchú, then I suppose the class was a success. I am still troubled by the students' resentment towards Menchú and her work, reflecting a backlash against multiculturalism and an unexamined response to the politics of "political correctness." Next time I will offer more historical preparation with Guatemalan history, geography, and politics (one suggestion in the evaluation was that this work would be more in line for a history course than a literature class). I will also have students discuss specific scenes rather than try to cover the book so generally. But as to their attitude, I don't know what I can do to prepare them to accept a story and a life as full and traumatic as Menchú's. How and why to teach *I, Rogoberta Menchú*, and in what environment, would be the next issues to address—and to remember that the best of plans expand into something even better when developed within the immediacy of classroom response.

NOTES

1. Theodore Adorno's notion that "to write poetry after Auschwitz is barbaric" serves as a critical foundation—about art and representation—for the Holocaust course. I would be interested in similar critiques for Menchú's work.

2. The syllabus continued as follows: Week Three/Poetry: selections from Emily Dickinson; Adrienne Rich's "When We Dead Awaken: Writing as Re-Vision," "Diving Into the Wreck," "I am in Danger—Sir—;" Audre Lorde's "School Note;" Lorna Dee Cervantes's "Poem For The Young White Man Who Asked Me How I, An Intelligent, Well-Read Person, Could Believe In The War Between Races;" Mitsuye Yamada's "Masks of Woman;" Gisele Fong's "Corrosion;" Elena Tajima Creef's "Notes from a Fragmented Daughter;" Chrystos's "Ceremony for Completing a Poetry Reading." Week Four/Short Story: Beth Brant's "Turtle Gal;" Charlotte Perkins Gilman's "Yellow Wallpaper;" Judy Grahn's "Boys at the Rodeo." Week Five/Novel: Toni Morrison's *Beloved*.

3. Found in Cary Nelson and Lawrence Grossberg, *Marxism and the Interpretation of Culture* (Urbana, Ill.: University of Illinois Press, 1988).

4. I know this is a generalization more applicable to earlier ethnographies, such as those by E. E. Pritchard-Evans, for example. Current work articulates just these problems and can be very enlightening for students.

5. I use both terms with reservation, since they have such different meanings when used in political debates of power that reflect positions and budgets in administrative offices, rather than reflecting intellectual concerns and pursuits.

6. For information on the video contact The Cinema Guild, 1697 Broadway, New York, NY 10019 (212) 246-5522.

14

WORLDING STUDENTS

STEVE MATHEWS

When postcolonial critics like Edward Said and Gayatri Spivak talk about "worlding," they are talking about texts.[1] By this concept, they mean the placing of the documents of culture in the world-historical context of Western imperialism. For them, aesthetic production must be read and analyzed with regard to its geographical placement in the history of Euro-American capitalism's colonization of the globe. In this essay, I want to think about the ways in which *I, Rigoberta Menchú*, as a decolonizing text, can be a pedagogical activator that situates the reader in these world coordinates of space and time. Thus, instead of a critical reader worlding the text, we have a critical text worlding the reader. Teaching, then, becomes an act of facilitation so that the text might more easily perform this cultural work.

These reflections stem from my experience teaching *I, Rigoberta Menchú* to University of Iowa undergraduates in a course on contemporary Latin American narrative in translation. Designed to give a broad overview of mid- to late-twentieth-century narrative literature, the reading list includes authors from eight different countries and a variety of cultural traditions. The divergence of a book like *I, Rigoberta Menchú* from, say, short stories by the Argentine Jorge Luis Borges, emphatically underlines what I communicate to the students in the course description section of the syllabus: "Contrary to many U.S. representations of it, Latin American culture is *not* a monolithic entity; therefore, our readings will lead us across multiple and shifting borders of ethnicity, gender, nationality, and politics." The course plan I follow crosses some of these frontiers with a definite geographical trajectory. We begin by reading Borge's "Tlön, Uqbar, Orbis Tertius," which creates a philosophically idealist, imaginary world, and finish with sections of Chicano writer Tomás Rivera's *Y no se lo tragó la tierra. . . . And the Earth Did Not Part*, an interwoven set of brief narratives about Latino migrant farm laborers working the harvest in the upper midwest, perhaps Iowa. The students' imaginations traverse territories from dreamt universes through the South American sierra to work camps inhabited by melon harvesters in Muscatine County. On the way, they pass through Guatemala.

However, this journey must not become a vacation nor the reader a tourist-voyeur; Rigoberta Menchú is not a tour guide. Though it is not always the case, one term I had a class comprised of white, mostly middle-class students between the ages of eighteen and twenty-four. This is not to say they were homogenous, only that none were Guatemalan Indians, nor, more generally, identified with a racially oppressed group. My course description always includes the following statement for discussion on the first day of class: "The emphasis we place on how cultural texts intersect with the world to produce meaning requires that we pay careful attention to the Latin American historical context as well as to our own positions as crosscultural readers." The patterns of identification and engagement enabled by the congruence of those reading positions with the pressures and limits established by the text itself, when combined with my own version of critical pedagogy, coalesced around three problems: land, Christianity, and violence. As our discussion coalesced around these three themes, the students began to develop an implicit critique of the facile exoticism of multicultural tourism. Before I consider the implications of this, let me present some details of these classroom conversations.

I, Rigoberta Menchú presents three basic modes of interrelation between human beings and the question of land. Early on, in the more ethnographic sections of the text, land is a sacred domain to which Indian groups relate through ritual and practice. It represents sustenance, communal identity, life itself. "Every part of our culture comes from the earth. Our religion comes from the maize and bean harvests which are so vital to our community (16)."[2] Land is also a place of suffering and pain. The families' forced annual migration to the coastal fincas and the severe exploitation they suffer there motivate demands for social justice. The text narrates several episodes of poisoning, malnutrition, and death that illustrate the extreme inhumanity of a brutal agricultural production system. Finally, the land tenure structure is openly displayed and analyzed as a motivation for antagonistic confrontation between opposed social groups. "After many years of hard work, when our small bit of land began yielding harvests and our people had a large area under cultivation, the big land owners appeared: the Brols. . . . [F]ive of them lived on a finca they had taken over by forcibly throwing the Indians of the region off their land" (103). The text makes strategic use of ethnographic description, storytelling, and socioeconomic analysis in order to detail the problem of territorial rights and land distribution that is the central focus of the Indians' struggle.

We began our discussion of this question with a ten-minute student presentation on land tenure and agricultural production in Guatemala: who owns which land, what is produced and why, who works for how much and where? Against the poststructuralist emphasis on the rhetorical construction of knowledge, against postmodernist distancing from "truth claims" and indeed, as I will discuss later, somewhat against the thrust of my own pedagogical efforts, most students continue to believe in brute, unmediated facts.

Within this context, we sought to understand the role of land in *I, Rigoberta Menchú*. Several students with ecological concerns spoke with profound respect and even awe at the bonds of love that united a community of human beings together through ties to the land. They lamented that such a profound connection to the earth as home seemed to have been lost in the United States. Several critiqued the instrumental use of land exclusively for profit or the dumping of poisonous waste in ways that clearly resonated with the text they were reading. As one student remarked, "Their bond to the earth brings them peace and happiness; you can't even drink the water in Iowa City because of the farm run-off." Of course, "Green" is currently fashionable and much of what was said contained strong elements of romantic nostalgia, but I was encouraged when several students pressed the discussion toward a consideration of social justice. They wanted to talk about their moral outrage at a system of land ownership and work that tossed aside human beings as so much detritus of the production process. In their efforts to understand systemic injustice they made the imaginative leap to farming in Iowa. Several students related vivid and painful memories of farm families who had been dispossessed of their land in small, rural communities. One woman raised the issue of the increase in corporate agriculture that had thrown many indebted farmers off their land. As the anecdotes piled up and students began to talk about people they knew, I moved to insist that it was only a rough analogy they were drawing and that we seemed to be risking over-identification between ourselves and others. Shaking their heads at me, at least two of them openly debated my caveat, insisting that the connection was a valid one, and ultimately suggesting that I just didn't get it. And in an important way, they were right, I didn't. In my teacherly resistance to the dangers of liberal exoticism, I failed to recognize their conceptual transition from relations of cultural identity to relations of economic structure and power. Without explicitly saying so, these students were talking about shifts in modes of production and the human costs of those shifts.

As we continued our discussion of land and justice, focusing again on the text, I learned that my trepidation was exaggerated by listening to their comments concerning the information about land, ritual, and identity given in the first few chapters. Aided by the ethnographic descriptions, they made it abundantly clear that they considered Rigoberta Menchú's culture to be markedly distinct from their own, that any similarities of situation were mitigated by this difference, and that any connection that was taking place could not be operating through the category of identity. Students also remarked at some length on the straightforward, antimelodramatic style of the stories that illustrate the horror of working conditions on the coastal fincas. "Deadpan" was their word. "She just lays it out there, she doesn't cry, she doesn't ask us to cry," said one man. "But she does ask us to be angry," replied someone; "At who?" another queried; "At the Brols," a woman stated; "Not just the Brols, all the land owners, the whole thing," said another woman.

In retrospect, I think this discussion helped me to see several things about transcultural understanding and the ways in which I, Rigoberta Menchú works to world its readers. In turn, awareness of how this process works in the North American classroom can help us see why we ought to push discussions about difference and diversity in a transnational direction, away from the 'nation' and into the 'world'. The model of multiculturalism that currently holds sway in the United States is a sort of neo-nationalist discourse that redeploys the language of pluralism to promote, ironically, a politics of assimilation and cohesion. On offer at present is a leveling rhetoric, a happy-family-of-man multiculturalism that raises differences only to manage and/or ban them in the end.[3] According to Henry Giroux, this conservative-liberal approach is motivated by the "spirit of displaying difference in order to displace it within a hegemonic project of national unity" (Giroux 1993, 5). The ideology operative here is one of national harmony; social conflict and relations of exploitation and/or oppression are evacuated out of notions of cultural diversity. Since, as Sacvan Bercovitch has argued, U.S. national ideology has long operated on a model of "dissensus," or the agreement to disagree (Bercovitch 1986, 632), to recuperate difference into an over-arching conception of unity, those of us who are critical of this understanding of multiculturalism suffer a categorical defeat if we accept the current geographical borders of the United States of America as significant markers in the debate about what a so-called multicultural pedagogy ought to look like. That is, whenever the category of the nation is readily available as a model for our understanding of "other" texts, real antagonism is too easily subsumed by the desire to all get along. Obviously, since no imaginable nationalist project in this country seeks to incorporate Central American Indians, if we bring a book like I, Rigoberta Menchú to the multicultural table in the U.S. educational system, the terms of the discussion are altered.[4] More interesting, however, is the way in which the text-reader complex that may appear while teaching the book presents a far more challenging model of crosscultural awareness.

The global corollary to U.S. liberal nationalist multiculturalism is an appeal to universal human experience and transhistorical nature. The commonsense belief that humanity is united by common bonds and therefore all differences are secondary frequently hides and naturalizes Euro-American normative ideology. However, as I witnessed in my students' responses, the text blocks this assimilationist reading and pushes students to see Rigoberta Menchú's culture as unavoidably different and somehow "pure" in that it derives strength and legitimacy from a relationship to land. We are confronted with a distinct, unassimilable "nature," one whose very presence unhinges the universalist pretensions of the notion itself. Furthermore, the text seems to produce a kind of Brechtian alienation effect in its refusal to allow sympathetic identification with poor, suffering people, as evidenced in the student's comment about "not crying" above.[5] As mentioned, students noted a distinct absence of pathos in the descriptions of loss and suffering, torture and death. The narrator does not permit a naturalistic identification with the characters in this drama; the easy path of catharsis is shifted to a more distanced perspective that requires thought and invokes ethos. The students correctly recognized that *I, Rigoberta Menchú* does not play upon notions of tragedy; it practices claims about injustice. Tragedy is about grief and sadness; injustice is about anger and vindication. Menchú's testimonial is an argument for transformation that demands more of the reader than sorrow and pity. Guilt is unproductive. "What she really wants," observed one student, "Is a revolution."

In their discussion of land, they began to move from the normative engagement with other-cultural texts that proceeds through the category of "identity" to another understanding that operates through something we might call "system," or to use their term, "the whole thing." They did not recognize themselves in Rigoberta Menchú's narrative, but instead began to see different people grouped on opposite sides of an important geographical boundary who are nevertheless caught up in a larger structure that displaces them both. Multiculturalism too often solicits sympathy and more rarely suggests empathy through some transmutation of gaps across cultural identity. *I, Rigoberta Menchú* perhaps posits a more useful approach that works through the intersections of systemic forces to suggest alliances and enable political solidarity. We belong to this system which, though it is currently masquerading under that ideological obfuscation, "the market," should be called by its historical name: capitalism. The difficulty is not with "bad" people; the problem, as the students learned through their reading, is not "the Brols" nor, in the 1980s vocabulary of liberal U.S. Central American solidarity activists, "Ronald Reagan." As Menchú narrates her growing awareness of a connection to Guatemalan ladinos, some students are able to draw parallels and make a leap of political imagination. Perhaps they can begin to construct a complex, nuanced "we" with Rigoberta Menchú.

Following our discussion of land, we moved on to a consideration of Christianity in *I, Rigoberta Menchú*. Most students had been raised in one Christian tradition or another, and all, of course, had experienced the Judeo-Christian norms and values that permeate the dominant culture in the United States. What *I, Rigoberta Menchú* did for some of them was to defamiliarize Christianity, to make them see it in a new way. We began with a challenging presentation by one of the more enthusiastic students about Liberation Theology in Latin America and Guatemala. Visibly moved by what she saw as a renewal of the message of egalitarianism and communalism for modern Christianity, she gave a highly partisan report that placed the issue of the connection between spiritual commitment and social justice squarely on the table before us. "Christian love," she said, "means reorganizing the world we live in, changing it to eliminate the suffering of millions of people now, not waiting patiently for an afterlife." After countering with some information on the growth of conservative, evangelical protestant sects in recent years, I opened the discussion by reminding them of the question of "transculturation." Previously, I had introduced the concept as borrowed by the literary critic Angel Rama from the pioneering ethnographer Fernando Ortiz when we read *Deep Rivers*, a novel by the Peruvian writer José María Arguedas that concerns itself with cultural hybridization and indigenous resistance in the Andes. According to Mary Louise Pratt, transculturation has been used "to describe how subordinated or marginal groups select and invent from materials transmitted to them by a dominant or metropolitan culture" (Pratt 1992, 6).

When I offered transculturation as a model for understanding *I, Rigoberta Menchú's* presentation of Christianity and, more specifically, Rigoberta Menchú's personal and political use of theology, many students were initially enthusiastic. They returned repeatedly to Rigoberta Menchú's statement, "I'm a catechist who walks upon this earth, not one who thinks only of the Kingdom of God" (79), and made the clear connection to tenets of Liberation Theology. They also cited statements like, "This is where you see the mixture of Catholicism and our own culture" (81), and "It was more like another way of expressing ourselves" (80), in order to get at the idea of selective cultural mixing. Students drew an analogy between Rigoberta Menchú's strategic decision to learn Spanish because she wanted to fight her oppressors with their own tools and her community's appropriation and reworking of Christian doctrine for much the same ends, as in the following statement: "We'd read a text and analyze the role of a Christian. This brought us together more and made us more concerned about each other's problems" (88). However, when I attempted to underline the importance of Rigoberta Menchú's mention of "reading" and "text" so as to point up the rhetorical nature of theological interpretation, I was opposed by several students, including the woman who had given the presentation on Liberation Theology. While we did have an interesting, if truncated, conversation about the sociohistorical power of script and "the Book" as well as cultural borrowing and resistance, these students' take on the transculturation of Christianity was clearly opposed to my own. Their position was that, whereas they understood my interest in dismantling claims to universality by showing interpretive conflict, they preferred to stake out absolute domains of right and wrong. They argued that Rigoberta Menchú and her faith community had captured the truth of Christianity, that the real power of transculturation was the recovery of original meaning and finally "getting it right." Ultimately, for them, the essence of Christianity was the demand for social justice, and they waved aside my focus on historical contingency and struggles over interpretive control by pointing to the moral power of Rigoberta Menchú's questions and demands—"Why did they spray poison when people were working there?" (89). I don't think they agreed to disagree with me; they thought I was just plain wrong.

A marked division in the way that we were talking about our object, which had been creeping in from the beginning of the term, now boldly asserted itself in this debate. Always careful to refer to the "text" or the "narrator" or to call the book by its title, I insisted on continually speaking about the constructed nature of the thing we had before us. We had framed our discussion of *I, Rigoberta Menchú* with an attention to the publishing industry, translation, interviews, Elisabeth Burgos-Debray, Rigoberta Menchú in Paris, etc. I gave a brief lecture on anticolonial critiques of anthropology's history and presented some skeptical perspectives on the truth claims of testimonial narrative in Latin America. My goal was to ask students to keep in mind the process of mediation and to deflect the naive belief that we somehow had direct access to the "voice" of an Indian woman. All of my good, teacherly intentions notwithstanding, most students dropped all distancing pretense when we began to talk about the transculturation of Christianity. The imperative of claims for justice combined with the text's refunctionalizing of familiar doctrine, and students' own ethical imaginations and religious commitments caused them to refer to her constantly as "Rigoberta" and to eclipse the problem of textual production. Certainly, the demand to eliminate injustice which was solicited through a cultural tradition most students recognized as their own proved to be a highly charged moment for the class. It represented a direct challenge to my skeptical approach and demonstrated the power of the testimonial's rhetorical address. Nevertheless, what I insisted on calling the "communicative effectivity" or some other turgid phrase and what my students called "truth" coalesced around the historical situatedness of the narrative. "Rigoberta" as a living woman serves as a locator for the reader, a marker of place and time that requires greater specificity than an anonymous narrator. The students' comments bore this out. They constantly referred to the religious meaning of concrete situations described in the book. In retrospect, it seems that the major emphasis of our discussion carried the specific evaluation of a situated ethics rather than the broad generalizing common to transhistorical moral injunction. The students' interventions were nearly always concerned with the why's and wherefore's of particular episodes and rarely broached vague notions of good and evil. However, the underlying tension between these two approaches to evaluative judgment would continue for the remainder of our discussions.

These conversations led directly to the question at the heart of both moral imperatives and strategic positionings: What is to be done? We began by considering the text's representation of the community's struggle against the Guatemalan security forces and the subsequent organizing efforts of the Menchú family. Our efforts to understand the extreme difficulties of putting together a peasant league to fight a viciously exploitative system led us to consider the question of tactics which, in turn, touched off a series of arguments about resistance and the legitimacy of violence that were to dominate the remainder of our discussion of *I, Rigoberta Menchú.*

Perhaps because the severity of state repression becomes an increasingly dominant theme as the testimonial progresses and possibly because the students found the narrator's descriptions of violence to be so stark and arresting in their unsensationalized presentation, the issue of violence became the early focus of our consideration of resistance. Several students raised the issue of legitimacy in this context. They seemed anguished and torn by what they felt to be a contradiction between the absolute moral injunctions against violence in what they understood to be a transformation of Christianity and an extreme situation where violence answered violence. Agonizing about the apparent need for self-defense and sympathetic to efforts at social revolution, a few of the "liberal" students nevertheless argued strongly that all killing was wrong and that violence only leads to more violence in an unending cycle. These forms of resistance, they claimed, were illegitimate. These statements provoked an interesting classroom moment by inciting the vociferous intervention of two traditionally conservative students who openly derided what they saw as their classmates' naivté. The liberal students immediately replied with the example of Ghandi and Martin Luther King, Jr., saying that positive change could only be achieved through nonviolent means. There ensued a serious debate in which, to my amazement, students I had thought of as quite conservative began to argue for the violent overthrow of illegitimate authority. Their reply to the Ghandi example was that the respective situations were widely divergent and the analogy simply did not hold. The example they preferred came from the text. They pointed to the episode of the army's attack on the village in which the old woman defends her hut with an axe and clubs a soldier (147).

Their attempt to force the discussion away from abstract principles onto the terrain of the grim reality of clearly defined situations allowed me to ask a question: What is violence without history? What appeared to be implicit in the conservative students' comments was the notion that a violent action only takes on meaning and thus can only be judged in the unique context of its enactment. All of this seemed rather straightforward, even familiar, to most students until one of them pointed out that the text was not making a case for self-defense as in a U.S. law court scenario, but instead arguing for communal-defense. This caused us to revisit a discussion we had initiated on the very first day of class on I, Rigoberta Menchú about the "we" and the "I." Many had remarked on the prevalence of communal commitments and collective undertakings while noting the difference this represented with respect to dominant modes of understanding in the United States. Throughout our consideration of the text, the difference between individualism and communalism had appeared, if only briefly. As a coda to our discussions of violence, it suddenly took on added importance. Following some of the arguments staked out in the text about Kjell's neoliberal agrarian reform, one man interjected the criticism that in a situation where there are claims being made in favor of community, the notion of individual rights is somehow inadequate.

Though I cannot say that this ever became absolutely explicit in the classroom, I suspect that more than a few students began to feel that individualism played a normative function and that its universalizing pretensions made transcultural understanding more difficult. That is, if we employ a Western notion of the individual "self"—which, not incidentally, fails to recognize its historical roots—in order to comprehend the justice-claims of collectivities that have been antagonistically related to that tradition, misunderstanding is inevitable. Also just under the surface of some students' responses was the idea that whereas individualism seemed to lend itself to abstraction, communal identity was grounded in specific historical junctures. In Menchú's testimonial, *these* Indian groups want *this* land, which they claim as theirs; and they do not pretend to speak for all groups everywhere for all time.

I feel secure in the assertion that a part of the class recognized this distinction because there ensued a short discussion of "rights" which proved to be the final spin-off of our grappling with the problem of violence and closed out our consideration of *I, Rigoberta Menchú*. Several students spoke admiringly of Rigoberta Menchú's ability to move beyond any narrowness of communal identification in a learning process that enabled her to connect to other Indian groups, ladinos, and industrial workers and miners regardless of their ethnicity. Another student remarked that this had come about because of the demands of organizing and the struggle against repression. Then someone said that it was because they were all concerned with human rights. "What are human rights and to whom do they belong?" I asked. Immediately, one woman remarked that it was hard to fit the image of community presented by the text with our commonplace understanding of human rights. Communal rights seemed distinct as a concept. In a rapid exchange cut short by those ever-present time constraints, one student raised the related issue of *structural* human rights and another made the connection back to violence by talking about *structural* violence. Both comments were offered in the terms of land rights and food production which of course we had been talking about all along. The attempt to talk about structure, for me, at least in retrospect, closed the circle to intersect with questions about "system." I ended the class by attempting to make a part of that system obvious. I stated—without comment and drawing upon what the students had felt to be Rigoberta Menchú's deadpan style in order to avoid the pathos of personal guilt—a series of facts and figures about U.S. government funding of the Guatemalan military during the 1980s.

Reading *I, Rigoberta Menchú* in the North American classroom can help students recognize their placement with others in a world-historical system that structures relations of difference into a complex whole based on the suffering of the many and the profits of the few. The text may facilitate what Fredric Jameson has, in another context, called "cognitive mapping." In my experience, their reading of the text helped students become aware of themselves globally. Further, it denied the naturalizing aims of a Euro-American ideology based on individualism and universalism that so often makes the teaching of other-cultural texts difficult in the United States. When combined with strategies of critical pedagogy, class discussions can be shifted from the vapid multiculturalism restricted to an identity politics towards a more useful geographical materialism that evokes a politics of locality-in-system.[6] It is worth remembering that exploitation is not just another synonym for oppression. This is not to reduce differential placement to systemic sameness nor to deny the specificity of local struggles, but we must not lose sight of those world connections that cut across lines of difference and exploit vast majorities.

One pedagogical strategy I learned myself from *I, Rigoberta Menchú* is that a rhetoric of guilt evocation is a mistake. Moreover, I think that in an important sense, it is wrong in that it obscures a larger truth. The normative left analysis of the "500-year system" is that white Europeans and Americans have oppressed indigenous peoples in a colonial relation that persists. This is correct, the genocide is real; yet, white guilt is a powerless response. Historically, in the Americas as elsewhere, colonialism, imperialism, and neocolonialism are all subsets of capitalism. Neoliberalism is not just a set of ideas about free trade; it is the name for the current restructuring of global space and capitalism's most recent, savage offensive against the world's peoples. A historically sensitive, internally differentiated alliance internationalism of we, the exploited, is the only powerful answer. Enabling this possibility is the work of worlding.

I write this on February 22, 1994, in Lima, Peru, a spot on the globe whose economy and democracy have been brutally impoverished by political violence and the IMF-mandated "reforms" designed for its "reinsertion" into the world financial system. Rigoberta Menchú has come to Lima this week for the *Primer Congreso Latinoamericano de Organizaciones del Campo;* she has come in solidarity with women workers, students, poor families, farmers, indigenous peoples; she has come to help organize transnational resistance to transnational exploitation. My hope is that perhaps, in some humble way, the North American classroom can also be a site for the globalization of solidarity in response to the globalization of the capitalist economy, a site where we begin to work for "free trade" in cultural production and understanding.

NOTES

1. For a more detailed discussion of "worlding," see Edward Said, *The World the Text and the Critic* and *Culture and Imperialism,* as well as Gayatri Spivak, *The Post-Colonial Critic* and *In Other Worlds.*

2. All quotes from *I, Rigoberta Menchú* are from 1984, English-language edition. Subsequent references are cited parenthetically in the text.

3. For critiques of happy-family-of-man multiculturalism, see my essay, "Multiculturalism and the 'Family of Man'," the *Toronto South Asian Review* 10, 3 (spring 1992); and Cary Nelson, "Multiculturalism without Guarantees: From Anthologies to

the Social Text," in the *Journal of the Midwest Modern Language Association* 26, 1 (spring 1993).

4. This is not to mention the problematic placement of disparate Latin American cultural traditions within the discourse of multiculturalism.

5. The narrator's refusal to divulge the secrets of her community also contributes to this distancing effect. By refusing to tell all, to bare her people's collective soul as it were, Rigoberta Menchú negates readerly voyeurism and disrupts the "human interest" conventions of *Reader's Digest*-testimonial prevalent in the United States.

6. See Janet Henshall Momsen and Vivian Kinkaid, "Geography, Gender and Development," in their edited collection *Different Places, Different Voices: Gender and Development in Africa, Asia, and Latin America* (New York and London: Routledge, 1993).

15

PASSION AND POLITICS
Teaching Rigoberta Menchú's Text as a Feminist

STACEY SCHLAU

> If in thinking of oneself as a voice . . . one sees oneself
> as inescapably changing the story one passes on . . . if
> one cannot tell that story without disrupting it . . .
> one's vocation is at once more difficult, more danger-
> ous, and much more interesting.
>
> —*Gail Griffin, as quoted in Fetterley 1993, 181*

When is too much not enough? For in some ways, *My Name Is Rigoberta Menchú and This Is How My Consciousness Was Born* is too much for the majority of the students where I teach.[1] Too much blood and gore, too much rhetoric and politics, too much indigenous culture. Yet I, like many other instructors, teach it precisely because it is too much. Intending to elucidate the economic, social, and political context of Guatemala that allows—even encourages—repression and state violence against the indigenous peoples, at the same time I try to generate sympathetic understanding of the text and the Quiché people. For the pedagogy explicit in the book leaves us limited choices in what we teach from it; either we recognize the exposé and condemnation of racial repression and genocide, and must be somehow politically engaged, or we miss the point. Of course, it is possible to teach the book as an anthropological text, a gold mine of Mayan customs and ceremonies, or as an example of postcolonial writing, forged from the European conqueror's legacy. But Menchú makes her purpose clear: to teach people of other countries about the socially and politically repressive situation of the indigenous peoples.

Yet many students deny the realities that seem to be repeated so often that they take on the character of a chant, a cultured formula. Perhaps this is because, as Henry Giroux has pointed out, "Culture in postcolonial discourse becomes something that Others have, it is the mark of ethnicity and difference"

(1991, 26).Or, perhaps it has everything to do with their socialization: family, media, religion, school.

The students at West Chester University mostly come from Catholic families; they tend to be the first generation attending college. Of course, African American and other persons of color, as well as returning women and men, form a small part of the student population. The majority, however, belong to the first group. These demographics have a profound influence on classroom dynamics, especially in terms of a world view that many sentimentalize as the "American [sic] way." Rarely does anyone, of their own accord, for instance, make the connection from the repression and genocide of the Quiché people to the acts of wholesale violence and deception against Native Americans in the United States. And most are horrified at Menchú's tale, but they hesitate to draw the obvious political conclusions.

Whatever the reason, the denial, if carefully challenged and understood, offers the possibility of deconstructing the centrality of dominant beliefs about Central America and the United States as "good neighbors" and offers another version of complicity and life for the vast majority of people in the hemisphere. But it must be done carefully, because there is great risk of students' coming away from the text with the idea that torture and mass murder occur only in those "primitive" countries and that the United States is a paradise for its citizens. The trick for me is to enact "[w]hat is best in people . . . a sturdy connection between respect for the self and respect for the other: reaching in and out at the same time" (Kaye/Kantrowitz 1986, 280).

Most recently, I taught Rigoberta Menchú's book in a general education course designed to be offered in English, "Contemporary Latin American Narrative." Primarily those students whose majors require a second year of foreign language study (proficiency equal to our fourth semester) or three courses designated "Culture Cluster" enroll. In fact, if it were not for the requirement, the class would not have enough students to be offered. Nevertheless, there were also, last time, two students with other reasons for taking it: a Latin American Studies minor and a International Relations major with an interest in women's and Latin American political issues.

In many ways, Menchú's is the capstone text of the semester. It was discussed last, this past time, and generated the most controversy of any work studied. And, this time, it was the only nonfiction piece that we covered,[2] having first read an anthology of short stories and then Isabel Allende's novel *The House of the Spirits*. The juxtaposition is possibly problematic, but I justify the choice by saying that I want to give students a taste of various types of narrative in Latin America today. Oral history, or testimonial literature, is one salient kind.[3] Which brings me to a critical point, about teaching class and race hierarchies in Latin America from and in the United States: in the classroom, engaging ethnocentric atttitudes must, I think, be contextualized in United

States-Latin America (especially Central America) political, economic, and military relations.

For a class in which 98 percent of the participants were fulfilling a requirement, this was an interested, prepared, and thoughtful group. There is no doubt that their participation made the experience the success that it was. Perhaps a factor in their participation was the format. Almost every class period, an hour and fifteen minutes, twice a week for fifteen weeks, included at least ten minutes of small group discussion on assigned themes and topics. Each small group then reported back to the class, which invariably generated more discussion. Thus, they played an active role in shaping the way each period turned out. By the time we read *My Name Is Rigoberta Menchú*, participants were used to and enjoyed the process.

Another assignment that turned out to be useful in generating active participation were "reaction papers." Handed in every two weeks, for twelve weeks, these were short (2–3 pages typed), thematic responses to the readings and discussions. It was in the reaction papers that several good insights about Menchú's text surfaced. Despite their complaints that this was not a "writing emphasis (W)" course (they need three courses designated as "W" to graduate), the reaction papers encouraged further thought, since they could not duplicate class discussions, but might take off from them. Thus, oral and written expression reinforced each other.

The students commented on the course in anonymous response forms that I created and asked them to fill out during the last week of class. Questions included: "What were your expectations of this class?," "Were they fulfilled? How or how not?," and "In what ways did or did not the class enrich your understanding of Latin American cultures?" One student said that Menchú's was "less of a story" than the other pieces assigned, which made it more difficult to keep up with the reading. Several offered their opinion that *My Name Is Rigoberta Menchú* should be read before *House of the Spirits*, because Allende's novel was a hard act to follow. The readings, claimed another, "although depressing were thought-provoking." Of the reaction papers, one student suggested, "I'd like to think of them as a diary of ideas, less structured, more freeformed so it's fairly simple in that sense." Of the small groups, the same person said that they "offered diversity."

When discussing *My Name is Rigoberta Menchú, and This Is How My Consciousness Was Born*, my experience and knowledge as a United States feminist and Latin Americanist play a critical role in the content and dynamics of the classroom. A speaker of Spanish with near-native fluency, a long-time student of third-world and especially Latin American women's issues, these factors color my presentation of the book. And, it goes without saying, how I position my subjectivity vis-à-vis the narrative has a direct impact on students' perceptions of it. And one primary task, as I see it, is "the demystification of institutional policies and practices that cloak social inequities" (Fine 1992, 90).

Nowhere is this more salient than in applying the theory and praxis of women's studies to *My Name Is Rigoberta Menchú.*

Women's studies is counterhegemonic in both theory and practice (Weiler 1988, 52). That is, the discipline was formed by and continues to operate as a critique of dominant social norms and a construction of new ways and means of transacting knowledge. Intellectually ambitious for many reasons, among the most salient of which are its interdisciplinarity and the willingness to engage in social critique, "Women's Studies as subject-matter reflects the particularistic, historical and contextual nature of our conceptualizations of human society" (Maher 1985, 34).

Indeed, an important tenet of women's studies implies that the very foundations of our construction of knowledge are narrow because their partiality has been taken for universality. Feminist philosopher Lorraine Code argues that "knowledge does not transcend, but is rooted in and shaped by, specific interests and social arrangements" (Code 1991, 68).

While Code is speaking of gender issues, her framework can be partially adapted to international concerns. That is, what can be useful in this line of thought is to use the category of difference creatively, as Audre Lorde pointed out long ago, and as the multiculturalism movement has elaborated since. Kathleen Weiler's advice, that we recognize that gender, race, and class conflicts are inherent to U. S. society, can also serve us well. She argues that recognition is not acceptance, and that denial and avoidance of these differences would be counterproductive. We should, she says, legitimate "this polyphony of voices and [make] both our oppression and our power conscious in the discourse of the classroom" (Weiler 1988, 144–45). Or, as Henry Giroux has written with a slightly different focus, "critical pedagogy needs to focus on the issue of difference in an ethically challenging and politically transformative way" (Giroux 1991, 48).

An example: Burgos-Debray's introduction is frought with contradictions and inconsistencies. While stating that she "became her [Menchú's] instrument" (Menchú 1984, xx) in the transcription process, she also lists no less than eight ways in which she shaped the text. Most students understood my point about how Burgos-Debray replicates race/class hierarchies in Latin America through her privileged position in the production of this book. And so does the publisher, by putting Menchú's name only in the title and listing Burgos-Debray as editor in the English translation and as author in the Spanish. The class dealt with the issue of problematic transcription and transformation by making several suggestions, most notably that the original tapes be sold, to avoid the editor's intervention. One student even envisioned a book on tape.

Through women's studies, I quickly learned that "changing *what* we teach, means changing *how* we teach" (Culley and Portuges 1985, 2). In fact, it is from my training in pedagogy through women's studies that I developed the small group and reaction paper techniques. Certainly, I try to offer what Janice Raymond has called "passionate teaching and learning":

The conveying of passion means that in style, content, and method, the professor communicates that she cares deeply about what she is saying, that teaching and learning are living, and that scholarship is a standing-point on a journey that recognizes other different standpoints. (Raymond 1985, 57–58)

It is easy to communicate the excitement one feels for one's subject matter if one allows the passion to surface, I think. Yet other tensions come into play.

As some have said about female instructors in general, issues of authority certainly play a critical role for students: "[a]s our maternal power is feared, our paternal authority is mistrusted" (Culley and Portuges 1985, 14).Perhaps Culley and her coauthors mean this in the sense that Dinnerstein did, on a profound psychic level. In any case, students' expectations of women professors appear to be different than those of men, no matter what we teach.

Also, in all classes, I want to provide a model for collaboration rather than competition and try to accomplish that through my behavior, as well as delineating prevalent behavioral norms in the class. For feminist teachers, it is important to "have a particular sense of themselves ... and [be] conscious of their actions as role models for students" (Weiler 1988, 115). The processes through which we communicate knowledge are as important as content. Therefore, I try to attain a norm of active, responsible participation in the classroom.

Part of the framework for that norm includes understanding education "as producing not only knowledge but also political subjects" (Giroux 1991, 47). The class itself, therefore, serves as a laboratory for understanding the social context of Menchú's and her people's world. Understanding the role that the intersection of class and race plays in their own lives, for instance, can help students to identify how it makes its mark in hers. I thereby try to enact the theory of my role as one of those "transformative intellectuals who occupy specifiable political and social locations" (53).

One important method in Quiché culture for making sense of and resisting in life is storytelling. Traditions are passed down through the *discurso* (speeches) from elders to the young. Menchú recounts, for instance, that elders make speeches when children come of age. Clearly, for the Quiché, "collective telling of stories is the foundation for seeing, and then challenging, patterns of systemic injustice" (Welch 1991, 89).

One aspect of the text that I emphasize is Menchú's account of women's speechmaking, as when they tell the trapped soldier that he must leave the army. Thus, the tradition of the *discurso* has been adapted to serve current needs for survival. Even if convincing only one soldier not to kill them does not stop the genocide, the women demonstrate the strength they derive from their culture through the collective articulation of concerns. Their case clearly demonstrates that "power is not only administered, but taken up, resisted, and struggled over" (Giroux 1991, 26).

At no time during class discussions in small groups and as a whole, did students challenge my assertion that Menchú constructs a master narrative, with her father as hero and herself as the central maturing individual. That is, she creates myths at the same time that she writes (speaks) a linguistic and political *bildingsroman*. Her-story, I tell them, comes to dominate his-story throughout, but most notably in the famous chapter 24, in which the public torture of her youngest brother and others leads not to indigenous submission, as the army officer had hoped and intended, but to resistance and rebellion. In their case, "even failed resistance bears powerful evidence of human dignity and courage" (Harrison 1985, 250).

While her experience was so different from theirs that the students did not relate her life to their own, they certainly emphasized the process of change in Menchú as she articulates more clearly a framework for political action, and then puts it into practice. And, they raised moral questions about whether or not Menchú was a terrorist, a question that Menchú herself raised on the first page of chapter 24 when she referred to the government's calling her family "foreigners" and "Cubans" (Menchú 1984, 172), and if she was, and if she advocated violence, was that justified? Filtered through media images of "Arab terrorists" and "communists," their responses engendered yet another discussion of the ideologies under and purposes of sterotyping.

Teaching the narrative this time brought many new insights, generated by the students. Several, in reaction papers, compared the Quiché situation with that of slavery in the United States. While the comparison does not totally hold, it demonstrated their visceral understanding of repression and state violence against the Mayan peoples.

But what generated the most heated debate (with many quite vocal students arguing against my position) was the notion, to which many firmly held for at least the first two-thirds of the book and several classes, that Quiché parents and elders were teaching indigenous children resignation and thereby contributed in a very real sense to their own oppression. After all, doesn't telling infants that they are going to suffer throughout their lives condemn them to that suffering? As the instructor, I felt caught between challenging the ethnocentrism of this line of reasoning and teasing out my argument about the book as a description of a gradual awakening to political discourse and action. I opted for the first, and held off on the second until the class had finished most of the chapters, when I raised the point again and asked them if they still felt that the Quiché preached resignation. Of course, they knew I—or Menchú—had set them up, but they took it with generally good grace.

There was less stereotyping of the Quiché than I had expected in the class. A measure of students' increased familiarity with the text and new rejection of exoticized images came when, as I passed around donuts as their 8:00 A.M. final exam began, a student joked, "Did you bring the maize?"

Even when I brought in a huipil,[4] because Menchú discusses the importance of dress, the students tried to decifer and understand the embroidered figures, but did not exoticize its wearers. Again, Menchú discusses the significance of dress to indigenous identity, so perhaps the text forestalled such behaviors. We did talk, though, about the politics (without using the word) of my owning a huipil, since the Quiché would not approve. Was I exoticizing or marginalizing? What did it mean that I, as a United States citizen, could even buy one?

Because most students in the class were U.S. Catholics, the controversial question of the possibility of religious syncretism raised another aspect of the exotic. Could the Mayans practice the indigenous rites and Catholicism at the same time and truly be both? One student argued, for several minutes in two separate classes, that they could not. He became so involved in this issue that he wound up writing a paper on the topic for a religion class. And, for the rest of us, the debate offered the opportunity to reflect on and draw conclusions with applications wider than this cultural situation.

Interestingly, several people talked about enjoying the chapters on customs and ceremonies interpersed throughout the narrative. One summed it up: "They let me see her as a real person." When the topic came up, others agreed that learning about Quiché culture helped to personalize Menchú's story. This was quite surprising to me, especially since the first time I read *My Name Is Rigoberta Menchú* those chapters seemed boring and unnecessary. Perhaps these students are more sophisticated than I was about the dynamic interaction between individual and culture. Perhaps they intuited that "the experience of marginality at the level of everyday life lends itself to forms of oppositional and transformative consciousness" (Giroux 1991 ['Postmodernism as Border Pedagogy: Redefining the Boundaries of Race and Ethnicity"] 251).Perhaps they found the chapters on customs a relief from the terrible scenes of repression and violence. Or perhaps they understood, as Alcoff has suggested in another context, that "the identity of a woman is the product of her own interpretation and reconstruction of her history, as mediated through a cultural discursive context to which she has access" (Alcoff 1988, 434).

In this class, because many students had taken other "culture cluster" courses about Latin America, they understood some major features of the politics, cultures, religions, and geography of Central and South America. This made their responses more informed. There is no escaping the feeling that the chemistry this time worked because of them. Certainly their participation fomented what we, as teachers, desire: passionate learning. Next time, I think the course will begin with *My Name Is Rigoberta Menchú*.

NOTES

1. I use this literal translation of the title throughout (rather than Ann Wright's, to which I object), since it emphasizes the individual more than the original Spanish. An ambiguity in my translation, however, which provides interesting class discussion, is that *conciencia* means both conscience and consciousness.

2. The controversy surrounding whether or not Menchú is telling "the truth" and where she makes up events is beside the point in this context, in which I use the text as an exemplar of the relatively new, hybrid narrative genre variously called "oral history" and "testimony."

3. There is no satisfactory, nonsexist term for this genre, but *oral history* seems more innocuous than *testimonial.*

4. *Huipil:* a traditional, hand-embroidered blouse, worn by indigenous women.

RIGOBERTA MENCHÚ AND MINORITY/NONTRADITIONAL STUDENTS

16

RIGOBERTA MENCHÚ'S TESTIMONY
Empowering ESL Students to Write

DAVID BLOT

ESL students on their way to becoming writers of college-level English face several important tasks. One of these is developing a conscious awareness that they have something to say that others want to understand and respond to. Another is the need to find a more articulate and expressive voice in communicating what is meaningful to them. ESL faculty are realizing more and more that stimulating reading goes a long way in helping students to achieve these goals. Thus, teachers are faced with the problem of deciding which reading materials will most powerfully and effectively move students to become more expressive and articulate writers.

Some books work better than others in engaging students in meaningful discussion and serious writing. One important quality of books that makes them work is their evocative power. In testimonial writing the author's or narrator's voice and the richness or immediacy of the text have a special power to tap students' creative spirit and draw forth deeply felt and deeply thought-about responses in writing. Of equal importance is the power of testimonial to validate ESL students' experience. Reading about people whose lives, struggles, and culture are similar to their own gives students a sense that the stuff of their lives is meaningful, worthy of being in print and considered by and responded to by others. Faculty who wish to empower students to become more fluent and clearer writers through the development and articulation of their own voices might consider including testimonials in their curricula. There are many effective testimonials that ESL teachers can use to inspire quality writing and learning. Carey-Webb's article in the *English Journal* contains an annotated list of important testimonials from many parts of the world. In my class I focus on two works: *Don't Be Afraid, Gringo*, the story of Elvia Alvarado, a Honduran peasant woman, and *I, Rigoberta Menchú*, on which this chapter will focus.

Don't Be Afraid, Gringo is a moving account of the oppressed poor in Honduras. Elvia Alvarado's political and social consciousness is raised through her training to become a community organizer and her subsequent work in the mountainous regions organizing women around issues of health and nutrition. Later she helps organize groups to "recover" land from the rich. Her dedication to her work is remarkable. She faces hunger, jail, and death as she struggles alongside her compañeros to make life better for her children and grandchildren. Alvarado does not pull any punches in telling her story. Her words are blunt and colorful and their meaning unmistakable.

Rigoberta Menchú gives a very poignant account of the hardships of a group of indigenous people living on the altiplano and forced to migrate to the plantations in the coastal regions to pick coffee and cotton for extremely low wages. Her testimony is filled with rich intricate detail about the life and culture of her people. Their culture is despised and they are marginalized, sought after only when their labor is needed to help make the rich plantation owners richer. Menchú has lived through years of oppression by a government intent on the extermination of the indigenous poor. Her attention to detail about birth ceremonies, marriage customs, daily life on the altiplano, and her people's relationship with nature serves to validate her culture and preserve the culture on record in case the ever-present possibility of total genocide becomes a reality. Menchú speaks so clearly, forcefully, and at times beautifully, that it is difficult, if not impossible, for the reader to remain uninvolved.

I, Rigoberta Menchú meets my four criteria for inclusion in an advanced level ESL curriculum. At Bronx Community College students must take several semesters of ESL and pass a proficiency exam in composition in readiness for college-level freshman English courses. Thus, writing is emphasized in ESL curricula. For the past several years ESL faculty have been making strong connections between the reading of whole texts and the development of students' writing ability. In this context I have found that the following criteria are essential for book selection:

1. A high level of interest stimulates intense discussion and keeps students reading.

2. The level of reading difficulty is within the range of student comfort. This may mean leaving out books with extensive dialect or colloquialisms. Aiming at students "comfort zone" is important because when the level of reading difficulty approaches the frustration point, students lose the internal freedom necessary for internalizing vocabulary, phraseology, grammatical patterns, and spelling.

3. Students can readily identify with the content and write about similar experiences in their lives or the lives of their families and friends. Effective reading will also stimulate students to broaden their thinking and dig for more information leading to expository writing from crosscultural, historical, psychological, or sociological perspectives.

4. Excellent reading material leads to writing that students perceive to be meaningful. In this way ESL students gain the knowledge that writing in college is serious, not simply something to be gotten through for the sake of passing English language proficiency exams.

Testimonial narrative in general and *I, Rigoberta Menchú* in particular meet these criteria especially well. Menchú's passion and clarity of voice engages the reader deeply and draws out powerful responses, both verbal and written. Carey-Webb, referring to the use of testimonials in classes of American students taught by American teachers, speaks of the "attempt to hear the voice of the voiceless." In my experience ESL students are able to attend to the voice of Menchú since their experience often closely parallels that of the third-world narrator. In reading the testimonial, students meet a person from a country and culture similar to their own with the courage to speak about her life experience. She serves as an example for students to do the same. In my class I build on their empathy to have them write "becoming pieces" where they attempt to see and feel a part of the world the way the author sees and feels it. The resulting depth of understanding provides a rich source for further writing.

To speak of the validation inherent in the use of Menchú's testimony is to reach an even deeper awareness of the evocative power of testimonial narrative for student writing. Reading this book and responding through "becoming pieces" and personal narrative serves as a process of cultural validation, necessary for students to become more self-confident and better writers. The instructor's choice of reading material representative of students' own background and experience validates the students themselves, letting students understand that they, their experience, and their culture are worthy of serious consideration. Their lives, culture, and viewpoint are worthy of appearing in print for others to enjoy, discuss, and respond to. The whole process is very affirming.

Materials have existed for years that are designed to help students become acculturated to "the American way of life." Examples include *Life in the U.S.A.: A Simplified Reader on American Culture* by R. Jordania, *Exploring the United States* by N. Hazelfield-Pipkin and J. McCarrick, and *Speaking of the U.S.A.* by B. Neustadt. Such books are important in ESL curricula. Yet the issue that needs to be examined is how to appropriately use culturally validating materials in our classrooms. Is there a contradiction between helping students understand and become acclimated to North American culture while also recognizing the value of their culture of origin and their experience of their own culture?

Rebecca Mlynarczyk and Steven Haber, authors of *In Our Own Words*, see no contradiction. Their book incorporates selections of writings by college students, much of it about experiences in their countries of origin. Students reading these selections and faced with the task of responding in writing are aided by the familiarity of the "words and worlds" expressed and by the implicit mes-

sage contained in the inclusion of student writing in an ESL text: "You are welcome here [in this course]; your writing is welcome here" (1991, vii). The
authors point to the difference in the writing of students using their textbook,
but they do not elaborate. Thus, the specific effects on student learning of culturally validating materials, whether they be textbooks or testimonials, remains
uncertain. What are the connections between such validation, increase in self-
esteem, and the improvement of writing skills? How might the content and
style of students' writing be analyzed to provide clues as to the effects of the validation process?

My class of twenty-four Latino students (Dominican, Puerto Rican, and
Honduran) spent the month of February 1994 reading Rigoberta Menchú's testimony and responding through discussion and writing. The rest of this chapter highlights their and my experience with this testimony, specifically its power
to evoke significant writing, the kind that grows out of personal engagement
and identification with a clear, forceful, and validating text. Several important
themes emerged for the students: Menchú's suffering, poverty, marginal existence, and communal life; her loss of childhood; her courage and hope; injustice, discrimination, and exploitation; language differences as barriers to communication and progress; and, finally, differences between the culture of the
Quiché Indians and the students' own cultures. These themes were explored in
the four kinds of writing that the students did.

BECOMING PIECES

After reading 100 pages of testimony, students wrote a "becoming piece" as an
in-class assignment. Students were asked to "become" Menchú for the class
period and, as Menchú, to describe her world and her feelings. Students began
their writing this way: "My name is Rigoberta Menchú. I live high up on the
Altiplano in Guatemala." Through their writing students were able to feel
deeply and express poignantly some of Menchú's pain, determination, and
insights. The following excerpts are representative of the extent to which students "got into" Menchú's world, the crucial first step in the process of identification and validation. Please note that here and throughout the chapter students' writing has been edited for grammatical correctness. Students' word
choice was generally left untouched.

My story is related to many other people in the world, especially to the
indigenous ethnic groups in Guatemala and in all of Latin America. I
have seen the exploitation of our community. I have seen my people
die in the oppressors' hands. This has made me feel sadness and anger.
I have been discriminated against in my own country because I look
different, and I speak another language and have a different culture.
(Josefa Amaya)

I, Rigoberta Menchú decided to learn and speak Spanish three years ago in order to tell of the oppression that my people have been suffering for almost five hundred years, so that the sacrifices made by my community and by my family will not have been made in vain. I am fighting for the recognition of my culture, for acceptance of the fact that it is different and for my people's rightful share of power. (Pedro Cabrera)

Sometimes I think they hate us because of our race, because we are poor. I hope to God all this suffering stops one day, but meanwhile I will continue fighting for the rights of my people. We are tired of being kidnapped, killed and abused and, if necessary, we are going to take up arms and fight this government. (Jesus Dominguez)

Every time that I remember how much we suffer because of these rich people, I get angry. They are living well because of us, and we are suffering and dying of hunger because of them. (Ana De Las Nueces)

My life has always been work and poverty. I do not remember that I ever had time to play with my siblings or neighbors. Being a child and having to think like a grown person is a trauma for all the children of my tribe. (Ilka Peguero)

Even though we are a very poor family, we are happy because we have the most important thing in life which is love. We also have a beautiful and united community. We are always there for each other. A lot of people think that money brings happiness but my community is proof that money doesn't bring it because we poor enjoy life more than a lot of rich people in Guatemala. (Ana, again)

EXPOSITION

The second step was for the students to analyze more carefully the situation of Menchú and begin to explore connections to their own world. Thus, the next assignment was to select a topic from their reading that interested them and write an expository composition. The students took this writing through a draft process, receiving feedback from classmates before revising and handing in their final version. Responses ranged from crosscultural comparisons to comparisons of social conditions to personal expository. Maria Molina wrote about the marriage customs among the Quiché and Dominican peoples that show respect for women. Zunilda Acevedo, in a composition entitled "Tools as Toys," explained how the Indian children of Guatemala grow up without play.

Joselyn Escarramon focused on the communication problem, the fact that the indigenous people of the altiplano can't defend their rights because of the language barrier. Iris DeLeon and Dania Lopez wrote personal accounts of discrimination in the United States. Iris was discriminated against at her job. For Dania it happened in high school. Finally, Angela Castillo compared the exploitation of the Indians in Guatemala with the exploitation of the Haitian sugar cane cutters in the Dominican Republic. Here is an excerpt:

> In the Dominican Republic also exploitation is one of the biggest problems. Every day a lot of people from Haiti immigrate there looking for a better change of life. Those people are submitted to a cruel exploitation. The Haitians work like animals cutting cane and they don't receive enough money to support themselves. However, they never complain because they need that miserable money.
>
> It is very painful to know how the Haitians after a hard day of labor are tricked by the people who weigh the cane. The Haitians don't say anything for fear that they will be deported to their country again. They continue working in the Dominican Republic because the economic situation in their country is worse.

The feedback and sharing process connected with this assignment provided a crucial time for students to share perspectives, knowledge, and insights. It helped to build communication and trust in the classroom so that students could move on to the next stage of the process of moving from cultural validation to enhancing self-esteem and confidence.

TESTIMONY

The next step was perhaps the most important for developing students' voice and confidence. Modeling on the very process Rigoberta Menchú went through, students were asked to write their own testimonies. The instructions were as follows: "Menchú spoke her truth about her life and that of her family and community. Write your own truth about your life in the context of your family and community. It doesn't matter how similar or different your life is to Menchú's." Students wrote a minimum of five pages. The writing again went through a draft process with students sharing their work with each other before submitting the final version.

Some students' testimonies confirmed Menchú's harsh childhood experiences. Boris Acosta recounted how he and his brothers grew up in the "care" of an aunt who took the money that his parents sent every two weeks for food. He and his siblings suffered hunger for years until one of his brothers died of malnutrition, and his father found out the truth. Boris wrote, "I don't think I was ever young in my childhood. I never had a chance to be a kid." Heydy Cabrera identified herself with Menchú at the age of eight because both of them developed work consciousness at the same age; Heydy was forced to assume the role of mother to her younger siblings when her mother took a job far from home. Gil Maldonado's father put him out on the street as a boy to start earning money where he worked as a shoeshine boy. Caridad Peguero suffered when at the age of seven her parents sent her away to boarding school. The strict life of the school plus the inability to see her family turned Caridad into a lonely and introverted girl.

Other students' testimonies served as counterpoint to Menchú's life: Marcia Velez, Angel Torres, Angela Estrella, and Angela Castillo recall their happy childhoods. Angela Castillo writes about the joy of playing with friends in a garden full of flowers, walking to school in the morning, receiving first communion, and singing in the choir. Even for those students whose lives were very different from Menchú, there were important realizations as they put together their own testimony. The childhood of Ana De Las Nueces was full of song and dance and pranks and fun; yet in her testimony she is conscious that her life contrasts sharply with those of many other children whose childhoods are buried in struggle, work, and hardship.

Finally, one student, David Gonzalez, was able to place his life in the context of his community. Going into extensive detail about community life, he recounts how his community lived for generations as farmers in a lush valley in the Dominican Republic. In 1969 the government forced his people up into the mountains to make way for a dam. In spite of this move the people continued to be united in their life and work. David says that this unity, characteristic of the community for generations, was noted by people for miles around.

While reading my students' testimonies, I was struck by how revealing many of them were. I decided to ask the students why they were so open with a professor that they had only known less than a month. Their answers fell into three categories. Several students who had difficult childhoods saw their writing as catharsis. They appreciated the opportunity to get their feelings out. Some students felt instinctively that the rule of confidentiality applied and that they could trust me. Other students felt that Rigoberta Menchú's trust and openness set an example for them. They said that Menchú gave her open testimony to an anthropologist whom she hadn't known previously. They also said that the content of her testimony served as a model for them to do the same. (NOTE: My students' trust led me to carefully elicit their permission to include their names, discussion of their writing, and the excerpts in this chapter. I showed them a draft of the chapter and gave them veto power over it. At their recommendation I also decided to keep the discussion of their testimonies general and not include lengthy excerpts.)

LETTERS TO RIGOBERTA MENCHÚ

The final piece of writing that the students did was to write a letter to Rigoberta Menchú. This was an important activity because it served to pull together the unit. Students were able to express their feelings about Menchú directly to her and tell her what she means to them personally and to the world. Students could begin the letter in one of the following ways:

1. You have taught me some important things about life.

2. I admire you very much.

3. I would like to help you.

4. I would like to invite you to come to Bronx Community College to speak to the faculty and students.

Most students wrote letters of admiration. Several said that they learned important things from Menchú. Two wrote invitations and two wrote suggestions as to how she could further her cause. Here are some excerpts:

My admiration for you is so great because I never thought that there could be a person in this world like you with a big capacity to love her people, with a big capacity to fight no matter against whom or what in defense of her community.

One of my dreams from now on will be to see you face to face to talk with you and feel your power to fight, your strong spirit and to tell you how much I admire you. (Ramona Acosta)

This story that you and thousands of Indians in Guatemala have lived has to be read by the world. Let them know that thousands of Indians are still struggling and dying in the mountains, that they are in need and starving and are still being exploited. I know that when you speak about your life and community, you want to touch each person in their heart in order for each one of us to become more united and humane. (Irene Vega)

Your whole life is like a school of courage. I learned from you that it is so important for everybody to be together in order to get the recognition of our rights. You have taught me that the struggle can never take a rest.

You have also taught me how hunger, exploitation and discrimination can be changed peaceably without violence because your struggle is teaching us only to be organized, to keep together in order to stop the injustice and to obtain a different life for everyone. (Julia Quezada)

If our culture were like yours, we would have a better world, maybe without war. (Yokasta Santos)

Rigoberta, you taught me that women don't have to be afraid or ashamed to overcome all obstacles interfering with success. I also learned that women have the power to fight against injustice and exploitation within our societies. (Mercedes Valdez)

One cannot help but be impressed by the power and seriousness of this writing. The students had something to say and found the voice with which to articulate thought and express feelings. The power of their writing clearly stems from the evocative nature of the testimony. *I, Rigoberta Menchú* resonated in the students' own spirits and called forth response. Through the reading, writing, and sharing we went through my students were able to identify with Rigoberta's world and to make connections with their own worlds, the world of their country of origin which they left behind but which is still very much with them, and the new world of the United States with which they are negotiating.

Much understanding came in the form of deepened reflection by the students on their own backgrounds. Recognizing how different many aspects of Menchú's culture were caused students to become more aware of their own cultures and to value them more. In this sense reading about a third-world person's life also gave them a new appreciation for their own life experience. Moreover, the testimony deepened their own human response to the suffering of others.

Most importantly, students were also empowered with Rigoberta Menchú's courage and hope. Many of the students, as is typical of so many students in urban colleges, have to fight against almost overwhelming odds to stay in college. They are single mothers attempting to raise their children alone and study at the same time, or they are husbands and fathers forced to work full time as well as study. At times under such pressure they get discouraged. Rigoberta Menchú's spirit served as a source of encouragement for them. Furthermore, many students readily responded to Menchú's desire to learn Spanish to be better able to communicate because they are right now in the struggle to learn English. They clearly see their English-as-a-Second-Language status as a barrier to economic and social progress in this country.

The connection between testimonial narrative and the writing development of ESL students was conclusively made in this course. My students were deeply moved to think and feel and write. In other contexts their movement of spirit might have expressed itself in song or dance or painting or sculpture. But, in my ESL writing course, my students wrote and wrote well. Indeed, my impression is that the writing of these students was better than the writing I received in previous semesters. I saw the written feedback they gave each other to help their writing consistently improve, and they enthusiastically performed extensive revision on their drafts. But above all, in the incorporation of testimonial narrative I came to hear my students' own voices and feel the power expressed in their words. In sum, I encountered new strength born of a felt need to communicate the richness of their thought and experience as it was called forth by the voice of Rigoberta Menchú.

17

TESTIMONY IN AN ADOLESCENT DAY TREATMENT CENTER
Rigoberta Menchú and At-Risk Youth

ANGELA WILCOX MOROUKIAN

> I really believe that if enough people learn more about places like your country, they will start trying to solve some of the problems. At first when I heard the title of your story I thought that nothing can be "like in the movies." Then I heard all of the horrible things that you and your family have had to put up with for many years. I do not think that any human being should be put through such hell.
>
> Thank you for making me realize that there are people who do not live like me. I know I haven't had to live through that. I will do my best to help in any way possible.
>
> —*Letter to Rigoberta Menchú from a student*

Tricia's letter to Rigoberta Menchú helps me remember why I have to teach. Tricia is sixteen years old; she has been kicked out of her house and is currently living with her boyfriend. Because she is often ill, or living too far from the school to make it in, she frequently misses attending. She happened to make it the week we discussed Guatemala and Rigoberta Menchú, and she was affected on many levels by the stories she heard. Tricia may never join in solidarity with the oppressed people of Guatemala, but she recognized, if only for awhile, that there are others who have survived more than she will ever have to live through. She also recognized in herself the ability to stand up and say no to abuse and oppressive experiences. She took a stand.

Tricia is one of fifteen students at the University Day Community, which is a day treatment center funded by Hennepin County, Minnesota, and connected with the General College at the University of Minnesota. The adolescents at Day Community are referred for a one-year stay by a court-appointed social worker for a wide range of reasons. Most of them have been truant, some for years. Some have been hospitalized for mental health problems, and some have probation officers and criminal records. There are students who come to us as a transitional site between residential corrections or chemical dependency treatment and public school. For all of these teens, day treatment is the least restrictive setting appropriate to their needs; they come to our program during the day, and they return to their families, or their group home, or their friend's house at night.

Because the teenagers who come to us have not been successful in the mainstream school setting for a variety of reasons, our classrooms must be flexible and adapt to the needs of individuals. Students don't attend lectures, take notes, do homework, or get tested at the end of a chapter. Instead, the classroom staff help students to choose projects they would like to work on, and then they study at their own pace. Periodically we will come together as a class to read, discuss, and write about a specific topic.

In addition to the standard academic classes, the students also study job-hunting and career-development skills, participate in group, individual, and family therapy, and explore the community and the outdoors through Experiential Education, a program that uses many of the Outward Bound philosophies to challenge at-risk youth to learn through experiences. Hand in hand, these pieces of the program attempt to build a safe place for teenagers to take some very threatening risks. We work with students who, in more traditional settings, do not go to school, who do not want to learn in an academic sense, who do not do what they are supposed to. Yet, what we find in our program is that when we respect them, listen to them, and study together things that make sense to their lives, they will come to school, even when they're sick. Indeed, they often compete with each other to complete more work, request to bring work home, and may even read books on their own, some for the first time in their lives. At University Day Community, we create community, where young people who have never known the meaning of the word begin to experience it for the first time.

What I have found in working with these teens who have missed nurturing, security, and discipline, is that the more material things are offered, the more they complain. If we order pizza as a treat, they can't understand why we wouldn't buy them sodas, too. If we cancel classes to have a celebration or to watch a movie, the party's too boring and we should have rented a different movie. I once joked with Julio that I was sure that if we offered them each a bar of gold, they'd complain because they didn't get two; he said "hell, yeah!"

However, when we brought the students to work on a house with Habitat for Humanity, they threw themselves into it. Andrea, who has obsessive-compulsive disorder and is terrified of getting dirty, spent the day lifting radiators, painting, and sawing, excited at the visible progress she made on this family's home. When we served breakfast at a local soup kitchen, the students were enthused and involved, talking to families and other volunteers, sharing stories with people they usually ignore on the street. Afterwards, Carrie and Hannah wanted to be assured that they could come back within the week.

When these students are given the opportunity to serve, to feel like they have something to give that is valuable, they can become capable, caring, and vital young people. At such times I recognize a potential in them that on the worst days I sometimes have to remind myself is there.

This pattern has emerged again and again with different groups of students over the four years of my teaching. They blossom when they are put in situations where they are able to help someone, but it seems to be nearly impossible for them to find such situations on their own. They need to be reminded, again and again, of the power they possess.

When we talk about future careers, some of the students cite brain surgeon or president as their choice, because of the power and money such titles imply. However, the great majority say that they want to teach, do social work, be a parol officer; they want to work with people like themselves, to help kids who need someone on their side. They know their own need to have someone stand up for them, to understand without judging, and they want to devote their lives to giving this back to other young people. Realistically, many of them won't finish high school, but I hope that the dedication of our staff and the security they feel as they work through one of their difficult teenage years will stay with them. I trust someday they will find a way to live their dream of sharing their stories and their pain to help other people make it through the bad times.

Creating curriculum for students like these is a challenge. Standard textbooks and mass-produced teaching materials may leave an at-risk student frustrated, alienated and isolated, eager to flee the classroom. In our program, we search for materials that build community. We need to create space for students' ideas, questions, imagination, and compassion. These kids understand what it means to be marginalized, to be punished for who your family is, the color of your skin, your gender, your age, the neighborhood you live in. Traditional perspectives on the world don't capture them as learners, because they have not inhabited a traditional position in this society. Instead, materials that speak with a voice of the "other" are essential starting points for us.

I first incorporated Rigoberta Menchú's testimonial into the classroom in 1990, using her story "Things Have Happened to Me as in a Movie," dictated to Cesar Chelala (found in the collection entitled *You Can't Drown the Fire: Latin American Women Writing in Exile*). I chose this story from a very powerful volume of writings because of the intensity of her testimony. I used this version of Rigoberta Menchú's testimonial rather than a chapter from *I, Rigoberta Menchú*, because it gave the basic history of her family, and was not quite as graphic in its detail about methods of torture and murder as similar sections of the book. This story was an appropriate length for reading aloud, holding the students' attention and leaving time for questions, discussion, and follow-up materials. What Rigoberta Menchú had to say cut through the boredom and defenses that students put up around themselves in the classroom. Kids who normally couldn't sit still in class were intensely involved, asking questions and responding. It was the most successful lesson in reading aloud that I had ever participated in, and it stuck with me.

Since Rigoberta Menchú was awarded the Nobel Peace Prize in 1992, I have continued to teach her story, supplementing it with a curriculum entitled "Rigoberta Menchú: The Prize That Broke the Silence," created by the Resource Center for the Americas, a Minneapolis organization that has been invaluable in assisting teachers in getting honest and applicable materials about Latin America for the classroom. I also show a BBC documentary about street children in Guatemala City called *They Shoot Children, Don't They?*, which is a compelling film for my students to see, as many of them have lived, at least once, on the streets.

Most recently, I taught Rigoberta Menchú's story in the winter of 1994, as our school was still struggling to recover from the two-week winter break. Students return to us with new traumas and problems after spending two weeks with old friends or in close proximity to family, and as they had been distracted and energetic, student learning had been frustratingly slow. I decided to bring up Rigoberta Menchú and Guatemala, in part to break this pattern and attempt to engage them in the classroom. Moreover, Rigoberta Menchú was also going to be visiting our community in several weeks, and I wanted to share her story in the hopes that some of them would take the opportunity to hear her speak. Though in the end, none of my students chose to give up their Saturday night with friends to attend the rally, I believe that hearing her story and knowing that she was a real person was powerful in itself.

Over a period of several days, I brought the students together as a group to learn about the history of Guatemala, the stories of the people, and the remarkable life of Rigoberta Menchú. These group lessons always begin with a struggle; students get into a pattern of coming to class, picking up their project, and working alone for fifty minutes. When I ask them to sit together at the table so that we can talk about something together, I am inevitably greeted with skeptical looks and mutters about how "boring" whatever we're going to be doing is. At such times I realize that part of being a teacher is also being a salesperson, trying to convince students that each new experience is worth buying into.

The pitch works best when the students can identify with the subject. They feel an almost immediate connection to anyone who has been mistreated, cheated, abused, marginalized, or ignored, and it is very easy to teach about the "underdog." Conversely, outside of the classroom, when I discuss the same stories with peers, I find that most middle-class adults seem uncomfortable with images of oppression, almost as if they believe that the victims must have done something to deserve it—Guatemalan Indians must have been communists or guerilla fighters to warrant such harsh treatment. In contrast, what continually takes me by surprise in my classroom is my students' ready willingness to believe that no one deserves to be mistreated. They know that you don't need to do something bad to be treated badly.

As we got more involved as a group in our exploration of Guatemala, students began to express their frustration over the fact that they had never heard about these things before. We talked about why it is important for people like Rigoberta Menchú to tell their stories, even with the enormous risks that entails. When they learned that the United States sent money to support the Guatemalan army, they were confused and outraged. To my initial amazement, not one student expressed disinterest or boredom with what we were learning, and every one wrote diligently about why it is critical to learn about people like Rigoberta Menchú. Anne, who had only been part of our community for a few days of the project, said that she felt it important "so others can help change things and learn how bad people can be." Shuttled from her parents house to her grandparents house, this young woman is now living in a group home because no one will take her in. She has been out of school for six months and has struggled much of her life to find a place that feels safe to her. Yet somehow, Rigoberta Menchú's story and the story of children in Guatemala touched her. She wrote a letter to our state senator, asking him to support the people of Guatemala and to give her information on where he stands on the U.S. policy in Guatemala. After she wrote the letter, she asked, as did many students, "Can I really mail this? And someone will read it?" The idea of making her voice heard came as a revelation.

Elizabeth had also joined our community recently, and had provided us with numerous challenges. She brought food to the classroom and passed it out, she talked, sang, and danced; she did whatever it took to get the attention of her peers and push the limits set for her in the classroom. I worried about having her as a part of this project because I didn't want her to make it impossible for other people to get involved.

In the end, she was one of the most engaged and interested students in the classroom; her writing showed more thought than anything she had produced to that point. What struck me most was that she seemed to feel a sense of responsibility about the U.S. relationship with Guatemala. When I asked her what she would want to tell Rigoberta Menchú if she could meet her, she responded: "I would tell her that I'm sorry that we didn't help and that I wish those things would never have happened." Many students responded to the injustices in the story, but not many were able to realize, as Elizabeth did, that they were part of a nation that was complicit with Rigoberta Menchú's suffering.

Andrea was out of school for over a year because of her fear of interacting with people, and this has been a struggle for her since she joined our community. Yet she is bright and aspires to make up the year of high school she missed and eventually go to college. When she heard Rigoberta Menchú's story and the stories of the Guatemalan people, her passionate feelings pushed Andrea to become quite outspoken. She talked about Guatemala to her other teachers, to her therapist, and to her family and friends. She came back to school and requested copies of materials that would give people information about Guatemala, the School of the Americas (a training school for Central American soldiers in Fort Benning, Georgia, that teaches counterinsurgency techniques and methods of torture). She drafted a letter to Representative Joseph Kennedy: "I fully support your actions concerning the School of the Americas. I would appreciate any information on how I can support your campaign to have our government discontinue their support for the Army School of the Americas." For Andrea, these were giant steps toward interacting with others, becoming an active citizen, and making her voice heard.

Julio is Salvadoran, orphaned in the civil war and raised in an orphanage until the age of five, when he was adopted by a couple in the United States. For years, whenever the topic of poverty, abuse, or Central America was discussed in a classroom, he checked out. He and I talked before I started this lesson; I wanted him to feel comfortable working in another room if it was too hard for him to participate. He thought it over and decided he would come to class but that he would have other work ready in a different classroom in case he needed to leave. I fully expected that to happen. What happened instead is that he was one of the most active participants in the group—his passionate responses and questions helped guide other students in their exploration of the topic. He wrote and talked about the fact that he had seen some of the same things. After hearing Rigoberta Menchú's testimony, Julio said that if he were Rigoberta Menchú, he "would want revenge and go kill a couple of soldiers myself." We discussed this desire for vengeance and how people like Rigoberta Menchú have to learn how to overcome these feelings and get on with the business of life. However, he was insistent, and for good reason. It was remarkable that he was still in my classroom. Through the unit, Julio took one more step in his journey to accepting his personal history, as well as bringing an invaluable perspective to our community.

One reason a lesson like this works in our program is because students are learning daily that what they do makes a difference in our system. Our program is structured to give students choices, to take their voices and allow them to shape many aspects of the community they learn in. We have a weekly group where students and staff gather to talk about the program and the community; what's working, what's not, who's involved and who needs to be. Students are able to see concrete examples of how their ideas can change their daily lives. The due process system we have in place allows students to challenge each other or the staff if they feel an injustice has been done. Students are given a chance to review some of the decisions staff have made and give reasonable input into how they believe it might be changed.

Because this structure is in place, I feel that students can learn about Rigoberta Menchú and Guatemala without feeling totally powerless and defeated. There is a model—and they are active in it—that shows them that organization, thought, work, and courage can make a difference. Most students decided to write to a senator or representative to state their feelings about U.S. policy in Guatemala. Gary insisted on writing to the president of Guatemala: "The reason I am writing this letter is because I saw a video about the treatment of people in Guatemala and I was mad after I saw it. I don't think it is right that anyone be treated as bad as they were. I saw little kids get beat up by police. I see things like that happen here and I think that is wrong too." Gary felt a sense of power, writing to the president of another country and telling him to change what he was doing.

Schools do not usually expect high-level dialogue or complex processing of issues from most of my students. Many of them read and write several levels below their grade level, and some as low as second or third grade. They are often pulled out of the classroom for therapy meetings, doctor appointments, or court hearings. Their education, though relatively "stable" compared to many of their histories, is still fragmented. Their lives outside the classroom often interfere with concentrating on the task at hand, no matter how interested they might be on a good day. Despite these factors, I can't let them off the hook. I want them to learn how to think, listen, and to put themselves in someone else's shoes. I ask them to give more than they think they can in the classroom.

Rigoberta Menchú now stands as a profoundly needed model of strength and courage to my students. Jacki said that she wants to tell Rigoberta Menchú that "she and her family were very brave people and I really admire that and look up to her." Rigoberta Menchú represents a people and a part of the world most of these young people never knew existed, and she tells a story that most of them never knew happened. Her story teaches them that people have lived through and survived the loss of family, friends, and country. It teaches them not only about Guatemala, but provides a link to stories of oppressed people the world over. It tells them that their own government played a part in terror and torture. As they read, discuss, write, and learn with Rigoberta Menchú, they develop our community and its relationship to the world. They begin to feel power in expressing themselves, and they find themselves ready to stand up and be counted.

TESTIMONIAL
CONSTRUCTIONS

18

TESTIMONIAL DICTIONARY TO THE READING OF *ME LLAMO RIGOBERTA MENCHÚ Y ASÍ ME NACIÓ LA CONCIENCIA*
In Search of Our Voice

RINO G. AVELLANEDA, KSENIJA BILBIJA,

LAURA G. GUTIÉRREZ, MYRIAM OSORIO,

STACEY D. SKAR, ANGELA G. WASIA

> Crucé la frontera amor
> no sé cuando volveré.
>
> —*Rigoberta Menchú, "Patria abnegada"*

The idea for this chapter was born out of a graduate seminar on women's writing, part of which was a study of *Me llamo Rigoberta Menchú y así me nació la conciencia*. We, a group that formed part of that seminar, chose the form of a dictionary in order to be able to address particular concepts that we found to be controversial in the study of this text and to offer definitions that include suggestions for utilizing cultural and linguistic differences both to enrich the process of learning and to improve the understanding of Burgos and Menchú's book.

The membership of our group comes from a rich variety of cultural and linguistic backgrounds. In fact, we are from different generations, genders, political ideologies, and family structures, and we all know what it means to speak another's language. More than once we have experienced crossing the boundary of our mother tongue and entering the wor(l)d of the Other. Thus, we know what it is like to gather the experience and memory in one language and then search for the tools in another in order to translate the feeling of being different. For years, we have been crossing back and forth the shaky linguistic bridge between two, three, or more cultures. In the process and at different points of our lives, we all made the conscious decision to become teachers of language and culture.

Our experience in the studying and teaching of *Me llamo Rigoberta Menchú y así me nació la conciencia* is as plural as our pedagogical approaches. Besides defining words that we thought to be of central importance to the reading of this text and its teaching in the North American classroom, this reference guide also includes some possible teaching strategies. These strategies can be applied to the study of a variety of disciplines and to deal with the numerous questions that arise in classes that focus on cultural studies. We have also included some testimonies of our own experiences with the text, specifically as they apply to cases of contextual breakdown.

Our familiarity with the teaching and studying of Burgos and Menchú's book ranges from third-semester Spanish language courses where students read one passage of the text in *Pasajes: Literatura* (edited by Mary Lee Bretz et al., 3rd ed., New York: McGraw-Hill, 1992), to a literature seminar for graduate students that included the Spanish version: *Me llamo Rigoberta Menchú y así me nació la conciencia* (4th ed., Mexico: Siglo Ventiuno Editores, SA de CV, 1988), to courses in history using the English translation: *I, Rigoberta Menchú: An Indian Woman in Guatemala* (edited with an introduction by Elisabeth Burgos-Debray, translated by Ann Wright, London: Verso, 1984). We understand our plurality of experiences and willingness to share to be our strength. Therefore, all of the definitions and teaching strategies that we offer here follow our collective effort and encourage a sharing of ideas and a cooperative collaboration not only between teacher and student, but also between students in and outside of the classroom.

The collective writing of this dictionary was quite similar to the way in which a testimony is created. In effect, we underwent several of the same processes that Burgos and Menchú experienced in the creation of their book, including the taping of our conversations and discussions. However, the format of our collaboration did not derive from a question-answer structure, but from a more open exchange. We noticed that our own words often appeared in other definitions, generating new contexts and new meanings. This has led us to conclude that although our first impulse in the seminar was to criticize Burgos's "organizing" and silencing of Menchú's voice, this type of manipulation is unavoidable. Being truthful to the "original" word is, if not impossible, at least extremely difficult. Moreover, we have seen our testimonial dictionary grow and become enriched by this collective effort, and we are aware that this is by no means a final version. In fact, we invite comments, new entries, experiences, and testimonies whether individual or communal to contribute to our project. We consider this to be not the end but only the beginning of discussions and testimonies that can add to an increased awareness of Menchú and Burgos's book, in particular, and of testimonial texts, in general.

The experience of collective writing made a significant impact on our sense of Academia. One Sunday morning when the outside temperature was 20 below zero and we had all left our homes and families in order to gather around the tape recorder, computer, some bagels, Menchú and Burgos's book (Menchú 1992 [1988]), and dozens of scribbled pages with our own thoughts and ideas, we realized that this urge that had made us all leave our warm beds is the meaning of Academia. It meant not always waiting for someone to finish his or her sentences, interrupting without apologizing, sitting in silence searching for that one right word that changes everything. It meant literally learning together and forgetting that hours were going by and that the outside cold was awaiting us. It also meant the freedom to say and explore, individually and collectively, without fearing a backlash of hierarchical power. As our project was nearing its completion, we tried to add more terms, to prolong the process and not break the enchantment of the collectivity. We hope that our words will carry on that magic to the readers.

America—Misnomer adopted by the United States and accepted around the world. The term pretends to describe the politically, economically, and militarily strongest nation in the continent but, in reality, denotes the conglomeration of nations and peoples that coexist in three continents and the Caribbean Sea. It is synonymous of cultural, artistic, musical, ethnic, and linguistic diversity, turmoil, guerrillas, territories as colonies, exploitation, violence, instability, extreme poverty and extreme wealth, struggle for land ownership, and peasant and indigenous populations. It is extremely important to be conscious of the differences between the English and Spanish usage of the false cognate "America." In the text, Burgos consciously questions the term *Latin America* by referring to it as "la llamada América Latina" (10) ("the so-called Latin America," xii). See GUATEMALA.

Anthropology—Academic discipline based on postcolonial desire to investigate, learn about, and "understand" the Other. It usually assumes the need to observe firsthand and record the cultural practices of that Other. Rigoberta Menchú consciously reverses this order in two ways. First, she decides to learn the language of the anthropologist. Second, she gives her testimony in Paris instead of in her own cultural environment. See BURGOS, MENCHÚ, SPANISH.

Author—Individual or corporation, dead according to Foucault, which possessing or assuming authority creates, produces, or offers an original version, a translation, a distillation, or a compilation of a story or stories about factual or fictional events in the form of mostly written works (i.e., novel, book, poetry). One of the most acute problems of testimonial writing is the near impossibility of pinpointing with accuracy who the author is: Is it the one who tells the story (Menchú) or the one who writes it down and structures it (Burgos)? This difficulty is particularly grave for those who expect a single author, a writer, and who have not learned to accept the concept of orality in its broader sense. In the case of our testimonial dictionary, we have attempted to eliminate one single authorial voice by translating our discussions into a dictionary form. See BURGOS, MENCHÚ.

Authority—Power exercised by one person over another on an intellectual, economic, political, social, personal, or gender basis. In relation to literature, authority is the assignment of that power to a person (author, witness) or to a version of events (personal truth). After the invention of writing, authority has been customarily ascribed in Western civilization to written versions more often than to oral ones. The fact that Burgos has the authority in the final version of Menchú's testimony leads many readers to assume that she enjoys a position of privilege. However, we wonder how the balance of authority was determined and maintained during the conversations she had with Menchú. See AUTHOR, BURGOS, CENSORSHIP, IRSE POR LAS RAMAS, MANIPU-LATION, MENCHÚ, POWER.

Book—Sacrosanct (after the Bible) form of writing that has become the authorized repository of knowledge and truth in Western civilization and which has been used as a means to "legalize" the versions of those who cannot produce written texts. It is composed of paper on which wor(l)ds are trapped between two covers and encompasses ideologies, dreams, and imaginations. Books are ideological instruments that contain beginnings, endings, language, stories, information, histories, narratives, fictions, lies, and voices. The final product of the conversations between Burgos and Menchú, transcribed and translated into various editions, acquired the form of a book. This process of legalization also occurs in academic circles that attempt to teach Menchú's testimony and that produce texts such as our dictionary and the book in which it is included. It should be emphasized to students that all of the versions of Menchú's testimony contain not only her ideologies, but those of other "authors," such as editors and translators. The version of the testimony that we read is titled *Me llamo Rigoberta Menchú y así me nació la conciencia.* See AUTHORITY, BURGOS, MENCHÚ, ORALITY, TRANSLATION, UNHEARD.

Boring—That which is not exciting or does not appeal to active participation or discussion. It is often perceived as too serious, unknown, or belaboring. Boring is what was of no interest to Burgos and was left out of the book. She explicitly states that, "Me han señalado que, al principio del libro, el capítulo sobre las ceremonias del nacimiento corría el riesgo de aburrir al lector" (18, emphasis added). (It was pointed out to me that placing the chapter dealing with birth ceremonies at the beginning of the book might bore the reader) (xx–xxi, emphasis added). Nevertheless, although Burgos comments that she did not heed that advice, she concludes that, "Una vez colocado el manuscrito en el orden que actualmente tiene, pude aligerar, suprimir las repeticiones sobre un mismo tema que existían en varios capítulos" (18, emphasis added). (Once the manuscript was in its final form, I was able to cut a number of points that are repeated in more than one chapter) (xx–xxi, emphasis added). Some of the less motivated readers may find *I, Rigoberta Menchú: An Indian Woman in Guatemala* "boring." For example, out of forty-six students in two sections of third-semester Spanish at the University of Wisconsin–Madison, about half said that they were bored by the excerpt that appears in *Pasajes: Literatura*. The other half was about equally divided between those that "did not care" and those that were genuinely "interested." See INTERESTING and PEDAGOGY.

Burgos-Debray, Elizabeth—Cultural anthropologist born in Venezuela and living in France who materialized the idea of writing down Rigoberta Menchú's life story. She recorded Menchú's voice on twenty-five tapes and transcribed them. In addition, Burgos not only wrote an introduction, a prologue, and a glossary to her version of Menchú's testimony, but she also chose epigraphs for the chapters of the book, and gave it a title. Moreover, she is listed as the author in the Spanish version although the English translation is catalogued in libraries under Menchú. Burgos has been criticized for giving incomplete explanations about what she eliminated from Menchú's oral account and for exercising censorship over Menchú's words in order to create the appearance of an organized and chronological life history. See AUTHORITY, CENSORSHIP, IRSE POR LAS RAMAS, ORALITY.

Censorship—Suppression or repression geared towards the elimination of unwanted aspects of the text. For example, while the Spanish version of Rigoberta Menchú's testimony ends with a seven-page-long manifesto of the Comité de Unidad Campesina (CUC) to which she belonged, the English version does not offer this document. Censorship is also a process through which any speaking subject constructs herself or himself by simultaneously releasing and withholding certain information. To a great extent this process is mediated by memory and by the way the subject wants to be perceived. Elisabeth Burgos admits changing some of the sentence structures produced by Menchú's recently learned Spanish and selecting the material from the tapes and organizing it. Moreover, Burgos channels Menchú's testimony with questions, but she does not publish them in the final version of the book. How much censorship does she exercise over Menchú's account? We asked ourselves why Burgos did not specify her intrusions to Menchú's testimony. We also wondered how much self-censorship Menchú applied to her own words. See ANTHROPOLOGY, BORING, MANIPULATION, POWER, SECRET.

Collective voice—Given the impossibility of a true collective voice, a community can achieve a distillation of its multiple voices into several representative ones, or, more commonly, into one authorized version. This distillation facilitates the political and propagandistic use of the version being offered because it allows the adoption of manichean positions that lead to a simplification of the "facts." Menchú intends to translate into Spanish from Quiché the collective voice of her community. Burgos ultimately writes a text that represents her own and Menchú's voices merged, hybridized. Our Testimonial Dictionary is an intent to create a text that would erase the presence of a single authorial voice and give meaning to the collective experience. We hope to have acheived this. See I, TRANSLATION, WE.

Dictionary—Conventionally, a compilation of a number of words in alphabetical order with an explanation of their meanings, roots, and syntactical use, including their synonyms, antonyms, and other details such as regional and standard use. It claims to be objective and functions as a tool to compensate for a lack of knowledge. It is considered to present the utmost authorized explanation of a word. A type of dictionary, a glossary, appears at the end of Menchú and Burgos's testimony in both the Spanish and English versions. Our dictionary does not attempt to be objective, authoritative, or definitive. Instead, it proclaims its openness. See AUTHOR, AUTHORITY, BOOK, GRAMMAR, WORD.

Discussion/Group discussion—Both the dynamics that allowed us to write this collective testimony and an exchange in a classroom environment to present the opinions, perceptions, ideas, or criticisms that students develop from the reading of a text. Pair discussion: Event that prompted Burgos to write her version of Menchú's story. Class discussions, either in pairs or groups, can lead to debate and are efficient strategies to avoid a teacher-centered environment. Their success depends, to a great extent, upon the interest of the participants. Discussions are a must to enrich everyone's understanding of a given text. In the case of Menchú and Burgos's book, they open avenues for the comprehension of Menchú's life and how her testimony impacts individuals across cultures and languages. A beneficial group discussion of Menchú and Burgos's book can begin with any of the entries included in this dictionary. See HIERARCHY, INTERESTING, LANGUAGE, PEDAGOGY, POWER.

Enemy—Person or persons at any level of the power structure who represent a real or imagined threat because they oppose one's being or ideology. For Menchú, the enemy has different faces: the "ladinos," the city, the government, and the army. See HIERARCHY, POWER.

Epigraph—Quotes taken from texts to open a discourse. This technique conditions the recipient to relate two different traditions. We asked ourselves why Burgos introduces epigraphs from *Popol Vuh*, *Hombres de Maíz*, *El libro de los Libros Chilam Balam*, The Bible, and Menchú's own testimony without providing any explanation, and we wondered if most of the epigraphs are used to give indigenous, "folkloric," flavor to the book or to universalize it. In the classroom, these questions could be addressed in order to make students aware of the effects that Burgos's employment of epigraphs has on the veracity of the testimony since it is questionable that Menchú herself had knowledge of the quoted sources. See AUTHORITY, BOOK, BURGOS.

Exam—Conventional way to verify that students know certain materials and are able to handle a quantity of information, structures and readings. Sometimes, students are able to offer criticisms and analysis in exams. Exams are a purportedly neutral and just objectification of an individual's knowledge and an exercise in which the student must answer the questions posed by a teacher, which reflect that teacher's mode of interpretation and particular ideologies. They are the most common method employed to test the level of comprehension and misunderstanding of Menchú's testimony. Testing students can reveal instances of contextual breakdown. For example, even though the problematic of authorship was central to the discussion of *I, Rigoberta Menchú: An Indian Woman in Guatemala*, in two sections of third-semester Spanish with a total of forty-six students, about 60 percent answered an exam question on the *Pasajes: Literatura* reading in one of the following ways:

(translated and paraphrased)

Question: Who is Rigoberta Menchú?

Answer 1:   She wrote a testimonial novel.
Answer 2:   She is the character of a story by Elisabeth Burgos.
Answer 3:   She is Elisabeth Burgos's maid.

These instances of contextual breakdown can be avoided by providing students with adequate background information. See BORING, DISCUSSION, PEDAGOGY, PICTURE.

Fiction—Subjective construct obtained by means of the imagination, which, however, represents experiencial, emotional, or intellectual truths translated into language. Although fiction is commonly considered to be separate from history, Burgos and Menchú's book challenges the traditional disciplinary boundaries between fiction and history by intertwining the historical value of testimony with various techniques of fiction to the point that they become inseparable. See AUTHOR, HISTORY, TESTIMONY, TRANSLATION.

Grammar—Rules governing the linguistic expression of a given language, generally assumed to promote understandable communication between manipulators of that language. Grammar is a way of showing the functioning of a language and usually represents a tremendous barrier to individuals expressing themselves in a language that is not their mother tongue. While Burgos corrects most of Menchú's grammar "mistakes," she maintains Menchú's quality of oral syntax in order to give authenticity to the testimony given by "alguien que acaba de aprender un idioma" (18) (someone [who] had just learned to speak a foreign language) (xx–xxi). Non-native speakers of Spanish who read the Spanish version of the text need to be encouraged not to translate because Menchú's testimony does not always adhere to written syntactical style. A small but significant percentage of students in our third-semester Spanish classes expressed their frustrations regarding the syntactical "mistakes" that Burgos does not correct. For this reason, we suggest that the issues of grammar and second-language acquisition be addressed before the actual reading. See LANGUAGE, QUICHÉ, SPANISH, TRANSLATION.

Guatemala—Central American country where the majority of the population is of indigenous descent and excluded from power. Of this population, 55 percent is indigenous and 44 percent mestizo. Among the approximately twenty-one different languages spoken in the country, one can find Quiché, Menchú's first language. The great linguistic variety has contributed to the isolation of the diverse populations. The economy of the country depends heavily upon cheap indigenous labor. Paradoxically, the labor source has been systematically exterminated, supposedly because of its support of armed opposition groups in the country. Even though the Guatemalan armed forces have violently suppressed the activities of those groups, the government remains politically weak. The country's political spectrum ranges from the ultra-right to the extreme left. Both advocate the use of violence in order to defend or alter institutional establishments. The Right legally participates in the political process, but the Left has been denied access to it. In terms of religion, the country is now a battleground between Catholicism and Protestantism and it is anticipated that, by the end of the century, the major religious persuasion in Guatemala will be Evangelical Christian. Although on the back cover of the English version, Menchú is identified as a "young Guatemalan peasant woman, already famous in her country as a national leader" (emphasis added), her primary national identity is Quiché. See AMERICA, MENCHÚ, QUICHÉ.

Hierarchy—An unequal distribution of power that is inherent to all human organizations and activities. For example, the author exerts power and stands above the subject of his/her writing. This power may be manifested in intellectual, economic, racial, religious, political, societal, personal, and gender forms. Within the context of Burgos and Menchú's account, there are, at least, two important points that readers should consider. First of all, one may wonder if Burgos manages or even attempts to erase the hierarchy that exists between her and Menchú. One can also consider the levels of hierarchies inscribed in the testimony (i.e., Menchú's community vis-à-vis other communities, the Guatemalan government, and the world). See BURGOS, CENSORSHIP, GUATEMALA, MENCHÚ.

History—As is the case with fiction, history is a written construct, but circumscribed by what historians call "evidence." Usually, history deals with those events that, because of their importance to a group of people, such as a community, city, or country, are considered a part of that group's formation and evolution. Furthermore, it is an attempt to recreate events in an objective manner with the ultimate goal of presenting the "authorized version" of what really occurred. In the case of oral history, however, the version of events is very difficult to document; as an example, we can cite the version offered by Menchú of her brother's death. It is important to note that in the case of *Me llamo Rigoberta Menchú y así me nació la conciencia,* it is not the history narrated by Menchú but the one mediated by Burgos that becomes a historical document that is neither part of the official history of Guatemala nor part of its national identity. During our discussions, we wondered why, given both Burgos's and Menchú's Marxism, there is no mention of former president Jacobo Arbenz (1951–54) and his reformist actions, but there are multiple references to the right-wing presidents who followed him: Kjell Laugerud García, Romero Lucas García, and the general Efraín Ríos Montt. Perhaps an answer is offered by the editorial classification of the Spanish version, "historia inmediata" (immediate history). See FICTION, GUATEMALA, MENCHÚ, ORALITY.

I—Personal pronoun that appears in the English title, but not in the Spanish version. It exemplifies the form in which the testimony is usually given and/or written. We should not forget that the empty signifier "I" could be filled with any identity and that strangely enough behind the "I" of *I, Rigoberta Menchú: An Indian Woman in Guatemala* two identities are hidden: Burgos's and Menchú's. In fact, Burgos states that she "allowed her [Menchú] to speak and then became her instrument, her double, by allowing her to make the transition from the spoken to the written word" (xx). (. . . dejando hablar a Rigoberta, y luego convirtiéndome en una especie de doble suyo, en el instrumento que operaría el paso de lo oral a lo escrito) (18). See AUTHOR, COLLECTIVE VOICE, WE.

Indian—Grave and fateful misnomer given to the inhabitants of the Americas by the sorely lost Columbus. While the English version employs the term *Indian* to classify Menchú's ethnic background, the Spanish version uses *indígena* (indigenous). In the history of the Americas, the word has acquired heavily negative connotations: savagery, ignorance, dirtiness, falsehood, poverty, inferiority, object, lack, inability, laziness, ugliness, shame, exploitation, oppression, ahistoricity, nonexistence. The word pretends to describe the human groups autochthonous to the Americas, which have been traditionally despised by and separated from the nationalistic, social, and political bodies of the region. Since many readers partake of these preconceptions, there exist at least two possibilities in teaching the Menchú and Burgos's story: class discussion of the stereotypes that the term amalgamates and avoidance of the word. Obviously, the former option opens avenues for mutual cultural enlightenment. See GUATEMALA, INDIGENOUS, NAMING.

Indigenous—The preferable adjective chosen by some to describe everything pertaining to what is autochtonous, such as culture, customs, language, religion, art, and traditions. It has been erroneously used as synonymous with Indian. In the Spanish version of the testimony, Menchú refers to herself and the people of her community as "indígena" (indigenous). However, in the English version, the translator opted for the adjective *Indian* most of the time. Why did Menchú (or Burgos) prefer the term *indígena*? Why did the translator feel that *Indian* was a better description? Is there a difference? See INDIAN, NAMING, QUICHÉ, TRANSLATION.

Interesting—Activity, reading, or assignment that awakens interest, involvement, enthusiasm, curiosity, empathy, passion, or desire. It is also that which Burgos determined to be of interest to the reader. Although the term *reader* is very broad, certain strategies can stimulate nonmotivated and/or less experienced readers. In a possible pre-reading activity, after some historical and cultural background is given, readers can be encouraged to create oral dialogues, assuming the roles of reporter (Burgos) and testimony provider (Menchú). They can base these dialogues on personal information or on what they think that Menchú's testimony would be like.

Step 1   Discuss the hybrid nature of testimony.

Step 2   Provide cultural and historical background as an introduction to the text.

Step 3   Divide the class into pairs.

Step 4   Model the activity with sample questions and answers and specify that the reporter may take notes. This activity could also be performed outside of class using a tape recorder.

Step 5   Give a time limit of approximately 5 minutes for the interview.

Step 6   Switch roles and repeat activity.

Step 7   Check "reports" orally in class and have testimony providers comment on accuracy. This report could be written at home if the activity seems too long to complete in class. The activity could serve to demonstrate some of the problems associated with authorship, authority, truth, orality, and manipulation as they pertain to testimonies. Furthermore, it allows students to participate actively in the problematizing of such concepts.

See BORING, DISCUSSION, PEDAGOGY.

Irse por las ramas—Necessary and untranslatable expression from Spanish (no nonpejorative equivalent exists in English) to underline one of the main characteristics of orality: that of creating byways born from the inherent human trait of association of ideas. It enriches any discussion with information that, otherwise, could not be considered pertinent. As such, it can be used effectively as an alternative method of teaching and learning. It stands at the opposite end of "volviendo al cuento" (getting back to the subject) and "¿Dónde es que íbamos?" (Where were we?). As we created our own testimony, we often slipped into topics that, sometimes, related to our goal only remotely and by association. How often did this happen to Menchú and Burgos? Did they talk about politics, daily experiences, female experiences? See CENSORSHIP, ORALITY.

Language—Do we exist outside language? How much is our vision of reality predetermined by the language we speak? In the case of Menchú, her community lives without most of Western technology and, for this reason, Quiché has no signs for that referent. However, learning Spanish opens new realms in Menchú's existence so that words such as "tape recorder," "camera," and "machine" enter her being. We also have to be aware of the importance of Menchú's decision to learn Spanish, the language of those who oppress the Quiché, in order to "save" her community. See NAMING, QUICHÉ, SPANISH, TRANSLATION.

Manipulation—Value-based suppression or addition to an Other, which is inherent to all forms of argumentation and translation and which is also essential to convince audiences of the "truth" or logic of one version or versions. It is the means to achieve ideological, political, philosophical, materialistic, or personal purposes. It embodies an application of authority in order to reveal only the things that one wants to be known or considers to be important or interesting. In the case of Menchú and Burgos's testimony, there are two levels of manipulation: Menchú produces and controls the original version, which she gives to Burgos, the necessary medium to get it into the form of a book. Unavoidably, Burgos then transcribes, organizes, edits, corrects, and publicizes her own version of Menchú's testimony according to her valuation of what is important or interesting. Perhaps there is even a third level of manipulation. After attending the symposium "I, Rigoberta Menchú" at the University of Wisconsin–Milwaukee, 25 March 1994, we became aware of the possible manipulative participation of the CUC (Comite de Unidad Campesina) in the production and publication of Burgos and Menchú's book. Although the text states that the original idea for the testimony came from one of Burgos's Canadian friends, the symposium suggested the CUC's clear political intervention in the creation of the testimony. See AUTHORITY, BORING, INTERESTING, NAMING, WORD.

Memory—The base of every testimony. It is selective, absolutely subjective, and can be manipulated either consciously or unconsciously. Menchú attempts to reconstruct her story based on her recollection of the key and formative moments of her life. To this, she apparently adds stories that are part of the official and collective memory of her community. See CENSORSHIP, FICTION, HISTORY, TESTIMONY.

Menchú, Rigoberta—Maya-Quiché political activist who won the Nobel Peace Prize in 1993 and who provides the raw material for the creation of the testimonial text that Burgos manipulates, organizes and signs. Menchú has recently returned to Guatemala after years of exile to continue her work with indigenous communities. During the armed uprising in Chiapas, Mexico, which began in January 1994, she mediated between the Maya community of Chiapas and the Mexican government. See BURGOS, NAMING.

Naming—Referring to an object, a place, or a person with a word according to what our social and intellectual formation has predetermined as appropriate. The act of naming is a manifestation of power because the named is shaped to conform to the constructs of the world as envisioned by the empowered. As we were discussing problems related to the book we caught ourselves referring to Menchú as Rigoberta and to Burgos as Burgos. Did we feel closer to Menchú or were we just projecting our supposed academic superiority? We also noticed that many critics were caught in the same trap. Two relevant examples are Doris Sommer's article, "Rigoberta's Secrets," (*Latin American Perspectives* 70, 18, 3 [summer 1991]:32–50) and Marc Zimmerman's article, "Testimonio in Guatemala: Payeras, Rigoberta, and Beyond," (*Latin American Perspectives* 71, 18, 4 [fall 1991]:22–47). See BURGOS, MENCHÚ.

Orality—This quality of oral expression pertains to communication. It is that which is not written and which the spoken word cannot transmit thoroughly. In it, associations play a fundamental role, creating a series of levels and paths of narration that vary in time, theme, point of view, and purpose. It is also understood to be the way in which peoples who do not have a written code of expression transmit their history and traditions. What is the relation between an oral and a written code of expression? Menchú's testimony is characterized by orality since she could not express herself in writing. The orality of Menchú's testimony required Burgos's manipulation, its transcription into a written code, in order to be published. Burgos's intervention encompassed "correcting" grammar and adding her own interpretations to the organization of Menchú's thoughts and expression. See IRSE POR LAS RAMAS.

Original—Concept closely related to the idea of the origin and to the quandary of not knowing where we came from. Western philosophy playfully approaches this idea by asserting it and, then, continually questioning it. Its value is established by contrasting it with a copy, which fits perfectly into Walter Benjamin's idea that the sacred text always eludes translation. In the case of Menchú and Burgos's book, the "original" voice is encoded on the audio tapes which, we speculate, are being kept by Burgos, and are outside public domain. We should not forget that Burgos is also part of that "original" voice since her questions dialogued with Menchú's own voice in order to generate the discussion that she organized into a book. See CENSORSHIP, TRANSLATION.

Pedagogy—Although pedagogical methods and needs vary greatly depending on the teacher and the class, we have chosen to define our plurality of strategies as that which provides for communal learning. In order to add to the plurality of pedagogical approaches used to teach Burgos and Menchú's text, we include the following strategies, which we consider fruitful:

> *Strategy 1* Students can be asked to interview members of the community, relatives, or even each other depending on their class objectives. In this process, they may use a tape recorder in order to obtain testimonies and then write them to share with their classmates.

> *Strategy 2* This activity could be adapted to many classroom environments: In groups, students may choose key words and concepts from the text, such as testimony, secret, community, and culture, in order to define how they are used or how they are problematic. As an alternative, students could be given a list of words. Working in pairs or as a class instead of in groups, they can write their definitions in English or Spanish, depending on class objectives. This strategy is similar to our experience in the compiling of this dictionary. We have found this type of communal sharing and learning to be truly enriching. See BORING, DISCUSSION, INTERESTING.

Picture—Accompanying any version of Menchú and Burgos's book will be pictures, either photographs or drawings, that affect the images that readers have of Menchú as well as of the relationship between her and Burgos. These pictures can be especially helpful to students that are reading the text in a language that is not their "mother" tongue. In our experience with *Pasajes: Literatura*, some readers assumed from the drawings that accompanied their textbook that Menchú could read (and therefore probably write) and that she was a maid (probably in Burgos's household). This contextual breakdown was not discovered until many students incorrectly answered an exam question. See EXAM.

Power—This is the driving force that determines the manner in which relations among people are established and which responds to the ever changing positions that a person assumes at different times and in different contexts. The possession of power gives one the ability to determine, control, and enforce not only one's own wishes, actions, words, or other self-expressions, but those of others. In Menchú's testimony, we see how two people manipulate the power available to them in order to achieve their individual and common goals. See BURGOS, HIERARCHY, MANIPULATION, MENCHÚ.

Quiché—The predominant language spoken by the largest indigenous group of Guatemala, which lives mainly in the southwestern highlands of the country. Quiché has not changed significantly during the last four hundred years and it has been kept "alive" through oral practice. With the arrival of Spaniards, the language was written down and encoded with the Spanish alphabet. One of the best known texts from Quiché is the *Popol Vuh* (*Popol vuh: The Sacred Book of the Ancient Quiché Maya*, trans. Adrian Recinos). See GUATEMALA, SPANISH.

Reader/reading—Term that describes those who read and/or decipher a text not necessarily in a critical way, bringing into the reading their own ideologies and perspectives and creating unique interpretations. Thus, the readers become active participants in the creation of a story-history and apply another level of censorship to the book, the words, the original, the translation, the history, or the fiction they read. Since there is no fixed meaning in any book, readers have the responsibility and power to create it. In the classroom, group discussions can be held to exchange impressions of how each student "reads" the text. See DISCUSSION, FICTION, HISTORY, STORY.

Reporter—Person who goes directly to the sources in order to obtain interviews or information about issues and, then, presents them in a purportedly objective way. The reporter is also a necessary and manipulating filter to bridge a gap in physical distance, cultural and linguistic differences, and knowledge. In the case of Burgos, she goes beyond the limits of reporting by including an introduction and making conscious changes in Menchú's testimony such as altering the original format of questions and answers, organizing the book chronologically in chapters, and maintaining possession and control of the recordings of her interviews with Menchú. See BURGOS, CENSORSHIP, MANIPULATION.

Secret—What remains hidden, unrevealed, and occult. In terms of language it is a notion related to the idea that only the original language contains one's real self, impossible to translate into the language of the Other. This original language is deconstructed as one learns another linguistic code. In the case of Menchú, she felt a need to insist on the fact that no cultural anthropologist or reader (intruder) can ever be able to uncover or decipher the Secret that only her community possesses. As a matter of fact, she ends her testimony by refusing to give in to the new identity that Spanish offers: "Pero, sin embargo, todavía sigo ocultando lo que yo considero que nadie sabe, ni siquiera un antropólogo, ni un intelectual, por más que tenga muchos libros, no saben distinguir todos nuestros secretos" (271). (Nevertheless, I'm still keeping my Indian identity a secret. I'm still keeping secret what I think no one should know. Not even anthropologists or intellectuals, no matter how many books they have, can find out all our secrets) (247). See ANTHROPOLOGY, LANGUAGE, QUICHÉ, TRANSLATION.

Spanish—Language brought by the Spanish colonizers of America. It was and continues to be imposed as the linguistic authority. Because of its socially central quality, ex-slaves, Indians, and their transcribers have been forced to use

Spanish to communicate with the society at large. Although Spanish is Menchú's second language, learned at the age of twenty according to Burgos, she acquired some knowledge of the language as a catechist at age thirteen. See LANGUAGE, QUICHÉ.

Story—Account that communicates thoughts, imaginations, ideas, ideologies, events, dreams, desires, and needs to an Other via oral or written means. In the case of the testimonial novel, it is the final version achieved through the modification of an oral testimony by the intervention of a supposedly neutral transcriber. This represents the creation of two versions of the story: one oral and the other written. Great care should be observed in class when teaching fragments of testimonial works in order not to convey the impression that those passages are short stories and are, therefore, products solely of the imagination. To avoid this contextual breakdown, students should be provided with appropriate background information regarding testimonial texts and Menchú's history. See AUTHOR, FICTION, HISTORY, TESTIMONY.

Tape recorder—Instrument representative of the power of technology, which contrary to the general assumption that it does so, never captures the totality of a testimony since it leaves out important nonverbal communicative patterns such as hand movements and facial expressions that are intrinsic to orality. The tape recorder serves as a source from which researchers, such as Burgos and our group, construct their own stories and those of their coauthors. Having used one to record our discussions, we consider it important to ponder how much its presence influenced Menchú's testimony and gave power to Burgos. Parallel to the secret kept within the confines of Menchú's culture, the contents of the recordings, nonverbal gestures and expressions notwithstanding, contain the secret of Menchú's testimony and anoint Burgos as its keeper. See ORALITY, REPORTER, SECRET.

Testimony—Written and/or oral account that relates a witnessed event or experience, which is subjective and influenced by emotions. It is important to keep in mind the sociohistorical religious and legal connotations of this term. Throughout the colonial period, the giving of testimony was a way for Indians to communicate with the Church and State. Menchú and others continue and enrich this tradition by telling their stories to the world. See MANIPULATION, ORALITY, SECRET, STORY.

Textbooks—The inclusion of Burgos and Menchú's book, whether in its totality or in fragments, in a second language acquisition classroom is an opportunity for many students to have their first "encounter" with a culture of the Americas that is often excluded from literary readings. Two textbooks that offer passages of *Me llamo Rigoberta Menchú y así me nació la conciencia* are *Pasajes: Literatura* and *Convocación de Palabras*. Both use sections of the testimony, but in contrasting contexts. The former selects chapter thirteen, "Muerte de su amiga intoxicada por la fumigación en la finca," and places it within the larger discussion entitled "La muerte y el mundo del más allá." The latter uses the first chapter of the testimony, "La familia," and places it in the section that has a homonymous heading. Our experience has been that many students consider Menchú's testimony to be fiction because they do not expect any readings in *Pasajes: Literatura* to be documentary. In fact, several of them assumed that the fragment offered was a short story and had a strong reaction to the orality of Menchú's account. *Convocación de palabras*, targeted for more advanced students, makes exclusive use of Spanish and includes another testimony, that of Domitila Barrios de Chungara. These elements help create a richer cultural, historical, and political context. A possible shortcoming of the fragmentary presentation of Burgos and Menchú's text is that cultural differences can be seen as folkloric, especially if the passages are accompanied by simplistic drawings or misleading pictures. These images can serve to discredit the authenticity of different cultural experiences. See BORING, EXAM, GRAMMAR, INTERESTING, PEDAGOGY, PICTURE.

Translation—Most commonly understood as the way to transfer meaning from one linguistic code to another (i.e., from Quiché to Spanish). However, in the case of a translation from an oral to a written code, it may also include the transposition of other semiotic systems, such as gestures or even thought processes. Although the general assumption is that faithfulness must give way to practicality, and that the translation is necessarily inferior to the original, it is important to bear in mind that language always gives more or less than the mind of the translator intends. Consequently, the new version in another language has the potential of being as powerful as the translated one. Menchú translates the experience of her community through a personal prism from Quiché into Spanish. Burgos transcribes that oral version into a written form of Spanish, which, in turn, is ultimately transposed into many other languages. At all levels of the translation process, the meaning suffers many changes, which can include the omission of whole sections such as the manifesto that appears in the Spanish version, but not in the English one. We all wondered if the Menchú in Quiché differs from the translated Menchú and to what degree the acquisition of Spanish changed her identity. Will *Me llamo Rigoberta Menchú y así me nació la conciencia* ever appear in Quiché? See LANGUAGE, QUICHÉ, SPANISH.

We—Pronoun for first person plural that assumes a certain collectiveness and embodies the unresolved tension of the voices that must be distilled into one authorized voice in order to communicate a communal experience. The entries to this dictionary are defined by speaking subjects from different backgrounds and experiences who are or have been at the crossroads of more than one culture and language. See COLLECTIVE VOICE, I, MENCHÚ, QUICHÉ.

Word—Written or oral linguistic representation of an object, a thought, or an idea. Menchú manipulates the spoken word to communicate her testimony to Burgos who, in turn, translates Menchú's expression into written form. See LANGUAGE, NAMING, TRANSLATION.

19

RIGOBERTA'S EARRINGS
The Limits of Teaching Testimonio

TACE HEDRICK

> In the eyes of our community, the fact that anyone
> should even change the way they dress shows a lack of
> dignity. Anyone who doesn't dress as our grandfa-
> thers, our ancestors, dressed, is on the road to ruin.
>
> —*Menchú 1984, 37*

When my Testimonial Literature class and I watched the video "Rigoberta Menchú: Broken Silence," my students noticed that Rigoberta, wearing her own Maya-Quiché *huipil* (blouse) and *corte* (skirt), was also wearing what were obviously Western-style, manufactured, seemingly un-Indian earrings. In fact it was my female students, trained as women are in a commmodity culture to be good observers of fashions and styles, who first noticed and had questions about that seeming discrepancy between the determinedly "Indianist" Rigoberta and her not-so-Indian earrings. A "trivial" detail such as this one, especially if it is a resistant one (the resistance caused by the proximity of seemingly opposing discourses—Western and non-Western, colonizer and colonized), may prove to be a point of fruitful discussion and thought. I suggest that the disjunctions and crossings-over of Maya-Quiché huipil and Western earrings might open up a space for exploration of those disjunctions encountered when a non-Western testimonio such as Menchú's meets up with a particular North American classroom.

In this chapter, I will examine two general aspects of teaching testimonio, with the idea of complicating what I feel are certain reductive ideas about the genre and its "place" in the classroom. My concern will be with the notion that testimonio, because of its associations with testifying and with truth telling, has an unambiguous *use value* (pedagogical and social) for readers' lives. Through an examination of some of the ways in which my female students in particular complicate and make partial the impact and meaning of a testimonio such as Menchú's, I hope to expand on unreflective ideas about the usefulness of testimonio to North American students. In other words, rather than assuming that Menchú's text can be presented as possessing a "wholeness" of purpose (itself a doubtful proposition) which could then be *useful* to the reader/student, the ways my female students relate to a testimonio like Menchú's are very partial, and complicated by their own lives as women who work, go to school, and in many cases are wives and/or mothers.

In his essay "Second Thoughts on Testimonio," John Beverley (1993) speaks of the "use" value of testimonio as "a concrete pedagogical issue, the use of testimonio has to do with the possibility of interpellating our students . . . in a relation of solidarity with liberation movements and human rights struggles, both here in the United States and abroad" (128). In the same vein, he continues, "testimonios have become . . . a discursive space where the possibilities of such an alliance can be negotiated on both sides without too much angst over otherness and othering" (128). In one sentence, Beverley casually dismisses that which I would consider essential to the understanding of the process of reading, especially the process of reading texts that do come from a culture completely "other," totally foreign, to the reader's own.

Before continuing with my reasons for needing such a category as the "other," however, I need to situate myself and my students: I am a professor of comparative literature who teaches mostly Latin American literature (in translation) in a small university situated in the politically and culturally conservative center of Pennsylvania. My population of students comes almost entirely from working-class families, and the majority of them work at least part time. As a whole, there are at least one-quarter "nontraditional" students, that is, older, returning students. In the Humanities Division in which I teach, most of these returning students are women, many either with young families or with grown families, some divorced. A common thread for all these various student populations is their propensity to stay put in this area: they are not a very mobile group. Latin America is in a very real way a completely other Dark Continent for my students.

Thus, to get back to Beverley's assertion, the question of reading any Latin American literature, much less Latin American testimonio, becomes not one of solidarity, or even complicity as other critics would have it (Sommer 1991b, 40; Shea 1993, 142) but a complex one of "othernesses" on the part of my students, of acceptances, resistances, and all the shades in between. It is this very real problematics of otherness that casts doubt on unreflective ideas of the "use value" for students of such an "othered" text as testimonio is itself. I would not, however, for this reason stop reading testimonios in my classrooms; so at the same time I would unsettle ideas of "use," I would like, also, to examine what it might mean for my students, especially my female students, to read and respond to *I, Rigoberta*.

THE DISINTEGRATION OF FORM:
CAN THE TESTIMONIO SPEAK?

It's hard for me to remember everything that's happened to me in my life since there have been many very bad times but, yes, moments of joy as well. . . . I must say before I start that I never went to school.

—*Menchú 1984, 1*

In reading *I, Rigoberta,* several of my students complained that they couldn't keep track of a temporal sequence of events in her narrative—partly a function undoubtedly of Burgos-Debray's editing, but also a function of an oral testimony that depends on memory and that is not necessarily schematized or mapped out beforehand. They also commented on a kind of "impersonality" of the text, something they couldn't quite put a finger on, but which prevented them from relating fully to her voice. Menchú's text seemed at times to lack the kind of affect they felt was appropriate to the conditions she was describing. Testimonios are, as almost all critics have noted (Sommer 1991b, 49; Beverley 1993, 130; Gugelberger and Kearney 1991, 11) a resistant literature; for example, *I, Rigoberta* works purposefully to hold the reader away from complete identification with Menchú or her people on several different levels. On another level is the difficulty Western readers have with the lack of "plot"; and still another, which I suggested to my class, is the possibility that Menchú is still keeping toward us the deliberately affectless face of subjugation, one which is careful to reveal few feelings to the outside world because to do so would be to invite vulnerability. Ariel Dorfman's "Political Code and Literary Code: The Testimonial Genre in Chile Today" carefully critiques Chilean testimonios for their "unreadability," the "disintegration of form, absence of suspense, and the abstraction of some experiences" (Dorfman 1991, 157, 159). Dorfman is quick to point out that these "literary" problems have to do with the situations of their authors: that, among other things, most of these testifiers wish to efface any narrative quirks of their own personal voice in order to make the communal nature of their plight clear, just as Menchú does: "The important thing is that what has happened to me has happened to many other people too. . . . My personal experience is the reality of a whole people" (Menchú 1984, 1). The result in terms of my classroom was that although many of my students come to my classes as relatively poor readers of literary texts, nevertheless their (more or less unconscious) absorption of a whole range of narrative conventions meant that they found that Rigoberta Menchú's text was not "good" literature. This, accompanied with the distance Menchú deliberately keeps, meant that my students felt in some ways that they couldn't "relate" to her narrative. Two of my students observed to me about their memories of reading *I, Rigoberta* that they felt "detached" from her narrative at first, although one of them felt that Rigoberta's "guard slipped" later on in the narrative. As another of my women students put it, Rigoberta "created a window" through which we as readers could look, but that there was "a glass" in that window that kept us separated from her. As my single African American student put it, she felt too far removed from Rigoberta's experience to feel "solidarity" with her, though as a woman of color she (my student) could empathize with Menchú.

"IT'S SCIENCE FICTION":
DEFAMILIARIZATION

> The teacher of literature, because of her institutional subject-position, can and must "re-constellate" the text to draw out its use. She can and must wrench it out of its proper context and put it within alien arguments.
>
> —*Spivak, "A Literary Representation*
> *of the Subaltern," 1988, 241*

Both Gayatri Spivak and John Beverley respond to subaltern writing from the point of view of defamiliarization. Beverley says, "At least part of [testimonio's] aesthetic effect—I mean this precisely in the Russian formalist sense of *ostranenie* or defamiliarization—is that it is *not* literary, not linguistically elaborated or authorial" (1993, 130). Here, Beverley uses an explicitly aesthetic effect to say that testimonio is not aesthetic, not a "literary" work—a relatively common stance among critics who wish to believe that there is a clear opposition between "nonfiction" (particularly historical nonfiction) and "fiction" (Georg Gugelberger and Michael Kearney in their "Voices for the Voiceless" call testimonio the "intentionality of regaining the real and the truth" [11]). For many critics, the testimonio is both used and *useful* because it is unfamiliar in both form and content, defamiliarizing. This means that the very unfamiliarity of the text has a shocking effect on the reader/student, "wrenching" or displacing her normal world view and thus allowing for a new look at what she thought she knew well. Beverley comes back at the use value of the testimonio from Menchú's side also, so that the testimonio itself stands as a form that serves both testifier and reader: "[w]e could say that Menchú *uses* the testimonio as literature without subscribing to a humanist ideology of the literary . . ." (1993, 134, my emphasis). Maureen Shea also assumes that reading *I, Rigoberta* "would *motivate* readers to find out more about the conditions of the indigenous Guatemalans, to learn how closely Menchú's testimony mirrors reality" ("Latin American Women" 148, my emphasis). We can see that these critics see the testimonio's defamiliarizing moments as *unambiguously* useful, motivating, "destroying complacency" (Shea 1993, 148)—but none speak of how this usefulness *actually* plays out, how firm or intermittent it is, in students' or other readers' classrooms and lives. However, I do not want to abandon the quality of strangeness of Menchú's text; there *is* a strangeness, and it comes from the testimonio's ambiguous place as a text: Is it history or fiction? Who are its makers? What will it do for/to us? As a way of seeing how all texts work to one degree or another to unsettle our habitual and habituated ways of seeing things, defamiliarization is a valuable concept.

One of my students, a woman in her late twenties, remarked in class one day that reading *I, Rigoberta* was, because of the alienness of Menchú's experiences, like "reading science fiction." Another student volunteered that Menchú's text "shifted paradigms" for her. Here I'd like for the moment to play on Spivak's use of the term *alien* in her quote above, coming back later to a more careful examination of the entire quote. I would argue that the testimonio comes to occupy a "proper context" in the classroom precisely as an alien, totally "defamiliarizing" *and* "defamiliarized" object. Obviously, there are two kinds of defamiliarization at work in what I am saying. To begin with, because of its status as an object in a college classroom, any literary text has already been assigned a "place" which I would argue from "experience" as a teacher all literature occupies to some extent: it is a "strange" thing, something which one does not "normally" read in the course of a life taken up with working, taking care of husbands and children, cleaning house, doing laundry, watching TV, being involved in the life of one's community and family. That is, a text in a classroom, because of the commonly perceived "alienness" of intellectual life (the *uselessness* of "booklearning" as opposed to "common sense"), can be categorized as that which has nothing to do with "real life"—as my students know their "real" conditions of money, jobs, and relationships. On the other hand, as an account of experiences unknown in my students' lives (torture, murder, forced labor, desperate poverty, constant fear) in a country or countries that seem distant at best if not completely unconnected to life in Pennsylvania, the testimonio "always already" defamiliarizes my Central Pennsylvanian student by its intrinsic alienness. Any ideas of the use value of testimonio I or my students might have had must begin to be mediated by this strangeness.

My students' comments on "science fiction" and "shifting paradigms" led me to think about the possible ways in which the genre of SF itself might illuminate my student's responses to Menchú's testimonio. Virginia Allen and Terri Paul's (1986) "Science and Fiction: Ways of Theorizing about Women" maintain that SF is a genre that uses cognitive dissonance to shift the ways the reader habitually looks at her world. In this essay, they note that "[g]ood science fiction creates situations that focus on anomalous aspects of human behavior and thereby arouse a high degree of cognitive dissonance concerning the reliability of familiar cognitive categories" (181). Allen and Paul go further than this, though; in their analysis of feminist science fiction (beginning, as Susan Gubar suggests, with "Mary Shelley's preoccupation in *Frankenstein* with the Monster, the other" [Allen and Paul 1986, 178]) they come to this conclusion: "[t]he conception of the alien within the self is more than a metaphor, however; it is a model of the feminine psyche" (179). As Paul and Allen note, fiction incorporates patriarchal assumptions; "and when those assumptions are repeated over a long period of time . . . they take on the status of reality in the popular consciousness" (181). When a woman comes to compare her feelings, ideas, and sense of self-worth against her own cultural (often unacknowledged or unconscious) assumptions, she herself, Paul and Allen suggest, experiences the "constant buzz of cognitive dissonance." That women are always already "alien" in patriarchy may give us a clue as to how my female students managed to situate themselves vis-à-vis the narrative in order to find, not a totalizing or totalizable use-value, but rather find points of contact with it—what Terry Eagleton calls "ways in which people *relate themselves* to writing" (1983, 9).

In showing that the unfamiliarity of Menchú's testimonio in fact unsettles what it means to find a text "useful" for students I find I must elaborate on the idea that the testimonio is not so much unmediated, "transparent" truth as it is a product of strategies of narrating and the cultural assumptions embedded in those strategies; as such, testimonio shares many characteristics with fiction. Terry Eagleton further blurs the line between fiction and nonfiction in his essay "What is Literature": "[p]erhaps 'literature' means something like . . . any kind of writing which for some reason or another somebody values highly. . . ." "Literature," Eagleton continues, "like the word *weed* is a *functional* term rather than one denoting a fixed 'being' of literature" (9).

The problem of the difference between the writing of "real" experience (fiction) and "literature" (nonfiction) was one of the first that my students and I attempted to face in our testimonial literature class, and they readily came up with instances where, for example, the experiencing of an event only meant that one's view of it was *subjective* because necessarily particular, rather than transparently and objectively true. Does this mean that the narrator's experience is in some way false? Don't we think history *is* history because it's objectively true? This knotty problem of what is transparent and what is mediated in a narrated experience like the testimonio is addressed by Maureen Shea in her "Latin American Women and the Oral Tradition: Giving Voice to the Voiceless," where she notes that "[o]ral testimonies do not merely report past events from an individual perspective; they also imply a personal interpretation of the past colored by a particular view from the present" (1993, 149); she calls this "documentary fiction," saying that the "reality represented is openly partial . . . a 'huella de lo real' (trace of the real)" (150). Were my students confused by discussions that try to see "literarary" and "nonliterarary" as existing at ends of a spectrum, rather than as binary opposites? Yes—sometimes they were. But a pedagogical strategy of confusion is often the only way to start with concepts that are unfamiliar to one's students; that is, one has to allow that a sense of confusion is "all right"—that to accept and begin to work with the unsettling feeling that there are no clear-cut oppositions is the *beginning* of thinking through problems of reading, of literature, and of history in different, more complex ways. As George Yúdice points out in his "*Testimonio* and Postmodernism,"

> I do not claim that testimonial writing suffers no problems of referentiality, but I do point out that it is . . . first and foremost an act, a tactic by means of which people engage in *the process of self-constitution.* . . . The ambiguity and confusion of the status of the testimonial is very significant because it indicates that there is a *shift taking place in the very notion of what is literary.* (1991, 18–19, my emphasis)

Testimonios are "acts," "tactics," but are also "fictionalized" because they are narrated: they are "'factual and fictional, and thus well equipped to deal with the elusive fusion of fact and fiction, which has become the matrix of today's experience'" (Shea 1993, 149). How we decide what is "literary" is changing, becoming less and less dependent on a master canon and a fixed way of judging which texts are "good" or "bad." The structural anthropologist Lévi-Strauss suggested the notion of *bricolage*, tinkering, to describe his methodological practice. In our own classrooms, we are more often than not *bricoleurs* (or *bricoleuses?*)—that is, we are tinkerers, handy-women, using tools and materials not "meant" for the job at hand—and for the most part—though I emphasize the partiality of this claim also—my students recognize, though they cannot name, the failure in their own lives of "master" discourses, meant to provide them with the tools of living, just as well as any academic can.

I would like to break in now, in the midst of this discussion on the "literary" status of testimonio, in order to talk a little more about my women students, which, for the exception of two men, made up my entire Testimonial Literature class. Out of eleven women, four were returning adults, three with children; all, as far as I know, worked at least part time. All of them had a sense of being "different" because as women they were attending college; the area they live in is conservative enough that that fact alone sets one, male or female, apart from the working-class, blue-collar, "Rust Belt" communities and economies from which they come. My female students especially are alive to the strange partiality of their present experiences as women, workers, mothers, wives, and students, and they know that they must pick and choose the parts of their experiences in school and at home they feel are important in order to begin to create an identity of their own as women; their master text, which has been the familiar (literally, in the sense of *family*) one of patriarchy, is failing badly. It is this sometimes contradictory, "openly partial" reality of the testimonio's status as literature and of my students' experiences inside and outside the classroom alike which I wish to stress. And it is at this partial and intermittent point that

I feel my female students begin to make a kind of contact with Rigoberta Menchú herself, a Maya-Quiché woman who is also outside her expected roles as a woman and who perforce negotiates (and I hope that this term does not empty her work and words of their very real faith and commitment, especially to Christianity) a strategy of "partial" moves, borrowing, as I will show, parts of "master" discourses to suit her needs—again, as George Yúdice notes that "in embracing Christ as the symbol of revolutionary consciousness and conscience, Menchú's community also embraces him as the most important of a panoply of 'popular weapons' ... which include both Christianity and Marxism, two master discourses which in the struggle for survival are made to yield their overriding authority" (1991, 29).

POINTS OF CONTACT:
THE "BADLY BROUGHT-UP DAUGHTER"

In reading *I, Rigoberta*, my students were quick to note that Menchú voices strong opinions about using Indian culture for "touristic" purposes, maintaining that it is wrong for example to take pictures of Indians and that "Indians have been very careful not to disclose any details of their communities. . . . We also find a ladino using Indian clothes very offensive" (9). I raised the question with my students of how to "use" Menchú's text (or, better, how *not* to use it): how to read Rigoberta while at the same time keeping our hands off her, trying not to appropriate her as merely exotic or to bring to her non-Western text the same expectations and narrative frameworks we usually do in reading Western texts. We could begin, I found, with Menchú's injunctions against others' appropriation of, or the Indian's abandonment of, her own traditional Maya-Quiché clothing. All of my students were familiar with buying beautiful, exotic, or unusual products of third-world countries at such chains of import shops as Pier 1, or even with buying quilts and other "souvenirs" of the Amish community here in Pennsylvania; these presented a familiar, concrete set of actions and objects for my students. Thus, our class as a whole could work on understanding how we as (relatively) privileged first-world subjects appropriate the physical, functioning, useful culture of others for "use" as decoration in our culture—buying a beautiful blouse woven to be worn and converting it into a pillow or a purse, or buying a quilt to use as a wall hanging, for example—and thus position a third-world, postcolonial, or even "outside" culture such as the Amish as merely entertaining, "colorful," or "quaint."

There is also another kind of appropriation which Rigoberta Menchú the Indianist knows is frowned upon by her community, yet which she feels she must do: learning "outside" ways of life so that she can make her voice, the voice of her community, heard by others outside Guatemala itself. A sense of confusion over the resulting disjunctions in her own life pervades the pages of *I, Rigoberta*. Although herself a "bad daughter," Menchú privileges the "purity" of those in her community who have not gone outside their community: for example, when she becomes old enough to travel and be an activist, she describes her initial confusion:

> I'd been a catechist since I was a child and had had a lot of ideas put in my head. It prevents us from seeing the real truth of how our people live. . . . I was very ashamed at being so confused, when so many of my village understood so much better than I. But their ideas were very pure because they had never been outside their community. (121)

As Sommers says, ". . . we can note here a hint of Rigoberta's 'descontructed' practice, in which the traditional categorical rigidity is simultaneously revered and sacrificed. For the price of the destabilizing distance from her community she earns some political clarity" (1991b, 36).

That destabilizing distance will result in Rigoberta Menchú being thought of, as she puts it, as a "badly brought-up daughter." She says, "When I saw my father, I was delighted and in front of all the *compañeros*, he said: 'This badly brought up daughter has always been a good daughter'" (Menchú 1984, 183). Her deliberate juxtaposition of the two terms *bad* and *good* make it clear that she understands the sacrifices she has had to make to be where she is, doing what she does; and the father's voice—male, authoritative, loved—makes her decision as a woman all the more complex and even poignant. The "authors," or producers, of testimonios are inherently "badly brought up" by the very fact of their speaking out: in Latin America, especially if the testifier is a woman, she has had to break the imposed silence of social and political forces both within and without her own community that mandate against the entrance of women into the public, political sphere. If Rigoberta had been a man, like her activist father, her political activities on behalf of her community would not have been deemed quite so culturally dangerous to her community itself. However, when Rigoberta wants to go to school, her father opposes it: "my father said he didn't agree . . . because I was trying to leave the community. . . . He said, 'You'll forget about our common heritage . . .'" (88). Having learned Spanish, become an activist, and moved out of the traditional ways of Maya-Quiché women, she is literally a bad *daughter* of her culture, one which imposes and enforces strict separation of gender roles: "The community is very suspicious of a woman like me who is twenty-three but they don't know where I've been or where I've lived. . . . A woman has no problem . . . as long as she obeys the laws of the community" (61, 78).

In this and other ways, Menchú's community is *conservative* in the literal sense of the word; although she remarks for example on her peoples' admixture of Catholic beliefs with their older Maya-Quiché religious practices (49), Menchú also makes it quite clear that her culture uses a rhetoric of purity to maintain its deliberately conservative outlook and, thus, protect itself from colonization and assimilation. The ritualized discourses of the community resist the very idea of mixing (often in more symbolic than actual ways), as in her description of the advice given by the elders of the community to a young couple on their wedding day: "For example, our grandparents say of Coca-Cola: 'Never let your children drink this dreadful stuff because it is something which threatens our culture . . ." (71). Bread made with egg, as the Spanish do it, is a "mixture, no longer what our ancestors ate . . . white men are like their bread, they are not wholesome" (71). This ritualized conservatism, which she identifies with being an Indianist, is much like the "nativism" Edward Said speaks of in his "Yeats and Decolonization" as having "led to compelling but often demagogic assertions about a native past . . . that seems to stand free not only of the colonizer but of worldly time itself. . . . To leave the historical world for the metaphysics of essences . . . is, in a word, to abandon history" (1990, 82).

What disturbs any closed rhetoric of purity is the presence already within the "body politic," so to speak, of foreign "organisms" or agents such as, in the case of Menchú's community, Catholicism. Catholicism has been incorporated into the Indian religious way of life; as such, this constitutes the kind of threatening "mixture" against which the community's elders speak. However, Menchú works *with* rather than against this seeming disjuncture between West and non-West, colonizer and colonized, by resorting to a more useful discourse: that of borrowing and appropriation. She says,

> By accepting the Catholic religion, we didn't accept a condition, or abandon our culture. . . . For instance the Bible tells us that there were kings who beat Christ. We drew a parallel with our king, Tecún Umán, who was defeated and persecuted by the Spaniards, and we take that as our own reality. In this way we adjusted to the Catholic religion . . . and made it part of our culture. (1984, 80–81)

In her testimonio, Menchú will appropriate specific Old Testament figures, such as Judith, whose story becomes a narrative framework to be *used* as the basis for real actions on the part of the women members of her community. In a broad sense, both her work as an activist and her testimonio itself are intertextual; and it is her interpellation of "outside" discourses into her community and into her testimonio that helps to provide for spaces of flexibility within both—spaces from which physically and psychologically the community could carry on its contestation of racist and genocidal practices. Yúdice notes that "[p]opular culture is thus constituted, not as the persistence of timeless customs, but as the adaptation to historical circumstances in order to survive and prosper" (1991, 27).

In spite of her own participation in her culture's struggle to maintain its traditional ways, Rigoberta also knows that to enter into history is to enter a postcolonial place where mixtures abound and where appropriations, borrowings, cooptings have, and perforce will continue, to occur. Like the mixture of Menchú's non-Indian earrings and Indian clothing, in the postcolonial space there is no "pure" place where one finds a "true" and original culture. As Rigoberta herself says,

> The only road open to me is our struggle, the just war. The Bible taught me that. I tried to explain this to a Marxist *compañera*, who asked me how could I pretend to fight for revolution being a Christian. I told her that the whole truth is not found in the Bible, but neither is the whole truth in Marxism, and that she had to accept that. (246)

FEINTS OF THE WEAK—NO "WHOLE TRUTHS"

Debra Castillo's *Talking Back: Toward a Latin American Feminist Literary Criticism* introduced me to Josefina Ludmer's essay "Tretas del débil" (Feints of the weak), which, according to Castillo, "takes the woman (writer) out of a narrow repertoire of options of representability and at the same time reevaluates the importance . . . of a rhetoric derived from the private sphere" (1992, 35). The "feints"—pretended blows, strategic moves to put one's opponent off guard—of the weak imply that the "weak" have their own kind of strength. This strength might be something like that of which Castillo speaks in her chapter on "Latin American Feminist Practice." There, she invokes the (woman) cook who no longer uses book recipes, but throws in whatever she has at hand, much like the *bricoleuse* invoked earlier in this essay: "[a] pinch of this, and a smidgeon of that" (36), a cook/woman/writer who takes "from tradition whatever is salvageable . . . borrow(s) from other writers what is needful and helpful" (36). The metaphor of the cook and recipe, however, as Castillo cautions, while it points to "an index of female creative power," also points to women's own sacrifices and consequent hungers in the role of all-nurturing "cook" (xiv).

My female students are women who come from a relatively restrictive working-class culture. One of the most deeply ingrained assumptions of this largely patriarchal culture is that women get married and raise children. (One of my returning students, a woman with a family and husband, put it this way about her own upbringing: "It wasn't '*if* you get married'; it was always '*when* you get married.'") Thus my female students paid close attention when I introduced the idea that the "personal *is* political," that is, the politics of patriarchy are woven through the entire range of experiences of both men and women, and the supposedly "private" sphere of the home itself is a microcosm of the politics presumably left outside the front door.

What especially got my students' attention was that many of the Latin American activist women and women's movements saw the "personal as political" in a somewhat different light from North American women's movements; that is, that, as Nancy Sternbach explains it, "[i]n a woman's testimony, that line between personal and political is often expressed in terms of her family; it is not unlikely that her role as mother compels her as testimonial subject to enter the public arena" (1991, 97). For my students, the banal objects of kitchen and motherhood were not connected with revolutionary or political action. The strictures and exclusionary tactics of patriarchy are deeply embedded in their view of the home: how can cooking be "political"?

When in Elena Poniatowska's *Massacre in Mexico* one of the many female participants in the demonstration that was to become the massacre in Tlatelolco is handed a milk bottle by another woman who admonishes her to use it against the soldiers, my students were fascinated, and several wrote about this one striking image, the presence of the personal in this highly political, "public" gathering of testimonios. When in her testimonio Menchú described the roles and duties of the women of her community, and the way in which women's work is seen to fit smoothly into the communal whole, my students were intrigued, but they were even more struck by her description of her community's "defense" techniques: "[t]he women brought salt, hot water, etc. . . . the weapons of the people: machetes, stones, hot water, chile, salt. . . . We've often used lime" (Menchú 1984, 127–29). The list: milk bottles, hot water, salt, chile, lime . . . *sounds* like a domestic recipe, but *works* like political, public action. This is not to say that I feel my female students have necessarily become more politically active or even aware by reading *I, Rigoberta*. In fact, I would venture to say that my students were not as a whole even *as* politically aware as Menchú herself is. However, as Ludmer puts it: "If the personal, private, and quotidian are included as a point of departure and perspective for other discourses and practices, they disappear as personal, private, and quotidian: that is one of the possible results of the feints of the weak" (quoted in Castillo 1992, 35).

Through her own "feints of the weak," Menchú's text might provide my female students with points of contact, various (and still ambiguous) places of relationship. This is especially true where Menchú demonstrates what my students feel, that women out of the home are "bad daughters." Here, they could begin to establish a relationship with her testimonio—and this in turn may become a "point of departure." After our class was finished, I informally asked my students about their responses to Menchú's testimonio, its possible "usefulness." Catherine, the African American returning student with a small child, said that reading *I, Rigoberta* had no usefulness in terms of "purpose"; that it wouldn't get anyone a job, for instance. But it did open up a new relation within her between her identity as an African American woman and other oppressed women of color whom she hadn't known about previously—Menchú's narrative could take its place in her consciousness as a North American black woman. For Cathy, a traditional college-age student, an orientation towards Menchú's text provided her with enough "cognitive dissonance" to see the ethnocentrism of her own culture. For Elizabeth, a returning student with a grown family, Menchú's text "opened a door" to her studies of third-world women's resistances to patriarchal systems of power.

CARVING OUT A PIECE OF THE ACTION:
WE ARE UPSTAGED

> In the *mise-en-sène* where the text persistently rehearses itself, writer and reader are both upstaged. If the teacher clandestinely carves out a piece of action (sic) by using the text as a tool, it is only in celebration of the text's apartness.
>
> —*Spivak 1988, 268*

When Spivak writes of "wrenching" the text out of its proper contexts and placing it within "alien arguments," she is advocating looking at a third-world text through the eyes of Western, first-world theory (feminism, Marxism, deconstruction) so that the text *itself* will show the limits of theory (241). In this chapter, I have tried to show that placing Menchú's testimonio within the "alien" *milieu* of a specific North American classroom can foreground the limits of our (uncomplicated) assumptions about the "use value" of such a text. In addition, the strangeness and unfamiliarity of the testimonio means that it too will keep an "apartness." Thus my beginning example of the Indianist Menchú's Western earrings, when used as an image of women's mixtures, appropriations, and confusions, might be an analogy for an intermittant, always partial "use" of her testimonio.

My students often speak, though they don't phrase it in this way, of the price they themselves pay for "book learning," for distancing themselves from conservative, anti-intellectual ideologies. They know that what they learn in my classes, for example, will distance them and make them seem strange to their families and coworkers. Thus their responses are always partial, continually upstaging my expectations as a professor; and we all find that Menchú's testimonio upstages us in its "apartness."

20

NOT JUST PLAIN ENGLISH
Teaching Critical Reading with I, Rigoberta Menchú

CLYDE MONEYHUN

An emphasis on critical reading in composition classrooms is growing in popularity. Reading texts critically does not merely provide composition students with subject matter for their writing, but engenders critical attitudes toward language and the world that will deepen their understanding of the act of writing itself. I encourage a critical faculty in my composition students by asking them to read with a sense of the writer's historical, social, and political context; to respond to texts with a sense of their own historical, social, and political context; to construct a rhetorical situation that contains both themselves and the text; and most of all, to become aware of the tensions and contradictions within the text, within themselves, and within their responses to the text.

For an introductory writing course I often teach at the University of Arizona, I like to assign autobiographies that raise social and political issues relevant to the students' own lives. In the past I have asked students to read Maya Angelou's *I Know Why the Caged Bird Sings*, Lorene Cary's *Black Ice*, Ernesto Galarza's *Barrio Boy*, Richard Rodriguez's *Hunger of Memory*, Mike Rose's *Lives on the Boundary*, and Tobias Wolff's *This Boy's Life*. I have found that these texts serve my purpose of fostering a critical sense in my students because all the writers construct their identities quite self-consciously against a well-defined historical, social, and political background.

I recently added *I, Rigoberta Menchú* to the repertoire of texts used in the course. I learned about the book because at my university, as at many others, it has become a popular text in Women's Studies courses, Native American and Latin American Studies courses, Cultural Studies, and Comparative Literature

Many thanks to the students in classes where I've taught *I, Rigoberta Menchú* who agreed to let me to refer to their work in this chapter, especially Sean DeGarmo, Sarah Keeter, Lynn Leon Guerrero, Geraldine McCabe, and Christina Wood.

courses. After a colleague distributed an excerpt from a chapter to her composition students, I decided to try teaching the entire book. I'm glad I did, because
the complexity of its subject matter and the wide range of possible responses
among North American readers created more challenges for my students and
myself than any text I had ever assigned. It presents just the kind of problematics that I look for in a text for a composition class, since it sets up contradictions between what students assume the text is saying after a first reading and
possibilities for other interpretations. With *I, Rigoberta Menchú*, I was able to
encourage students to question their assumptions about the stability of meaning in any text and in a world they know chiefly through texts. In this chapter
I will sketch some of the intricacies that reading *I, Rigoberta Menchú* presents,
especially to first-year composition students, and I will explain how I taught my
students to experience and deal with these issues for themselves. I hope that
what I say about Menchú's book can be extended into a more general approach
to critical reading, particularly the reading of increasingly popular "multicultural" texts.

Few of my students at the University of Arizona have ever encountered a
text as complex as Menchú's, and few of their high school teachers have taught
literature in the context of the problematics of translation, genre, or rhetorical
intent, all issues that figure prominently in a critical reading of the book. One
of the first questions I raised concerned the mediations of Menchú's narrative,
first through the editing of ethnographer Elisabeth Burgos-Debray, then
through the rendering of translator Ann Wright. (See the first reading journal
assignment in appendix 1.) I stressed I. A. Richards's view of translation as a
negotiation not simply between languages but between mind sets and world
views, so students can recognize that the experience of reading Wright's version
of Burgos-Debray's version of Menchú's version of her life is several times
removed from whatever we might recognize as Menchú's "real world." We
talked about the different intentions and audiences associated with each of the
three writers involved in the production of the text.

I was particularly anxious for them to understand Menchú's testimony not
as a quaint relic from the past but as a product of a late-twentieth-century
world that they share with her. I introduced the idea of the book as "autoethnography," Mary Louise Pratt's name for texts created in the midst of the cultural and political turbulence of "the contact zone": "[I]f ethnographic texts are
those in which European metropolitan subjects represent to themselves their
others (usually their conquered others), autoethnographic texts are representations that the so-defined others construct *in response to* or in dialogue with
those texts" (Pratt 1991, 35). In short, I encouraged them to understand
Menchú's testament as neither a "pure" rendering of Indian life untouched by
European influences, nor a corrupted version of Indian life discredited by
European influences.

As we read and discussed the book, I supplemented it with a number of texts, including a documentary film, that familiarized them with the situation in Guatemala and events in Menchú's life since she wrote the book. The documentary, *When The Mountains Tremble*, features Menchú as an on-screen narrator and includes material on events not covered in the book, such as demonstrations and uprisings in urban centers and the involvement of the Reagan White House in arming and training the Guatemalan military. I also placed on reserve a copy of *Harvest of Violence* (Carmack 1988), one of the best of several anthologies available on recent historical and political events in Guatemala. (See especially Robert Carmack's "The Story of Santa Cruz Quiché," 39–69, and Beatriz Manz's "The Transformation of La Esperanza, an Ixcán Village," 70–89.) The first semester I taught Menchú's book was fall 1992, just when she happened to win the Nobel Peace Prize. Several students brought in newspaper accounts of the event, including one in Spanish (a first language for a number of students in any class in Tucson), as well as other articles about the Guatemalan situation from the international pages of local newspapers, and we added these to the packet of background materials.

I also made a series of writing assignments that are part of the ongoing journal students keep throughout the course. (See appendix 1.) The questions ask students to read, summarize, and respond to portions of the text in fairly straightforward ways. I commented on these journal entries myself and also asked the students to exchange and comment on one another's writing. I invited students to rewrite the entries if any comments prompted them to change their minds about anything they had said. The midterm exam was more of a challenge, asking questions that grew out of in-class discussions and my comments on their written work. In these comments and discussions, I tried to complicate their uninflected views of the text and I challenged them to read the text in more sophisticated ways.

For example, I often encouraged students to examine what I perceived to be their misappropriations of Menchú's text. By interpolating selected pieces of Menchú's story into their own master narratives, they tended to nullify important differences between her experiences and beliefs and their own.

One student linked the Quiché belief in the nahual, or protective animal spirit (Menchú 1984, 18–20), to the Christian concept of guardian angels. I praised her for trying to understand Quiché beliefs in terms of her own, which is after all the only way any of us begins to understand cultures alien to us. At the same time, I asked her to examine differences between the belief systems that gave rise to these two very different relationships to the spiritual world. The student later wrote that the nahual seemed more more immediate, much more of a spiritual presence in the everyday material world, than Christian angels. While angels can seem remote, the student wrote, it would be "very special to have a nahual and know that they are my protector." Thus, beginning from the assumption that Menchú's spiritual beliefs can be understood within the framework of Christianity, the student was able to draw crucial distinctions between the docrines of her own culture's religion and those of Menchú's. My hope was that the student would carry this critical ability to other reading she did about cultures different from her own.

Other students tried to make sense of the political situation in Guatemala from within certain popular versions of American history. One read Menchú's racial attitudes across the narrative of the American civil rights movement, identifying her negative attitude toward ladinos as racial "prejudice," a kind of false consciousness to be overcome through "education." We discussed the civil rights movement, specifying the forms of discrimination it fought against: the systematic oppression of African Americans in housing, education, the political system, and the job market. It became clear to the student that Menchú's "prejudice" did not take these forms and perhaps should not be called "prejudice" at all. Using these ideas, I asked him to define the differences between Menchú's racial attitudes toward ladinos and the racial prejudice of a middle-class, white American who would deny civil rights to people of color. We also talked about the difference between a white American "overcoming racial prejudice" against people of color and Menchú learning to distinguish between ladinos who were oppressors and ladinos who were just as oppressed as the Quiché.

Other students understood the armed rebellion of the Guatemalan peasantry in the context of the American revolution, referring explicitly to the doctrines of the Declaration of Independence. As one put it, "She and her people have the right to take charge of their lives." While I agreed with their general sentiment, I challenged their reinscription of the events in Guatemala as another myth of freedom-loving patriots in the tradition of the Founding Fathers. I asked them to brainstorm differences between the American upper-class revolt against a distant colonial power and the Guatemalan lower-class revolt against a racist, terrorist government. I hoped they would come to read texts in their historical specificity, in this case to distinguish between a ruling colonial elite institutionalizing its power and a colonized native people trying to survive genocide. The myths of righteous revolution are powerful in the United States, however, and my students seemed to resist distinguishing between the Minutemen of 1776 and Guatemalan insurgents of 200 years later.

In addition to reinscribing her story into master narratives alien to her context, a second response to texts such as Menchú's that I saw among my students was a tendency to go to the extremes of either complete identification with her or complete exoticization of her. Anuradha Dingwaney and Carol Maier talk about their distress over the "repeated appropriation" of third-world cultures in many academic settings "under the cagetories of the familiar (same) or the unfamiliar (different)—which inevitably seems to characterize student/reader responses" (1992, 47). Patrick Hogan calls for a reading of works by writers who are unlike us that "allows for freeing oneself from narcissistic constraints and experiencing what one is not—but still on the basis of what one is" (1992, 189–90). I tried to steer students toward a response that recognized both similarities and differences between themselves and Menchú, a response that embraced their shared humanity but acknowledged crucial differences as well.

For example, one student wrote, "Reading *I, Rigoberta Menchú* made me think of the values I live by from when I was born and of things I was taught by my parents." I wanted her to complicate this simple identification, and so I asked which Quiché values she had in mind. At first she replied, "Don't lie, don't use bad language, always be respectful." In elaborating further on the rules her parents taught her, she realized, "Well, I am now 19 and I have disobeyed them in each one of those." This led her to observe, "Just reading about the cultures that Quiché people had, I know that they would never ever disobey what their parents tell them. It is so strange how people's cultures vary from one another and how they are more strict or lenient." The student was inspired to go back to the book and read the opening chapters, which define the cultural values of family obligations, with a new understanding of the possible differences between herself and Menchú.

When a Navajo student wrote, "My people have the same values" as the Quiché, she had little trouble giving examples: respect for nature ("the mother of man"), thankfulness to the natural order for life and sustenance, the preservation of these values through ceremony. I encouraged her to explore these similarities further in her continuing reading of the book, but I also asked her to account for differences between her own personal situation and Rigoberta Menchú's by considering the different histories, cultures, and present politics of the Quiché in South America and the Navajo in North America. This led, later in the semester, to a research paper on the negotiation of water rights on Native American land in northern Arizona, which she placed in the context of the struggles of all native peoples in North and South America, but at the same time specified differences in the ways domination came about for her people and the ways in which it is being fought.

Another student began with an opposite approach to the previous two, putting Menchú at arm's length by writing, "Menchú's people have some interesting values," pointing as examples to Quiché rituals surrounding death and the interesting fact that they are an affirmation of life, and also to the Quiché people's suspicion and mistrust of outsiders. It occurred to me as I read his response that the values he pointed to did not seem as exotic as he made them appear. When I asked, however, he had trouble answering my question about how these Quiché values might overlap with any in his own culture. We talked first about American funeral customs and then about the strong strain of xenophobia in the American character, but in the end the student insisted on Menchú's essential difference from himself. His reaction made me wonder if some readers have too much invested in the belief that their cultural "others" are too "other" to acknowledge the common bonds of humanity.

And finally, a third response my students started with in their interpretation of the book was turning a blind eye to its radical politics. They expressed
the belief that "the good guys" in the Guatemalan struggle are pretty much
like the good guys in American struggles for civil rights and women's liberation. One student wrote, "The poor had to stick together to overcome and
defeat the rich, no matter what their differences." At the same time, most of
them had trouble following the line of such thinking to its conclusion—in
Menchú's case, a leftist revolution that would bring the poor to power and
redistribute the wealth of Guatemalan society. Their thinking was momentarily confused in a productive way when I pointed out that United States has
long supported the government of Guatemala in its suppression of the rebellion, providing both training and arms to the Guatemalan military. Viewing
the documentary *When the Mountains Tremble* was particularly enlightening
for some students, with its scenes of Guatemalan troups descending upon
remote mountain villages in American helicopters, wearing American uniforms and carrying American rifles. Interestingly, few students chose to
answer the midterm exam question that pointed to such issues. It drew their
attention to a scene in the film where Reagan lobbies Congress to send aid to
the government of Guatemala to help it "fight communism" and "build a better democracy," and asked them whether in their opinion "the Guatemalan
army's war against 'subversive' Indians and poor ladinos is a war to 'fight communism' and 'build a better democracy.'"

My students also had trouble transferring their warm and fuzzy feelings of
solidarity with the distant Quiché to any oppressed groups closer to home. The
issues of injustice and righteous rebellion that they understood in the abstract
in the case of the Quiché had little to do in their minds with the widening gap
between rich and poor in the United States, the rights of undocumented workers, the drug trade, the Los Angeles riots. Victor Villanueva mentions a similar
tendency among students (and their teachers) in the curriculum he designed
for a basic writing program. Discussions of *Child of the Dark* by Carolina Maria
DeJesus, a barely literate Brazilian woman, "turn on the cultural," not the political: "Students enjoy the dialogue. But there seems to be no dialectic, no sus-
tained probing into the conditions that relegate certain people to the ghettos
and others to the 'burbs in disproportionate numbers" (Villanueva 1993, 93).
My students were passionate in their denunciation of the Guatemalan's oppression of the Quiché and warm in their support of the rebellion, but told me, as
one student put it in his end-of-the-semester class evaluation, that discussions
extending the political implications of the Guatemalan struggle to the American scene were "off the track."

I didn't want my students to see the qualities I pointed to in their writing
as "amateur's mistakes." I always encourage my writing students to see their
ideas as part of a continuing conversation that includes both less experienced
student writers and more experienced professional writers. Therefore, I

emphasized to my students that I considered their reactions to the book to be on a continuum that includes published critics. I told them that I faulted many published essays for their misappropriations of Menchú's text in the service of a not entirely appropriate master narrative, and I placed on reserve many of the works I mentioned. For example, some feminist critics, while adding crucial perspectives to our understanding of the book, tend to reinscribe its meaning in the text of mainstream Western feminism, particularly literary and academic feminisms (Moya-Raggio, Meese). I also pointed out how some anthropologists and ethnographers echo my students' dual tendency to identify with Menchú and exoticize her at the same time; Rosemary Feal both distances Menchú's text by placing it in the genre of historically remote American slave narratives and domesticizes it by referring approvingly to the tendency of ethnographer/collaborators to lose their own identify in that of their informants. And I explained my belief that, like my students, not enough critics writing on *I, Rigoberta Menchú* have taken its radical politics seriously. Claudia Salazar's otherwise excellent discussion of Menchú's violation of the Western dichotomies of public/private, personal/political, and theory/practice does not point to the most likely source of Menchú's inspiration in this area: practical revolutionary theory, which can be traced in a direct line from Lenin (in "What Is to Be Done?") to Rosa Luxembourg (in *Reform or Revolution*) to Gramsci (in *The Prison Notebooks*) to Mao (in "The United Front in Cultural Work") to Che Guevara (in *Venceremos*) to Paulo Friere (in *The Pedadgogy of the Oppressed*) to the compañeros, or comrades, who trained Menchú and whom she joins in her book as a revolutionary theorist.

Before we are finished reading and writing about *I, Rigoberta Menchú*, some of my students do solve some of the interpretive problems I've been describing. For one in-class writing activity, for example, I asked students to work in groups and write collaborative paragraphs based on their responses to one of the journal assignments. The following class period I asked groups to exchange paragraphs and to rewrite the paragraphs they received, offering a written explanation of the changes they made. One group originally wrote:

> In the beginning of *I, Rigoberta Menchú*, Rigoberta and the other Indian tribes were naive of the cruelty of ladinos. Rigoberta's prayer stated, "We cannot harm the life of one of your children, we are your children" (58). Later in the book as Rigoberta becomes older and more civilized an old lady said to her, "I've got a surprise for you. I've killed a soldier" (146). This statement contradicts the prayer of the Quiché people, but after the old lady had done this everyone was happy and wanted to live again.

The group that rewrote the paragraph made several changes, among them making the meaning of the last sentence clearer by replacing it with another: "By the violent act of killing the soldier, Menchú's organization demonstrated a direct contradiction to their earlier beliefs." More important, however, was a change they made to the third sentence, which they explained in terms of subtle shades of meaning, not just clarity: "We changed the sentence 'Later in the book as Rigoberta becomes older and more civilized . . .' to 'As Menchú traveled, she became educated and learned about self-defense.' You are assuming she was savage instead of just uneducated." Such students have adopted a sophisticated attitude that avoids interpreting Menchú's story through the haze of an inappropriate master narrative (the savage and the civilized) and, instead, approaches it in a way that respects its own conception of itself (a journey of personal enlightenment, a narrative of the political education of an entire people).

Most gratifying to me has been the sometimes delayed reactions of students who carry a critical attitude toward texts with them into other settings. I've run into students from previous semesters who have told me that the experience of reading Menchú's text as we did in the class has caused them to think more critically about issues raised in other courses ranging from American immigration policies to English-only laws, from the right-wing alliance of church and state to the Gulf War. One student mailed me a copy of a paper she wrote on Menchú for an introductory anthropology course in which she reads the traditional rituals that the Quiché struggle to maintain as "a form of resistance" to their oppression, an essentially political act that locates them as dangerously active agents in a modern setting. Such a reading is a far cry from the initial exoticizing view of some of my students that the Quiché are "preserving an ancient culture," an explanation that drains the act of all political meaning and locates them as passive historical curiosities in a safe, quaint, unreal distance.

General reactions to the book and my approach to it were reflected in the students' end-of-the-semester course evaluations. Three trends emerged. First, except for one student who said that he found the book boring and fell asleep every time he tried to read it, response to my choice was overwhelmingly positive. Most preferred it to the other two books we read (Rodriguez's *Hunger of Memory* and Wolff's *This Boy's Life*), partly, I think, because its very difficulty provoked such interesting discussions in class and in their writing. One woman said it was her "new favorite book." A second kind of comment concerned the personal involvement I had insisted upon as a prerequisite to truly critical reading and thinking. As one student put it, "This course has helped me to take my personal experience and combine it with my understanding of a text to create an essay." I was very glad to see that at least one student thought I did a good job of tolerating the very wide range of responses to the text that emerged from the class:

> Most teachers have a set paper that they want written. If you don't write exactly what they want, you don't get a good grade. Clyde is not like that. He realizes that each student has different views and that

those views will not be the same as his or anybody else's. He allows his students to express what they find out when they read on their own and grades them on what they wrote and not on what they did not write.

The third kind of comment is the most interesting to me, from the point of view of composition pedagogy, because it concerns students' perception of what "English class" is all about and the way in which writing is in fact often taught, and the failure of the class to meet those expectations by not being business as usual. First, nearly all the students who mentioned the effects of the class on their writing also mentioned its effects on their reading, like this student: "I think my writing skills and understanding of reading material improved dramatically." Such comments reflect the crucial link in the students' minds between the critical reading they did in the course and the writing that grew out of the reading. To others, the emphasis on critical reading and thinking made the class seem something other than an English class. One said, "I noticed that the class was not just plain English. We discussed many things about the world and the society we live in," and another added, "I liked how the class opened our minds with the help of our peers and teacher. At times, it seemed like it wasn't even an English class. It was that interesting and fun." One student said, in a clever passage that begins with a tongue-in-cheek criticism of the class:

> I didn't learn the technical structure of a paragraph. I didn't learn where and where not to put commas. I didn't learn how to spell. But I learned so much. I learned how to put my thinking into a paper. I learned not just to write a bland, no-thought paper but instead learned how to put something of myself into a paper.

Comments like these say volumes about how irrelevant students think most "English classes" are to the goal "putting thinking into a paper," about what a surprise it is to be in a composition class that challenges their expectations with critical reading and thinking, and about how hungry students are for such a pedagogy.

The original Spanish title of Menchú's book is *Me llamo Rigoberta Menchú y así me nació la conciencia* (literally, My name is Rigoberta Menchú and this is how my consciousness was born). Her use of the word *conciencia* shows her understanding of the revolutionary concept that Freire calls *conscientização* and defines as the growing awareness that the order of things is not inevitable or fated and can be changed. First, however, we must "emerge" from "submersion" in the ideology that constructs the order of things as the only possibility, so that "intervention" to change the status quo is literally unthinkable:

Men *emerge* from their *submersion* and acquire the ability to *intervene* in reality as it is unveiled. *Intervention* in reality—historical awareness itself—thus represents a step forward from *emergence*, and results from the *conscientização* of the situation. *Conscientização* is the deepening of the attitude of awareness characteristic of all emergence. (Freire 1992, 100–1)

As Menchú puts it, "[W]e realized that it is not God's will that we should live in suffering, that God did not give us that destiny, but that men on earth have imposed this suffering, poverty, misery and discrimination on us" (Menchú 1984, 132). One of her first revolutionary duties when she began traveling with her father was to "explain to the children of the community that our situation had nothing to do with fate but was something which had been imposed on us" (119).

To foster truly critical reading in my students, I want them to see that their responses to written texts are in many ways the products of the man-made ideologies that they accept as natural. I want them to see that their understanding of "the real world" is mediated through particular texts, and that they carry these understandings with them to the reading of other texts. I want them to learn to question every understanding they believe they have about a text, so that their understanding is not dictated by an unchallenged master narrative, by the narcisstic belief that everyone is pretty much the same, or by knee-jerk political prejudices. I want to them to locate themselves in relation to the text in a realistic way, asking themselves, "Who is the author? Who am I? How are we similar? How are we different? What are our relative places in the broad cultural and political systems that both connect and divide us? How does our relationship influence what the author says to me and how I make sense of what is said?" I want my students to realize that the meanings of texts, like the meanings of life, are highly unstable, and that it is within their power to negotiate many more meanings than what has been made to seem the most obvious. And from my students' reactions to the course, I would say that they are both capable of learning these things and eager to do it.

21

"THIS IS MY TESTIMONY"
Rigoberta Menchú
in a Class on Oral History

MERI-JANE ROCHELSON

I taught *I, Rigoberta Menchú: An Indian Woman in Guatemala* for the first time in 1993–94, in a two-semester interdisciplinary honors seminar called "Inhabiting Other Lives." Given the title and asked to build a course around it, I found autobiography to be a natural choice. It was important to me (and in keeping with the goals of the honors program) that the students have an academically rigorous experience that would also incorporate intensive independent work. The reading list I developed included Benjamin Franklin's autobiography, the narratives of Frederick Douglass and Harriet Jacobs, World War I memoirs by Vera Brittain and Robert Graves, Elie Wiesel's *Night*, Maxine Hong Kingston's *The Woman Warrior*, and *The Autobiography of Malcolm X*, along with *I, Rigoberta Menchú*. As I taught Rigoberta Menchú's testimony, however, I quickly saw that it would be one of the defining texts of the course, not only through its power as testimony, but also in its interweaving of personal, political, cultural, and historical narratives. In a class that was to spend the second semester writing oral history in independent projects, *I, Rigoberta Menchú* became both model and inspiration.[1]

The students read *I, Rigoberta Menchú* in its entirety, along with the editor's and translator's introductions, during the first semester of the course. Up until that point the readings had been arranged chronologically, so that by the time the students began Menchú's book they had already read and discussed

I wish to thank Stephen M. Fjellman, for encouraging me to teach *I, Rigoberta Menchú*; and my students—Brian Abramson, Carmen Albu, Carmelo Blanquicett, Nadine Charles, Colleen Fallas, Christina Groom, Walter Henao, Lauren Hunchak, Daisy Jacob, Lana Kelsick, Marvine Laurent, John Marek, Michelle Mui, Jeick Nahmias, John Preval, Kirill Resnik, and Ingrid Wynter—for enriching me with their energy, their enthusiasm, their stories, their lives.

Franklin's autobiography, the slave narratives, the World War I accounts, and the Holocaust testimony. While it seems to me curious now that I disrupted chronology to place Menchú's story before those of Maxine Hong Kingston and Malcolm X, both of which dealt with events of an earlier period, my choice was motivated by the feeling that Menchú's history and culture possess both an extremity and a foreignness that align it with the accounts of trauma immediately preceding it in the course. Indeed, one of the comments made in class discussion that found almost universal support was that it was hard to believe Menchú's experiences had taken place so recently (in our own lifetime, as one student noted) and so close to us geographically. Menchú's testimony served as a stimulus for discussion of a great many issues: the meaning, purpose, and value of traditional culture, in society in general as well as in the Central American context; the history and culture of the Quiché themselves, and the ignorance most of us have had of their situation; the role of the anthropologist or historian in recording oral history, and the importance of finding (and for the transcriber, recording) an authentic voice in making one's history known.

The students wrote journal entries on all their readings in preparation for class discussion, which, in the case of Menchú's testimony, occupied two full class periods, plus an additional class led by a guest speaker. For two of the students, Menchú's testimony evoked revelations of their own family histories. A nontraditional-age student reported that Menchú's story reminded him of the experiences of his mother, a Colombian Indian whose father had been kidnapped and killed in the crossfire of a civil war. Another student, whose father was the child of a European immigrant to Argentina, wrote that Menchú's narrative brought to mind her maternal grandmother, a South American Indian whose experiences had been considered unimportant by her descendents. (It would have worked well for the purposes of this chapter if these students had gone on to produce oral histories of their Indian forebears. As it happens, however, the first student had a spring term schedule conflict and the second chose to interview her father. Life is messier than art, and the influence of *I, Rigoberta Menchú* on students' projects was not quite so direct.)

Other students commented favorably, in their journals, on the rich culture and simple lifestyle Menchú described and reacted with horror and anger at the treatment of the peasants by ladino landholders and finca owners and the military. These themes were taken up in class discussion, which also considered some of the more difficult issues raised by contradictions between Rigoberta Menchú's apparently wholehearted support for her culture's values (of endurance of hardship, secrecy, and separation from modernity) and the compromises she herself had to make with those values in order to be an effective revolutionary. Rigoberta Menchú's emphasis on community, her repeated insistence that she was speaking for her group rather than for herself, was recognized as distinctive in terms of autobiography and as part of the revolutionary status of her testimonio.

Another major difference between *I, Rigoberta Menchú* and texts read earlier in the semester was that this narrative was originally oral rather than written, a fact that had significant relevance for students who were examining and experiencing autobiography as a genre—and who would be spending much of the following semester preparing an oral history document very much like Rigoberta Menchú's. The essays of both the translator and the editor were thus especially important insofar as they delineated procedures. Menchú's narrative as we receive it is, after all, mediated by Elisabeth Burgos-Debray, who gathered the data in Spanish, in Paris, "every day for a week," finally accumulating twenty-four hours of taped conversation (Menchú, xv), and, for English readers, by the translator, Ann Wright.

Because this mediation has drawn criticism, I will state at the outset the assumptions and definitions that were implicit in my conception of the oral history projects that the students would carry out. The term *oral history* itself has been controversial, as at least one definition reveals. John Beverley distinguishes between oral history and testimonio—the form of Rigoberta Menchú's narrative—to the detriment of the first:

> In oral history it is the intentionality of the recorder—usually a social scientist—that is dominant, and the resulting text is in some sense "data." In testimonio, by contrast, it is the intentionality of the narrator that is paramount. The situation of narration in testimonio has to involve an urgency to communicate, a problem of repression, poverty, subalternity, imprisonment, struggle for survival, implicated in the act of narration itself. (1992, 94)

My own definition of oral history in fact has more in common with Beverley's description of testimonio. It is taken not from the context of social science but, rather, from its use by archivists of Holocaust survivors' memoirs, which have been collected to maintain a first-person record of the survivors' wartime experiences. Those oral histories (audio and video tapes and their transcriptions) generally have no mediation and resemble testimonio in their function of bearing witness. This subject-centered and subject-driven oral history was the kind I wanted my students to help create.

For their projects, the students were asked to interview a person of their choosing, obtaining at least four or five hours of interview tapes. They would then transcribe the tapes and organize their transcriptions into a coherent narrative, as far as possible in the subject's own words. It would be up to the student "editors" to decide how to organize the material, and how closely to stay with the subject's characteristic language (including whether or when to keep or omit grammatical errors, slang, foreign words, and so on). In this respect, their role would resemble Elisabeth Burgos-Debray's—and would provoke, in them and in me, questions similar to those that have arisen regarding her role as editor.

Unlike the narratives recorded by my students, in which preserving memory was more central a goal than initiating change, Rigoberta Menchú's testimonio is a revolutionary act. Elisabeth Burgos-Debray, a first-world anthropologist who interviewed Menchú in Spanish, the language of her oppressors, has been seen as usurping or appropriating that revolutionary discourse. However, Burgos-Debray has been defended even by commentators well aware of the revolutionary status of Rigoberta Menchú's testimony. John Beverley asserts that "in the creation of the testimonial text, control of representation does not flow only one way" (1992, 100; see also 99). Because Menchú determines what she will and will not tell, because she is "in a sense exploiting her interlocutor in order to have her story reach and influence an international audience," the anthropologist becomes a facilitator rather than a colonizer (100).

Thus, while the introductory chapters by Wright and Burgos-Debray resemble the "authorizing" prefaces and afterwords that abolitionists appended to slave narratives (and even the introduction by François Mauriac, to *Night*) in that they serve as bridges from the dominant culture to the "strange" narrative that will follow, they differ from those others in the degree of self-consciousness with which they perform the bridging function. Unlike William Lloyd Garrison or Lydia Maria Child, Wright and Burgos-Debray are not attesting to the veracity of the account or the reliability of its narrator. Unlike Mauriac, they do not mainly stand in admiring awe of the story that will follow their words. Rather, they recognize the role they themselves play in bringing that story to a wider audience, and thus their comments on method give the reader important guidance in interpreting the narrative.

In designing a project that would enable my students to look at history through a first-person account, I sought to place them in a similarly facilitating position. And far from being inclined to impose their own cultural interpretations upon the narratives they received, these interviewers were well aware of their status as students just starting out, given custody of the life stories of people considerably more experienced than they. We spent a great deal of time on how to listen, and when and what to ask.

Burgos-Debray's account of how she came to know Rigoberta Menchú and gained her confidence provided a context in which to discuss what the relation between narrator and transcriber should be, and allowed us to consider issues of cultural difference and appropriation of discourse. In no case did my students replicate the first-world/third-world pairing of Elisabeth Burgos-Debray and Rigoberta Menchú. The closest examples might be of those students, upwardly mobile by virtue of their university status, who interviewed their working-class parents and grandparents. Still, Burgos-Debray's narrative provided a sense of the baggage that goes along with telling someone else's story and created an awareness in the student interviewers of the responsibilities their position entailed. A student who interviewed a Holocaust survivor reflected as follows on the limitations and responsibilities in her role:

I found myself feeling guilty as I was interviewing [my subject]. She is a fascinating person, who I believe could speak to anyone and have them learn from her, regardless of how much she speaks. Her life goes back sixty-six years and I was interested mostly in the worst part of it. I didn't ask what her best friend's name is, what she would have liked to be as a professional, what she likes most about living in Venezuela.[2]

(In fact, this student did record a limited narrative of her subject's life before and after the Holocaust years.)

I found, and remarked on the fact, that Burgos-Debray's tone seemed condescending in her descriptions of Rigoberta Menchú's clothing and her "open, almost childlike smile" (Menchú, xiv). Her descriptions of the stages of their developing trust and friendship, while obviously sincere, reflect the fragility of those bonds. And yet, the interviewer/transcriber's comments at the end of the introduction are poignant as she explains what she herself gained from the project: "[Rigoberta] allowed me to discover another self. Thanks to her, my American self is no longer 'uncanny'" (xxi). Claudia Salazar alludes to this byproduct in defining Burgos-Debray's task as, in part, "to articulate the antagonistic and complex process of the formation of the 'cultural imaginary'—or ethnic unconscious—of the ladinos (descendents of the Spanish colonizers)" (1990, 8).

The care with which Burgos-Debray and Wright set forth their roles and explain their decisions reflects each one's awareness of the extent to which an oral history project is inherently collaborative. At the same time, the compiler and translator understand that while their contributions facilitate the dissemination of Menchú's narrative, they are also charged with preserving its and Menchú's integrity. Both John Beverley and Claudia Salazar note approvingly Burgos-Debray's decision to "correct the gender mistakes which inevitably occur when someone had just learned to speak a foreign language [because it] would have been artificial to leave them uncorrected and it would have made Rigoberta look 'picturesque'" (Menchú 1984, xxi; Beverley 1992, 99; Salazar 1990, 8). This consideration of how to handle levels of language was a point we discussed in class during the first semester's reading.

My students encountered the issue again during the second semester, in Studs Terkel's *Working*, whose narratives often re-created working-class dialect. There were cases in which I believed Terkel had unnecessarily retained grammatical errors and mispronunciations; I felt they obscured the meanings of his respondents' words and detracted from his speakers' dignity, mimetic though those expressions might have been. Several of the students disagreed and said they felt the exact reproduction of the respondents' language added to its "flavor." When it came time to organize their own transcripts, however, it was evident that most students had found a middle road in which distinctive expressions and speech patterns were retained in the context of a generally grammatical presentation. While I am not naïve enough to think they were uninfluenced by my earlier statements on Terkel and Menchú, some of their "editor's introductions" suggested that as they wrote out the transcripts they found their own levels of comfort. The student who interviewed (in English) a Holocaust survivor who had settled in Venezuela described her decisions this way:

> I found it necessary to make multiple grammatical corrections, most consisting of switching nouns, verbs, and adjectives. The Spanish language places these in different parts of the sentence than English. Nouns were made plural or singular where necessary. Words were included in brackets by me, making better sense of what was said. Some awkward phrases were left where the meaning was not disturbed by them.
>
> The extensive vocabulary is exactly the same. [My subject] has a very well-formed vocabulary, even in English. She has read hundreds of books in many languages. Although she never finished school, I found her to be more educated than many college graduates. (Albu, 6)

Another student, who interviewed her grandmother in St. Kitts, commented similarly:

> I did not have any problems with language or dialect. My Grandmother is very eloquent and well spoken naturally. She prides herself on her vocabulary and speech skills. Truthfully, I in many instances wrote word-for-word what she said, including my questions as part of her answer so as not to leave the reader lost. I did include all the local dialect, which was mainly for flavour here and there, that she used. Properly educated West Indians rarely use bad language—only in areas to "spice" up the story, which is exactly [how] Grandmom used it.[3]

My comparisons of transcripts to final narratives show few differences between the two in many of the papers, which may suggest that changes were made silently in the process of transcribing the audio tapes. Burgos-Debray's statement on organization was influential. Reporting that she had tried several different arrangements of story and information, Burgos-Debray ends by saying that she ultimately followed a chronological organization, with chapters on Quiché ceremonies inserted according to Rigoberta Menchú's own placement of them in her recollections. My students tended to opt, as well, for chronological arrangements that stayed close to the story as recorded.

Rigoberta Menchú's use of Spanish and the subsequent translation into English were discussed as factors that brought her story to a wide audience while simultaneously distancing that story from its origin in Quiché language and culture. In class discussion we found that distance from the reader results at times, too, not only because of the "repetitions, tense irregularities, and sometimes convoluted sentences" left by Ann Wright to recreate Rigoberta Menchú's difficulties with a recently learned language (Menchú, translator's note), but also through Britishisms incorporated by the translator herself, which occasionally added—for American readers—an unexpectedly formal or inappropriately "foreign" tone. Two of my students translated from the Spanish of relatives interviewed, and one student employed a translator who was present at the interviews.[4] In the one case in which I had access to both the Spanish transcription and the English re-creation, I could see that the student frequently condensed the original, in particular omitting much of the dialogue quoted by the speaker. My own sense is that elements of the speaker's tone— her humor, her warm and casual style—were maintained, although her volubility was not reflected in the English presentation. But the precise role that the editor and translator should take in this kind of decision making remained something to be negotiated on the individual level, and something never fully resolved in class discussions. This lack of resolution was itself an important lesson in the oral history project, and made real to the students the ambiguity of the borders between autobiography, biography, and mediated account.

If I were to teach the course again I would use *I, Rigoberta Menchú* much more directly as a model for the second semester's work. I would still, however, keep the two companion texts I introduced in the second half: *Ready from Within: Septima Clark and the Civil Rights Movement*, edited with an introduction by Cynthia Stokes Brown, and *Like It Was: A Complete Guide to Writing Oral History*, by Brown and based on her experiences in writing *Ready from Within* (although it was published earlier). Both books were useful in providing an additional model of oral history and step by step practical instructions for the interviewer, such as what features to look for in a tape recorder and what kinds of specific questions might elicit extensive replies. In its own right, *Ready from Within* is a fascinating account of a crucial but underrecognized participant in the voting rights movement of the 1960s.

I also included on the syllabus selections from Studs Terkel's *Working*, and had the students write a short paper on a section not discussed in class, in which they would, among other things, discuss Terkel's decisions as an oral historian. My intention was to give the students an example of oral history that was more "modern," more reflective of their own experiences. What I hadn't realized was how much has changed in American life since I first read the book when it appeared in the early 1970s. Assumptions about gender roles seemed (oddly though encouragingly) dated, and the apparently compulsive comments of Terkel's subjects on race (whether or not elicited by his unprinted questions) reflected the attitudes and expressions of an earlier stage of awareness. The animus toward college students in many of the accounts seemed nearly incomprehensible to the students in my class, and I needed to do a brief Vietnam-era orientation. So while the readings in *Working* were interesting and fun, they ultimately were less essential than anticipated. What they did convey effectively was the need for sensitivity in transcribing dialect and imperfect grammar and usage. As I have noted, the students engaged in heated discussions on this issue, one that they were encountering immediately in their own interview sessions.

But much of what was reinforced by these later readings was already present in *I, Rigoberta Menchú*. Elisabeth Burgos-Debray's explanation of her editorial choices anticipated many of the same decisions my students would face:

> When we began to use the tape recorder, I initially gave her a schematic outline, a chronology: childhood, adolescence, family, involvement in the struggle. . . . As we continued, Rigoberta made more and more digressions, introduced descriptions of cultural practices into her story and generally upset my chronology. I therefore let her talk freely and tried to ask as few questions as possible. (Menchú, xix)

The problems of organization that obsessed my students as they worked to tame wide-ranging transcriptions are anticipated as Burgos-Debray describes her efforts to integrate descriptions of ritual into the chronological account: "I inserted them at a number of different points, but eventually went back to my original transcript and followed the order of Rigoberta's spontaneous associations. . . . Once the manuscript was in its final form, I was able to cut a number of points that are repeated in more than one chapter" (xx).

The most successful projects in my class followed Burgos-Debray's methods. The students were required to turn in their transcripts along with the final oral histories, so I could see where questions had been deleted and transitions subtly added while the subject's language and emphasis were for the most part maintained. The one student who began by incorporating her subject's hesitations and false starts quickly saw that "um"'s on paper are much more distracting than in conversation.

Several papers might have benefited from greater attention to Menchú's narrative itself as it presented cultural traditions. In class, during the initial reading of *I, Rigoberta Menchú*, we discussed at length the importance of community in the lives of the Quiché and the near-sacred significance of such daily acts as making tortillas and putting on clothing. In teaching the course again I would emphasize, during the second semester, the chapters devoted to birth, coming of age, marriage, and funeral rituals. Through attention to these I would encourage students, first, to allow their subjects to discuss at length such customs or similar details of daily life in their own backgrounds and, second, to present such cultural narratives at length in their final oral histories. One student elicited from her grandmother, the daughter of Lebanese immigrants to St. Kitts, descriptions of island foods and holiday customs, such as making new curtains for the house at Christmas (Kelsick, 5, 22). Joined with the chronological history of her life, these details give a picture of the way of life in which she took part and create a commemoration of traditions that may erode with passing time. Emphasis on Menchú's example would encourage this kind of documentation. The plain speech of Menchú's narration, and the poignancy which that plainness evokes, were apparent as well in many of my students' narratives. Perhaps one can say that this is just the way people talk, but I believe that the power of Menchú's voice helped my students resist the frequent temptation to "make it sound better" or more impressive. Nothing could have been more impressive than the voices I heard in their writing.

The guest lectures that accompanied the reading of Menchú's testimony reinforced the lessons of the text. Janet Chernela, an anthropologist at FIU, introduced the students to the Wanano Indian culture of Brazil, thus placing the customs, values, and behaviors of the Quiché in a wider context. She focused, too, on the role of the anthropologist or ethnographer in gathering data, encouraging student interviewers to have respect for their own questions, whose answers are infinite. Remain attentive, she told them, and you'll end up with much more information than you can use. Maria Firmino, a graduate student who has worked with members of the Maya community in Miami, spoke with the class during the second semester and emphasized the importance of testimony to cultural preservation and historical accuracy. Bernice Wiener, director of oral history projects for the Holocaust Documentation and Education Center, reinforced these points. Using videotapes of actual interviews with Holocaust survivors, she also demonstrated to the students good and bad ways of dealing with emotionally sensitive material in an interview, stressing the importance of knowing when to be silent, when to stop asking a question, as well as when to push on.

The final projects revealed that the students had learned a great deal from the models they had used and advice they had received. Some used the oral history assignment as an opportunity to learn more about their family backgrounds and about relatives to whom (they were sometimes surprised to learn) they became much closer in the process. In addition to the young woman who interviewed her grandmother, three students interviewed their fathers, one her mother-in-law, and one her great-grandmother. Three students interviewed Holocaust survivors: a Jewish student who interviewed an older cousin, an African American student, and a non-Jewish student from Romania who interviewed a Romanian Jewish survivor.[5] Other students interviewed a professor who is a World War II veteran; an advisor who, as a successful African American woman, was an influential role model; an admired karate instructor; a Peruvian immigrant; and a leader of the South Florida Seminole tribe. While some students chose to interview a person of similar background to their own, others intentionally sought out other ethnicities or histories about which they wanted to learn more. Students were required to write an introduction to their oral histories, in which they would recount not only their goals in the project (including what they learned and what surprised them) but also their procedures—the decisions they made regarding levels of language, organization, and what to include or exclude. All the students were required to present their subjects' stories orally to the class and were encouraged to bring in photographs, videotapes, or any other visual aids—which they did, with excellent results. Photographs were appended to several of the narratives in their final projects.

In part because I saw it as academically sound (giving the students a broader perspective on their subjects' histories) and in part to make up for the limited role they would have in editing, I required the students to compile a brief bibliography of secondary works related to their subject's home area or participation in historical events. Information from these sources would be used in creating "editor's notes," discussions to be interspersed in the narrative, while also set off from it, as a way of providing the reader with needed background or explanations. Although each student was required to (and did) submit the bibliography in advance, this in many cases was the least successful part of the project. While some students effectively incorporated secondary and primary information, in most of the projects the editor's notes were cursory, at best. But the primary accounts—the oral histories themselves—were in nearly every case detailed, complete, and powerfully moving. The influence of Rigoberta Menchú's testimony was apparent to me in the remarkable work I received.

I asked the students to write thank-you letters to the people who had given them so much of their time, energy, and emotion, and to send them each a copy of the oral history after submitting it to me.[6] I hope the letters they wrote conveyed to their recipients what the students made clear to me, often indirectly: that not only did they learn a great deal from the narratives they heard and recorded but that they also gained a sense of their own accomplishment and achievement in documenting this testimony. In addition, their role as chroniclers of the lives of participants to greater or lesser extents in twentieth-century history gave the students a clearer view of their own relation to those larger currents. One student who interviewed a Holocaust survivor concluded that she herself would now be one more "witness" to refute the deniers.[7]

One may question, of course, whether it is really possible to "inhabit other lives." One may question the possibility of accurately presenting testimony in a document produced through collaboration with an outsider. My own view, supported by the student oral histories I read and heard narrated, is that the gain in knowledge and understanding is well worth the effort, however imperfect the result (and frankly, I hesitate to use the term *imperfect* to describe the work I encountered). At a time when restrictions on Haitian immigration were being debated in government and the press, it was useful and important for all of us to hear the testimony of a student's father who had emigrated from Haiti a generation ago. This moving account of his life and views was prefaced by the student's modest statement that "he lived a rather uneventful life; unlike all the other subjects people use to interview, nothing traumatic or remarkable happened to my father, it was just business as usual."[7] *I, Rigoberta Menchú* allowed my students, as far as possible, to inhabit the life of the Quiché people. But it also helped give them the tools to enable other voices to be heard.

NOTES

1. Page numbers referenced in this chapter are from Menchú 1984 unless otherwise indicated.

2. Carmen Albu, editor's introduction, "If Not for the Flames" (unpublished paper, 1994), 7. While all the interview subjects were told by the students that their professor would read the oral histories, I did not ask for permission to quote them in this chapter. Therefore, I have limited my quotation to the students' introductions, and have concealed the names of the people whose stories are told.

3. Lana Kelsick, introduction to "The Biography of [My Grandmother]: A Legend, A Lady" (unpublished paper, 1994), no page.

4. This last seemed to me a less than ideal arrangement, although the translator was both trustworthy and committed to the project.

5. I am grateful to Rositta Kenigsberg and Bernice Wiener of the Holocaust Documentation and Education Center, whose offices are located at Florida International University, for their generous assistance in introducing these last two students to their interview subjects.

6. In *Like It Was*, Brown makes a point of advising students *not* to present their work to the subject before submission to the instructor, although she adds that the subject should be allowed to review the manuscript before any publication (1988, 44).

7. Nadine Charles, "A Rose among Ashes: An Oral History of the Life of [ ]—A Jewish Survivor of the Holocaust," (unpublished paper, 1994), ii.

8. John Preval, introduction to "The Life of [My Father]" (unpublished paper, 1994), no page.

COMPARATIVE
STRATEGIES

22

RIGOBERTA MENCHÚ'S TESTIMONY AS REQUIRED FIRST-YEAR READING

JONNIE G. GUERRA AND
SHARON AHERN FECHTER

This chapter details the use of *I, Rigoberta Menchú: An Indian Woman in Guatemala* as a required text in a first-year general education core course at Mount Vernon College, a liberal arts institution for women located in the nation's capital. The course, "American Culture and Identity in the Global Context," received national recognition from the Association of American Colleges in 1991.

In the late 1980s and early 1990s, the faculty at Mount Vernon College undertook the reform of the general education requirements in order to strengthen the liberal arts core of the institution. As educators at a women's college, faculty recognized that one contributing factor to the "chilly climate" for women in higher education was what Adrienne Rich, as well as other feminists, has described as the "almost total erasure of women's experience and thought from the curriculum" (Rich 1979, 232). It became apparent that even at a women's college, traditional liberal arts study carried out through discipline-specific distributional requirements placed emphasis on how men perceive experience and what men think is important. Thus, our top priority was to create the cornerstone for a multi-year vertical core in liberal studies that would orient students to the liberal arts within the context of an interdisciplinary course that highlighted women's lives, dilemmas, and choices and exposed students to "great issues" through the reading of texts written by women.

Since the mission statement committed the college to encourage students to develop a global perspective, the faculty team sought texts that would represent cultural diversity and expand students' understanding and appreciation of cultures other than their own. The team's definition of "cultural diversity" encompassed differences that were the consequence of class, gender, race, ethnicity, and historical period as well as of geopolitical structures. Our intention was to locate works that would invite comparisons of different assumptions about and perspectives on women's lives from book to book and culture to culture, as often as possible through the portrayal of conflicting cultures within individual texts.

Faculty involved in the design and development of the new course included specialists in language, literature, women's studies and social science, all of whom shared an interest in women's testimony, oral and written. Previous experience had convinced us that the narrative structure and personal voice of testimony made it a form of reading accessible to first-year students on many levels. Because of the multiple dimensions, such texts also promised to raise issues that would broaden the course focus to other liberal arts disciplines—economics, philosophy, political science, and anthropology, to name a few. Moreover, we believed that, more than other forms, testimony allowed women's voices to be heard unmediated.

As the syllabus took shape, the course became a consideration of the cultures of the Americas emphasizing the evolution of pluralistic values through the study of individual lives and social change over time. The thematic center for the course was the quest for freedom and justice as a continual process carried out by figures representing diverse cultural backgrounds. We wanted students to consider how identity is forged by the complex interaction of cultural history, family experience, factors like gender, race, and ethnicity, and the values and mores of particular cultural contexts. We also wanted them to investigate how social change occurs and the role of individuals in the creation and rebuilding of systems—social, governmental, economic, religious, and ethical—to achieve the ideals of freedom and justice.

Rigoberta Menchú's testimony was chosen as a powerful means of accomplishing several of the course's intended goals. First, the use of her narrative helped us to expand the definition of "American" culture to include cultures of the Americas beyond that of the United States. It also presented issues of class, race and ethnicity, and gender that were relevant to the course's thematic center. Rigoberta's life and her struggle, as well as her own choice of testimonio as her preferred vehicle of communication clearly illustrated the way in which social change is effected through the life of an individual as well as through the individual lives whom the witness/narrator represents. Just as important, her testimony provided an excellent opportunity to relate historical phenomena to contemporary outcomes. Topics introduced early in the course involving cultures of precolonial America would gain historical relevance within *I, Rigoberta* and its contemporary setting. Themes that spiraled throughout the course regarding women's lives, work, and witness—from Native American creation myths and Harriet Ann Jacobs's narrative of her life in slavery, *Incidents in the Life of a Slave Girl*, to the diaries of pioneer women and the autobiography of union organizer Mother Mary Jones—would find new meaning through the touchstone of Rigoberta's story.

At first, our discussions of Rigoberta's testimony were focused upon traditional themes—family, personal relationships, community—and how these might be used to make connections to other works. We felt that the students would be engaged by Rigoberta's explanations of cultural practices among the Quiché Indians and hoped they would grasp the timelessness of her world vision through their exposure earlier in the course to pre-Columbian cultures in general and cultural values in particular. We were sure that parallels between Rigoberta's life and relationships and the lives and relationships of women in these earlier cultures would be readily drawn and accessible to first-year students.

As we became increasingly convinced of the importance of the sociopolitical content and implications of the work, this focus became more prominent in our deliberations about how best to use Rigoberta's testimony as the culminating reading of the course. We were concerned that, no matter how compelling Rigoberta's story of the political struggle in Guatemala, our students would find it difficult to relate to immediately and perceive a comfortable distance between themselves and the reality of the situation Rigoberta was describing. Thus, our pedagogical dilemma became the need to shorten this distance: to focus their attention on the importance of testimony as a vehicle for social and political change as well as to provide a detailed but concise delineation of the struggle in Guatemala and of human rights issues in general.

While some scholars insist that Latin American testimonio came into being as a narrative genre, of which Rigoberta's work is but one example, in the 1960s (Beverley 1992, 93), others find a very close relationship between Menchú's testimony and the American slave narratives (Feal 1990, 105). Citing Olney's summary of the formal features of slave narratives included in *The Slave's Narrative* edited by Davis and Gates, Feal notes that Rigoberta's tale communicates an urgent social message in the form of an appeal in the present. This is, of course, virtually identical to Jacobs's narrative and narrative intent. The narration of both of these witnesses clearly contains the elements cited by Beverley as the hallmarks of testimonio; that is, both contain an *urgent* need to communicate and both express a problem of repression, poverty, subalternity, imprisonment, and a struggle for survival (Beverley 1992, 94).

Menchú's narrative begins and ends with her declaration of intent:

> My name is Rigoberta Menchú. I am twenty-three years old. This is my testimony. I didn't learn it from a book and I didn't learn it alone. I'd like to stress that it's not only *my* life, it's also the testimony of my people. . . . what has happened to me has happened to many other people too. My story is the story of all poor Guatemalans. My personal experience is the reality of a whole people. . . . The world I live in is so evil, so bloodthirsty, that it can take my life away from one moment to the next. So the only road open to me is our struggle, the just war. . . . That is my cause. . . . That is why I've travelled to many

places where I've had the opportunity to talk about my people. (1984, 1, 246, 247)

Similarly, Harriet Ann Jacobs declares:

> I want to add my testimony to that of abler pens to convince the people of the Free States what Slavery really is. Only by experience can anyone realize how deep, and dark, and foul is that pit of abominations. . . . Reader, it is not to awaken sympathy for myself that I am telling you truthfully what I suffered in slavery. I do it to kindle a flame of compassion in your hearts for my sisters who are still in bondage, suffering as I once suffered. . . . In view of these things, why are ye silent, ye free men and women of the north? Why do your tongues falter in maintenance of the right? God bless those, everywhere, who are laboring to advance the cause of humanity. You may believe what I say; for I write only that whereof I know. I was twenty-one years in that cage of obscene birds. I can testify, from my own experience and observation, that slavery is a curse to the whites as well as to the blacks. (Jacobs 1987, 1–2, 29–39, 52)

Importantly, both narrators understand the inherent danger involved in the act of testifying. Harriet Ann Jacobs writes under the pseudonym Linda Brent and intentionally masks the identities of both people and locations. Rigoberta asserts "I am still keeping my Indian identity a secret. I'm still keeping secret what I think no one should know. Not even anthropologists or intellectuals, no matter how many books they have, can find out all our secrets" (1984, 247).

What, in the first year, was a spontaneous exercise generated by student interest in the comparisons between the texts became a planned in-class assignment in the following year. Beginning with the observation made by one student that Rigoberta's memories of her childhood life on the finca called to mind "Harriet Ann Jacobs's fears for herself and her children when Dr. Norcom plotted to send them to his son's plantation," we asked the class to break themselves into small discussion groups to explore similarities and differences between the women, their lives, and their testimonies. The idea was for the groups to brainstorm for fifteen minutes, then to select three key similarities and three key differences to share with the class as a whole. A second-year addition to the assignment asked the students to pinpoint specific textual illustrations to support their comparisons and contrasts. The discussions that this assignment precipitated were illuminating to the students and even caused us to see the works in provocative new ways. Through a summary that includes some student-generated ideas and insights about the lives and texts as well as some issues that raised questions or caused confusion for students in our discussions, we hope to demonstrate the possibilities for using *Incidents* and *I, Rigoberta* together in a women's studies or interdisciplinary humanities course.

One specific connection between the testimonies, cited frequently by the students, was the cruel, dehumanizing treatment of their people, including family and self, that both Harriet Ann Jacobs and Rigoberta Menchú detail graphically. Such treatment, the students realized, represented both a cause and an obstacle to each woman on her quest for freedom. All of the students, even those who were international, claimed familiarity with the American Civil War and its causes, yet, for many, knowledge of the peculiar institution of slavery was superficial at best. Those who had not been exposed previously to the genre of slave narratives were horrified at the atrocities against slaves Jacobs presented in *Incidents*, both the stories of brutal physical abuse collected in the chapter "Sketches of Neighboring Slaveholders" and the prolonged tale of psychological abuse Jacobs described herself enduring from the age of fifteen when Dr. Norcom, her master, began his persistent campaign to gain her submission to his sexual demands. About the sexual harassment and abuse of slave women in particular, students knew virtually nothing; their interest in these topics was keen, no doubt in part because current events had heightened their consciousness about harassment issues generally. If most of the students could empathize with Jacobs's personal dilemmas and outrage, admire her courage, and savor her victory over her oppressor, others were resistant readers and, denying any contemporary relevance, distanced themselves from the issues raised by her testimony. In their minds, slavery was wrong, but, in the words of one student whose response was typical of the minority opinion, "Slavery belongs to a different century and could not happen in our country today."

Reading Rigoberta Menchú's testimony to the oppression of the Indians in Guatemala posed a challenge to such a complacent attitude, and, no doubt for this very reason, some students deemed it "too morbid" and "depressing." Students openly acknowledged their shock when, during the introductory lecture on Guatemalan history and politics in the twentieth century, they learned about the traditions of torture that were customarily employed by the government against political dissidents. But only after they read Rigoberta's moving accounts of the torture and death of her sixteen-year-old brother burned alive in front of his family and of the kidnapping, torture, rape, and murder of her mother—in which Rigoberta painstakingly names every atrocity that was inflicted on her beloved family members, did many students grasp fully the meaning of the term *human rights violations* that had figured centrally in the history outlined for them. Writing about the testimony in their journals, many students admitted to their acute discomfort with Rigoberta's story, noting that they had become physically sick from the descriptions, had cried, or felt anger. Many also commented on the strength of character that enabled Rigoberta, after witnessing her brother's death and losing both parents to the revolutionary struggle, to relive these terrible moments in creating her testimony. A few, however, responded politically rather than emotionally, expressing a desire to do "something" on behalf of Rigoberta Menchú and the Guatemalan Indians. At that time, Mount Vernon had a chapter of Amnesty International on campus, and several students began to attend the group's meetings. To our knowledge, no other political action resulted. Overall, like Harriet Ann Jacobs, Rigoberta Menchú became for our students a role model for personal courage, though a number candidly admitted doubt about their own abilities to endure such suffering and abuse as had been routine in the lives of these two women.

An important mark of the women's courage was, in the students' eyes, each one's decision to become a fugitive, and this similarity between them also was regularly cited in class writings and discussions. Ironically, however, we found ourselves needing to intervene when students attempted to pit the two figures against each other for the purpose of judging whose suffering was more gruesome or whose life as a fugitive was nobler. For homework, we assigned the students to review the testimonies for specific passages in which the women analyzed their dilemmas and explained their choices *in their own words*. As a starting point, we suggested that they look again at chapters 16, 21, 29, and 41 in *Incidents* and chapters 17, 19, 32, 33, and 34 in *I, Rigoberta*.

In the next class, the students presented and debated their findings, a process that enriched their understanding of both texts. This brief summary outlines their conclusions, but does so in our own more polished prose: Both women chose a fugitive life out of necessity. Harriet Ann Jacobs became a runaway slave out of determination to save her children from slavery and, to a lesser extent, to foil Dr. Norcom's plot to make her his concubine. Once Jacobs accomplished her immediate ends, her focus turned to the existential indignities associated with slavery, particularly being identified as the property of another human being and therefore capable of being purchased and sold. In contrast, from the beginning, Rigoberta's fugitive existence was politically motivated, a part of her revolutionary mission to save her people from exploitation and discrimination. Indeed Rigoberta's only hope to remain alive was as a fugitive. Unlike that of Harriet Ann Jacobs, Rigoberta Menchú's testimony did not conclude with an end to her fugitive existence and a celebration of freedom but rather with a renewed commitment to the revolutionary struggle of her people.

Part of the success we had in teaching these works was due to their dramatic aspects: portrayals such as Harriet Ann Jacobs's escape from slavery and living conditions for seven years in an attic crawlspace, coffin size, above her grandmother's house and Rigoberta's narrow escape from death in Huehuetenango after she was spotted on the street by soldiers who called her by name and pursued her in their jeep. For traditional-age student readers whose tastes had been shaped by their television viewing more often than not, the testimonies of Harriet Ann Jacobs and Rigoberta Menchú offered sufficient suspense and adventure to engage and hold their attention. Frequently, in fact, students commented in class, sometimes in self-surprise, that they had not stopped reading until they finished one or the other of the books. Such testimony on the part of students constitutes a significant recommendation for teaching both texts.

An important theme throughout "American Culture and Identity in the Global Context" was the role of education and literacy in shaping the figures we studied as well as their quests for freedom and justice. One topic that we introduced for student reaction, because it had been overlooked in the initial discussion of similarities and differences between *Incidents* and *I, Rigoberta,* was the empowerment each woman experienced as a result of language, literacy, and storytelling. The students knew from our study of *Incidents* earlier in the semester that Harriet Ann Jacobs had received no formal education and was literate purely by an accident of fate: although it was against the law for slaves to be taught how to read and write, Jacobs had learned both from her first mistress. Together we had traced how Jacobs had used her literacy, first, to trick Dr. Norcom into searching for her in New York while, in reality, she was hiding in her grandmother's garret and, later, to help the "two millions of women at the South, still in bondage, suffering what . . . [she] suffered" (Jacobs 1987, 1) by writing her life chronicle with its impassioned personal testimony to the sexual exploitation of slave women.

When the students thought about Rigoberta Menchú, they recognized both similarities and differences from Harriet Ann Jacobs with regard to the theme of language and empowerment. Like Jacobs, Rigoberta never attended school. However, it was not until she reached the age of twenty that Rigoberta, helped by nuns, learned to read and write and to speak Spanish. Her decision to learn Spanish was consciously made and politically motivated, intended as a strategy that would both assist her as a political organizer and enable her to tell her story to the world. Rigoberta recognized and articulated her need to dominate the language of her oppressor, much as Harriet Ann Jacobs did. At the same time, and without violation of her own cultural and political values, she would be able to communicate the urgency of her message as well as broaden her horizons and communicate with other oppressed peoples. In an interview conducted prior to the Quincentenary, when Rigoberta was asked what significance learning Spanish had upon her own cultural identity, she responded:

> I learned Spanish because I needed to; when I left my Quiché community I realized that otherwise it would be impossible to share experiences with brothers from other places. Understanding the language of a people means the possibility of understanding their universe, their world, their ideas. Spanish has given me the opportunity to know something about the lives and struggles of other peoples, from South Africa to the Amazon. Also, I have seen how important it is for the

natural leaders of a community to learn a universal history that
enables them to develop a solider, broader consciousness. I value
Spanish as a means of communication and of learning. I wish I could
speak more languages. (Yáñez 1992, tr., 97)

The point we wanted to get across to students was that Rigoberta, like Jacobs,
was persuaded to recount her history not for personal gain, but to establish a
public record documenting the oppression and victimization of her people.
Just as important, each woman's testimonial broke silence on a taboo subject
and forced readers to confront what had heretofore been carefully hidden or
purposely suppressed from public knowledge.

When we asked the students to comment about drawbacks of testimony,
they came up with several insightful ones. One student suggested that the
author could implicate other people and get them in trouble. In response, several of her peers remembered ways in which both authors had exercised caution
to avoid creating risks for others. Harriet Ann Jacobs had used pseudonyms
throughout her narrative, even for herself, and Rigoberta had omitted information that she thought might put other compañeros in danger. Another student noted that the audience might prefer not to know about the events an
author was bearing witness to in his/her testimony. This observation provoked
a heated discussion of the advantages, burdens, and responsibilities that
accompanied knowledge, and though producing no resolution, it certainly
gave the students much food for thought. So did our reminder to them that, by
the turn of the century, Jacobs's testimony was regarded as a false slave narrative
and not restored to credibility until Jean Fagan Yellin, in the 1980s, authenti-
cated Jacobs's authorship and confirmed the people, places, and incidents
detailed in Jacobs's story.

A final thematic area that we explored with our students was gender. Since
this topic had been one of the foremost in course discussions throughout the
semester, the students were virtually conditioned to think about it, regardless
of the text they were reading. In our comparative study of *Incidents* and *I,
Rigoberta*, each work provided a provocative touchstone for the other as far as
the gender issues it raised. During our engagement with Jacobs's text, we had
provided the students with some background on the cult of true womanhood
that influenced how women were viewed and viewed themselves in the nineteenth century. Under the terms of this ideology, a woman was expected to be
sexually ignorant and to remain a virgin until her marriage. For Jacobs to tell
her story, then, she had to reveal her own disgrace: as a single woman, she not
only possessed sexual knowledge (the consequence of being sexually harassed
by Dr. Norcom and then, in assertion of her autonomy, of deliberately becoming the mistress of another white man, lawyer Samuel Sawyer), but also had
borne two children out of wedlock from her illicit liaison with Sawyer. On the
one hand, Jacobs expressed genuine sorrow and humiliation about her past life;

on the other, she assumed full responsibility for her actions and courageously planted in the minds of her readers the suggestive seed that slave women should not be judged by the standards of white morality as long as their sexual exploitation remained legally sanctioned under slavery.

In turning to Rigoberta's testimony, we asked the students to develop a cult of true womanhood according to the traditions of the Quiché Indian culture. This journal assignment elicited a variety of responses ranging from descriptions of traditional clothing, methods of tortilla making, and courtship practices to cultural beliefs about women's relationship to the earth and definitions of machismo. The students agreed that a typical Quiché woman could expect her destiny to include marriage, motherhood, and a hard life. Rigoberta's mother passed along these expectations for women to her daughters, but she also encouraged her children, regardless of gender, to participate in the revolutionary struggle. The students came to understand the depth of Rigoberta's political commitment through a consideration of what she gave up in order to dedicate her life fully to the struggle. For Rigoberta, the competing obligations of her life—as a Guatemalan Indian woman, "to multiply the seed of . . . [her] ancestors"(1984, 224); as her parents' daughter, to serve her people as a revolutionary leader—could not be reconciled. Her testimony records her renunciation of both marriage and motherhood and her regret in making this choice. Some students argued that Rigoberta's traumatic memories of the deaths of her brother, father, and mother seemed to have left her with a profound fear of further loss; by her own admission, they pointed out, she did not ever "want to be a widow or a tortured mother"(225). Their sense of her morbidity arose from Rigoberta's apparent belief that, if she achieved personal happiness through new family relationships with a husband or children, she would inevitably become vulnerable to a reversal of fate.

The comparative approach to Rigoberta's testimony was a fruitful one. The power of Rigoberta's narrative voice and her role as protagonist of her testimony, coupled with her explicit and urgent need to communicate, found resonance in the life and witness of not only Harriet Ann Jacobs, but also of other "representative" American figures whose lives we investigated. For the final examination, students were asked to consider the effect of an individual's culture (ethnic, familial, religious, etc.) and historical period on the development of his/her identity in an essay that discussed Rigoberta Menchú and four other *real life* (the very heart of testimony) people studied during the term. Not surprisingly, many of them chose to include Harriet Ann Jacobs as well. That they were able to make important connections among the witnesses/narrators we studied was testimony to us that we had been able to eradicate the distance between Rigoberta Menchú and themselves. In fact, the student who wrote the following spoke for many of her peers when she evaluated *I, Rigoberta* as "excellent, because I know more about Guatemalan culture and their agony." As feminist scholars and teachers, we were pleased with the success of our comparative approach to Rigoberta's testimony for another reason. Treating *I, Rigoberta* in conjunction with Harriet Ann Jacobs's *Incidents in the Life of a Slave Girl* helped our students view each work as part of a tradition of women's writing. It was important to us that our students recognize that women's voices are powerful and articulate sources of testimony on issues significant to their historical times and places. Too often women students are exposed only to the polemical writings of men and come to understand concepts like freedom and justice from an exclusively male perspective. When given the opportunity to explore women's writing on the same topics—most often, as in the case of *Incidents* and *I, Rigoberta*, in the form of personal testimony rather than straight polemic, women students experience an enriched engagement with history and culture and a new appreciation for the role women have played in their creation.

A WINDOW OF OPPORTUNITY
An Ethics of Reading Third-World Autobiography

JANET VARNER GUNN

I will never forget the first time I stood in front of a university classroom in the fall of 1966. It was packed with the composition students I would be teaching as a part-timer at a large urban campus in Chicago. Names like Mary Ellen Arpino, Lois Leposky, Joan Krishko, and Ron Sigada reminded me of my own classmates back in the western Pennsylvania mining town where I was born. Part of the Anglo-Saxon minority in Portage, I had grown up feeling both superior to and excluded from the Italian and Eastern European Catholics whose lives I observed with both fear and envy through the window of my Republican childhood.

Those people were the "foreigners," according to my great-Aunt Mary who had come to the United States from Scotland when she and my grandmother were still toddlers. Annie Dillard's western Pennsylvania childhood was spent in fear and envy of the Irish Catholic Jo Anne Sheehys who, in Dillard's *An American Childhood* (1987), ice-skated in the winter street outside her Point Breeze house in Pittsburgh. In my own adolescence, I was in awe of the Mary Ellens and the Joanies whose bodies glided with their own "radiance" across the teen canteen dance floor.

As soon as I began calling the roll on that first day of composition class, I knew that I would be canceling most of the supplementary texts I had added to the anthology of essays departmentally required for all composition sections. I would make room on the syllabus for my students' lives. The course, I hoped, would be a larger window on American ethnicity.

After leaving Chicago for Chapel Hill some ten years after I began my teaching career, Annie Dillard's autobiography, had it been published by then, might have been the model of the book I wanted to write about growing up in western Pennsylvania. Having left the flat plain of the Middle West, I found myself again in the Back Country whose low mountains chained down the Alleghenies to the Carolina Piedmont. But instead of writing my own autobiography, I returned to graduate school at the end of my first year in North Carolina so that I could develop a theory of autobiography that employed the writing of others.

Four years after publishing my dissertation, I left for a city among other hills halfway around the world. Divorced by then and taking my first sabbatical since starting out in that Chicago classroom, I decided that I wanted to turn fifty in Jerusalem, not Greensboro, North Carolina, where I was a tenured professor of religion and literature. It was on my subsequent return to Jerusalem that I first read Dillard's *An American Childhood*. Having taken the sabbatical to begin a book on holocaust autobiography, I later went back to Jerusalem to work and study on the Palestinian West Bank.[1]

It was in the third world, then, that I first read Annie Dillard's autobiography and, as it turned out, began writing my own. I say, "as it turned out," because I didn't realize how much of my own life was implicated in a book I began to write about a Palestinian refugee family. Gaining access to the life of that family was not a matter of getting outside my own window but of acknowledging that it was there: I was looking at them from somewhere. How the window of my own life both blocks and facilitates the telling Palestinian lives was part of the story I wanted to tell.

The information I have been supplying thus far is not personal background but critical foreground to the more explicit argument I want to develop about an ethics of reading third-world autobiography, which begins with the reader, not with the text. Defining the location of that reader is the first interpretive task for such an ethics. The next interpretive task requires the interrogating of that location. Defining and interrogating the reader's location finally affords the reader what Edward Said calls a "wider optics"—a new and expanded location that can move interpretation toward transformation or what George Yúdice (1989) has called an "ethics of survival," which engages the autobiographical activity of the first-world reader as well as the third-world text. Along the way, I will be addressing the differing functions of the "other" in first- and third-world representations of selfhood and identity.

I, Rigoberta Menchú: An Indian Woman in Guatemala is the third-world autobiography I want to use. A life history set in a country that accounts for more than half of the disappeared in Latin America, *I, Rigoberta Menchú* is a counterstory that works against such disappearance to the extent that it testifies to the appearance of her people on the stage of history and names the harsh reality in which they live. It is furthermore a resistance story about directing that history and transforming that reality.

Life stories like Menchú's emerged in Latin America after the Cuban Revolution and were elicited by other more privileged women like the Venezuelan anthropologist Elizabeth Burgos-Debray, who edited and inscribed Menchú's story. She interviewed Menchú in Paris, where the Guatemalan had been invited in 1982 to participate in a conference sponsored by the 31 January Popular Front. The organization's name commenorates the day in 1980 when Menchú's father and other early leaders of the Committee of Campesino Unity had been burned to death during their peaceful occupation of the Spanish embassy in Guatemala City to protest military repression in their villages.

Latin American women like Burgos-Debray were trying to overcome their own marginality in a patriarchal culture. Through such testimonials as Menchú's, they wanted to show that oppressed people were subjects and not merely objects of national histories. The inscribers of these testimonials were also raising questions about the negative aspects of the concept "third world" with its connotations of dependency and racial backwardness. They were helping to redefine "third world" as a positive term of radical critique against colonalist policies both inside and outside Latin America.[2]

When I returned to my teaching career in the United States, I decided to use *An American Childhood* as a point of embarkation for the course on third-world autobiography, which I team-taught with an anthropologist.[3] An auto-biography like hers, we agreed, could be useful in defining our own location since most of us, like Dillard, had had a middle-class American childhood. More than that, Dillard would help us to measure the distance between our lives and Menchú's, in their differing modes of self-representation as well as their material conditions.

In beginning the course with Dillard, we began to appreciate some of the differences between what I called "autobiography of nostalgia" and the testimonial. The former represents a mainstream tradition of self-writing in the industrialized West and North. A strategy of recovering what would otherwise be lost, autobiography of nostalgia is directed toward the past. The autobiographer's identity depends not only on recovering this past but on individuating his or her experience of the past. Childhood memories are especially important since it is in that period that the process of individuation has its start. That process is experienced as separation, painful but necessary to establish a self/world boundary that must be kept essentially intact to assure the unique individuality on which identity is based. Growing up requires the self's outward movement into the world, but in such a way that a sense of boundary is maintained and even sharpened by experiences of otherness. The other, alluring but dangerous, continues to reset those limits that keep alive one's sense of having a self.

Unlike nostalgic autobiography of the first world, the testimonial's understanding of selfhood is based on collective identity, not individuality. Early in her account, Menchú is quick to insist that her "personal experience is the reality of a whole people" (Menchú 1984, 1). What follows in the first half of her book is the description of rituals that establish the bond between the community and each of its members. Those rituals begin with the practice of the mother who, "on the first day of her pregnancy goes with her husband to tell . . .

elected leaders that she's going to have a child, because the child will not only belong to them but to the whole community" (7).

Like other third-world autobiographies, the testimonial is oriented toward creating a future rather than recovering a past. It is a form of utopian literature that contributes to the realization of a liberated society based on distributive justice. A form of resistance literature as well as utopian literature, the testimonial resists not only economic and political oppression, but also any nostalgic pull toward an idealized past—pre-Hispanic origins, for instance, which promise false comfort. To resort to such indigenism would implicate Menchú in the very culture from which her testimonial wants to free itself.

While autobiography of nostalgia welcomes and, in fact, needs the other, the testimonial has to find ways of deconstructing it, since otherness in the third world is the most basic structure of colonial control. It is a construction by means of which the oppressed are kept "barbarian" and the colonizer securely defined as the bearer of civilization's burden. The operative existence of the other justifies a colonialist structure of domination.

Through autobiography of nostaligia like *An American Childhood*, I tried to define and establish the location from which the first-world reader listens to the voice of Rigoberta Menchú. The reader I constructed is a reader very much like myself some fourteen years ago when I developed a theory of autobiography based on the self-writing of Thoreau, Wordsworth, and Proust—all of them writing in the romantic tradition of an Annie Dillard and all of them members of a culture that already has a voice (Gunn 1982). Although I raised questions about an autobiographical tradition that privileged the private and ahistorical self, it was not until I spent time in the third world that I began to see that another set of questions had to be raised about the "narrative space of familiarity" that my very choice of texts constructed (Kaplan 1992). That space was, first of all, defined by the first-world citizenship of my informants. To be sure, I ended my project with Black Elk, but even there I was reading his testimonial out of the location I had established by means of the others. It is that location I began to interrogate with the help of Menchú.

Were the reader to respond to Menchú from an unexamined mainstream location in the first world, she would, I think, be disturbed or simply incredulous at the suffering that fills Menchú's world and frustrated at how little she could do to alleviate that suffering. She might conclude much like Jane Tompkins (1987) did in her essay on American Indians: "The moral problem that confronts me now is not that I can never have any facts to go on, but that the work I do is not directed towards solving the kinds of problems that studying the Indians has awakened me to" (77). Such limits must be acknowledged in establishing an ethics of reading third-world autobiography that gets us beyond a conventional ethics of altruism to an "ethics of survival."

An American Childhood epitomizes a nostalgic mode of self-representation. The following passage illustates several of its main characteristics:

How much noticing could I permit myself without driving myself round the bend? Too much noticing and I was too self-conscious to live; I trapped and paralyzed myself, and I dragged my friends down with me, so that we couldn't meet each other's eyes, my own loud awareness damning us both. Too little noticing, though . . . and I would miss the whole show. I would awake on my deathbed and say, What was that? (Dillard 1987, 155)

Replete with echoes from Thoreau's famous words about going to the woods to live deliberately, Dillard's passage underscores three features associated with a mainstream autobiographical tradition of the industrialized world. First of all, its "loud awareness" calls attention to a Cartesian singularity of consciousness. Second, the passage calls attention to an aesthetics within which individuation and style are coterminous. Third, Dillard's exact noticing combines with exact expression to situate the passage in a tradition that privileges inner selfness as both the spring of artistic activity and the starting point of ontological reckoning. The world is significant to the extent that it enters and is ratified by one's consciousness: Dillard writes, ". . . things themselves possessed no fixed and intrinsic amount of interest; instead things were interesting as long as you had attention to give them" (79).

Nostalgic autobiography seems to hold out the promise that memory can achieve perfect rapport with the past. Dillard writes her autobiography to rescue the sensuous details of her childhood from what she calls a "cave of oblivion." She understands memory to be an empty space individually filled rather than a cultural activity practiced in and informed by a historical and ideological situation. In order to maintain a centered "I" by defining itself against the other, Dillard's autobiographical agenda has to remain fixed. In the sense that Menchú's testimonial "I" represents the communal and resistant "we," its agenda must remain open.

The comfortable Pittsburgh neighborhoods of Point Breeze and Squirrel Hill where Annie Dillard had her American childhood are worlds away from the inhospitable mountains and fincas of Guatemala where Menchú grew up. Even so, Dillard has her dangerous places: the "dark ways" of the Roman Catholic Sheehy family, the "greasy black soil" of Doc Hall's alley, the Frick Park bridges under which the bums had been living since the Great Depression, and, in the earliest memory of all, her own bedroom into whose corners a slithering, elongated "thing" would burst nightly to search her out. In the process of figuring the "thing" out as the lights of passing cars, young Annie was "forced" to what she calls "the very rim of [her] being, to the membrane of skin that both separates and connects the inner life and the outer world" (21).

In the daily mapping of her world, it is important for Dillard to name those experiences of what might be called the other but at the same time to keep them on the outside of that membrane. Like the ice-skating figure of Jo

Anne Sheehy whom she watches from the "peace and safety" of the Dillard house, they are experiences that take place on the outside of her skin's rim—dark, dangerous, criminal, but also beautiful, mysterious, and "radiant." Dillard's child is careful to keep the membrane virginally unbroken, but she needs nonetheless to be taken to her "edge" with that combination of "desire and derision" that communicates the anxiety involved in the construction of otherness (Bhabha 1983, 19).

Not surprisingly, Menchú's autobiographical agenda is quite different. But in a world more literally dangerous, it is surprisingly more open. The telling of her story is a matter of cultural survival. In telling that story to Burgos-Debray, she makes it clear that she used the story of her own past as a strategy for organizing her people against landowners and the larger system of oppression whose interests they represented. "I had some political work to do, organizing the people there, and at the same time getting them to understand me by telling them about my past, what had happened to me in my life, the reasons for the pain we suffer, and the causes of poverty" (Menchú 1984, 162).

In no way unique, Menchú's story is intended to elicit recognition and, in naming the suffering she shares with her people, to deliver them and herself from muteness. Such muteness is a product of oppression. As recently observed by a fellow member of the Committee of Campesino Unity, "a person can be poor, dirt poor, but not even realize the depth of their poverty since it is all they know" (MacGregor 1990, 132). To take notice of the oppression and to give it a name is the first step beyond it. Noticing, it turns out, is an even more important activity in Menchú's culture of silence than it is in Dillard's culture, whose voice is secure. But it is a noticing of material conditions, not a noticing of noticing.

Menchú's testimonial is a story of resistance as well as a story of oppression. More precisely, her testimonial is itself an act of resistance. Solidarity growing out of resistance as much as membership in a community of the oppressed produces the circumstances of her identity. Menchú has to be reminded of these circumstances by a twelve-year-old when she is on the verge of hopelessness following the torture deaths of her brother and then her mother. "A revolutionary isn't born out of something good," the young girl told her; "[she] is born out of wretchedness and bitterness." The twelve-year-old goes on to add something very foreign to an autobiographer of consciousness like Dillard: "We have to fight without measuring our suffering, or what we experience, or thinking about the monstrous things we must bear in life" (Dillard 1987, 237). Menchú's testimonial is instead an autobiography of conscientization.

Menchú leaves behind the communal rituals that have long anchored her and her people in order to enter resistance activity that keeps her on the run outside her own community. Far from mourning her loss, she opens herself to new and potentially conflicting strategies of survival, especially in learning Spanish and turning to the Bible. Spanish is the language of her enemy; those who learn it, as her father cautioned her, often leave the Indian community. The

Bible had been used by many priests and nuns to keep her people "dormant while others took advantage of [their] passivity" (Menchú 1984, 122). Menchú, however, uses both, especially the Bible, as "weapons." Far from being "an unlikely, movie-set world" as it was for Dillard, the Bible became a document by means of which Menchú could understand her people's reality. Moses "gets pluralized and Christ turns into a political militant" (Sommer 1988, 123). Biblical stories allowed Menchú and her people to give yet another name to their oppression.

Instead of constructing a single map within whose boundaries a Dillard can hold safely onto a sense of individual identity, Menchú superimposes many "conflicting maps" in a collective and incorporative struggle for communal survival (Sommer 1988, 120). Yúdice notes (in words that echo liberation theologian Enrique Dussel), "her oppression and that of her people have opened them to an unfixity delimited by the unboundedness of struggle" (1989, 229).

Dillard's autobiography set side-by-side with Menchú's testimonial raises a new set of issues that can move us in the direction of Yúdice's "ethics of survival." A third-world testimonial like Menchú's serves to destabilize the nostalgic structure of autobiography based on a *loss* and *recovery* ostensibly beyond the marketplace that gives force to those very terms. More important, it lays the ground for exposing otherness as that construction that keeps women, blacks, Jews, Palestinians, and Guatemalan Indians in their subordinate place.

In order that interpretation become transformative and reading of third-world autobiography be ethical, we need to reinsert texts into political cultures and what Raymond Williams calls the "life of communities" (Said 1991, 82). The Pittsburgh of the Fricks and Carnegies is also the Pittsburgh of the unemployed steelworkers and the black slums. That the latter are outside Dillard's ken has everything to do with the fact that the former are not. Gerald Graff has reminded us that "what we don't see enables and limits what we do see" (1992, 47). He was offering a personal account of how his teaching of *Heart of Darkness* has changed as a result of confronting a very different reading of the text from the third-world perspective of the Nigerian novelist Chinua Achebe. Simply out of sight from this or that location, huge chunks of the world are blocked out.

Dillard's memories of Pittsburgh block out the Polish and Slovak steelworkers and the Hill District ghetto except, in the case of the latter, as a place where boarding-school boys carouse. To acknowledge such unavoidable blocking is to open the way for examining the emancipatory potential of autobiographical practice in testimonials like *I, Rigoberta Menchú*. With that "wider optics," we might find a way of breaking through the membrane of critical isolation and solitude to an ethical criticism practiced "in solidarity with others struggling for survival" (Yúdice 1989, 229).

Cornel West identifies as an Enlightenment legacy "the inability to believe in the capacities of oppressed people to create cultural products of value and oppositional groups of value" (1984, 17). In any ethical reading of third-world autobiography, the racism inherent in this legacy must be exposed and rejected.

George Yúdice turns this legacy on its head when he concludes his essay "Marginality and the Ethics of Survival" by defining "ethical practice" as the "political art of seeking articulations among all the 'marginalized' and oppressed, in the interests of our own survival." "We need not speak for others," he says, "but we are responsible for a 'self-forming activity' that can in no way be ethical if we do not act against the 'disappearance' of oppressed subjects" (1989, 230–31).

Autobiography like *I, Rigoberta Menchú* calls on first-world readers to take responsibility, not for the third world but for the locatedness and therefore the limitations of our own perspective. Acknowledging those limitations might contribute to the survival of us all. The ultimate window of opportunity is to stand with Menchú and, acknowledging the cost borne by the third world for our own selfhood, to affiliate at the borders between us.[5]

NOTES

1. I've discussed my move from West to East Jerusalem in "A Politics of Experience: Leila Kahaled's *My People Shall Live: The Autobiography of a Revolutionary*," in *De/ Colonizing the Subject: The Politics of Gender in Women's Autobiography*, ed. Sidonie Smith and Julia Watson, University of Minnesota Press, 1992.

2. Among those policies, one would have to include the billions of dollars in foreign aid that the United States has given to Central American countries like Guatemala despite their human rights records. As U.S. citizens, we are thereby complicit in the story Menchú tells. That political fact is part of our location as readers of her story.

3. I am indebted to Professor Judith-Maria Buechler of Hobart and William Smith Colleges, with whom I hashed out many of my ideas.

4. *Conscientization* is a term used by Paulo Freire. In my use of it here, I am talking about an autobiographical process that takes place in and on the world and serves as an instrument of the world's transformation and not simply of the self's representation.

5. I am especially appreciative of Caren Kaplan's argument that as a matter of "staying alive," cultural autobiography (as "outlaw-genre") "works to construct both 'safe' places and the border areas of coalition politics where diversity operates in crisis conditions to forge powerful temporary alliances." See her essay "Resisting Autobiography: Out-Law Genres and Transnational Feminist Subjects," Smith and Watson.

24

SUPPLEMENTING THE STANDARD CURRICULUM
Twain's Connecticut Yankee *and Menchú's* Indian Woman of Guatemala

GERALDINE T. RODRIGUEZ

The suburban community where I teach high school English in southwest Michigan is homogeneous and traditionally conservative, made up primarily of middle-class descendants of Dutch and German farmers and professional families from nearby urban areas. Our curriculum matches our community; the literary units of the sophomore English course I teach, for instance, are almost exclusively Eurocentric. Nonetheless I feel strongly that our students should be sensitized to other realities, and, in November 1993, I introduced selections from Rigoberta Menchú's oral history, *I, Rigoberta Menchú: An Indian Woman in Guatemala* as a comparative study with one of the more traditional works approved for our curriculum, Mark Twain's *A Connecticut Yankee in King Arthur's Court.* My purpose was to begin to integrate multicultural themes into my teaching and draw my students' attention to relevant questions of social injustice.

I began this project with apprehension since I feared that reading such a controversial and "radical" text as that by Rigoberta Menchú might pose problems in a community where some members had difficulty accepting even canonical works like *The Adventures of Huckleberry Finn, Catcher in the Rye,* and *Of Mice and Men.* Consequently I decided to move cautiously, present the material objectively, and allow the students to reach their own conclusions both about social injustice and what role or roles they might play in addressing it.

Rigoberta Menchú's story has a special significance for me because in 1986 I had the opportunity to live in her country. My husband, a college professor of Spanish, taught as a Fulbright Professor at a private university in Guatemala City, and as representatives of the U.S. government, my children attended an international school that served the needs of the State Department and their families. It was during that year in Guatemala that I opened my eyes to the pathetic social conditions of its indigenous population and their desperate struggle for equality and justice. Outside the new apartment house in which we lived there were always impoverished Indian women attempting to sell their beautiful and painstakingly hand-woven fabrics. Inside our apartment we were expected to house, in a pathetically small room, our own Indian servant girl. When my personal discomfort with the arrangement led us to provide private quarters for her, to pay her a living wage, and to invite her to join our family meals, we found ourselves shunned by some of the wealthy Guatemalans who had initially welcomed us. I haven't been able to forget this experience and the personal relationships formed through it.

I decided to insert a selection from Menchú's testimony between the otherwise disconnected and certainly more conventional works that I usually teach. Thus with my sophomores I used the film version of *To Kill a Mockingbird* to introduce a thematic unit on social injustice that would end up including both Menchú and Twain. Harper Lee's story could, I thought, provide my students with a more familiar context for discussion of social injustice and its various faces in our society. The film, like the novel, depicts the unjust indictment of an African American hired hand accused of raping a poor, white teenager in a small, rural town in Georgia during the Depression. After viewing the film, each student wrote a personal response to the film's handling of prejudice and inequality. We discussed the film from a historical perspective seeking to understand how Americans fought to overcome social inequality and injustice. Through their writing and discussion the students seemed to conclude that social injustice can be resolved only when someone in power takes a stand against the wrongs and works to address them. Their thinking was not entirely disempowering, however, because they reasoned that individuals in a democracy are responsible for bringing pressure on the government to work against unjust forces. But even as the class agreed on *what* must be done, the students began to realize the difficulty of *how* to do it. This is where *To Kill a Mockingbird* proved especially useful because it served as an entrance point for discussion of the African American civil rights movement. Drawing on the story and a special day of recognition of Martin Luther King Jr.'s birthday, we viewed films and discussed examples of courtroom challenges, sit-ins, marches, demonstrations, and nonviolent confrontations that established a wide range of choices for citizen activism.

Following our examination of *To Kill a Mockingbird* and citizen involvement, I provided my students with two chapters from *I, Rigoberta Menchú*—chapter 1, "The Family," and chapter 4, "First Visit to the Finca: Life in the Finca"—and briefly outlined some of the historical, geographical, and biographic elements needed to understand them. In the first chapter, Rigoberta introduces herself and provides background on her family and community. She describes their abject poverty as well as their strong Mayan identity as a people forced to survive within a culture from which they are excluded from economic and political power. In chapter 4 Menchú powerfully describes the exploitation and inhumane and perilous conditions that Mayan workers must endure on the finca (plantation) eight months of the year. Taken together, these two chapters could provide my students with a awareness of the bitter social injustice that persists in Guatemala today.

Because of my own familiarity with the country, I was able to share with my students some of my personal experiences. While in the country I had visited several villages inhabited mostly by old men, young children, and the indigenous women who worked long hours weaving their magnificent textiles. Meanwhile, their husbands, sons, and brothers were dispersed from their communities, forced to find work on the fincas located in the highlands or along the coast. Still others from the villages had to leave their children with family members and seek work as domestic help with affluent families in the capital. As Menchú describes in her chapter on being a maid in Guatemala City, domestic workers in Guatemala are expected to live in their employer's home and be available to them twenty-four hours a day. I had learned first hand about these exploitative domestic relationships where the employer provides the worker with a meager place to sleep, a bit of rice, beans, and fruit, and a monthly salary of 30–40 quetzals (no more than $15 to $20). Because of the long distance, time restraint, and financial burden of traveling back to their villages, many domestic servants are unable to see their children or families for many months. Lacking legal protection, servants travel home only at the discretion of their employers.

Before we began the reading I provided students with a short vocabulary list and study questions, and students were encouraged to share their responses to the questions orally to initiate our first, informal discussion. The next class period I formed small discussion groups of four or five students to individually respond to several key questions, share their comments with each other within the group, and, finally, have a representative from each group share their group's consensus on a particular question for whole class discussion. The questions I chose attempted to move from more traditional language arts concerns to the issues of culture and politics raised by the reading. I asked students to try to determine Rigoberta Menchú's audience and purpose, analyze her use of detail about her culture and that of the ladinos, consider what she learned from her experiences and the ways that her autobiography could contribute to her struggle in Guatemala.

To these questions there were a variety of responses. One group felt that, "She writes to anyone who would listen because she wants to get her story to everyone . . . and tell us what it is like to be a majority, but treated like a minority." Others felt that Menchú "attempts to educate and inform people around the world of the lifestyle she endures . . . a lifestyle of prejudice and pain. . . . She hopes to change people, make them understand how she feels." The same group felt that Menchú's autobiography contributes to her fight because it "influences others' reactions and feelings, their sympathy and understanding [of the problem her people face] and fight for change [which will] help Mayans as well as others gain equal rights." One group believed that "Rigoberta Menchú's autobiography can make people aware of her peoples' struggle and possibly the rich and the finca owners will become enlightened to the plight of the workers."

One group of students suggested more definite actions as a result of her autobiography: "Rigoberta's autobiography can help her struggle because it can wake people up to what is going on, and they can also join the effort. This could be achieved through letters to the government, the organization of aid to the Mayans, boycotts, and also through revolution." A more militant group of students added: "We think civil war [between the ladinos and the Mayans] is the only way out."

In spite of their own sheltered backgrounds and their lack of exposure to the injustices of a society that produces the kind of suffering Rigoberta Menchú documents, my students showed great interest in the Mayans' plight, were sensitive and compassionate to the needs of these oppressed people, and proved to be fervent and sincere in their desire to execute change and right the wrongs they read about. Many suggested ways they themselves could influence change, yet, at this stage, their recommendations were usually overly simplistic or unrealistic. After our brief encounter with the issues they still didn't understand very well the difficulties the Mayans face attempting to empower themselves through education or standing up to the forces of the political and economic system. As Americans they take their privileges for granted; they were unaware that these privileges are not guaranteed rights for all people. As their teacher and guide in these discussions I, too, was frustrated by an inability to provide simple solutions to the complex problems. Although I mentioned the demonstrations and uprisings that took place in Guatemala in the early 1980s, I did not expose my students to the overwhelming tragedy and violence of that era as Menchú presents it later in the text—I was not sure that it would inspire hope. We did discuss, however, the currently ongoing dismantling of apartheid in South Africa as a positive example of how public pressure and economic sanctions did influence change. This was more useful as it facilitated an awareness that people could contribute as individuals to systematic change through the exposure of injustices.

Mark Twain's satiric depiction of medieval chivalry, A Connecticut Yankee in King Arthur's Court, served as the next text in the unit. For three more weeks we continued to focus on the theme of social injustice, this time as Twain portrays it in his not so fanciful rendition of medieval society. One important point expressed by the main character of the novel, mysteriously transported back in time, was that even though living conditions have improved greatly since the Middle Ages, his present-day world was still full of poverty and injustice. Another theme Twain emphasizes is how those in power are often unable or unwilling to see the needs of the poor and powerless. For example, even though the Yankee brought social reforms and the technological advances of the nineteenth century to sixth-century Britain, they had little effect on the social and economic conditions of the period. My students noted that it wasn't until the Yankee and King Arthur disguise themselves as commoners and set out across the country among the common folk that the king realizes that his own laws are unjust, favoring those who enslave others. On their journey, they encounter a lack of sufficient medical care, unsanitary living conditions among the poor, slavery, crime, and an unjust legal system. Indeed, King Arthur and the Yankee themselves become enslaved unjustly, and the King realizes that as a commoner he has little control over his fate. Ironically, the King's character changes in this section of the novel. He displays a new bravery, compassion, and awareness of injustice and develops for the first time what we saw as a real nobility.

Twain's optimism that oppressive systems can be changed when those in power make it happen reinforced the student's original analysis of social injustice. After reading and discussing the novel students were asked to write an essay comparing and contrasting the elements of social injustice portrayed in our standard canonical work, *A Connecticut Yankee in King Arthur's Court*, with the depiction of the same subjects by Rigoberta Menchú. As a concluding portion of their essay, students were also asked to comment on ways that they, as members of a democratic society, could effect change in the exploitation and social injustice in Guatemala. The outcome of my approach to curricular change is indicated by the following selections from these student papers:

> In his novel *A Connecticut Yankee in King Arthur's Court*, Twain exposes many social injustices. These injustices are still present in today's society. They are slavery, massive differences in status and wealth between social classes, racism, and a few people having all the power. . . . Twain depicts extreme wealth vs. extreme power in the Yankee's wanderings with Arthur. . . . In Arthur's court, Arthur has all the power, and the people have nothing to say about it.
>
> In *I, Rigoberta Menchú*, the Indians have no power, no wealth, live in poverty and are subject to someone else's will at all times. . . . When they vote, it is not theirs, but a workboss' or a man with a gun. The only difference is that the Indians know they are enslaved and can do nothing about it.
>
> As a people, we of the United States can help by urging our government to put a stop to this. Economic pressure could be put on the offending government or even military pressure. America's Civil War was fought for the same reasons as this . . . all the Indians need is a means of fighting back. . . .
>
> In *A Connecticut Yankee in King Arthur's Court*, Mark Twain reveals to the reader that social injustices were very much present in sixth-

century Britain. The existence of poverty and disease shows us that people were not given equal opportunities in King Arthur's Camelot. The woman and child with smallpox will never experience a life better than the family they were born into could give them.

Centuries later, Rigoberta Menchú tells us these horrible conditions still exist in *I, Rigoberta Menchú: An Indian Woman of Guatemala*. Because of their heritage, her family is forced to do degrading work for little or no salary. They must bear the unbearable when they travel to the finca. They have absolutely no say in the government of their country and are denied an education. There are many similarities between the hardships faced in sixth-century England and twentieth-century Guatemala. During both time periods, a social class is exploited and robbed of their humanity.

Even though my students still have a long distance to travel to master the issues, I ended the unit with satisfaction. I had exposed my students to literature that was not an established part of the curriculum, demonstrated that the incorporation of minority views can lead us to rethink the meaning of canonical works, and tied our language arts studies together with a meaningful purpose. As a class we experienced directly the power of literature to influence and heighten social awareness. As students read and discussed the examples of social injustice in the various texts, they began to realize both that solutions are never simple and that each individual must determine to influence change through awareness, commitment, and action. My modest experimentation with transforming the curriculum has enhanced my belief that, with whatever students we teach, we must instill the desire for change.

REFLECTIVE TEACHING

25

BRIDGING THE GAP
*Modes of Testimony
and Teaching
Central American Politics*

DANIEL GOLDRICH

For all of the social problems I have cared about as a teacher and as a citizen, one of the toughest hurdles is bridging the identification gap between the well off and the poorly off, the more powerful and the less powerful, those presently alive and future generations. Central America represents this challenge well. The various forms of testimony are intrinsically and instrumentally one of the best means of bridging the gap of which I am aware.

With the term *testimony,* I refer to the telling of their story by people whose lives have been most affected by a problem or situation (such as repression by the National Security State). Keck and Sikkink (1992, 10), writing on "international networks on the environment and human rights," describe how activists interpret facts and such testimony in a way that makes political action possible. They frame the issues in terms of right and wrong, and they appeal to shared principles. In so doing, they often redefine what had been "technical" matters (promoting national security through appropriate foreign policy, for example), properly the province of "qualified experts," obviously a highly limited elite, as political issues properly the concern of a much broader set, citizens.

What are the dynamics here? It is a cliche that we are flooded with information by the various media. None of us can take in and act on much of it— Rwanda, Haiti, AIDS, homelessness, species loss—so we become numb to much of it, we desensitize. But personal testimony is harder to turn off. Here's a real human being, this is someone's real experience. This dynamic is heightened if the testimony is presented in a social setting focused on it, where connections are made between the presenter and the audience, where the values and principles shared between them are noted. This makes it even harder to turn off. In such a setting, a shocking personal crisis can be created. We've heard it. Do we let it in or try to shut it out, restoring our safer, more comfortable world? Shutting it out will take more energy than in the case of a TV abstraction (there is a psychic cost). But if we let it in (suppose it's Rigoberta Menchú)—after all, she's a fellow Christian, a woman, a person, she's a victim, in part at least, of U.S. government policy (the overthrow of a constitutional democracy considered procommunist in 1954 leading to the U.S.-supported evolution of the National Security State), there's a 1992 version of 1492 going on here.

Then, an awful question arises, "What do I do, what can I do, what should I do?" This is a crisis of personal responsibility. Testimony can generate this dynamic. It tends to generate, I believe, a sense of guilt. I'm aware that guilt has a bad name with many people contemporarily, but I think guilt arises in a process beginning with the perception of the gap between the ideal and the real, right and wrong, and through testimony such as Menchú's, the question appears, "What should I do?" The psychohistorian Robert J. Lifton terms this the anxiety of responsibility (1973).

In the course I teach on Central America at the University of Oregon, there's no one answer presented to that question. But I do attempt to make clear what the high costs of the prevailing arrangements are for Central Americans and for us, and to explore the costs and benefits of some alternatives. The students are encouraged to consider how and why so many Central American and U.S. people acquiesce in the situation, but also how and why a substantial number of Central Americans and U.S. people struggle to find a way to make change.

In this course Central American dissidents are not presented only as victims, but as people struggling to create an effective response. This leads to a critical question. What accounts for people being able to take profound risks that render them (and those close to them) highly vulnerable to terrible death? The inquiry points to an examination of liberation theology, which rooted deeply in the region from the late sixties onward, and involves the students and me in a sensitive, even sweaty inquiry into matters of faith, hope, and spirituality as they have developed in Central America. I have found that religion and spirituality are among the most controversial subjects for inquiry in the basically secular humanist culture of the academy. As we try to understand how they function in the region, the students often revisit their own histories. Our process of working through development issues—clarifying standards, considering reality and the ideal/real gap, and probing alternatives—has an analogy to the liberation theology process used by many base communities, though the spiritual quality remains a diffuse aspect. We explore the idea that a strong sense of community, an identification with the community across time into the future allows activists to act for that imaged future even though the acts may lead to their own death. We consider the question, What else can account for this, the phenomena reflected in the lives of the Menchú family? We try to put ourselves in the place of others in this situation, for example, those who become numb, those who cleave to the traditional Church—a comfort in a harsh world, those who seek out other religions. We look at competing political currents in relation to the changing political roles of women, indigenous, and other important ethnic groups.

In contrast, another major theme of the course is the living legacy of cold war anticommunism in U.S. politics, in the stances of the range of politicians and the discourse of the mass media. U.S. policy is assessed in relation to its impact on democracy, equity, and sustainability, and we trace the emergence and impact of grassroots oppositional politics in this country. We look at the rise of the Central American Movement in U.S. politics, seeking to expose the National Security State and, in some parts of the movement, seeking support for Central American opposition groups, parties, and so on. The rise and dynamics of the sanctuary movement, sister cities (and sister universities, clinics, parishes, etc.), Witness for Peace, rapid response networks, and alternative media are explored, as are some citizen campaigns that reinforced Reagan's policies, such as Adopt-a-Contra, and religious advocacy for ultraconservative Central American regimes.

Throughout the course, the question is posed, What connects us with Central America? It is pretty easy to trace how the United States affects Central America but intriguing to explore the other side of it (for example, the role of the destruction of the Central American environment on the generation of refugees and the impact of the latter phenomenon on racist nationalist political responses in the United States).

An orientation, unfamiliar to many enrolled in the course, is stressed from the beginning: The student is considered a citizen, with the responsibilities inherent in that role. This seems particularly important to emphasize in view of the extreme inadequacy of U.S. policies and politics on Central America with reference to democracy, equity, and sustainability. That is, the situation is so dire, ignorance and disinterest so widespread that the hours we devote to the inquiry take on an unusual importance. Furthermore, we are all reminded that our counterpart academics in Central America often cannot avail themselves of the opportunity to analyze their national reality in the classroom or have paid dearly for having done so. Thus a certain *presence* is demanded of the student—not just class attendance, but being there psychologically in the sense of active engagement, as if one's thinking matters.

The students explore the ways in which United States citizens learned to bring the Central American issues home, through the sanctuary movement, the Witness for Peace approach, and sister cities. Sanctuary, of religious and sympathetic nonreligious local citizens, came to provide a home and support in hundreds of churches and cities for Central Americans fleeing official repression and in danger of being detained and deported by the Immigration and Naturalization Service. The achievement of sanctuary status reflected protracted processes of gaining members' and citizens' attention and commitment and then the official support of church and city officials. The risks were uncertain but high. In the initial years, the government viewed sanctuary as illegal, infiltrated communities, and carried through a set of highly publicized trials of sanctuary workers, who believed they had morality and law on their side. What seems to have given the movement its energy and commitment was the *direct presentation* of the testimony of victims of the National Security State (Coutin 1993). Suddenly in the early eighties, Salvadorans and Guatemalans appeared to tell their story at Sunday mass, at civic meetings, and with growing support at city council sessions, generating processes similar to those described earlier concerning crises of personal responsibility in social context.

Witness for Peace also brought the issues home. It recruited local or special focus delegations from all over the United States to visit Nicaragua. Typically, a delegation would meet with a broad social and political range of Nicaraguans, building in exposure to intensely contentious issues. Most of the delegates' days were spent in an active war zone, sharing the arduous conditions of the campesinos, in part by living with such families for a few days. They were shepherded by long-term WFP workers, stationed in the conflict zones to gather relevant information and document human rights abuses. Upon returning home, the participants were committed to *telling what they had seen and heard* as widely and as intensively as possible, through local media, meetings, and newsletters of organizations of which they were members, at work, with their Congressional delegations, and in public demonstrations. Their actions were typically moved by the sense of urgency generated by the impact of the war and economic embargo on people who now had a *name,* a *face,* and the status of *friends.*

Another grassroots variant in the effort to develop direct citizen-to-citizen communication was the sister cities relationship, established between more than eighty-five U.S. local communities and Nicaraguan counterparts during the 1980s (Chilsen and Rampton 1988, 125–34). The relationship requires an educational political process to attain official status. Once established, "sisterhood" provides interested citizens a markedly lower barrier to participation than sanctuary—with its attendant risk of government prosecution—or Witness for Peace—entailing the personal risk of entering the war zone. Sister relationships typically involve the exchange of delegations. While expensive, the exchanges promote *enduring* ties, not quite so dependent on the urgency of crisis, yet with the *reinforcement of personal ties over time.* Some paired communities have learned how to communicate powerfully but more cheaply by making and distributing videotapes to each other. Such a relationship is sufficiently broadly cast—community to community—that a wider base may develop over time, beyond the activism over crises. One can imagine such a relationship over time bridging the North-South gap with exchanges between high school students, various economic or occupational sectors, women's groups, environmental activists, as well as purposely cross-sectional delegations.

Over the course, there are some compelling juxtapositions. For example, the students explore U.S. mass media treatment of Central America. We review the way the El Mozote massacre (of Salvadoran campesinos) was handled or written off by the press and politicians in 1981 against what was revealed by UN human rights analysts in the early 1990s, the subject of a powerful "60 Minutes" segment (Sixty Minutes 1993). By the mid-eighties, alternative (critical) media had become available so that dissidents' arguments about mass media could be assessed, focusing on critical events or benchmarks. Such is the case with Fairness and Accuracy in Reporting's (FAIR) "Extra" issue on Central America (1987) and Herman and Chomsky's analysis (1988).

We read the powerful writing on Central America and foreign policy of Jeane Kirkpatrick (1979, 1981), who became a central policy maker herself with the inauguration of the Reagan administration. Her failure to refer to, much less account for the National Security States (disguised as "traditional autocracies") or her labeling the *FMLN* (Salvadoran guerrillas) as of the Pol Pot type evoke a strong reaction from those who have read about the operations of the National Security State and independent human rights organizations' assessments of who is responsible for the vast bulk of abuses in the region. Or, we review the State Department's White Paper on Communist aggression in El Salvador (U.S. Dept. of State 1981), which commanded prime-time attention of the U.S. public in February 1981, and the students ask, "Where are the accounts of the state's murder and other acts of repression against grassroots Christian activists and clergy, or the state's violent, fraudulent manipulation of two presidential elections in the 1970s?" (Petras 1981; Bonner 1984). Or we review the Kissinger Commission Report to the President on Central America (1984), note its call for U.S. professionalization of the Central American militaries ostensibly to preclude their abuse of the civil population, and the students ask, "How can the commissioners endorse this without accounting for the previous quarter century of U.S. programs to professionalize Latin American militaries since the onset of the Alliance for Progress in 1961?" (LeoGrande 1984).

Perhaps the most important juxtapositions are policy analyses or speeches of "statesmen" and the testimonies of Central American citizens, for example, the speeches of Ronald Reagan on Central American policy and Rigoberta Menchú's account of her life.

We read other participants' writings, such as Charles Clements's (a U.S. Vietnam veteran and doctor who worked in a largely guerrilla-controlled zone of El Salvador for a year), and Witness for Peace accounts of the Contra war's impacts on Nicaraguan villages (Clements 1984; Griffin-Nolan 1991).

Here is a sample of direct accounts presented to the class. Menchú herself has visited the campus to present her work. A visitor, Mira Brown, close associate of U.S. engineer Ben Linder, murdered by the Contras, reports on the progress of their Integrated Rural Community Development Project in the heart of the conflict zone in Northern Nicaragua. A Sandinista campesino activist who had never before been out of his remote rural region describes his experience. Five years later, and after the war deaths of two sons, he returns for an update on his town, now controlled by the opposition coalition.

Central America has also been brought much closer to home by university community members relating important personal experiences. A linguistics professor, working across a five-year span on Nicaragua's Atlantic Coast to record the language of a small Indian group, became a close observer of a key peace process (virtually uncovered by our mass media). She reported how a government initiative transformed a war into a painstaking grassroots consultation, eventuating in a constitutionally based regional government with substantial autonomy. The students thus learned of a political breakthrough regarding inter-indigenous and -ethnic relations with little precedent in post-Conquest American history (Goldrich 1987).

A course alumnus reported on his military intelligence work in Central America, an account that generated useful conflict with my experience, my position. Another reported on his recent tour, focusing on the reminiscences of local community members regarding the way they have brought their initially much more conservative priest around to their socially progressive activism. This reminded us of how much the political culture of the Church has changed over recent decades. Another, active in our university's sister project with the University of El Salvador, described his delegation to support their counterparts at a particularly intense juncture. This provided an opportunity to understand the excruciating Salvadoran reality through people with whom the class members could readily identify. And I constantly draw on my experiences.

GOING TO CENTRAL AMERICA

I usually work through participant observation in activities that seem important to me. Over time, my teaching of Central America led to a more profound involvement. I found I couldn't just teach this as a "service" course and let it go at that. The testimonies such as Rigoberta Menchú's went deeper, occupying me emotionally more and more. The more I let it in, the more I had to face the nightmare images of Guatemalan and Salvadoran death squads, the more I had to struggle with despair and to understand, as a lifelong secular humanist tempered by considerable work experience with the American Friends Service Committee and with militant pacifists, how activists in Central America could continue to struggle in a hopeful way amid the carnage. I had to face my own fears of deeper involvement—going to Central America seemed more and more necessary, but I had to go through my own process of preparation. I had been virtually paralyzed emotionally by the relentless, hideous repression imposed by the military on Chile, a country in which I had lived and worked in the sixties, and one that had set a standard for me in political openness. I felt

I had to be ready to face the repression of my Central American counterparts without collapsing and to get through my own fear of what might happen even to a U.S. citizen in Central America who crosses the National Security State. I had a good reason not to go—I was thoroughly occupied in environmental political activities, research, and teaching that passed the test of worthwhile work. But Central America occupied more and more mental space. As more and more friends returned from Witness for Peace delegations to Nicaragua and sanctuary/human rights-related delegations to El Salvador, and my own involvement in Central American solidarity grew, my ambivalence intensified. What shifted the balance, I think, is that I was watching my returning friends very carefully and I saw the joy that characterized them in that work. They were also desperate, harried, horror ridden, but above all, they were joyful in their work. It is not a phenomenon or term commonly used by academic people, but I knew what I was seeing in my friends (friendships built over the decades, through Vietnam, civil rights, and countless community activities in common). And so when one of those friends told me he was leading a delegation to El Salvador, I felt the time had come. I had to understand that phenomenon through my own direct experience or I would be increasingly inauthentic in my role of teaching about Central America.

In fact, those eight days were one of the richest experiences of my life. We encountered a panoply of people representing the political range. Here is but a sample of what I learned. We met after mass with people from a Christian base community, who calmly described their work, ongoing though they were losing fellow members to repression for their community participation. We met with young lawyers leading the independent human rights commission. Their simple offices were filled with photo albums of death squad victims found by the side of the road or in notorious body dumps. Searching through these albums was often the only way family members could have the certainty of knowing what had happened to their disappeared. I watched an old man looking there for his son. I listened to the young people describe their work in a way notable for the lack of egoism nor any dramatic presentation of their experience—straightforwardly, calmly. Above them on the wall was a photo of one of their commission's founders, who had been murdered by the military as she gathered evidence of repression in a rural area. They knew what their own chances were and, awesomely to me, they went about their work. We visited an in-town refugee camp, an old church crammed with women and children, hot and smelly—an assault on the senses. We heard testimony from a young woman in late pregnancy about fleeing the rural bombing to give birth in relative safety. Her eyes were terrorized and outraged, and I can see them very clearly still.

After a while, I could open up enough to realize that in an adjoining room, a priest was saying mass, in which many of the women were participating, relating the trials depicted in the Bible to their own experience. Days after, it came through to me that these "victims" were *transcending their victimization by actively construing their experience, by using their traditional texts in current context to distinguish between right and wrong, and to go that crucial liberation theologically informed step further: to consider what they could do about it.* (Later, they took a great risk in demonstrating in the streets for a series of demands.) Despite thinking that there was probably a better way to use this time slot, I went along with the others to a Baptist orphanage. The children had been collected here and there, survivors of bombings, abandoned or lost in war's chaos. I watched the staff holding and cuddling kids, carefully feeding them, creating a *home* for them in the torment of El Salvador. That night, in our Quakerly reflection, it came through to me in a revealing flash that utterly shook me that I had come to El Salvador having prepared myself for *the quality of death,* and what I was experiencing was *the quality of life amid death* that had come through to and so transformed my friends. And as I worked through the experience in the next months, I came to understand that these Salvadoran persons were so committed to their community and so believed in its ultimate capacity to make an equitable peace that they could do their daily work in the face of death, for many the high probability of their own death. *The community and life would go on.* You may imagine that the experience raised the energy level of my teaching.

In 1987 I completed a period of eighteen months' preparation to colead a Witness for Peace delegation to Nicaragua. The war was at its height. Working in local solidarity organizations had helped me through my own fear of entry into the Contra war zone. From this experience, similar in intensity and value to the Salvadoran, I make one observation. Everywhere, we encountered grassroots leaders working in new organizational activities that seemed critically a part of a development process. Our conversations revealed biographies of people whose talent had led to their coming to do things and hold positions they could not have imagined before the Revolution, and for which their counterparts in much of Central America were dying. Whatever the problems and relative failings of the Sandinistas, they had created a tremendous amount of opportunity for ordinary Nicaraguans to act in support of democracy, equity, and sustainability. It has remained for the U.S. solidarity movement to learn that through its own experience and tell it to fellow citizens back home.

My most recent visit was to participate in an international environmental meeting in Managua in 1989. I had the opportunity to observe an appropriate technology project sponsored by the small farmers' association. In a situation of extreme governmental fiscal crisis (that has become much worse), this minimal cost, farmer-to-farmer project trained people in sustainable agricultural practices generating rapid returns, which they then returned home to teach their neighbors. It has been important to me to know this alternative and teach about it in view of a national Nicaraguan situation that has deepened desperation.

These descriptions of the use and impact of testimonial literature, testimony, and other direct presentations of Central American reality to bridge the North-South gap are not intended to convey that the perspectives expressed represent *the truth*. Innumerable important questions remain open—for example, concerning effective and appropriate strategies for changing the structures of repression, inequity, and environmental destruction. But the key point is that such approaches seem to *raise the probability* that those who witness the testimony will feel themselves compelled to respond. Of those so affected, some seem moved toward an active (activist) orientation. This may seem a vague or imprecise observation. But I suggest that the problem of identification involved—that is, *being able or moved to place oneself in the distant, less powerful person's situation*—is so crucial, and apparently so difficult to generate that these forms of direct presentation are worth considering. The course doesn't prescribe a response. It does provide information about many people in Central America and the United States who are creatively struggling in various ways against repression and for democracy, equity, and sustainability. These provide models not so much for particular approaches as for the struggle to find *one's own* active orientation toward the U.S.-Central American relationship. Employing the terms of Lifton, such people undergo a process of animating guilt, coming to life around one's guilt.

THE SHIFT OF FOCUS FROM WAR TO "NORMALCY"(ECONOMY)

As Central America's war crisis has shifted formally toward electoral democracy, all of the basic problems but war remain. The global economy is increasingly the crucial determinant of most Central Americans' lives, though the National Security State apparently is far from dismantled. But the global economy is less overtly dramatic, more technical, more impersonal, and less understood both in Central America and the United States than the problems of the preceding era, and even less critically analyzed by the mass media in the United States.

So teaching about Central America has to shift, too. Students must learn more economics about trade and investment, topics offputting to many. I have been worrying and exploring how to do this.

My own research and participant observation has refocused over the years toward the impact of global and hemispheric integration on democracy, equity, and sustainability. The current direction of economic integration is overwhelmingly toward reducing barriers to capital investment and increasing corporate access to resources. This type of heightened market economics has been very rough on wages and the environment in Central America, at a point where the situation of labor and the environment is disastrous. The declining regional economy is desperate for foreign capital, and thus, despite deep impoverishment and environmental deterioration, political decision makers do not set conditions on corporate activity to promote equity or environment. This is a tough problem on which to mobilize attention, and daunting with regard to generating a politics of alternatives.

Since Mexico has gone further down the road of international economic integration through the North American Free Trade Agreement (though Central America is trying hard to follow in its footsteps), and the outlines of the impacts of economic integration, and political responses to that, are discernible, I am concluding the Central American course by exploring that. It would be logical to include a focus on the 1 January 1994 uprising by Mayan Indians in Chiapas. They were protesting NAFTA's and the Mexican government's sacrificing of small farmers in the interest of large-scale agribusiness. In addition, they were rejecting their increasing impoverishment and the perversion of electoral democracy by forces quite similar to those of the Central American National Security State.

I will link to this discussion how the economic nexus has generated an interesting cooperative relationship among similarly broadly based citizen coalitions in Mexico, Canada, and the United States. They have been concerned about the way in which this particular version of economic integration undermines democracy, equity, and sustainability. Because many environmentalists, labor activists, small farmers, and human rights activists throughout North America have seen how NAFTA deregulates corporations in a standard-lowering competition, they have been able to come together not only to oppose NAFTA and support forms of integration more appropriate to their values, but also to work together in a broad grassroots-based effort unparalleled in North-South relations. There has been increasing interchange among them, with Mexican maquiladora workers seeking solidarity for raising standards by touring and telling their story directly to U.S. and Canadian communities, and U.S. and Canadian delegations mostly of workers touring the maquiladora cities, hosted by their Mexican counterparts, to report home what they have seen and heard. Whether these phenomena of *testimony and witness* evolve to include more extensive inter-community relationships such as occurred during the 1980s over the Central American crisis is an important question. What is particularly intriguing here is the fact that the issues underlying economic integration affect such a broad proportion of the citizens so directly that the potential for grassroots impact on policy is correspondingly high. And the more this North American political phenomenon evolves, the more likely North American citizens will grasp and perhaps respond to Central Americans' contemporary economic dilemmas.

APPENDIX: COURSE ORIENTATION, LOGISTICS

My teaching, research, and community activity has evolved in a fairly integrated way from my general approach to the use of my professorship. The value base has come to be democracy, equity, and sustainability. I have come to see the interface between political and economic power as crucial for these values in my time, and have tried to formulate work that would advance them. That meant studying and participating in processes that seemed to me strategic for them, and out of that study and participation came the courses—problems in U.S. political economic development; theory and practice of environmentally oriented, community-controlled economic development; Latin American politics, including a focus on the North American Free Trade Agreement and tri-national citizen efforts to promote democracy, equity, and sustainability in relation to the Agreement.

As a student of Latin American politics for many years, I was of course aware of the increasingly murderous politics of Central America and of the new Sandinista experiment. But no one on my campus was teaching about this, despite the urgency and despite the growing interest in it on the part of the most politically acute and sensitive students. So, more or less on the margin, I put together an experimental course on the Central American crisis.

Given the wretched state of the national "debate" on Central America, I organized the course assuming virtually total student ignorance of the region. I begin by defining development in terms of the dynamics of promoting or retarding democracy, equity, and sustainability, and I invite the students to consider this key definition critically. With such a base, we can analyze any society over time or compare any set of them. Here the focus is Central America, in global context since the conquest, but especially the post–World War II period. The key cases are Guatemala, Nicaragua, and El Salvador. The rise of the National Security State is described, along with the regional impact of the Cuban Revolution, and U.S. cold war anticommunism in the U.S. National Security State repression against proponents of change and other *anticipated* sources of subversion is documented, as are the struggles to create political alternatives, U.S., Latin American, Soviet, and Cuban governments' involvement in regional politics are traced, as are North American grassroots politics of the solidarity sort.

The response to the course was substantial, so I've taught it twice a year. Through the eighties, it grew to a size of 175, or about 350 per year; in the nineties, that has dropped off by about one-third (surprisingly little to me in view of the virtual disappearance of Central America from the news media). Thus I've worked with over 3000 students on Central America. The numbers *are* important to me for two related reasons. First, though I have a strong bias against big class limitations on individual participation, the need for educating citizens about Central America has seemed great enough to justify the tradeoff. Second, I found early on that if people read even a little of the academic literature on this region, the gap between official rhetoric and policy rational and the horrendous costs visited on Central Americans generates an energetically critical perspective on the part of most people. So the more students in PS 235 the better.

A continuing paradox was that the approach and materials gave rise to unusually intense personal reactions, yet the large class size prevented many students from dealing with much of it during intense class sessions or office hours.

A few years into the course, a student suggested that we find a way to offer an optional discussion group to work over the issues more intimately. We found a set of class members who would prepare for and lead such discussion sessions, provided they demonstrated their capacity to understand Central American politics and articulate the issues, as reflected in exams or high quality of classroom participation.

Since then I've worked with a set of such course graduates every term. We offer small discussion groups for one credit, meeting one hour a week. The discussion leaders are credited for their work. I meet with them to prepare: how to generate and facilitate discussion, how to clarify but not minilecture, how to use the knowledgable student's participation without discouraging the relatively ignorant but involved student, how to work with conflict to clarify the issues involved, how to deal with the problem arising from a student's feeling disbelief or disloyalty to the United States by entertaining this information (in response, we raise questions about what serves the people of the U.S. and Central America better—looking into the facts as best we can ascertain them and analyze policy critically, or accept official formulations).

Many discussion leaders have undertaken this task as part of their activism on issues relevant to Central America, though activism is *not* a requirement for the position. Both the students noted earlier for their presentations to the class were discussion leaders at one point. Another was a Mexican Purepecha Indian woman, working on campus to bridge the gap between the Mexican American and Native American student organizations, paralleling an inter-ethnic political distance common throughout the Americas.

Two other discussion leaders had worked together as environmental advocates, as well as having taken a leading role in community education on the environmental issues of the North American Free Trade Agreement. Beyond their discussion task, they recruited and trained students—class volunteers—to arrange the campus visit of the previously noted Nicaraguan local appropriate technology project leader. We learned a great deal from him about both the project and creative peace making. For example, he's a locally well-known Sandinista activist, just the sort of person targeted by the Contras for assassination during the war, a problem persisting in areas such as his since the formal end of that war. Despite losing two sons in that war, he has been disposed and able to develop goals in common with the local police, former Contras, who now warn him about periodically impending dangers.

A final example is provided by a young woman who initiated what became a series of special discussion groups across the years on women in Central American society and politics. She had come to me dissatisfied with the way the Central American reality was presented in class, too undifferentiated by gender experience. She had learned a lot about Latin American women and was willing to assemble special materials for and organize a new discussion option that would educate the participants and me so that we would be able to interject this dimension more adequately into the course. She led the first such group so effectively that a series of women have followed her model, each adapting the approach. The "successors" have varied in background on the issues, one having had considerable experience working with Latin American women on a community project to provide each other crucial support for daily life problems. This option has become a rich and important class tradition.

It seems to me that the chance to lead these groups has provided an important opportunity for students who become so deeply involved in Central America that they want to do educational work, though my original motivation was to provide a smaller-scale work site for students stuck with a large class.

26

RIGOBERTA MENCHÚ
AND LATIN AMERICAN
CULTURAL HISTORY
A Professor's Journal

TERESA LONGO

I teach *Me llamo Rigoberta Menchú y así me nació la conciencia* (*I, Rigoberta Menchú*) in a course called "The Cultural History of Latin America" at The College of William and Mary in Virginia. The course is one of the offerings of the Spanish Section of William and Mary's Modern Language Department. In my six years at William and Mary I have come to define the cultural history course as an investigation of cultural production—painting, music, film, literature, and philsophy—in the context of Latin American history. My students tend to be college juniors and seniors majoring in Spanish and/or Latin American Studies. They begin the course well prepared linguistically: all have several years of preparation in Spanish language, composition, and conversation courses; many have studied abroad. In most cases, the students have also done a significant amount of reading by the time they take this course: they know Borges, Cortázar, and Isabel Allende; they may even have studied Mariátegui and Ariel Dorfman. When we get to the first chapters of Rigoberta Menchú's testimony, however, students invariably say, "I have never read anything like this before. Menchú is so different, so exotic and interesting. She talks about the most basic things— like corn and water—in a way I never imagined." By the time we have spent a few weeks on the Guatemalan activist's work, most students no longer find Menchú exotic or mythical. They do, however, discover that her work is important, moving—and real. By the time we finish the course, students also tend to conclude that what Rigoberta Menchú says in *Me llamo Rigoberta Menchú* is profoundly connected to many aspects of Latin American culture—issues such as democracy and justice, international solidarity and U.S. involvement in emerging nations. The following pages summarize entries from my journal on the teaching of Rigoberta Menchú. As I wrote them, I discovered that my own teaching, scholarship, and personal understanding of Latin American culture (not unlike that of my students) have been deeply influenced by the work of Rigoberta Menchú. I also discovered that although I attempt to "teach Menchú" in the first three weeks of the semester (between 22 January and 12 February) I am never able to *complete* this goal: on 15 March and 30 April, Menchú's name continues to surface and her work continues to teach.

SYLLABUS

LA HISTORIA CULTURAL DE LATINOAMERICA

I. Las civilizaciones antiguas y su herencia

Enero

m 20 Introducción; García Márquez, "La soledad de America Latina"

v 22 leer *Me llamo Rigoberta Menchú y así me nació la conciencia* capítulos 1 y 2; ver el video: *Popol Vuh*

l 25 leer *Rigoberta Menchú* . . . caps. 3 y 6

m 27 leer *Rigoberta Menchú* . . . caps. 7 y 8; empezar a analizar el texto

v 29 *Rigoberta Menchú* . . . caps. 9 y 10; entregar los diarios

Febrero

l 1 *Rigoberta Menchú* . . . caps. 15 y 17

m 3 *Rigoberta Menchú* . . . caps. 23 y 24

v 5 *Rigoberta Menchú* . . . caps. 27; video: *When the Mountains Tremble*

l 8 *Rigoberta Menchú* . . . caps. 29 y 30

m 10 *Rigoberta Menchú* . . . caps. 32 y 33; informe: "El norte"

v 12 *Rigoberta Menchú* . . . caps. 32 y 33; entregar trabajo analítico I; analizar la conclusión del texto

l 15 Cristóbal Colón y Fray Bartolomé de las Casas

m 17 Hernán Cortés y Bernal Díaz de Castillo en *Cronistas de Indias*

v 19 Elena Poniatowska, *La noche de Tlatelolco*, primera parte: "Ganar la calle" pp. 13–25, 37–47

l 22 Poniatowska pp. 58–69,

m 24 Poniatowska pp. 84–91, 97–108

v 26 Poniatowska pp. 150–59; segunda parte, "La noche de Tlatelolco" 163–71; entregar los diarios

Marzo

l 1 Poniatowska pp. 178–89, 196–205; informe: "Los olvidados"

m 3 Poniatowska pp. 235–43, 264–73; informes: "Art and Revolution in Mexico" y "Portrait of an Artist: Frida Kahlo"

v 5 Examen de medio semestre

II. Revolución y modernidad

l   15   César Vallejo, *El tungsteno* pp. 9–37

m 17   Vallejo pp. 37–63

v   19   Vallejo pp. 64–85; entregar los diarios

l   22   Vallejo pp. 86–108; trabajo analítico II

m 24   Vallejo pp. 109–34

v   26   Domitila Barrios de Chungara, *Si me permiten hablar*, informe: "The Aymara of Bolivia"

l   29   *Si me permiten hablar*

m 31   *Si me permiten hablar*

Abril

v   2   *Si me permiten hablar*, entregar los diarios

l   5   *Si me permiten hablar*

m 7   Ernesto Cardenal, "Hora 0"; informe: "Roses in December"

v   9   Ernesto Cardenal, "Hora 0"; informe: "The Uprising"

l   12   Video: Miguel Littín, "Alsino y el condor"

m 14   "Alsino y el condor"

v   16   García Márquez, *La aventura de Miguel Littín clandestino en Chile* pp. 7–30; informe: "Inside the CIA: Subversion"; concluir y entregar los diarios

l   19   García Márquez pp. 30–56

m 21   García Márquez pp. 57–80

v   23   García Márquez pp. 81–106

l   26   García Márquez pp. 107–36

m 28   Garcia Márquez pp. 137–52;

v   30   informes: "El mojado"; "The Buried Mirror V: Unfinished Business" y Rebeca Chávez, "Una entrevista con Rigoberta Menchú; trabajo analítico III

Monday, 25 January 1993: point of view and culture. Classes started last week. I introduced students to the issues of the course with a reading of García Márquez's Nobel Prize acceptance speech, "La soledad de América Latina" (The Solitude of Latin America). I asked them to react in writing to Márquez's statement that "the ravages of life are not the same for all. . . . Why think that the social justice sought by progressive Europeans for their own countries cannot also be a goal for Latin America, with different methods for dissimilar conditions?" One student responded that he was taking this course because he wanted a Latin American perspective on issues, like democracy and justice, which he has learned from a Western, first-world point of view.[1] For this student, reading *Me llamo Rigoberta Menchú* is a good place to start. In addition to their reading, I have asked the students to see selections from the animated film *Popol Vuh* and to think about the presence of ancient Mayan thought in Menchú's testimony. We will begin discussion of chapters 1 through 8 on Wednesday.

Wednesday, January 27: tradition. The traditions of Menchú's ancestors—traditions recorded in the ancient *Popol Vuh*—are important throughout *Me llamo Rigoberta Menchú*: by maintaining their ancient traditions, the Maya Quiché also maintain their ethnic identity. The *Popol Vuh* film[2] begins with the statement, "Hace mucho tiempo, antes de la era cristiana, los pueblos de la cultura maya de Guatemala y México relataban la historia de la creación—del nacimiento del sol y de la luna y de cómo germinó el primer grano de maíz" (A long time ago, before the time of Christianity, the Mayan people of Guatemala and Mexico told the story of creation—they spoke of the birth of the sun and the moon and of how the first grain of corn germinated). Today, a student noted the presence of dual imagery, like sun and moon, throughout the *Popol Vuh*.[3] With this as a starting point, we tried to determine whether the same kinds of dualities—indicative of the ancient Mayans' world view—resurface in the beginning chapters of Rigoberta Menchú's narrative. Clearly, duality is a presence in the epigraphs from the *Popol Vuh* and the *Chilam Balam* that the editor Elisabeth Burgos has placed at the beginning of chapters.[4] Duality is also significant when Menchú presents herself to her readers: "Me llamo Rigoberta Menchú ... *Mi situación personal* engloba toda *la realidad de un pueblo*" (My name is Rigoberta Menchú ... *My personal situation* encompasses the entire *reality of a people*) (1988, 21, emphasis mine). And duality continues to be important as Menchú explains her parents' responsibilities in the community: "En la comunidad de nosotros hay un elegido, un señor que goza de muchos prestigios. Es el representante que toda la comunidad lo considera como padre. Es el caso *de mi papá y de mi mamá*" (In our community an individual is elected, a man who enjoys a lot of prestige. He is the representative that the whole community treats like a father. This is the case of *my father and my mother*) (27, emphasis mine). I suggested that while the dualities, like mother/father and individual/community, which appear in *Me llamo Rigoberta Menchú* do echo the teachings of Menchú's ancestors, there are also moments of divergence. I cautioned the students to observe, as they read, both the instances in which Menchú clearly adheres to ancient thought and the times when she finds it necessary to break away.

Friday, January 29: divergence. Continuing our discussion of tradition, I asked students to do close readings of passages from chapter 9, "Ceremonias de la siembra y de la cosecha" (Ceremonies of Planting and Harvesting). One student wrote an analysis of the following selection in which Menchú elaborates on these Maya Quiché celebrations:

> ... cuando viene la cosecha ... se inicia el primer día cuando se recoge la mazorca, tanto la mazorca como la demás cosecha que tiene que dar la pequeña tierrita ... y se hace una ceremonia donde ... van a comer juntos los de la comunidad. Las mujeres recogen el fríjol y los hombres recogen la mazorca y todos recogemos las frutas de toda nuestra siembra (... when the harvest comes ... the first day of gathering the corn begins, the corn like the rest of the harvest that the dear earth gives ... and there is a ceremony ... where all the community comes to eat together. The women gather the beans and the men gather the corn and we all gather the fruits of our sowing). (78)

This student noted that, here, as Menchú focuses on the community's identification with the earth and the joys of planting and harvesting, her narration seems to correspond to the world view of the ancient Maya Quiché.[5] Nevertheless, although she narrates in the present tense, Menchú's current lifestyle as an exiled advocate of indigenous rights can no longer correspond to the binary rhythms of nature. In her analysis of this passage, my student has touched on one of the most compelling issues of Menchú's testimony: in the context of the narrator's twentieth-century life story, a "clear adherence" to the world view of the ancients may be impossible.

Monday, February 1: intervention. In order to further contextualize the students' reading—especially of chapter 15, "Cárcel del padre" (Jailing of her father)—I lectured on Guatemalan history today.[6] The students reacted with considerable interest to two points in particular: (1) that in support of United Fruit's opposition to the Arbenz administration (1950–53), U.S. Secretary of State John Foster Dulles and Allen Dulles of the CIA organized the invasion of Guatemala that ended Arbenz' presidency; and (2) that from 1953 to 1992 the vast majority of Guatemalan presidents were colonels or generals in the Guatemalan army. On the first point, most students found it curious that Rigoberta Menchú never explicitly mentions U.S. involvement in Guatemala in her narration. Nevertheless, as one student remarked, Elisabeth Burgos does suggest, albeit subtly, a U.S. presence in some of her epigraphs. At the beginning of chapter 9, for example, Burgos quotes Miguel Angel Asturias's *Hombres de maíz* (Men of corn): "Sembrado para comer es sagrado sustento del hombre que fue hecho de maíz. Sembrado por negocio es hambre del hombre que fue hecho de maíz" (Sown for eating is the sacred nourishment of the man who was made of corn. Sown for trade is the hunger of the man who was made of corn). According to my student, in its critique of capitalism the epigraph implicitly denounces U.S. involvement in Guatemala. On the second point, students found it extremely significant that Menchú portrays the heroic figures of her narration in stark opposition to the army officials who rule Guatemala. This is clearly the case in Menchú's portrayal of her father: in contrast with the long list of faceless dictators who promote racism and poverty, falsify elections and divide the country,[7] Vicente Menchú emerges as both a compassionate human being and a leader who sacrifices himself for the community.

Wednesday, February 3: oppression. For today's class, students read chapter 23, "Tortura y muerte de su hermanito quemado vivo junto con otras personas delante de los miembros de la comunidad" (Torture and death of her little brother who was burned alive with other people in front of members of the community). This is, by far, the most difficult chapter to teach. Students reacted in various ways to the burning alive of Rigoberta's brother: they expressed indignation, disbelief, anger (some of it directed at me for making them read this), and, in a few cases, a desire to "make things different." For me, the difficulty in teaching the chapter lies in trying to balance or temper the students' emotional responses with what I perceive to be one of my responsibilities as an educator—that is, to approach texts in a "scholarly and academic fashion." I think that an emotional response to Menchú's description of torture is both natural and important: it is precisely this emotion that helps the students stop seeing Rigoberta Menchú as an "exotic, romantic, mythical Indian." But in order for them to also start seeing Menchú as an intelligent, articulate spokeswoman whose cause includes promoting international solidarity with oppressed Guatemalans, they need to go one step further. This additional step requires a serious attempt at objective (relatively objective) textual analysis in response to the question, How do Burgos and Menchú achieve solidarity with their readers?

Friday, February 5: transcultural communication. As a companion piece to this morning's reading (chapter 27, "Sobre la muerte" [On death]) students watched the documentary *When the Mountains Tremble.* The film, narrated by Rigoberta Menchú, examines civil war and ethnic survival in Guatemala. I am beginning work of my own on this piece: since it was produced by U.S. filmmakers (Pamela Yates, Thomas Sigel, and Peter Konoy of Skylight Pictures) but narrated by Menchú, I am primarily interested in studying the images relevant to the text's transcultural composition.[8] I had asked the students to think about scenes in the film that indicate either a coming together or a clashing of cultures. We ended up focusing on a scene that does both: a section of *When the Mountains Tremble* in which the filmmakers document the aftermath of a government-sanctioned massacre of the indigenous inhabitants of a Guatemalan village. Viewers see close-up coverage of dead bodies; we also witness the intense human reactions of those who survived. Many students thought the scene brought them closer to an understanding of repression in Guatemala. They argued that by making us share the grief of the survivors, the filmmakers use their work to promote a sense of solidarity and compassion that transcends national boundaries. Others were troubled by the U.S. film crew's coverage of the massacre. They felt that by filming the intense grief of these Guatemalans so closely, "we" (U.S. citizens by association with the U.S. filmmakers) had, again, intervened where we don't belong.

Monday, February 8: women and solidarity.[9] I focused today's discussion on the analysis of chapters 29 ("Enseñanzas recibidas de su madre" [Teachings of her mother]) and 20 ("Sobre la mujer" [On women]). Many students, especially the women, stated that these were the chapters that most strongly promoted a sense of transcultural solidarity with Menchú. One student noted that the epigraph to chapter 29, a statement by Menchú on equality in the revolution, immediately draws North American and European women—accustomed to the struggle for equal rights—into Menchú's cause. Another student argued that her identification with Rigoberta began to solidify when Menchú described her departure from the traditional responsibilities of Maya Quiché women—a departure that resulted, to a certain extent, in a separation in identity between Rigoberta and her mother. According to this student, the mother/daughter separation is a common process in our culture, and although Menchú's circumstances are different from our own, the pain of the process is not so far removed.

Wednesday, February 10: exile. We are nearing the end of *Me llamo Rigoberta Menchú.* . . . The students discussed Rigoberta's exile today. They agreed that like her statement on feminism, Menchú's comments in chapter 33 ("El exilio" [Exile]) also promote international understanding and sympathy for her cause: when she is forced into exile, Menchú not only separates from her family, she also distances herself from her culture and her community. That distancing requires a new definition of community—one that eventually includes European intellectuals like Elisabeth Burgos, Nobel Peace Prize committees, and students of cultural history.

Friday, February 12: concluding Me llamo Rigoberta Menchú. Students finished their reading of Menchú's testimony and turned in midsemester papers today. The titles include "Las armas del pueblo según los indígenas de Guatemala" (The Weapons of the People According to the Native Americans of Guatemala), "El discurso emotivo en *Me llamo Rigoberta Menchú y así me nació la conciencia*" (Emotive Discourse in *I, Rigoberta Menchú*), "Elisabeth Burgos y el establecimiento de la solidaridad" (Elisabeth Burgos and the Establishment of Solidarity), and "Los secretos del pueblo" (The Secrets of the People). While all of these are important topics, the last is particularly relevant when it comes time to conclude the text: for this reason, I asked the student who had written the paper on "the secrets of the people" to lead the discussion on the book's final chapter. She began with Menchú's closing remarks:

Mi causa se radicaliza con la miseria que vive mi pueblo. . . . Por eso
es que yo he pasado por muchos lugares donde he tenido oportunidad de contar algo sobre mi pueblo . . . en toda mi narración yo
creo que doy una imagen de eso. Pero, sin embargo, todavía sigo
ocultando mi identidad como indígena. Sigo ocultando lo que yo
considero que nadie sabe, ni siquiera un antropólogo, ni un intelectual, por más que tenga muchos libros, no saben distinguir todos
nuestros secretos (My cuase becomes radical with the misery that my
people live. . . . This is why I have visited many places where I have
had the opportunity to relate something about my people . . .
throughout my narration I believe I give an image of this. Nevertheless, I continue hiding my indigenous identity. I continue hiding what
I believe that no one knows, not even an anthropologist, nor an intellectual, for as many books as they might have, they can't find out all
our secrets). (271)

The student in charge of the discussion asked her classmates what effect this
conclusion had on them: Why had Menchú worked so hard to build international solidarity with her readers in order to distance herself in the end? While
a few students felt that this was a tactical error on Menchú's part ("Doesn't she
need our understanding?"), others strongly argued that Rigoberta's closing
words were extremely astute: She does need international understanding, but
she also needs to maintain control over her own situation and to resist "well
meaning" interventions from abroad. The text's closing words, therefore, stress
respect and self-determination over international unity.

Monday, February 15: Rigoberta Menchú and Elena Poniatowska. After the
students conclude their readings of *Me llamo Rigoberta Menchú,* I like to have
them study selections from Elena Poniatowska's *La noche de Tlatelolco*
(Massacre in Mexico). Like Menchú, Poniatowska recalls the words of the
ancients as she constructs her narration of contemporary history—the events
of 1968 that resulted in the massacre of hundreds of university students and
their supporters in the Plaza de Tlatelolco in Mexico City.[10] Poniatowska
reveals, for example that as family members mourned their slaughtered loved
ones, they read aloud from Nahuatl texts that mourn the conquest of Mexico.
Some students noted that in both Guatemala and Mexico "conquests" seem to
extend well beyond the sixteenth century.

Monday, February 22: Rigoberta Menchú and Cristóbal Colón. We began
reading Colón today. As a bridge between the last month's discussion and our
investigation of the fifteenth- and sixteenth-century Spanish chronicles, I had
planned to mention ideas from an article I wrote during the Quincentennary
on Rigoberta Menchú's response to 1492.[11] Well, my prompting wasn't terribly
necessary because as soon as I opened the discussion of Columbus's diary,

students noted its impact on *Me llamo Rigoberta Menchú*.[12] They were quick to observe, for example, that throughout his diary Columbus describes America's indigenous peoples as "other": perhaps, our initial reactions to Menchú as romantic and exotic are as old as 1492.[13]

Monday, March 15: Rigoberta Menchú and Karl Marx. It has been almost a month since we finished our discussion of the sixteenth-century Spanish chronicles and a month since Rigoberta Menchú's name has come up in class. But, today, I lectured on Marxism and a student remarked that although Menchú never declares an adherence to Marxist thought (in fact, she is careful not to do so), Marx's words do seem to echo throughout her text: the Marxist notion that "the history of all ... society is the history of class struggle"[14] is certainly present in Menchú's narration of conflicts between land owners and peasants, the formation of the CUC (Comité de Unidad Campesina [United Farmworks Committee]) and the farmworkers May 1 march on the Guatemalan Capital.

Friday, March 26: Rigoberta Menchú and Domitila Barrios de Chungara. Today, we began reading *Si me permiten hablar ... Testimonio de Domitila* (Let Me Speak ... The Testimony of Domitila). Students immediately noted the thematic and stylistic similarities between the story of the Bolivian mineworkers and *Me llamo Rigoberta Menchú*: Rigoberta's declaration that her personal experience is "the reality of a whole people" clearly resembles the selection from Domitila entitled "Lo que clama mi pueblo" (What my people cry out for).[15] But the students perceived differences as well. On the issue of feminism, for example, they remarked that while Rigoberta tends to draw her first-world readers into her cause, Domitila sets up boundaries in order to clarify her own position as radically different from that of her readers.[16]

April 16: Rigoberta Menchú and Miguel Littín. We are working on an analysis of *La aventura de Miguel Littín clandestino en Chile* (The Adventure of Miguel Littín Clandestine in Chile). Miguel Littín is an exiled Chilean filmmaker who returned to Chile in 1985 to film "the reality of his country after twelve years of military dictatorship" (García Márquez 1986, 1). When the filming was complete, Littín went back into exile in Madrid where he produced—for an international audience—his story of life under the Pinochet regime (1). In our discussion of this text, a student observed that Miguel Littín's work is remarkably similar to that of Rigoberta Menchú: both have turned exile into a weapon of resistance.

Wednesday, April 28: Rigoberta Menchú and García Márquez. Back in January, I used García Márquez's "La soledad de América Latina" (The solitude of Latin America) to introduce students to the issues of this course—issues like solidarity and intervention, justice and survival. And for the past few months, the students have been keeping journals on their "outside reading" of

Márquez's *Cien años de soledad* (One hundred years of solitude). Today, I decided to begin drawing the course to a close with a discussion of the last lines of the last page of this book: "porque las estirpes condenadas a cien años de soledad no tenían una segunda oportunidad sobre la tierra" (because races condemnded to one hundred years of solitude did not have a second opportunity on earth) (García Márquez 1970, 432). The issue, here, as my students suggested, is that unlike the mythical Buendías, many Latin Americans, like Domitila Barrios de Chungara, Miguel Littín, and Rigoberta Menchú, have seized their second opportunities to resist oppression and to create more just societies.

Friday, April 30: Rigoberta Menchú and The Cultural History of Latin America. Today was the last day of class—the day when I step back and turn the discussion over to the students. One student had prepared an oral presentation on Rigoberta Menchú and the issues of the course. She began by showing a videotaped interview with Menchú by the Cuban filmmaker Rebeca Chávez. In one of the most passionate moments of the interview, Menchú makes a statement about her role in history: "Fuimos tejedores de vestidos bonitos y ahora somos tejedores de la historia" (We were weavers of beautiful clothes and now we are weavers of history). When the student in charge of the presentation asked for an interpretation of this comment, the class offered the following remarks: "It's clear from the contrast between the past (*fuimos* [we were]) and the present (*somos* [we are]) in this statement that Menchú's identification with her ancestors has changed—it had to change." "Yes, and the subject of her remarks is changing too: Rigoberta's 'we' is a reference to herself and to her father, but isn't she really talking about Guatemala in general?" "Well, her community has grown, so she's also talking about Domitila and Miguel Littín . . . she's weaving it all together." "I guess that's what we're doing too."[17]

Monday, May 10: border crossings. Exams have been graded. Papers have been read. I am beginning to focus on my research again. While I revise my article on transcultural imagery in *When the Mountains Tremble*, I am thinking a lot about the poem "Crucé la frontera, amor" (I crossed the border, love) with which Menchú concludes her narration of this documentary. Indeed, Menchú has not only crossed the borders that divide nations and races, she has challenged us all to seriously consider the validity of those divisions. Just yesterday, I read a report in *The New York Times* ("Nobel Laureate Rallies a Community") on Menchú's recent address to Salvadoran refugees living in Long Island. The issues important to Menchú—issues of identity, equality, and survival—are pertinent to Salvadoran refugees and to long-term citizens of the United States as well. When I teach the cultural history course next spring, I may ask the students to bring their discussions back home again—to do some questioning of recent events in this country in light of Menchú's work. For the time being, however, my writing calls. Fortunately, the border between teaching Cultural History and writing about Rigoberta Menchú is a pleasant one to cross.

NOTES

1. García Márquez won the Nobel Prize for literature in 1982. On the first day of the cultural history course, I use Marina Castañeda's English translation of Márquez's acceptance speech, which was published in *The New York Times* on 6 February 1983. In addition to the issues of justice and difference mentioned by this student, Márquez's comments on solitude and solidarity are also relevant in the teaching of *Me llamo Rigoberta Menchú.*

2. The film, produced by the University of California–Berkeley in 1989, uses animation taken from the drawings of classic Mayan pottery. It begins with the creation of the world according to the ancient Maya and ends with the victory of the hero twins over the evil lords of the underworld.

3. On duality, see Dennis Tedlock's introduction to the *Popol Vuh* where he writes, for example, that the first people modeled from corn dough, the first Quiché leaders, were dual entities—the mother/fathers of their lineage (47).

4. See, for example, the epigraph preceding chapter 15: "Acopiad el *grano y las semillas* y juntad los retoños que tiempos de sequía y de hambre avecinan" (Gather together *the grain and the seeds* and gather the sprouts because times of draught and hunger are near) (128, emphasis mine). These epigraphs also suggest an additional area of interest to the students—the role Burgos plays as editor of the text.

5. The harvest scenes in the film *El norte* (The North) also provide some intriguing insights into this chapter. In addition to the imagery that stresses the Maya Quiché's identification with the earth, there is a circularity present in the film that, like Menchú's narration, emphasizes the rythmns of planting and reaping.

6. In *Modern Latin America,* Skidmore and Smith (1989) provide a complete and concise analysis of Guatemalan history beginning with the arrival of the Spaniards in 1501. The information in the lecture noted here comes from this text.

7. Menchú addresses these issues directly in chapter 17, "Autodefensa en la aldea" (Self-defence in the Village).

8. *When the Mountains Tremble* was produced in 1983 and re-released with additional narrative by Menchú after she won the Nobel Peace Prize in 1992. For additional information, see Erik Barnouw, *Documentary: A History of the Non-fiction Film* (300–2) and Alan Rosenthal, "*When the Mountains Tremble*: An Interview with Pamela Yates," in Rosenthal (1988). My article, "*When the Mountains Tremble*: Images of Ethnicity," in a Transcultural Text" is forthcoming in the University of Minnesota's *Hispanic Issues* series.

9. On feminism, solidarity, and Menchú's narrative, see Elizabeth Meese, "(Dis)Locations: Reading the Theory of a Third-World Woman in *I, Rigobera Menchú*," in *(Ex)Tensions: Re-figuring Feminist Criticism.*

10. See also Poniatowska's *Fuerte es el silencio* (*Strong is the Silence*), in which she describes conditions in Mexico that stimulated the 1968 student movement.

11. In "Authority and Reconquest," in *Me llamo Rigoberta Menchú y así me nació la conciencia,*" I argue that Menchú appropriates the language of authority used by the Spanish chroniclers in their accounts of the discovery and conquest of America. This dialogic appropriation is part of Menchú's struggle for the reconquest of her culture.

12. I should note, here, that I organize the readings in this course thematically, and not chronologically, in order to stimulate these kinds of comparisons.

13. On this topic, see Todorov (1984), *The Conquest of America* and de Certeau (1986), *Heterologies: Discourse on the Other.*

14. See Marx and Engels (1992), *The Communist Manifesto,* page 3.

15. The narrator as spokesperson for the people is one of the most obvious and consistent characteristics of testimonial writing. See John Beverley, "The Margin at the Center: On *Testimonio,*" in Sidonie Smith and Julia Watson (1992), *De/Colonizing the Subject.*

16. This is particularly true in the selection from Domitila's narrative entitled "En la Tribuna del Año Internacional de la Mujer" (On the Platform of the International Year of the Woman].

17. I am grateful to the students of Spanish 311 who so willingly engaged in many hours of discussion on this topic. Special thanks to Susan Clifford, Tracy Devine, Michael Lambert, and Michelle Osborne for the insightful research papers mentioned in the February 12 journal entry, "concluding Rigoberta Menchú," and to Megan Maher for the presentation on Menchú that concluded the course.

27

TRAINING TEACHERS WITH RIGOBERTA MENCHÚ
A Computer Conference

ALLEN CAREY-WEBB

INTRODUCTION

My principal responsibility in the English Department at Western Michigan University is offering a 400-level course entitled "Teaching Literature in the Secondary Schools." Designed for English majors and returning students who will be student teaching the following semester in either high school or middle school language arts, the course is one part of a complex program. Western Michigan University is one of the largest teacher training institutions in the country; the English department alone has 310 declared majors with a secondary education emphasis. In addition to carrying full loads and finishing up their English programs, many of my students are employed more than twenty hours a week to pay their own way through school. By the time they arrive in my class they have a reasonable command of English skills, an introduction to traditional literature, and a commitment to enter a career that is neither glamorous nor remunerative, but personally rewarding and socially significant. At the same time, their backgrounds and experiences are often limited. Nearly every student that enters my class has grown up either in one of Michigan's rural small towns or in one of its protected suburbs. Few have traveled, and for my students—overwhelmingly white and middle class—the Western Michigan campus and the close-in berg of Kalamazoo may represent the most racially and socially mixed environment they have encountered.

This chapter contains an edited transcript of a computer conference discussion of pre-service secondary English teachers on the subject of teaching Rigoberta Menchú's testimonial. Preceding this transcript is an introduction that describes the purposes of the course in which the conference took place, the relevance of *I, Rigoberta Menchú* to this class, and the way computer conference technology was used. Following the transcript there is a brief conclusion.

Thus, as I see it, the single most important objective as I work with these aspiring teachers is to broaden their interests and range of vision so that regardless of where they end up teaching—either in communities like those they came from or in more racially and socially diverse environments—they will be able to make their language arts teaching meaningful to their students and to a changing world. Toward this end I have found no ready-made approach or easy answer. Instead, by experimenting with syllabi and methods in every section of the course, I hope to create relevant learning that will stretch, enrich, and sharpen my students' understanding. Some sections of the course have drawn on educational thinkers with critical thinking agendas, such as Paulo Freire, Henry Giroux, Gerald Graff, and Terry Eagleton. Other sections have been more practical, examining "real world" case studies involving a variety of students and classrooms. I have also used teacher narratives of transformative teaching experiences, such as the recent collection edited by Mark Hurlburt entitled *Social Issues in the English Classroom*. Always in this class we develop and explore a variety of issues in a problem-posing format. I encourage us to examine pedagogical strategies for working with literature by minority authors, and at the same time consider ways to integrate minority literatures with more traditional works. In this effort I have found it necessary to make the historical relevant to the contemporary, to move across disciplines, and to borrow eclectically from other traditions and approaches. Since I share the general concern that young people lack historical understanding, in my literature methods course I utilize a "history across the curriculum" approach. (Howard Zinn's *A People's History of the United States* has been particularly useful in this regard.) In this class we also read books that help us discover and reconsider the traditional "boundaries" of Language Arts teaching, works such as *Annie on My Mind*, an adolescent novel about two young women falling in love with each other, or *Half Humankind*, a collection of vituperative street pamphlets from Shakespeare's day about the role of women in society, or *Monster*, Kody Scott's recent autobiography of life as a member of the Crips in South Central Los Angeles, or, relevant to *Teaching and Testimony*, *I, Rigoberta Menchú*.

Particularly when preparing aspiring teachers, I believe that the way I run my own class is just as important, if not more important, than the content I choose to include. In Teaching Literature in the Secondary Schools I have attempted to decenter my authority by forming collaborative student groups. These groups take on responsibility for the different units of the class, for which they choose and order books, design classroom activities, lead large and small group discussions, assign and evaluate written work. These groups have also invited special speakers to the class, set up panels of area teachers, developed complex role plays, organized community projects, made school observations, attended conferences, created case studies, and so forth. I find this collaborative teaching approach very demanding of all of us, requiring hours of group meetings outside of class, extended phone consultations, extra reading to develop curriculum, written responses to each other's assignments, and so on. I have learned that as professor, resource, and facilitator, I need to remain in active dialogue with the students throughout the process. Yet, while this student-directed learning is unpredictable—part of my own pleasure in the process is that I don't always know what will happen next—there can be no denying the variety, the energy, and the devotion that the approach has generated. As students move from the beginning of the semester, where some are uncertain, even trepidacious, to the end when there is usually a general enthusiasm for the approach, I observe a consistent improvement in the design of class activities and an increasing self-confidence and openness to experimentation. Students become more and more willing to disagree with the professor (and sometimes even ignore him! See the confer transcript below). The team teaching experience itself becomes a crucial part of the course, something that prepares aspiring teachers for participation in their future roles as members of a department or curriculum development teams, as coteachers, and, most importantly, as orchestrators of collaborative learning in their own classrooms. As it unfolds over the semester the group process becomes a matter for discussion and analysis, something we do in individual and group meetings, on the computer conference, and, in recent sections, on the final exam.

The sense of ownership and responsibility for curriculum development that emerges in English 480 is something that I view as especially important for aspiring teachers in the 1990s. Today public school English teaching is ever more constrained by anxieties over job security and a narrowing range of nationally marketed standardized textbooks produced by a shrinking handful of publishers. Some school administrations and teachers seem to find the "pre-approved" textbook approach safer and more comfortable than the earlier tradition of teacher selection of individual works, materials, and assignments—and they are encouraged in this view by the powerful marketing efforts of the publishing houses that present their books as teacher tested, up to date, and cost effective. Yet, I remain convinced that the best English teachers are not curriculum takers, but curriculum makers, willing to develop generative thematic concepts and thoughtfully explore established orthodoxies. I hope that by taking my class all of my students will become more courageous, inclined to strategically resist the encroachment on the classroom of textbook manufacturers and curriculum standardizers. Thus, one of the primary purposes of my pre-service training is to help aspiring English teachers recognize the limitations of traditional, prepackaged textbooks and behaviorist, cookbook methodology in favor of developing curriculum in a dialogic interaction between students and contemporary issues. My approach does not call for English teachers to jettison "the canon" or disciplinary skills and knowledge. Instead, I believe aspiring teachers need to better understand the historic processes of exclusion and canon making and the political negotiations involved in designating certain skills as "abstract" or "neutral."[1] Moreover, while I affiliate myself with the multicultural movement, I respect Cornel West's admonition that new literatures should not simply be added to an expanded canon, but that an incorporation of minority perspectives needs to include "a wholesome reconsideration of the canon already in place" (19).[2] With an understanding of the dynamic nature of canonical change, teachers and students can examine together what has been taught, what should be taught, and how to collectively formulate a responsible and responsive learning content and process.

Given my students and my approach to Teaching Literature in the Secondary Schools, *I, Rigoberta Menchú* presents itself as a useful text. Foremost, perhaps, is the fact that Menchú's deep and abiding commitment to democratic social change—despite extraordinary adversity—offers inspirational reinforcement for my student's initial motivation for entering teaching, their belief that they, too, can make a difference. Tragically, teacher training and the customary activities of public school teaching often put an enormous drain on idealism. The acquiring of technical knowledge about adolescents and school systems, navigating the complexities of the university—often while holding down outside employment—and the enormous responsibilities and lack of support for classroom teachers can overwhelm enthusiasm. Though I don't think this emerges very well from the computer conference below, it is possible for *I, Rigoberta Menchú* to remind my students that if some of the poorest and most desperate people of the world can band together to resist oppression by a despotic military government, so can they, in their own less dire situations, join with others in the effort to improve their world. Indeed, in most of the courses where we have read it, *I, Rigoberta Menchú* has supported my students' conviction that teaching and learning can and should be powerful, engaging experiences.

I also believe that *I, Rigoberta Menchú* is a text that will extend my students' perspective and concerns, facilitating a vision of teaching within a more global frame—even if, at first, they find it strange and difficult to relate to. By the time students arrive in my class they have a background in traditional works and New Critical approaches that can be augmented, even defamiliarized, by this testimonial of a Guatemalan peasant woman. Indeed, *I, Rigoberta Menchú* allows students to explore themes and issues that they haven't focused on in their other course work but that are broadly relevant to multicultural and cultural studies teaching, such as oral and autobiographical traditions, the complex interrelationships of politics, history, and culture, tensions between assimilation and minority cultural identities, experiences of oppression and inequality, the organizing of resistance, and the relations between local, minority, national, and international cultures. As they consider these issues, via Menchú, these prospective English teachers can become directly involved in some of the most current questions in the academic study of literature and can learn to contextualize them within a pedagogical framework and their own vision of the classroom. This effort is partly documented in the computer conference reprinted below. In my course students come to wonder what they will be asked to teach in the public schools, how students, parents, and administrators may react to curricular innovation, and how to justify their own risk taking. As they put together plans for the kind of teaching they hope to do, the urgency of Rigoberta Menchú's story ought to challenge them to develop meaningful connections between their classrooms and the world.

We have not used *I, Rigoberta Menchú* in every section of English 480 and when the book has been inserted things work out differently every time. In my view no section of the class has yet taken full advantage of what the testimonial has to offer to aspiring teachers, and this may be as much due to the way I have been teaching as to the students. The fall term of 1993 (from which the computer conference transcript below is taken) seemed in particular to reflect some lack, discontinuity, and incompleteness in grappling with Menchú's words. I initially planned this course to focus on the theme "Multicultural Democracy and the Teaching of Literature," with the notion that we might be able to draw on the changing South African political situation currently dominating the news in order to reflect on the pitfalls and possibilities of teaching literature in the rather less volatile, multicultural democracy of the United States. With this theme in mind I proposed a wide range of student-led units with open possibilities for a variety of reading. From this menu of choices students decided to focus on (1) the pedagogical issues involved in teaching literature from South Africa (the major reading they chose included *Cry the Beloved Country* and *Kaffir Boy*); (2) literature and materials about the founding of new worlds (included *Utopia*, *The Tempest* and *Morning Girl*); (3) teaching about slavery (included *Huckleberry Finn*, Frederick Douglass and Linda Brent's slave narrative, Nat Hentoff's adolescent novel *The Day They Came to Steal the Book*, *Satire and Evasion: Black Perspectives on Huck Finn*); (4) race and American justice (they assigned Malcolm X's *Autobiography*); (5) sexual orientation and literature teaching (included *Annie on My Mind*); (6) poverty and homelessness (they included *Rachel and Her Children*); and, (7) a final unit called "making change." It was for this last section of the course that the student leaders decided to use *I, Rigoberta Menchú* as a way to revisit many of the central themes of the course, and, simultaneously, examine the process of social change described in the story. As a starting point the group leaders decided the class should consider whether or not *I, Rigoberta Menchú* was "literature" that could be taught in the public schools—a relevant question since the title of my course would seem to imply that if it isn't "literature" it doesn't belong in the secondary English curriculum. This question served as a starting point for the last unit, and since it was posted by one of the student leaders on the computer conference a week in advance of the scheduled discussion, the first comments in the conference represent student contributions before any whole group meeting on the topic. For this final week-and-a-half long unit the student leaders asked their classmates to do a great deal: read *I, Rigoberta Menchú* and two additional articles, write a journal entry, a computer conference entry, and a three- to five-page lesson plan. Since it was the hectic final week of a very busy semester, with other projects due and a final exam a couple of days away, the reading of Menchú's story was hurried. (Compared to the truly fearsome workload of the typical secondary English teacher, however, I suppose they still had it easy.) Moreover, time was not taken for these students to explore the background of the story in Guatemalan history or Mayan culture. These limitations did affect their responses, and the alienation from the text that some of the students manifest provides a starting point for my own ongoing reflection on and reformulation of the class. Nonetheless, the conference transcript demonstrates that they still managed a rich, multifaceted discussion marked by the strong feelings any classroom encounter with Menchú seems to produce. At times they are sharply critical of *I, Rigoberta Menchú*. Yet, as these students listen to each other they complicate and develop their thinking, often advancing approaches that compare well with the teaching described by many of the more experienced teachers contributing to *Teaching and Testimony*.

Since many readers may be unfamiliar with the incorporation of computer conferences into instruction, it is necessary to give a bit of explanation of my use of the technology. Since I first experimented with bringing a computer conference into my courses (in the winter term of 1993), the approach has quickly become an integral part of my teaching repertoire, providing an additional space for thoughtful and completely interactive communication. By the end of each course my students have, in effect, collectively written hundreds and hundreds of pages of responsive discourse closely tied to the central themes we are studying. While there is intense, dialogic conversation on the "confer," there is no interrupting, which seems to make participation more comfortable, in particular for some of my women students. The confer simultaneously involves students closely with course content and offers them a high degree of independence and freedom. Students are often more open about what they say on the confer than in class, and, after they become comfortable with the format, they begin initiating items for whole class discussion. The few students who come to the class already familiar with confer are usually delighted that the class will include one.

The computer conference for the 1993 fall semester of Teaching Literature in the Secondary Schools turned out to be about average in length. It included forty different items of discussion, most of them put forward by students. The average item had over 50 responses, some items as many as 134; over the term the conference was accessed 1491 times by students in my class either from terminals on campus or via modems from their home computers. Except for two training sessions early in the term, all confer time was "outside of class." I let students know that I expect at least forty minutes of quality time per week on the confer—and the system includes a built-in mechanism for me to check up on this. I would say that item 38, the item on teaching Rigoberta Menchú, develops somewhat less and is somewhat less interactive than many of the other items, perhaps because students kept returning to the opening question. The conversational tone of this confer item is typical. For publication in *Teaching and Testimony*, fifteen redundant entries were removed (indicated by the numbering) and several that do appear were slightly edited.

THE COMPUTER CONFERENCE

ITEM 38

11/30/93 16: 53
David DePeal
Well, gang! Here it is. . . . Your confer question for the Making Change unit: Is *I, Rigoberta Menchú* literature? Would you teach it? Why/Why Not? How might it be taught?

51 RESPONSES

11/30/93 23: 56
38: 1) Christopher Roberts
In my opinion, this book is an ethnography and would be suitable material for an anthropology class. And this particular ethnography is most certainly not the most well-written or interesting one I've read.

12/03/93 21: 22
38: 6) Allen Carey-Webb:
Might we teach ethnography in "literature" classes? Can we always clearly distinguish "ethnography" from "literature"? (I actually don't see my own teaching as strictly limited to "literature," but think of what I do more as a form of "cultural studies.")

12/06/93 14: 38
38: 8) Beth Moore
Yes, it is literature. Would I teach it? Maybe, it would have to depend on the class that I was working with. I may only teach parts of it. It is a hard text and long, in my opinion. The perspective is very interesting, though.

12/06/93 15: 36
38: 10) Anne Schipper
I found *I, RM* ponderous reading. Thoughts were too scattered. I never could quite keep up with the time sequence. I don't think I would teach the book. I would definitely use excerpts dealing with Indian life, culture, and the persecutions still going on. I think I would pick a book that was more interesting (*Let Me Speak?*) and collect pieces from other testimonial literature. I would

introduce it with a video ("El Norte" is a really good one). Maybe I could create a unit on testimonial lit and could culminate in students giving their own "testimonial."

12/06/93 22: 02
38: 11) Christopher Roberts
Anyway, I would never teach *I, Rigoberta Menchú* in a high school English class; the writing is poor and tedious and it reads like a chemistry textbook. I might use excerpts to lead into relevant grassroots (local) issue discussions, but probably not even that. This book is not interesting enough to hold the attention of the average high school English student.

12/07/93 00: 18
38: 13) Thea R. Mann
I ditto Chris's opinion.

12/07/93 00: 58
38: 14) Denise Wright
I believe that *I, RM* is literature. However, I am not convinced that I would use the book as a whole in my classroom. Excerpts would be beneficial, especially to emphasize the oppression and lives of Indians. I feel the book is informative, but it does lack something that would make high school students interested in it. Possibly because it's not romanticized, turned into a story that's "sure to sell." Does American society REALLY want to read about a child being burned alive in front of their family? I don't think so. But I would use excerpts from the book, to get some serious reality across to the students.

12/07/93 12: 57
38: 15) Melinda Hagaman
I agree that *I, RM* is literature. However, I agree with Denise that I would not teach the entire book in my class. I thought the things that happened were terrible, but I felt like it was just fact, fact, fact. The oppression that occurred caused feeling, but I think Rigoberta's feelings shown more explicitly would have been more powerful. Nonetheless, I would take excerpts from the book to use in different units. I think the different chapters/parts could be used in units on women, oppression, and changes. This would especially be good if I was stuck with an already established curriculum. The reading could be supplemental to what we were already doing.

12/07/93 14: 36
38: 16) Susan Cunningham
I feel that I could teach *I, RM* in the classroom. I'm not sure that I would teach it as whole, but I feel that high school students may find it more interesting than some of the dull overdone stuff that some teachers assign. This is real and it is still going on. As Anne suggests maybe it could serve as a lead in to stu-

dents writing their own stories about themselves. Maybe students would be refreshed by the "not perfect writing" and really get into it. I don't know, but I think I would have really enjoyed this much more than most things that I was forced to read in high school.

12/07/93 16: 45
38: 17) Jennifer Purkiss

I am going to have to give pretty much the same response here. I would not teach the book as a whole, but would surely use parts of it. I, too, think that having the kids do a sort of testimonial would be a great idea. The best part of using this would be that this is something that is happening now—today. . . .

12/07/93 17: 11
38: 18) David DePeal

Okay. We seem to be running into a consensus here about teaching only sections of the book. Now let me throw ya a monkey wrench. Doesn't teaching only part of a work detract from the original meaning and bastardize it? Would you show art students only Mona Lisa's smile? How can you only teach a portion of a work?

38: 21) Tom Morris

Dave: To your new question, partitioning the book does not make it less effective. Everything you read has been edited—this is not the only version of *I, RM,* although it may be the only published version. Every sentence, paragraph, and chapter carries its own meaning to be studied, and yes, art students are looking at Mona's smile.

It's obvious from their comments that a few people were unaffected by *I, RM,* and that a few were extremely moved. I would rather use this in a culture class than a literature class, because it's merit is buried in the actual events that took place, not her tale. It might fit into some literature curriculums, as a biography for example. But we might have to include Iacocca or Sam's book.
12/07/93 20: 29

38: 22) Anne Schipper

That might not be an all-bad idea, Tom. They are definitely part of America as we know it today. And if UCLA can ask Milliken to teach a course on corporate business!!! ("And class, we now are going to do a unit on how NOT to live. . . .")

12/08/93 11: 02
38: 23) Sherri Ouellette

I think that I would consider using *I, RM* in a lit class, but I agree with quite a few of the people who previously stated that they would only use portions of it in their class. I think this book has many merits, and I think portions could be effectively used in a unit on women, making change, or even manipulation. The way our government manipulates us into believing things that benefit only the government itself is astounding. I think having students read parts of this book and then asking them how they feel about the idea that Rigoberta and her family were considered "guerrillas" would be effective. This could fit in well with the idea of how we are manipulated into believing that Columbus was a hero, especially with the Indian culture tie in.

12/08/93 15: 22
38: 24) Meredith Johnston

Due to its directness and real-life situations, testimonial literature allows students and teachers alike to experience the power of language. Furthermore, testimonials or passages from testimonials, Dave, work well when studied in connection with the more traditional or canonical literature. Therefore, using only certain pieces of literature not only compliments various other works, it adds to the effects and results these pieces have on the reader.

12/08/93 15: 22
38: 25) Denise Wright

Although teaching the whole book might be a nice way to spend a six-week period, I don't feel that it will benefit the students to read the whole book. We are college students and some of us find it difficult to stay focused or interested in the book, so how do we expect high school aged students to stay on-task with it? It wouldn't be censoring the work either, I don't believe. By giving the students excerpts of the book they are learning the story and oppression etc., but there wouldn't be as much despised by the students if they only read segments of the books.

12/09/93 11: 02
38: 28) Tom Morris

Whether the teacher loves a book or not, some of the students are going to lose interest with any topic. My sophomore English teacher was obviously interested in Native American culture, a unit that a few of us stumbled through due to a lack of excitement. Studying Guatemalan culture would have a wonderful appeal to some students, so why couldn't the book be included on an outside reading list, as Allen suggested in class Wednesday?

12/09/93 12: 01
38: 29) Allen Carey-Webb

In my previous experience many students initially have difficulty stretching themselves to relate to the Quiché-Mayan culture, but as we discuss the story, read aloud passages, examine the way that the Native Americans see the world my previous students have usually connected with the book and have been anxious to have others read it or to teach it themselves.

I see what has turned out to be an emphasis on testimonials in this class as a worthwhile experiment that may end up diversifying the more "traditional" materials I tend to assume you all have been getting in your other English courses. Perhaps the curriculum at Western has changed more than I realize, however, and "multicultural" materials have become a more dominant form. On the other hand, maybe we are weaned on one kind of literature and, because it is familiar, seek to return to it ... still I wonder why? Whose interests are being served? How have our own backgrounds effected our taste in literature? Why? How might we develop new tastes? Should we?

I am interested in your responses. I need them, in fact, as I am sure the reaction of this class to the testimonial will play a part in the book I will soon be working on. (If you don't want me to quote what you say on the confer, let me know, as I will be tempted to directly incorporate your thoughts and reactions in the project.)

12/09/93 14: 50
38: 30) Daria Moskwa

I think that *I, Rigoberta* is literature, but I do not think that I would teach it. It is possible that I do not have a complete picture of the book, as I have not yet finished it. The fact that I can always find something to do (like washing the dishes) when I should be reading it, tells me that I am not interested enough to teach it. For some reason (and maybe part of it is end of the semester burnout/ senioritis), I cannot get excited about this book. There have been books that we've used in this class that I couldn't stop talking about—*Rachel and Her Children* and *Malcolm X,* for example—and I think that my time and my students' time would be better spent with something that I could be excited about. I would, however, offer *I, Rigoberta* as an optional reading for my students— maybe they could get excited about it and teach it to their classmates with an enthusiasm that I just don't have.

12/09/93 15: 15
38: 31) John Glasgow

Hello! I share in Allen's surprise at the class reaction—not all of it, specifically that some found it boring! This book very much moved me. I felt that I did get to know her as a person, and her culture, perhaps some of it based on inferences. I was appalled, shocked, and had trouble putting it down—it was almost like putting my conscience aside. Yet I can understand how it might be boring. But hey, although I have read and watched, on video and in theaters, "Romeo and Juliet" many times, I still get teary-eyed at the end. I guess I am just naturally emotional.

The book is literature. I do not see any way around that. I believe I would like to teach it, once I know more about the context and history associated with it. However, I do not know where I would teach it. I think college is very appropriate (but it is too long for just one-and-a-half weeks; especially immediately prior to finals week!). It is the type of book that not only cries out to be read and understood, but is a book that requires thought and, relatively speaking, slower reading. For example, I began each chapter by looking up the Spanish word meanings in the back of the book, write them near the words in the text, then read. Laboriosity!

In high school, I probably would agree that passages (i.e. chapters) might be more appropriate for that reading level. I am not so sure how I might go about choosing which ones, however. I think the book can add a new dimension to a student's understanding of, as Anne so eloquently expressed it, this great and glorious nation of ours. There are atrocities that the future voters need to know about—not only to change the world if they wish, but to hear the truth, and form intelligent decisions based upon exploring all of the angles. As some of you suggested, the text might fit better into other classes, e.g. anthropology or social studies. Why not use it in conjunction with these classes, i.e. get together with the other teacher and see if it can fit into an integrated curriculum?

12/09/93 15: 48
38: 32) Tammy Bobell
Well. . . .

Sorry that anyone was offended by the "B" word in association to Menchú, (you know—boring) but I had a hard time getting into it. Would I teach this in an English class? No. Why?

1. I didn't like the book, and as such can't feel justified in teaching it. I don't feel that I could get excited about Menchú, and I know that the kids would sense that lack of enthusiasm, therefore probably not getting into it themselves.

2. I don't think that could make it relevant to the lives of my students. If its not relevant, why learn it? "Hamlet" is at least relevant in that he is a kid, his mom remarries and he hates his step-father.

3. I didn't find this to be an exceptionally well-written piece of literature.

4. I'm afraid that this would only reinforce stereotypes of Latin Americans that my students may already have. Poor, migrants, barbaric, etc.

12/09/93 16: 31
38: 33) William deDie

This book was informative, frustrating, sometimes angering, and very depressing. It is very much an oral story, loaded with sidetracks and antedotes. The problem is the organization. It seems so circular. By the end of the book, we were talking about what she learned as she was coming of age. Besides, most of the specific cultural information was needed to know the significance of these peoples' actions, such as when using cut flowers.

The violence in this book is very graphic, and much harder to read than a fictional novel where you know it is not real. The decisions she made involved tough choices, sometimes even having to reject her own cultural values. This would be very hard in the tight-knit community in which she lived.

If a teacher was going to use this book in a high school class it would have to be in a very special situation. *I, RM* cries out for historical context, particularly of Central America. It would be irresponsible to teach this book without this information. Also, the teacher would have to make sure the students came to understand the world view and values of this culture. These two things are so radically different from twentieth-century America that students might have problems relating.

There are problems I see arising when using this book in a high school class. I agree that it is important to look at the U.S. involvement in Central America and in other places as well. But how do you handle the contrast between what the U.S. news media tells people and what this book tells people? I know there is more than one side to every story, but when you realize that the military commanders were trained in the United States, this means that they have the same ability to do the same to any single person who tries to make changes. R's society supported her, housed her on her travels, and helped to protect her, but what in the United States do we have to compare with these numerous communities of people all under the same oppression?

In this country, we are so concerned with ourselves we often neglect the concerns of the masses. And when those masses rise up, they are beaten down just like in Los Angeles. What people supported them? How were they portrayed on the news media? And isn't bringing the pictures of those protesters being beaten into our homes during meal time the same thing as bringing all the peasants to the city to watch the torture and executions?

If this book were to be taught in our future classrooms as a way to consider making social change, would it be realistic for our students? Few if any students in the United States would ever consider rejecting our society's values and travel around the country to drum up support. And look at the personal benefits Menchú gained, to see her family jailed and murdered, to watch others harassed, to be in a constant state of danger, and finally exiled. When teaching about social change, these seem to be some high expectations for us to present to our students, threatening examples of the sacrifices necessary to make change.

I can see how she was inspired by the Bible, but in today's classroom you cannot assume the Bible stories of Moses and Ruth are known by your students. In fact at a Latin conference, a couple of professors told me that all Biblical illusions in literature are meaningless to their present students, and it is over the next generation where we will decide if the classical mythology is lost also.

And as for other classics that could be taught with Menchú's story, what about as a companion to Upton Sinclare's *Jungle*, or an affirmation of George Orwell's *1984*. Neither extremely upbeat books.

12/09/93 16: 43
38: 34) William deDie
 I know my last response sounded really depressing, but the part of this book that really sticks in my mind is where RM questions why she should marry and bring children into the world only so that they will have to work as hard and endure all she has to. Because you know, she is not the only person in the world to have ever questioned that either.

12/09/93 18: 10
38: 35) Anne Schipper
 As I said in class, it was not that *RM* was not interesting. But it lacked passion. It was told in such deadpan fashion that it also left me, the reader, without much feeling. I suspect translation and editing are the chief culprits here, because I cannot believe RM told this story in a flat, emotionless monotone— and yet, that's how it comes across. That's why I could not give it my full attention for very long. And that's why I would use excerpts. It is an important story to tell. The violence needs to be presented because kids get so much exposure to violence Hollywood-style that the tendency is to believe it's all just make-believe. There was a murder on our corner this summer. At the trial, one of the defendants said they didn't mean to kill Christopher Ricketts. They "just wanted to scare him." They have seen so many murder scenes where the actor dies and then is reincarnated in another movie that they can't fathom that when you shoot bullets at people they are going to die—for good. *RM* is real. And it is NOW.

12/10/93 10: 29
38: 36) Steve Griffin
 Sure, *I, Rigoberta* is literature. As we've discussed, it's a testimonial type of lit. Oral traditions are (were) extremely important in the histories of native Americans, Africans, and African Americans, and other peoples of color (for lack of a better term). I think it would be useful for us to study oral traditions as English teachers, especially given the current oral tradition, if you will) of rap/hip-hop. I don't know if I'd teach Menchú. I agree with several others in the class that students may have a hard time getting into it. I might use it in a senior level Eng. class if I thought my students would get into it. Also, I think it could be useful if I taught it while doing an integrated unit with another teacher for a class like history, soc., modern problems, and other soc. studies courses. Finally, I am sure I would make the book available as an option for a group project or an individual paper where students were choosing their own books.

12/10/93 11: 11
38: 38) Denise Wright
 I feel that we, as a nation, have been so attached to the television and the excessive romanticizing of personal testimonials that when we're exposed to a

work such as *I, Rigoberta Menchú* we end up comparing it to the last Sunday night mini-series on the life of so-and-so.

I feel testimonials are a very powerful way of teaching people about other cultures and the difficulties of life. However, our nation doesn't want to open our eyes to Guatemala, we'd rather look at Ethiopia or somewhere that is further away than Guatemala. (Safety in distance.)

12/10/93 11: 43
38: 39) Teresa Smola
I would probably not use the whole *I, RM* in a high school class. It was too long and dry, and as Anne said, it lacked passion—the one quality that might be able to draw readers into the story and make it more personal. While it was not boring or unimportant I also have to agree that the feeling of the story was lost in the translation/organization.

I, RM is literature and could be used in class as one example of a testimonial in an attempt to demonstrate oral tradition. Testimonials are very strong because they tell the story of a person who actually experienced a segment of history—something we do not get from traditional history texts. Oral history is an excellent way to draw students into the past and introduce them to the fact that history consists of real people like themselves, not just the political leaders that get written about in most history texts. Allen mentioned in his article works by Studs Terkel, which I find much more interesting than *I, RM.* His translations of the interviews he has conducted reflect the true speech and emotion of the person being interviewed and they are easy to sympathize with, hate, love, envy, etc. Terkel also demonstrates how one experience in history gets translated into several different experiences, depending on the person being interviewed.

We might be able to use examples such as these to let students write their own testimonials and conduct oral history assignments with people in their community. And I think it would be an excellent idea to use any testimonial in conjunction with the history that surrounds it—collaborating with another teacher.

12/10/93 13: 20
38: 40) Doug Martin
Wow!
Some really exciting thinking is taking place here. I must admit, I was not immediately impressed with the style in which *I, Rigoberta Menchú* (See? I know how to SPELL it.) was written, but I had to keep reminding myself that it was first, an orally transmitted story, and second, it had to be translated from Spanish into English. I did appreciate the few Spanish words I learned (I kept getting cravings for Taco Bell after reading about all the tortillas and tamales); it really added some spice to the story. Once I got into it, though, I realized the power of this genre of literature. The testimonial can be an extremely powerful

tool, especially with young people, many of whom have their own testimonials of poverty and sadness. Like *X* and *Kaffir Boy*, Menchú is the voice of one person acting for a group as a whole. It's important for our students to know their voices are important and can make a difference and that someone is always listening. I would not, however, use the entire book, but I would certainly use some of the most powerful parts, and I wouldn't dare think of even starting to teach it without educating myself and then, my students, on the history behind the story.

Bill, I really liked your response, too. However, I have yet to find an ANTE-DOTE (more commonly known as antidote) in my copy of *I, Rigoberta Menchú*. (I could have used some the other night when I carelessly mistook a bottle of Liquid Plumber for my bottle of olive oil. The pasta primavera I made was a bit strong, but man, the dishes sure cleaned up easily!) Just kidding, Billy.

12/10/93 14: 35
38: 43) Tom Morris

Allen, the comments about senioritis are worth looking at. After all, for some of us this is THE LAST BOOK WE WILL READ in college. The positioning of the unit was poor, too, and the fact that it was crammed into three days (thanks to my group, sorry) left some of us wondering whether to read that book or the other. I think if you try this unit earlier next semester you'll see better results from that class.

As for those of you who called the book "boring," stand by your opinions. No piece of literature should affect all readers the same. I am proud to say that I have laughed at passages while those near me cried. We all bring some of our own experiences into what we read.

12/13/93 17: 03
38: 44) David DePeal

In evaluating the presentation of *I, RM*, I have come to realize that some essential aspects were definitely lacking. I was not REAL enthused about teaching it, and I think that that attitude does have a way of seeping into the minds of the those that you are teaching. But, more than that I believe that our group was criminal in its neglect for background and history. THIS BOOK CANNOT BE TAUGHT WITHOUT IT. The result was an even greater apathetic response.

12/14/93 10: 57
38: 46) Allen Carey-Webb

Well, maybe someday when you all have more time again, you will pick up RM's story and read it again. You might not find it as dry a second time. I also recommend a visit to what we call "third-world" countries. Maybe there, too, things will just seem too depressing, too different, impossible to take it. Life really can be overwhelming, yet the luxury to choose not to have to confront it is a luxury we ought to examine.

12/14/93 11: 12
38: 47) Julie Ringold
I am amazed by some of the comments that I have read on this confer item concerning *I, Rigoberta Menchú*. I realize that everyone has their opinions, and the right to teach what they want—but what about the students in your class-rooms? Don't they have a right to be exposed to a story like this? Don't they have a right to know about the incredible circumstances that these people must live through every single day? How can anyone say that they were not affected by this book, or that it was boring? It is one of the most powerful books I have ever read, and I thank Allen for bringing it to my attention. I was reading the sections in the book where Rigoberta's brother and mother were tortured and killed. I was crying so hard that I could barely read the words on the page. Try and think of your own mother or sibling going through something like that. I cannot even imagine. I definitely plan to teach this book in my future English classroom, because I think my students will never be the same after having read such a book.

12/14/93 11: 49
38: 48) Tammy Bobell
Julie—how can I say that I wasn't affected by *I, RM?*—because I wasn't.

12/14/93 14: 32
38: 51) Janie Sare
Better late than never, I guess. I have to agree with most of the comments that I would only teach a part of the book and not the whole thing. The power of *I, RM* is in its testimonial style. I would want to test the water by having the students read a few chapters and see what their reaction is. If they showed a lot of interest then I wouldn't hesitate in teaching the whole work, however if their reaction is the same as this class than I wouldn't want to push it. I guess what I'm trying to say is that I would try doing a few chapters and then let the students decide.

CONCLUSION

The responses of these aspiring teachers at Western Michigan University are multifaceted and contradictory; I offer here only the briefest comment.

As with my previous experiences using *I, Rigoberta Menchú* with aspiring teachers, there were students who were profoundly moved by the story, anxious to learn more, perhaps teach it themselves at some point in the future. Some students had concerns about how testimonials would "fit in" to current high school literature curriculums—I would like all students to engage more richly with the question of what is literature, how it has been defined historically, and how our understanding may evolve. Several students express alienation and estrangment from *I, Rigoberta Menchú*. This response can be explained, in part, by a shortage of time for reading the work and exploring background. Yet, it is interesting that the word *boring* comes up in other chapters in *Teaching and Testimony*. *Boring* is a word that I sometimes hear when students confront a particularly difficult text, one beyond their comfort level. There are, of course, many aspects of *I, Rigoberta Menchú* that make it difficult for my students. They struggle with oral narration and the documentary, testimonial style. As they point out, they need more contextual background. It may pose challenges to their world view or their conception of the role of English teacher. For those students interested in teaching Menchú, for those who are uncertain, and in order for all of us to reflect on teaching, I look forward to sharing the wisdom and experiences of the contributors to *Teaching and Testimony* with my class. I believe that this book, along with Menchú and other testimonial narratives, can play a role in training teachers.

NOTES

1. The politics of literacy skill pedagogy is explored in *Critical Teaching and the Idea of Literacy* by Knoblauch and Brannon (Portsmouth, N.H.: Boynton Cook, 1993).

2. West, Cornell. "Minority Discourse and the Pitfalls of Canon Formation." *Yale Journal of Criticism* 1987.

28

RIGOBERTA MENCHÚ'S SECRET
Culture and Education

JOHN WILLINSKY

Like many readers of *I, Rigoberta Menchú: An Indian Woman in Guatemala,* I was left shaken and uncertain about the commonplaces of my life, especially my life as a teacher. In trying to make something of this reading, to move forward from the experience of the book, I have set out to examine how the book unsettles our typical notions of cultural diversity and integrity. What became increasingly apparent to me was that the fascination with distinctions of *culture,* which we bring to the story of "an Indian woman in Guatemala," is in itself both decidedly inadequate and a typically educational response to the life and story of Rigoberta Menchú. This cultural reading did little more than distance her, placing her curiously apart from me, that I might learn from and appreciate this rich source of difference. She was a representative of the Other, an object lesson out of the annals of anthropology, that allowed me to possess an understanding of the emblematic culture of the Quiché Amerindian. It was this sense of gazing onto a new world that, in the shadow of the Columbus Quincentenial, Menchú repeatedly interrupted. Just as we are caught up in the fetching of water in earthenware pots or the use of maize leaves in making tamales, she breaks out of this cultural display by speaking of the "horror film that was my brother's death" (Menchú 1984, 181) produced, in all of its terrifying effects, by the military regime that had overthrown the elected leftist President Jacobo Arbenz Guzmán in 1954, with support from the United States Central Intelligence Agency (Golden 1992). I found this disturbing coexistence between the anthropology of culture and the politics of terror raising serious questions about how our conception of culture might be entangled in a web of colonial and racial interests deeply invested in the production of difference.

"This is my testimony," Menchú declares in the text's opening lines, "I didn't learn it from a book." The case for her readers is different, given our good fortune. We are to learn it from a book. And so begin the paradoxes raised by Menchú's bearing of witness, this setting of herself apart, that still has a way of drawing witness and reader closer together, while calling into question the reader's, shall we say, "educational" interests in the Amerindian people. For me, as a teacher, Rigoberta Menchú's distrust of our bookish and schooled lives unsettles our best intentions to teach the young about those living far away and next door. I emerged from reading *I, Rigoberta Menchú* struck by a sense of how poorly prepared I was to help students live in, and understand, a world in which Latin American cotton and coffee comes out of the suffering recounted by Menchú. It would seem particularly callous to say that what separates Menchú's life from our own is that we inhabit different and distinct *cultures*. That is, I do not deny that the differences between us are real enough and that those differences in food and work are cultural in nature. What I am taking exception to is only the degree to which we regard those differences as defining a separate and integral form of life, a coherent and autonomous culture, that serves to distinguish "us" and "them." It seems presumptuous to think that our responsibility, as educated citizens, is to study the culture of the Quiché Amerindian in the hope, as it is often said, of learning more about ourselves.

Rather than invoke notions of a distinct culture represented by Menchú's life, it seems far more to the point to speak of differences in economic and political well being, to take up matters of human rights and personal safety. Concepts such as neocolonialism would seem more promising for understanding how Guatemalan coffee makes its way to the shop around the corner and Menchú's story arrives at the bookstore next door. The testimony of this woman presents a particularly powerful challenge to education's assimilative urge, in a will to know that is capable of turning the testimony of others into "learning experiences." This process of educational commodification needs to be related to colonial patterns of anthropological inquiry that form a persistent element of the European intellectual heritage. At issue here for me is the drawing of attention to *I. Rigoberta Menchú* because of the way it can interrupt this particular manner of regarding "less-developed" peoples that continues to contribute to a colonizing treatment of indigenous peoples around the globe. Or to put it another way, how absurd it would be to stand up at the end of the school assembly and thank Ms. Menchú for sharing her story with us today, in light of how much richer we are for it.

To consider, as I propose to do in this paper, how Menchú's book unsettles *the educational regard for culture* may seem particularly ill advised for someone who is not given to the neoconservative celebration of a national "cultural literacy." I fully appreciate that multiculturalism and other cultural diversification approaches have become rallying cries for progressive educators keen to address the prevailing forces of structural inequity. Even allowing for the fact that multicultural programs have often amounted to little more than food-and-festival celebrations, and that they have been superseded by far more pointed antiracism programs, they have done a good deal to expand the cultural inclusiveness of curriculums and classrooms over the last two decades

(Donald and Rattansi 1992). So it is with some caution and in an exploratory frame of mind that, coming out of a reading of *I, Rigoberta Menchú,* I want to question what we have made of *culture* in constituting a fair and essential set of differences between self and Other, one culture and another. My goal here is not to insist that we attend instead to cultural universals, which are no less a part of the anthropological study of the Other; it is to make this process of constructing *difference* and *universal* the subject of inquiry. This work grows out of an earlier article in which I introduced instances of what I term the educational imperative of European imperialism, especially as it still haunts the study of other cultures in Canadian schools (in press). Menchú's book has brought me that much further along in realizing that our very conception of culture is, to a degree educators seldom consider, an artifact of imperialism and the legacy of an age that gave rise to our well-traveled and -schooled view of the world. This is not, then, an extended review of Menchú's book, giving as it does too little attention to its accomplishments, but an effort to think about culture and education through her words and life. It seeks to serve Menchú, not by presuming to affirm or validate her book, but by extending its vision to the educational realm in which I work.

The current manner of thinking about culture emerged during the age of empire that marked the late Victorian period. Christopher Herbert, in examining the origins of this manner of framing human differences during this period, finds that culture originally stood for more than the sum of social practices and beliefs: "Culture as such is not, therefore, a society's beliefs, customs, moral values, and so forth added together; it is the wholeness that their coexistence somehow creates or makes manifest" (1991, 5). Culture posited the distinctiveness of other people in terms of an essence or wholeness that operated as part of a symbolic order by which the European could position its manifest destiny. Where the Amerindian had originally been demonized and infanticized by the Christian invaders, as a preparation for their conversion, by the nineteenth century they were regarded as operating within a scale of "natural" differences that found their expression in the new sciences of evolution and culture (McGrane 1989, 94). Darwin provided a biological basis for the study of cultural distinctions by holding that "all true classification" was genealogical and "that community of descent is the hidden bond which naturalists have been unconsciously seeking, and not some unknown plan of creation, or the general enunciation of general propositions" (1962, 23). Within a few years of the publication of Darwin's work, E. B. Tylor set a new-born anthropology in pursuit of humanity's "community of descent" that lay waiting in the living museums of culture afforded by the colonial empire. He pointed out how "savage and barbarous tribes often more or less fairly represent stages of culture through which our own ancestors passed long ago, and their customs and laws often explained to us, in ways we should have hardly guessed, the sense and reason of our own" (1913, 388). In his history of discipline, Bernard McGrane speaks of a nineteenth-century "anthropology [that] transformed the Other into . . . a concrete memory of the past" as if "to overcome time by extending our memory" (1989, 94). What was to go missing from this emerging science of society, accompanied by a colorful literature of fiction and travel adventure, is the degree to which the European process of contact, conquest, and coloni- zation shaped the lives and cultures of those it touched, even as this science constructed a particular sense of culture that minimized, where it did not deny, the influence of these fearsome encounters.

Today, anthropologists, all too aware of this legacy, have begun to turn their curious gaze onto their own practices of "writing culture" out of their field experiences in a process of constructing particular sets of difference (Clifford 1986). For my part, I want to ask how the very concept of *culture*, so central in our regard for others, actually works to stabilize—as a "true classification"— the differences and distances that appear in a book such as *I, Rigoberta Menchú*. To what degree does the concept of culture continue to bear the legacy of its symbolic formation during Europe's colonial resolution of the globe? If it is indeed the case, as Herbert (1992, 4) holds, that "the racial component" was "effectively expelled [by Franz Boas] from responsible anthropology in 1911," it is still worth thinking again of the continuities between conceptions of *race* and *culture* that gave rise to anthropology's interested take on the world. To consider Menchú's life in anthropological terms, or as a teacher might use excerpts from the book in a unit on Amerindian culture, is effectively to set her off and apart; it appears to be a way of explaining or naturalizing the distance between people. This concept of culture, shared by anthropology and literature alike, does seem rooted in an earlier science of race that sought to distinguish differences among people at a biological point that falls just short of the species level, Black from White, Amerindian from European, Jew from Christian.

Another relevant feature of anthropology's historical constitution of the Other is its tendency to treat women as cultural fixtures within the domestic sphere, in ways that Rayna Reiter (1975) brought to the fore in her breakthrough collection, *Women in Anthropology*. Anthropology's interest in the Amerindian was, of course, preceded by a European "conquest" often directed at native women, in a sordid history of rape, concubinage, and polygamy. The conquering heroes created a legacy of "miscegenation," which the women and their children were made to bear within a Latin American caste system that became part of the governing apparatus of the colonial forces (Mörner 1967). Through these various relationships with the European, many Amerindian women came to play a prominent role in what Stephen Greenblatt terms "the strategic symbolic oscillation between self and other" by which the conquistadors and Church sought to position them as go-between and translator, lover and whore, savior and betrayer (Greenblatt 1991, 141–45). Mary Louise Pratt describes how among Latin American women, in general, there has long been this sense that "as mothers of the nation, they are precariously other to the nation. . . . Their bodies are sites for many forms of intervention, penetration, appropriation" (1990, 51). The case is all the more so for indigenous women, who as mothers of the mestizo peoples, have come to signify, in Pratt's terms, a continent "conquered (feminized) and coopted (seduced) by the Spanish" (59)

Menchú takes up her own place within this mediating process by, on the one hand, decrying the forced prostitution and punitive rapes visited upon the women of her community as part of the plantation economy that underwrites the country's relations with the first world, just as she details the special suffering of mothers and widows for the *disappeared* who are victims in the fight to "protect" Guatemala in its American-backed fight against communism. On the other hand, she acts in this book as an informant, offering up a finely detailed picture of her people to her Western readers. She offers the sort of private insights into the personal spheres typically identified with women's texts, while with her own life rejecting its key elements of marriage and childbearing, in the name of a people's political struggle, having seen what combining the two can mean through the instance of her mother's tragic life. This living within and outside of the culture arises at other points as well. For instance, Menchú describes elements of what she terms the "machismo" of her people, adding that it "doesn't present a problem for the community because it's so much part of our life" (Menchú 1984, 14). Yet this masculine privilege is *not* so much a part of her life that it can pass without comment. She is living within the "oscillation between self and Other" described by Greenblatt, as it rises from the continuing influence of the European "encounter."

A second and related reason for thinking about the colonial status of cultural distinctions, if a second reason is needed, is the role played by *I, Rigoberta Menchú* in the "culture wars" being fought on American campuses. For the students chanting, "Hey, hey, ho, ho, Western culture has got to go," as they marched with Jesse Jackson and later occupied the university president's office at Stanford in 1988, Menchú's book represented just the sort of cultural diversity needed to redress the monolithic edifice of Western Civilization represented by a first-year requirement at Stanford. For the conservative forces that rallied to the defense of that edifice, including the then Education Secretary William Bennett, who appeared on the campus to denounce "the forces of ignorance, irrationality, and intimidation," it was obvious that the assignment of a book by an unlettered peasant woman in a survey course demeaned a great university (McCurdy 1988, A2). Perhaps the strongest critique of the new program and Menchú's place within comes from Dinesh D'Souza, whose forceful book, *Illiberal Education* (1991) forms a second reference point for this paper.

It does appear that conservative and liberal interests alike accept that differences among human beings naturally flow out of the inherent distinctiveness of cultures. Culture has become the lens for fixing the Other, as a transparent device that has been ground and polished over centuries of evolving theological and scientific inquiry. Today, on the educational front, we find that the basic issues of this debate are by no means restricted to higher education; schools in many areas face similar conflicts over policies for multicultural education and rainbow curricula that affect the lives of many children. While I take obvious pleasure in disposing of D'Souza's well-received complaints against Menchú's book, this is preliminary to redressing two aspects of how her book unsettles typical notions of culture through issues of identity, the first concerning the secrets she keeps and the second the Catholicism by which she lives. D'Souza' antagonism toward Menchú may blind us to the fact that something complex is at stake in their related stories of successful authordom in the West, each of which contributes in its own way to an effective critique of a regard for cultural autonomy. Setting out how thoroughly amiss D'Souza is in his treatment of Menchú's book may also allow, I am hoping, a little more light to fall on the side of the angels.

MENCHÚ'S THREAT TO WESTERN CIVILIZATION

Dinesh D'Souza's best-selling *Illiberal Education: The Politics of Race and Sex on Campus* argues that free speech and academic standards in American higher education have been seriously endangered by the development of affirmative-action programs and a more culturally and sexually diverse curriculum. The book's third chapter, "Travels with Rigoberta: Multiculturalism at Stanford," covers with some dismay a Rainbow Coalition's modestly successful efforts in 1988 to change the Western Civilization requirement of first-year students at Stanford University. This meant that "the relative importance of Western thinkers would be correspondingly reduced," by D'Souza's calculations, ". . . to make way for new, non-Western voices" (1991, 61). He builds his case, which often includes this sort of opposition between "thinkers" and "voices," "important" and "new," on one of the eight optional tracks developed as part of the "Cultures, Ideas, Values" (CIV) replacement for the Western Civilization courses. In the estimation of John Searle, a Stanford philosopher who saw the process as a compromise between interests, seven of the CIV tracks are "quite similar to the originals," while only the eighth, "Europe and the Americas," demonstrates a considerable effort to broaden the cultural reach of the curriculum (1990, 39). Searle concludes that "the report of the demise of 'culture,' Western or otherwise, in the required freshman course at Stanford is grossly exaggerated" (39). D'Souza disagrees. He focuses exclusively on this track, reprinting its suggested reading list, while misleadingly suggesting that these are "the kind of works that dominate the current curriculum"; the list includes Menchú and other Spanish American, African American, and American Indian authors, along with a lesser number of figures from the European canon (D'Souza 1991, 70). Typical of D'Souza's complaints is that the changes sacrifice chronological or thematic order to the "ideological coherence" (70). This has the effect, he points out, of reducing such figures as Shakespeare "to colonial, racial and gender-related forces," although the course outline, which he cites at some length, specifically identifies *The Tempest*, a play for which critical considerations of colonialism and racism have long been a part of the scholarly tradition (71).

D'Souza seizes on Menchú's book as symbolizing all that is anathema to the university's commitment to Western Civilization as the common culture among us. The chapter's title, "Travels with Rigoberta," appears to be an allusion to her as a deluded fellow traveler and trendy jet setter, and it is true that, during the struggle at Stanford, she was a political exile appearing at the United Nations to make representations on behalf of her people, returning home for a brief visit in 1988, only to face arrest and extended interrogation. D'Souza's reading of the book appears to have been partial at best, as he misrepresents Menchú's politics and the "massacre" of her family, which he frames as "*reportedly* carried out by the Guatemalan army," thereby calling into question her testimony (71, emphasis added). He presents her development as a feminist, "then a socialist, then a Marxist," as if to recall the irrevocable descent from marijuana to the harder stuff, while completely omitting her commitment to Christianity. He challenges her authenticity: "Does Rigoberta's socialist and Marxist vocabulary sound typical of a Guatemalan peasant?" (72). The obvious answer for D'Souza is that Menchú (who is referred to by her first name alone and is not included in the book's index) does not represent the peasants. Her book is thus something of a hoax that has taken in the "queasy but cooperative liberals" at Stanford, as D'Souza refers to the faculty supporting the revised curriculum (84). It does seem a particularly cruel judgment, given the deaths of her brother, mother, and father in the cause of representing the Guatemalan peasants. But then for D'Souza, Menchú is little more than a cultural fake, an ideological distortion of a people who have no business messing with modern politics, or as he puts it, "she embodies a projection of Marxist and feminist views onto South American Indian culture" (72). The ideological reduction that threatened Shakespeare is acceptable when dealing with Menchú. This tyranny of cultural integrity—she does not "sound typical of a Guatemalan peasant" (72)—is about keeping others properly contained within the anthropology of essentially distinct and primitive differences.[1]

If D'Souza ultimately holds to the immensely reasonable proposition that "the cosmopolitan society is only possible when human beings acknowledge their differences and take them seriously," he is unshakable in his faith that this can be best accomplished by "the teaching of the classics" (91). It is another sort of faith in a culture distinguished by the best that has been thought and said, which Matthew Arnold made famous in the last century as all that could keep us from anarchy (Arnold 1969). How precisely does the substance of this culture serve D'Souza? Toward the conclusion of "Travels with Rigoberta," D'Souza provides one answer by calling on *The Merchant of Venice* as proof that "the Western tradition offers powerful and moving treatment of the issues of slavery and equality" (1991, 90–91). That he need only refer to Shylock's famous speech, "Hath not a Jew eyes?" does suggest the value of a readership informed by a common knowledge of classic texts. Yet this point of a shared *cultural* literacy, which E. D. Hirsch has made so much of, proves only peripheral to D'Souza's argument, receiving short notice in his concluding chapter (232–33). Rather, D'Souza holds up Shylock's speech as "one of the most moving indictments of prejudice known to literature" (90). Without disagreeing, I do wonder what sort of sense it makes to compare, as D'Souza implies, Shylock's speech and Menchú's testimony on their ability to move us in their indictments. D'Souza goes on to claim that Shylock's "eloquent protest against anti-Semitism challenges the ethnocentric principle by replacing it with a principle of justice based on equality" (90). While D'Souza acknowledges that Shylock's famous speech refers to only the most basic of human functions, he still feels justified concluding that Shakespeare "articulates through Shylock the very basis of modern liberal society" (91).

D'Souza celebrates Shakespeare for upholding a universal truth, while dismissing Menchú for her failure, in his eyes, to be representative of the "South American Indian." How much less culture bound is Shakespeare's portrayal of Shylock, beginning with the speech D'Souza cites, as it ends by foreshadowing the exaggerated revenge to be wrecked by this Shakespearean Jew: "The villainy you teach me, I will execute, and it shall go hard but I will better the instruction." By the climatic court scene in the fourth act, Shylock is made fiendishly insistent on a pound of flesh. This maleficence is met, in the playwright's scheme of things, by Shylock's forced conversion to Christianity, as merciful punishment for murderous intent. Still, it hardly amounts to "the very basis of modern liberal society." Does the play uphold the universal "principle of justice based on equality," as D'Souza claims, during the centuries it played before its largely Christian audiences? Shakespeare has turned to dramatic purpose a complex interplay of cultural prejudices, resolving them decidedly on the side of a less-than-tolerant Christianity, and, as such, the play might be thought to be an impoverished indictment of anti-Semitism. Its demonizing and eventual colonizing of difference bears comparison with what D'Souza makes of the feminist, not to mention Catholic, Menchú.

D'Souza's point stands that Shakespeare and other canonical figures are not "oblivious to issues of racial and ethnic difference, or incapable of addressing with considerable subtlety questions of equality that concern us today" (90). Yet in Shakespeare's case especially, it seems a little absurd to argue that this took place "because Western thinkers have been forced to confront difference much more than thinkers in other, more culturally homogenous, less cosmopolitan, traditions," unless one counts as a delayed confrontation the expulsion of the Jews from Britain some three centuries before Shakespeare's day. Let us indeed turn to Shakespeare, but not because his indictment of racism transcends his era, nor as it exceeds those of less dramatic and poetic skill. Let us, rather, examine the ways in which Shakespeare's sharp representation of cultural engagement with difference becomes the source of a dramatic tension that confronts and comforts the audience's beliefs, as they emerge slightly shaken but ultimately reassured. Shakespeare does "the work of culture" by symbolically resolving the demonic through conversion, in a comedic dissolution of difference. Where D'Souza puts his faith in the encompassing adequacy of the classic, he ultimately diminishes them by skimming thematic fragments from their surface, leaving undisturbed the work's place within the history of Western thought. Could this be the sort of cultural literacy that Matthew Arnold was attacking when he spoke of "the culture which is supposed to plume itself on a smattering of Greek and Latin [and Shakespeare]" while serving principally as "an engine of social and class distinction" (1969, 45)?

This detailed treatment of D'Souza's arguments against the assigning of *I, Rigoberta Menchú* in a university survey course may seem an extended digression. Yet rebutting D'Souza is the very least I can do, in my bookish way, to see that Menchú's testimony is not discounted nor her book kept from the curriculum. However, I also want to note that, in a strange way, D'Souza and Menchú represent different sides of the same coin in a postcolonial engagement with the symbolic work of European culture. The parallels are found on the back covers of their respective books. Dartmouth educated and currently a research fellow at the American Enterprise Institute, D'Souza refers to himself as "brown skinned and of Indian decent" (xviii), and his picture on the back of the paperback smiles out at us no less than Menchú's does in her back-cover photo, although he wears a white shirt and striped tie compared to her woven shawl and beads. It seems all too telling that he stands before the obligatory shelves of books, while she stands in a Paris garden with her amanuensis, Elisabeth Burgos-Debray. It is on this matter of appearances and ethnicity that D'Souza concludes his treatment of Menchú and her book in terms that fall just short of contempt:

> Her very appearance and tribal garb are a rebuke to European culture; for Rigoberta to style her hair, or wear a suit, would be to corrupt her with Western bric-a-brac. As it stands, she is an ecological saint, made famous by her very obscurity, elevated by her place in history as a representative of oppression. Now is her turn to be canonized—quite literally, for her to enter the Stanford canon. (73)

Such is D'Souza's privilege to be able to attack her "rebuke to European culture," as he might be said to serve as Menchú's opposite in representing a cultural engagement with the West. D'Souza would seem to have had opportunities Menchú missed, again pointing to the ways in which cultural difference and distance, as both D'Souza and Menchú supporters hold, may not be the primary issue in understanding who fits best within the larger curriculum. D'Souza and Menchú are both at once Other to this culture and now fully part of it. Through the courage and articulation of their opposed political convictions, they have become part of the educational apparatus as intellectual celebrities, with their paths inevitably crossing in airports and on university campuses. At times I thought that the question for D'Souza—as it may be for all writers even as it is perhaps their fear—is, Why didn't this woman of color, Rigoberta Menchú, write the book that I have written, or lived the life that I am living? How is it that she, and those who support her work, have turned on a world that offers a great deal to those who afford it the respect that it deserves? Menchú did not have the opportunities that would have led to another sort of book, and what she has created for us to read is given with a great wariness and a striking determination to protect herself and her people against the West's claim on her, against its anthropological interest in her life-as-culture.

MENCHÚ'S SECRETS

Early in the book, after carefully setting out the rituals that attend the birth of a child in her Quiché community, Rigoberta Menchú established the fact that she will not be telling us all: "We Indians have always hidden our identity and kept our secrets to ourselves" (Menchú 1984, 20). This element of *secrecy* proves to be the Quiché's most powerful weapon against the forces mounted against them both literally and in a more general way. It alone steels them against the outside, even as it brings on further recriminations against them for not willingly giving up this final aspect of themselves:

> That is why we are discriminated against. We often find it hard to talk about ourselves because we know we must hide much in order to preserve our Indian culture and prevent it from being taken away from us. So I can tell you only very general things about the *nahual* [a shadowy protective spirit, usually in the form of an animal]. I can't tell you what my *nahual* is because that is one of my secrets. (20)

On reading this, the immediate question for me was what could it possibly mean to know Menchú's nahual? What if she had named the secret of her identity? When she explained how parents did not share the nahual with a child until they thought the child was ready, I wondered if that had to do with the way one can be shadowed, and sometimes overcome, by parental expectations? But I gradually realized that the symbolic work here was about both naming and keeping the secret. The secret-that-will-not-be-named is a principle of control by which the Quiché resisted Western efforts to know and possess the Amerindian. If Menchú had identified her nahual, in the same way that she revealed how children are kept from their new baby siblings or as she named the prayers that are offered up to mother earth ("Mother Earth, you who give us food, whose children we are . . ."; 57), it could not possibly mean as much as her declaration that there is a realm of her life that will not be revealed to the curious reader.

Each child in Menchú's community is admonished at ten years of age to keep her people's secrets in homage to those who have suffered the conquest. The elders tell the child directly, "The Spanish dishonored our ancestors' finest sons, and the most humble of them. And it is to honor these humble people that we must keep our secrets" (13). What is there left to hold onto, to spirit away, when everything else has been taken or devalued? Menchú's people have found this one weakness in the conquering spirit of the dishonorable Spanish, and that is the power to frustrate to some small degree the broadly European desire to map the world in its every corner, to capture the mysteries of its every secret. Such is the educational imperative that follows the path cleared by sword and cross. *I, Rigoberta Menchú* also appeals to this will to know, even as it treats this knowing with suspicion as part of an imperial legacy.

After Menchú's community successfully eludes the government army during their first raid on the village, she announces to the people, "This is a great victory for our secrets, no one has discovered them" (147). The secret of their hiding places represent a deeper hidden strength among a people who at first did not know how to use the few guns they captured. The secrets are fetishized, as things in themselves—"we must keep our secrets"—just as they remain the weapon of choice in moments of civil disobedience against the enormous cultural forces of the West: "When we began to organize ourselves, we started using all the things we'd kept hidden. Our traps—nobody knew about them because they'd been kept secret. Our opinions—whenever a priest came to our village we all kept our mouths shut" (170). Traps and opinions, and opinions-as-traps, describe the cultural landscape Menchú's people have had to inhabit for centuries. Missionaries had been the first to make a study of Amerindian life, as they sought ways to eradicate their pagan faith and steer them away from their idols: "To preach against those things," wrote the sixteenth-century Franciscan Bernardo da Sahagun, "and even to know if they exist, it is necessary to know how they used them in the time of their idolatry" (cited by McGrane 1989, 18). Western interests in knowing the Amerindian have created this thin economy of cultural capital (through anthropology, "primitive" art, and tourism), which the Quiché have worked to what little advantage they could. Menchú is quick to calculate the consequences of this long-term strategy by which her people have kept to themselves, generalizing it to the larger regard paid to the Amerindian:

> This is why Indians are thought to be stupid. They can't think, they don't know anything, they say. But we have kept our identity because we needed to resist, we wanted to protect what governments had taken away from us. They have tried to take our things away and impose others on us, be it through religion, through dividing up the

land, through schools, through books, through radio, through all things modern. (170–71)

Michel Foucault, in his excavation of the human sciences that arose out of the European Enlightenment, speaks of how ethnology and psychoanalysis share "a common concern to pierce the profound enigma, the most secret part of human nature" (1970, 378). For the ethnographer, the secret part of the self, long lost to the civilized sensibility, is found in the primal Other, the savage mind, which is then seen as one of the (educational) resources of the empire, like so much antique gold and silver, readily available to the slightly adventurous intellectual. Menchú's secrets are about refusing this European urge to use the Other to fill out the "positivities," as Foucault names them, that constitute "man" and "culture" as unequivocal and coherent objects of knowledge. The particular knowledge of humankind at stake here concerns, of course, the origins of the European, while one of the primary benefits of this attention for the natives was to be subjected to a colonial or mission education that was intended to bring them out of themselves, as Other. Against this, Rigoberta Menchú and her secrets resist, in the same spirit in which her father advised her and her siblings not to go to school: "'My children, don't aspire to go to school, because schools take our customs away from us'" (169). This cultural struggle, as this book makes clear, is not so easily determined. The cruel irony, however, is that both ethnographic and psychoanalytic inquiry regard "the most secret part" as closed to the subject. That is to say that Menchú's very act of protecting the secrets of her people becomes, in this order of things, symptomatic of the real and deeper secrets that will always lie outside of her untrained, unlicensed reach. The will to know operates through its own institutionalized and governing body for intervening, in the name of the human sciences, in the lives of Others.

Menchú has had to deal cautiously, sparingly with the secrets that remain to her because of the anthropological interest in the Amerindian. She has learned how to traffic in this interest, just as she acquired Spanish at the age of twenty; these are the means of engaging and resisting this imperial shaping of her homeland. Her closing sentences, as arranged by her editor, offer a final rebuke of Western interests in forms of knowing the Other that has done so little to serve the Amerindian:

Of course, I'd need a lot of time to tell you all about my people, because it's not easy to understand. Nevertheless, I am keeping my Indian identity a secret. I'm still keeping secret what I think no one should know. Not even anthropologists or intellectuals, no matter how many books they have, can find out all our secrets. (247)

As readers come to the final page, the point at which they might commend themselves for having made her story their own, Menchú abruptly slams the book shut in their face with a bang. She feels compelled to testify both to and against this intellectual tradition that seeks to define the secrets of each culture, a tradition that repeatedly invented and betrayed the Amerindian, that did little to contradict the culture of terror and degradation used by the governing classes to make the colonies profitable. In the opening and closing of this text, Menchú takes a stand against the books that have done little to interrupt the reality of her family's pain as they paint a vivid picture of life among the Amerindians. After her people have long been subject to this book trade in anthropology and social studies, Rigoberta Menchú has found a way to turn the elevated desire of the educated imagination to her advantage. A decade after the publication of *I, Rigoberta Menchú*, this Noble Peace Prize winner is able to join 2,500 of her exiled compatriots in a rickety bus caravan from Mexico that brings them joyously home to Guatemala. While she has kept the secret of her Quiché identity, there is another side to her that she is equally adamant about proclaiming, in a baptismal process of identification that has long shaped the spiritual geography of European interests in a new world.

MENCHÚ'S CATHOLICISM

As Menchú describes how hard the community worked at remaining true to their ancestors through the ceremonies of births, marriage, and death, there emerges a parallel story, which took me aback, of their Catholicism: "A lot of people (in fact almost everyone in my village) are Catholics, devout Catholics. We have rosaries, novenas, we celebrated God's word, the lot" (84). At the age of twelve, Menchú took up the role of catechist, acting, as she puts it, "as a Catholic missionary, in the community" (84). Without knowing what the Spanish words meant, she memorized the verses of the catechism, teaching them to others in her community between the visits of the priest and amid the celebration of the Mayan traditions conducted in the name of her ancestors. In fact, through it all, Menchú and her family's Christianity never falters, although in her case it moves in its expression from catechism to liberation theology. When one pauses for a moment to recall the stories of compassionate refuge found in Latin America churches, the murdered Jesuits caught in the struggle for social justice in El Salvador, then the place of this Christian faith in this Amerindian struggle begins to pose less of a problem to the reader searching for cultural coherence. Yet it still appears to be a troubling point for those who encounter her story, as Menchú is the first to recognize, judging by the explanations she provides for it. In editing the book, Burgos-Debray forestalls Menchú's personal declaration of Catholic faith until the story is well underway; D'Souza (1991), in attacking the book's place in the university curriculum, ignores her Catholicism completely; Barbara Harlow (1987), as a sympathetic reader, treats it as a passing feature of the people, rather than a central aspect of Menchú's life; and, for Menchú, "I am a Christian and I participate in this struggle as a

Christian. For me, as a Christian, there is one important thing. That is the life of Christ" (132).

Menchú's encompassing faith is not constrained by a jealous and dogmatic God who refuses to share the heavenly throne, nor by a Catholicism that is governed by Papal decree. Her religious tenacity and encompassing faith constitutes its own challenge to the search for the cultural distinctions that are often assumed to exist among people. In discussing her faith, she remains aware that others may consider this embrace of Catholicism an abandoning of her culture. She is quick to point out how it is a matter of selective assimilation. The Quiché welcome Christianity as the opening of another avenue to the spiritual realm: "It was more like another way of expressing ourselves. It's like expressing ourselves through a tree, for example; we believe that a tree is a being, a part of nature, and that a tree has its image, its representation, its *nahual*, to channel our feelings to the one God" (80). The distinctiveness of culture here, we might say, is in its defiance of the dichotomy between pagan and Christian. Her need to explain this embrace of the oppressor's religion, to proclaim and stand by her expanded faith, forms another aspect of what is confounded in trying to assimilate her life under the rubric of cultural difference. As the story continues, along with the reasons for her faith—"Throughout his life Christ was humble" (132)—she comes to the divide between the poor and the rich within the Church: "I think even religions are manipulated by the system, by those same governments you find everywhere . . . it's clear that a priest never picks cotton or coffee" (133). In explaining why her people fail to comply with all of the ordinances of the Church, she invokes the language of political resistance that is enacted toward an institution implicated in the conquest: "We don't want to because we know that they are weapons they use to take away what is ours" (171). By way of effecting something of a reversal in the colonial pattern of exploitation, she makes her own uses of Catholicism, turning aspects of this European religious treasure to her advantage, if only by asking a renewal of its spiritual mission.

As part of her spiritual journey, Menchú joins with concerned nuns, priests, and lay people in a struggle to build a "Church of the poor which is at war" not only with the state but the "Church of privilege" (234). The nuns and priests provided money, much of it raised in Europe, to hide her father from the military, while she herself found shelter in a convent. With the Bible, Menchú appears to possess almost a Protestant regard for its unmediated capacity to guide the faithful reader. In referring to its usefulness, she draws attention to the scarcity of cultural resources in her life that might assist with coming to terms with the conquest:

We started using the Bible . . . it was because we found in it a document to guide us. It's not that the document itself brings about the change, it's more that each one of us learns to understand his reality and wants to devote himself to others. More than anything else, it was a form of learning for us. Perhaps if we'd had other means to learn, things would have been different. (135)

Here, as at other points in describing her faith, Rigoberta Menchú is speaking gently, asking for our understanding of how she and her people have sought a reliable guide to centuries of a seeming failure of humanity on the part of those who carried this Book with them in their conquest. Toward the end of her story, she describes her decision to join the Vicente Menchú Revolutionary Christians, named in memory of her father. If she is fighting for peace and justice in the name of a religion that may have seemed, at times, to have betrayed her people, she still feels that she had always been wisely guided by her father who was himself very much a Christian ("He never confused what Heaven is with what Earth is"; 234). She saw the formation of a Church of the poor as a beacon for her cause, all of which gave a special focus to her work as an organizer among the people:

My job is above all carrying papers into the interior or to the towns, and organizing the people, at the same time practising with them the light of the Gospel. . . . I have tried to explain this to a Marxist *compañera*, who asked me how I could pretend to fight for revolution being a Christian. I told her the whole truth is not found in the Bible, but neither is it found in Marxism, and she had to accept that. (246)

With the particular mystery of Menchú's Christianity before me, I turned, as she might have guessed, to (the books on) the place of the Church within history of the conquest to better appreciate what seemed the secret of this other side to her identity. Out of my own secularism, I needed to recall how this Catholicism, as both a force of conquest and a source of resistance, has inextricably formed part of the Latin American landscape of Amerindians for nearly half a millennium.[2] A remarkable aspect of this religious history is how the Amerindians used the Latin alphabet and Catholic faith to argue for native interests in the name of Jesus Christ. The Andean writer, Guaman Poma, objected to the injustices suffered in the name of a falsely ascribed cultural gap, pointing to how his people were descendants of Adam and followers of Christian law. He insisted that "one must remember that Castile is Castile because of the Indians" (Adorno 1986, 24), in a theme echoed three centuries later by Frantz Fanon—"Europe is literally the creation of the third world" (1965, 81)—the full truth of which is still being charted and contested (Blaut 1992). The Mayan *Book of Chilam Balam* proclaimed that the second coming of Christ would surely end colonialism, at which point the Spanish "shall be asked for their proofs and titles of their ownership, if they know them" (cited in Jara and Spadaccini 1992, 33).

Without entering into the theological questions posed by the pantheistic nature of Menchú's Christianity, I do think that what originally disturbed the Church at the time of the conquest, and may well continue to disturb us for different reasons, is how the mixed faith of her people unsettles the apparent cultural coherence and unifying principles of Christianity. Menchú's faith represents an alignment of deities from across cultures and continents, drawing on the superior moral forces that are available; her faith appears to disregard the properties and proprieties that give organized religion its character, and operate as among the most predictable cultural boundaries. So it is that the *Popul Vuh*, the Mayan book of the Dawn of Life, sets out without censure the ancient word on the Quiché "amid the preaching of God, in Christendom now" (Tedlock 1985, 71). So, too, Menchú's embrace of her ancestors and their secrets occurs within this new spiritual landscape. Following in the path of a number of Amerindian writers, she testifies to a faith in Christ that appears to contradict the concerns about cultural loss found in such critics of the conquest as René Jara and Nicholas Spadaccini, who write that "Christianization represented the erosion of Amerindian social, familial, and sacred structures, the loss of Indian contact with rhythms of nature, that in a last turn of the screw, was tantamount to the breakage in the link between social persona and individual self" (1992, 40). Another version of this is found in Dennis Tedlock who, in his introduction to the *Popul Vuh*, refers to Mayan people using "the symbolism of Christian saints as a mask for the ancient gods" (1985, 27). The truth is that Menchú uses the Bible without referring to this other sacred work of her ancestors. If the Bible was made available by the same forces that suppressed Mayan texts, her particular faith in Christ is still no mask. Certainly, Christianity posed a serious threat, as Jara and Spadaccini argue, to the Quiché-Maya people, forcing them to give up their children for a Christian education, while confessing that their own ways were a sin. The alternative to this heavenly offer was the sort of demonization that D'Souza performs on Menchú, as he describes her as progressively feminist, socialist, and Marxist, while overlooking the basis of a faith that might confound his denunciation of her. She has found what is good and what gives her strength within the Catholic faith in a way that again has its parallels with D'Souza's own coming to terms with the spread of European culture. He has found his form of incorporation by taking advantage of the opportunities he has had within American educational and political structures, no less so, I suppose, than the generations of my family have, as Jews escaping Europe for this "new world" and being culturally transformed by it. The Christian-Amerindian response to the conquest is far better cast as a selective absorption or incorporation, rather than an "erosion" or "mask."

Among the most dramatic instances of the vitality to this incorporation comes with the Procession of the Virgin and other Christian celebrations that effectively preserve aspects of pre-Columbian life in Catholic guise (Gisbert 1992). Rigoberta Menchú, after noting that "the actual fiestas that our ancestors celebrated probably no longer exist," identifies the "Dance of the Conquest" as her favorite Christian fiesta (204–6):

> Oh! Wake, my country, wake!
> And from your volcanoes hurl fire,
> Burn and destroy the conqueror
> Who comes to put us in chains.
> Wright 1992, 58

I realize that her community's choreographing of Columbian history is still something of a nostalgic writing of the encounter, but the creative play of the fiesta is about undermining the sanctimonious integrity of cultures, Catholic or aboriginal: "And that's how today in our towns we have fiestas for our patrons, for saints and images, because the people absorbed all this and made it their own" (Menchu 1984, 205). There is then, that level of integration into the cultural landscape that makes Christianity part of what it can mean to be either a loyal or disaffected Latin American. The Church was there in the village; it spoke of compassion and communion; it sought to minister to the people, keeping to the fore the image of the man who sacrificed his life for those who believed in him.[3]

Menchú, in finding her own peace within the immensity of the Church, found her way to what has proved to be among most significant responses of the Church to its complicity in the conquest—a theology of liberation. Beginning in the late 1960s, a group of concerned priests and nuns have espoused a "liberation theology" that seeks to redefine the Church's mission in terms of "the aspirations of oppressed peoples and social classes," as the Peruvian priest Gustavo Gutiérrez has described it, calling for a "witnessing" of poverty on the part of the Church, in exchange for acting as "an accomplice of the external and internal dependency of our peoples" (1973, 139–40). Although Menchú does not refer to liberation theology by name, the resemblances are striking. Ofelia Schutte describes the movement's development of Christian base communities (*comunidades de base*) "that combine critical reflection on the Scriptures with organized political action on social issues directly affecting the well being of their communities" (1993, 159). In just this way, Menchú is participating in a reformulation of the Church's mission within Latin America. The political importance of this theological position has become all the more important in recent times.

In an interview granted to Richard Wright in 1990, during a visit to Canada, Menchú raises objections to "a veritable invasion from the fundamentalist sects—evangelicals closely tied to the American right. . . . They are directly attacking the roots of Maya" (Wright 1992, 274). Catholicism fails to pose such a threat in Menchú's eyes. Her strong blend of politics and faith continues to confound simple and discrete notions of culture, while selectively engaging with the invading forces in what for her is an ongoing encounter "Our struggle [did] not begin in 1992 and neither will it end in 1992" (274). The strength Menchú and her people have been able to find in their faith, giving rise to an alternative sense of the Catholic mission, certainly bears comparison with the contribution of the African American church to from its influence on the fight for civil rights to its contribution of the Gospel sound to pop music.

Ethnographers have coined the term *transculturation* to cover the sort of "discontinuities" that I found in Menchú's life. It is used, Pratt explains, when a marginal group appears to break with its own cultural traditions by taking up the ways of the dominant culture (1992, 6). In identifying this break with common conceptions of cultural coherence, the term points to anthropology's interests in the integrity of the Other as constituting a set of cultural distinctions that set "them" apart from "us," in ways bounded by the colonial divisions of cosmopolitan/indigenous, civilized/savage, modern/ancient, European/Amerindian. The dichotomies reveal the dependency of the prized cultural form on the Other, as the search for the missing side of an equation might be thought to justify those long troubling journeys around the globe. It speaks to the necessarily multicultural sense by which for centuries now peoples have come to know their place in time and space. To hear Menchú tell of her life, in its own multicultural form, disrupts what is, in effect, a cult of authenticity that still informs educational, as well as anthropological and aesthetic, interests in indigeneous peoples. This veneration embodies, as Pratt points out, "an exoticist tendency [that] distances, objectifies, and dehumanized indigeneous peoples (1992, 61). The desire to "possess," whether through study, travel, or collecting, the pre-Columbian (and prelapsarian) integrity of these cultures might also be seen as an effort to expiate the terrible violation that followed in the name of imperialism. It speaks to multicultural dependency often on the grounds of the mutual benefit to be gained by both indigenous and European peoples.

The benevolent expression of this particularly multicultural construction of the world has taken many cultural forms within the European imagination. Think of Paul Gaugin during the last century, trying to capture the Eden-like qualities of primitive culture in the Polynesian island, coming to proclaim during the final years of his life, "I am a savage. And civilized people sense it. There is nothing surprising or baffling in my work except for that 'savage-in-spite-of-myself' quality" (Cachin 1992, 124). But if that is the artist from the Age of Empire, consider Clifford Geertz, who not too long ago identified anthropology's need "to grasp firmly the essential character of not only the various cultures but the various sorts of individuals within each culture, if we wish to encounter humanity face to face" (1973, 53). Geertz may have moved on to a postmodern rejection of such essential characterisations, but there remains a need to appreciate how deeply this sense of culture pervades our common understandings.[4] This profound sense that deep within Europeans lie the

Other, and that, in the particulars of the Other's life, Europeans can come face to face with their own humanity, their own darkened heart, represented a way of moving beyond conquest and conversion, providing its own moral economy for the educational interests of scholarship, school, travel, and publishing. In skillfully resetting her interview with Menchú as a form of autoethnography, Burgos-Debray has created an ironic prisoner of an anthropology torn between the search for primitive specifics and cultural universals. That artists, anthropologists, and educators are now questioning earlier, colonial ways of charting the world through European eyes, supports a reexamination of how colonialism has itself long been an interpretive tool that has figured in the curriculum at Stanford, no less than in the elementary school down the street.

Having come this far, it is indeed difficult to imagine how to break out of the colonizing pattern. Education forms its own culture of redemption for the first world, and it does not take much imagination to realize that this chapter is no less a part of that redemptive effort. Whether to preserve the heritage of Western Civilization or absolve it of past sins, the common theme is that education will make us free. I remain concerned that the celebration of cultural diversity that marks multicultural initiatives not be allowed to obscure the colonial constitution of self-and-Other or the degree to which the great European library is the product of these imperial designs. What teachers such as myself also need to learn from Rigoberta Menchú is how to ask again about the conceptual function of *culture* as a source of recrimination and exclusion, is how to return to the curriculum, and other forms of representational machinery, to search out what may well be the educational secret of this manifest identity. It is not enough, I feel, to follow Greenblatt's hopes for the New Historicism, in cultivating "the eyewitness' surprising recognition of the other in himself and himself in the other," in the hope of recovering the "wonder that remains available for decency as well as domination" (1991, 25). This is still to use the other, after Gaugin and Geertz, as a mirror on one's own identity in which the civilized being stands in a knowing relationship to the other. I am inclined to think that there is more promise, especially of an educational sort, in turning this sense of wonder back onto itself, onto what Greenblatt names "the European representational machinery" that initially put aboriginals on display in the capital cities of Europe, that subjected their language and customs first to priestly inquiry and then scientific study, and that visited their societies with versions of Western schooling intent on reconstituting the world in its own image (24). The pedagogical intent here is to become a student of culture with an eye to how the concept itself has been constructed and used in the ordering of the world.

A few decades before Menchú met Burgos-Debray in Paris, Roland Barthes visited a popular photographic exhibit there entitled "The Great Family of Man." With stunning shots from around the world, the exhibit sought to portray the twin aspects of culture, human *diversity* and *unity,* through a series of common everyday themes. In his ongoing efforts to demythologize the elements of popular culture, Barthes objected to the seductive quality of the pictures, noting that "we are held back at the surface of an identity, prevented precisely by sentimentality from penetrating into this ulterior zone of human behavior where historical alienation introduces some 'differences' which we shall here quite simply call 'injustices'" (1972, 101). The sentimentality that confines us to selected surfaces in the construction of difference also manages to distance the observer in ways that are no less important to the perpetuation of injustices in places such as Guatemala. This study of the culture of the Other is part of an education that divides up the world, even as it divides each of us within the always multicultural dimensions of our own lives. After reading *I, Rigoberta Menchú*, I feel we need to turn greater attention to the schools' contribution to the particular production of "differences" that relate to the distancing and injustice, to the continuation of colonialism by other means. The schools' best prospects may no longer lie in the study of cultural difference, except as we also examine how the curriculum itself has also, and continues to, construct these differences. The educational regard for culture that would set apart the life of Rigoberta Menchú as "an Indian woman in Guatemala," contains, in effect, the secret of this educational imperative that fails to examine its own motives, an identity that I, like D'Souza, have worked hard to include myself within, to qualify as one of "us," as opposed to "them." This secret is one that we, in turn, have long refused to name, however much it has defined our way of knowing the world and our place within it. The naming of this secret is itself an initial act of good faith. It seems worthwhile joining with Rigoberta Menchú in starting a renewed education in the meaning of culture.

NOTES

1. If we must go multicultural, D'Souza also insists, then we need not forsake the standards of high culture: "Non-Western societies have, of course, created works of literature and art of the highest order" (73). His counterinstance proves an interesting one, as he turns to the Bengali poet Rabindranath Tagore, for whom he is happy to cite Yeats's own seemingly colonial judgment that here is a poet who "managed to capture 'a whole people, a whole civilization' and he did so grandly, nobly, without polemic" (73). D'Souza fails to mention that Tagore, Nobel Prize winner and author of eulogies to Shiva and Shakespeare, resigned his English knighthood to protest the British military measures taken in the Punjab "disorders" of 1919, thereby joining Shakespeare, Yeats, and D'Souza in keeping politics closely entwined with the poetics of Western culture (Thompson 1925).

2. The missionaries preached that the Amerindian's ability to accept the Lord affirmed their humanity, while the papal bull of 1537 declared that the Amerindians were human, "true men," ready to receive the Christian faith (McGrane 1989, 14). On the other hand, the Dominican Bartolomé de Las Casas (1992) called in the sixteenth century for the restitution of Amerindian land, backed by descriptions of the barbarous

cruelty of the Spanish invaders, to the Franciscan Diego de Landa, who tortured and drove a number of Amerindians to suicide before conducting his celebrated *Auto de fé* in 1562 that destroyed great quantities of Mayan hieroglyphic rolls and spiritual icons (Jara and Spadaccini 1992).

3. When Salman Rushdie visited Nicaragua in 1986, he came across the painting *Cristo guerrillero* by Gloria Guevara, and was struck by how its vivid and transposed image of Christ helped him to understand how it was that this highly conservative religious force could prove the road to revolution: "Three peasant women, two kneeling, one standing, wept at the foot of the cross, upon which there hung a Christ-figure who wore, instead of a loincloth and crown of thorns, a pair of jeans and a denim shirt. The picture explained a good deal. The religion of those who lived under the volcanoes of Central America had always had much to do with martyrdom, with the dead" (1987, 19).

4. In a recent review, Geertz lays low anthropology's object of desire: "Descriptive reports of 'organic' societies governed by 'integrated' cultures, settled shapes, and solidified structures 'real as a seashell,' grow unpersuasive. Stark 'great divide' contrasts between 'modern' and 'premodern' societies, the one individualistic, rational, and free of tradition, the other collectivistic, intuitive, and mired in it, increasingly mythical, summary, and simple-minded. The very idea of a bounded, self-contained community, 'We, the Tikopia,' 'The People of Alor,' becomes suspect; that of a seamless way of life, 'The Balinese Temper,' 'The Cheyenne Way,' dubious altogether. These are no petrified survivors from the world we have lost; just hapless castaways, neglected, and vulnerable, on the one we live in. The anthropological 'science,' if it is a science, seems to have lost its object" (1994, 3).

Appendix 1

TEACHING MATERIALS FOR
I, RIGOBERTA MENCHÚ

JOURNAL ASSIGNMENTS BASED ON
I, RIGOBERTA MENCHÚ

CLYDE MONEYHUN

Journal 1

Read Menchú viii–xxi ("Translator's note" and "Introduction"). You will learn there how the book was written. Summarize the process described by the editor (Burgos-Debray) and the translator (Wright). Comment on the way the book was written. Whose book is it?

Journal 2

Read Menchú 1–90 (chapters 1–13). In these opening chapters, before she tells of her extensive contact with ladinos and with other Indian groups, Menchú carefully defines the cultural values of the Quiché people. Summarize the main features of her people's values, and explain them using specific examples from the book.

Journal 3

Read Menchú 91–121 (chapters 14–16). In these chapters, Menchú continues to explain the relation of the Quiché people to "the outside world." What is that relation? What is the place of the Quiché and of Indians in general in Guatemalan society?

Journal 4

Read Menchú 122–226 (chapters 17–31). From her sheltered beginnings in an isolated village, Menchú eventually travels and comes to know many different kinds of people. Her first beliefs about and attitudes toward ladinos and other Indian groups change markedly. Explain the change in her beliefs and attitudes, using specific examples from the book.

Journal 5

Finish Menchú (chapters 32–34, 227–47). Near the end of the documentary film *When the Mountains Tremble*, Rigoberta Menchú says that her people were brought up to believe that suffering was their fate, but that she has learned that they have the right to take charge of their lives and "fulfill their potential as human beings." Her autobiography *I, Rigoberta Menchú* documents many other ways in which her people abandon or modify their traditions and values in order to survive. Discuss these ideas, referring to specific passages from the book.

DISCUSSION QUESTIONS FOR THE FILM
WHEN THE MOUNTAINS TREMBLE

CATHERINE COLLINS

1. What relationship does the film argue existed in Guatemala between the military and big business?

2. Just after the discussion of the death of Menchú's father, young military men are interviewed. They are uncertain about why they are fighting. What does the inclusion of this segment do to our sympathies for particular characters? A similarly powerful argument comes from the interviews with the Catholic Cardinal. What points are the film makers making?

3. Explain the economic motive for repression in Guatemala. How does the film suggest the military and the United States contribute?

4. How is the baptism ritual linked to the guerrilla's cause?

5. How does the female guerrilla justify a change in gender roles in the indian society? How persuasive do you think her message is? Why?

6. How does the United States aid the Guatemalan military? Pay attention to the framing in the scene where the village women are in mourning. What do you see in the background of the final shot in that sequence?

7. Compare and contrast the portrayal of Guatemala in the film and in the testimonial.

8. How does the film portray the guerrillas? Does the portrayal lead you to rethink assumptions or stereotypes about guerrillas? Do you find the film's portrayal convincing? Why or why not?

9. Why were so few of us aware of the atrocities being committed in Guatemala before we began reading Menchú's book and saw this film?

MENCHÚ AND THE AMERICAN MEDIA

ALLEN CAREY-WEBB

The following article describing the burning of the Spanish Embassy in Guatemala (when Rigoberta Menchú's father was killed) appeared on the third page of *The New York Times* on 1 February 1980. Compare and contrast the portrayal of the events in this article with that in *I, Rigoberta Menchú.* What conclusions can you draw?

36 SAID TO DIE IN GUATEMALA PROTEST

GUATEMALA, Jan 31 (UPI)—A fire killed at least 36 people today in the Spanish Embassy, where Indian peasants had been holding the Ambassador and several others hostage, according to Red Cross officials.

The only survivors of the fire, which authorities speculated was started by a gasoline bomb accidentally dropped by one of the Embassy occupiers, were Ambassador Máximo Cajal y Lopez and an unidentified man. Both were reportedly injured.

Among the people initially reported as dead were the former Guatemalan vice president, Eduardo Cáceras Lehnhoff, and a former Guatemalan foreign minister, Adolfo Molina Orantes, as well as Mr. Cajal's secretary, Jaime Ruiz del Arbol.

"The bodies were burned so badly we can't tell the peasants from the embassy people," said one Red Cross official as he poked through the rubble of the mission's second floor, where most of the victims were found.

A United States Embassy spokesman, Jack Gallagher, said, "The Second-story windows had bars, which resulted in tragedy." He said there were unconfirmed reports that at least five of the Indians were "armed terrorists."

The Red Cross said it had found 36 bodies. At least four appeared to be embassy employees and one was identified as one of the peasants who had taken over the embassy and captured the hostages at noon.

The peasants, Indians from the Quiché region 186 miles west of Guatemala City, had been demanding a meeting with Government officials to air their complaints of army repression against Quiché Indians.

Witnesses, contradicting early Red Cross reports that the fire started shortly after policeman stormed the building, said the blaze was well under way by the time the police rushed inside in an apparent attempt to help the victims. Some 2,000 people, many of them poor Indians, have been killed in political violence in Guatemala since May 1978, according to a report released last September by Amnesty International, the London-based human rights organization.

Appendix 2

FILM/VIDEO RESOURCES

Many of these films/videos are available from NISQUA (Network in Solidarity with the People of Guatemala): 1500 Mass. Ave. NW #241, Washington, DC 20005; (202) 223-6474.

El Basurero (The Dump). Johnathan Treat. 30 min. About Guatemalans who live at the city dump and their efforts to improve their lives.

Caminos del Silencio. Feliz Higes. Alba Films. Guatemala News and Information Bureau. 1987. 59 mins. Communities of resistance who fled army to create new societies.

The Dark Light of Dawn. Edgardo Reyes. Guatemalan Human Rights Commission. Educational Film and Video Project. 1987. 28 mins. Human rights and military oppression in Guatemala.

Death Squads in Guatemala. Educational Video Network Inc. 1990. 23 mins. Attests to the "truth" of Rigoberta's narrative.

Devil's Dream. Mary Ellen Davis, Productions B'Alba. 1992. 68 mins. Focuses on the performance of a traditional popular drama.

El Norte. Gregory Nava. Cinecom International Films; dist. by CBS/Fox Video. 1984. 141 mins. A visual and moving depiction of the life of the Quiché that examines the experience of refugees who flee to the United States. One of the best choices for the North American students. Menchú and Arturo Arias assisted with production.

Guatemala: The Hidden Holocaust. BBC 1984. 52 mins. Spanish priests story of twenty years in the highlands.

Guns for Guatemala. Gene R. La Rocque. Center for Defense Information. 1989. 30 mins. Exposé of U.S. Colt Industries sale of M-16s to Guatemala.

If the Mango Tree Could Speak. Patricia Goudvix, New Day Films. 1993. 58 mins. The consequences of war and poverty on Central American children.

Out of the Silence: Fighting for Human Rights (Guatemala Version). Chuck Olin Associates. 1991. 34 mins. Focus on CERJ; interview with Rigoberta Menchú.

The Long Road Home. Andrea Leland. 1992. 30 mins. Guatemalan Refugees in Chicago and Chiapas.

Rigoberta Menchú: Broken Silence. Felix Zurita. Films for the Humanities and Sciences. 1993. 21 mins. Follows up on the Nobel Prize and organizing effort for indigenious rights in the Americas.

Todos Santos: The Survivors. First Run/Icarus Films. 1989. 58 mins. The effect of war on a Guatemalan village.

Under the Gun: Democracy in Guatemala. Patricia Goudvis and Robert Richter. 1987. 60 mins. Human rights, land reform, military control in "democratic" Guatemala.

Voices from the Darkness. Johnathan Treat, Sun Productions. 1993. 45 mins. Women's struggle for human rights and social justice in Guatemala.

When the Mountains Tremble. Skylight Production. 1983. 83 mins. Rigoberta Menchú's story.

Appendix 3

GUATEMALAN RESOURCES/ACTIVISM

CHRLA (Center for Human Rights Legal Action). 1601 Connecticut Ave. NW #612, Washington, DC 20009; (202) 265-8712. CHRLA does international legal work in defense of human rights in Central America.

EPICA (Ecumenical Program on Central America and the Caribbean). 1470 Irving St. NW, Washington, DC 20010; (202) 332-0292. EPICA is a faith-based educational and solidarity organization offering books, reports, videos, delegations, and speaking tours.

Guatemalan Human Rights Commission/U.S.A. 3321 12th St. NE, Washington, DC 20017; (202) 529-6599. GHRC/USA publicizes and organizes campaigns to end human rights abuses in Guatemala.

Guatemalan Partners. 945 "G" St. NW, Washington, DC 20001; (202) 783-1123. Guatemalan Partners is an educational and material aid organization with a particular focus on health and community projects in Guatemala.

Guatemala Scholars Network. Marilyn Moors, Route 1, Box 55, Friendsville, MD 21531; (301) 746-4057. An organization of scholars whose field of research is Guatemala dedicated to bringing out voices and information from Guatemala. Affiliated with LASA (Latin American Scholars Association).

NCOORD (National Coordinating Office on Refugees and Displaced of Guatemala). 59 E. Van Buren #1400, Chicago, IL 60605; (312) 360-1705. NCOORD serves as a clearing house for information on refugees and the displaced, and provides a forum for developing comprehensive strategies in the United States to benefit these populations.

NECA (Network of Educators on Central America). 1118 22nd Street NW, Washington, DC 20037. NECA provides resources for classroom teachers on Central America, coordinates tours, speakers, and a human rights emergence response network.

NISQUA (Network in Solidarity with the People of Guatemala). 1500 Massachusets Ave. NW #241, Washington, DC 20005; (202) 223-6474. NISQUA is the national coordinating office for Guatemala solidarity work and organizes delegations, speaking tours and campaigns in defense of human rights and popular organizations.

Resource Center of the Americas. 317 17th Ave. SE, Minneapolis, MN 55414; (612) 627-9445. Educational and resource center for educators on the Americas. Publishers of *Rigoberta Menchú: The Prize that Broke the Silence* (An activity-based educational packet on the relationship between Guatemala and the United States for grade 7 to adult).

CONTRIBUTORS

Rino G. Avellaneda is a graduate student in the Department of Spanish and Portuguese at the University of Wisconsin–Madison, specializing in Contemporary Latin American Literature, with an M.A. in Latin American History at Vanderbilt University. His studies concentrate on the exploration of male representation in literature written by women and he is currently developing a multimedia work on Colombian reality.

Luis O. Arata is associate professor of Modern Languages at Quinnipiac College. He received a Ph.D. in Romance Studies from Cornell University, was a Postdoctoral Fellow at the Center for Twentieth-Century Studies of the University of Wisconsin–Milwaukee, and a Visiting Faculty Fellow at Yale University. His published books and articles have been in the area of modern theatre, Latin American cultural studies, and Maya literature, from an interdisciplinary perspective. His most recent previous publication was a chapter entitled "In Search of Ritual Theater: Artaud in Mexico" in *Antonin Artaud and the Modern Theater*, Gene A. Plunka, ed. Associated University Presses, 1994.

Arturo Arias, Guatemalan by birth, is professor of Humanities at San Francisco State University. Co-writer for the screenplay for the film *El Norte* (1984), his most recent book in English is titled *After the Bombs* (Curbstone Press, 1990). Author of four novels in Spanish (*Después de las bombas,* 1979; *Itzam-Na,* 1981; *Jaguar en llamas,* 1989; *Los caminos de Paxil,* 1991) and winner of the Casa de las Americas Award and the Anna Seghers Scholarship for two of them, he is a specialist on ethnic issues, a subject that is a central theme in both his fiction and his academic work. He is presently a Humanities Fellow at Stanford University.

Gene H. Bell-Villada was born in Haiti and grew up in three Spanish American countries. He is professor of Romance Languages at Williams College. His articles and reviews have appeared in *The New York Times Book Review, New Republic, In These Times, Monthly Review, Salmagundi, TriQuarterly,* and *The Nation.* His books include *García Márquez: The Man and His Work* and *The Carlos Chadwick Mystery,* a novel. Forthcoming titles are *Art for Art's Sake and Literary Life: How Politics and Markets Helped Shape the Ideology and Culture of Aestheticism, 1790–1990,* and *Abortive Romances: A Novella and 13 Stories.*

Stephen Benz is professor of English at Barry University in Miami Shores Florida. Coeditor of *Teaching and Testimony,* he is author of *Guatemalan Journey* an account of his two years as a Fulbright Scholar in Guatemala.

Ksenija Bilbija is assistant professor of Spanish at the University of Wisconsin–Madison. She has translated a book of short stories by Luisa Valenzuela and co-translated a book of selected stories by Mario Benedetti from Spanish to Serbian. Her critical essays on Contemporary Latin American Literature have appeared in *Confluencia, INTI: Revista de Literatura Hispanica, Journal of Interdisciplinary Literary Studies, Revista Chilena de Literatura, Modern Poetry in Translations, Journal of the Fantastic in the Arts,* and *Studies in Latin American Popular Culture,* among others. She is currently working on a book *Literary Dolls: The Promethean Dream in Contemporary Latin American Fiction.*

David Blot is assistant professor of English as a Second Language at Bronx Community College (CUNY). He earned his Ph.D. at Fordham University in 1991 in Language, Literacy, and Learning. His publications include three writing texts for ESL students published by Heinle & Heinle.

Allen Carey-Webb is assistant professor of English Education at Western Michigan University. His Ph.D. is in Comparative Literature from the University of Oregon. Co-editor of *Teaching and Testimony* he is working on books on literature and national identity and on cultural studies and secondary English teaching. Essays have appeared in *English Journal, College Literature, American Literary History,* and *Amerindian Images and the Legacy of Columbus.*

Catherine Ann Collins is professor and chair of Rhetoric and Media Studies. Ph.D., Speech Communication, University of Minnesota. She has published articles in *Critical Studies in Mass Communication, Southern Speech Communication Journal,* and *Central States Speech Journal,* among others. She is carrying out research on narrative framing in environmental reporting, media representations of the intifada, and political argumentation and co-directed the World Views program 1993.

Sharon Ahern Fechter is associate professor of Spanish and English as a Second Language and is currently serving as associate dean of Continuing Studies at Mount Vernon College in Washington D.C. She holds a Ph.D. from New York University. Her research interests include Latin American women writers, the contemporary Spanish theatre, curriculum development, and topics in second language acquisition.

Daniel Goldrich teaches political science at the University of Oregon. He studies the politics of the environment, of the inter-American region, and of Mexico and Central America. His current focus is transnational grassroots citizen organizing in support of democracy, sustainability, and equity. He has been an activist in efforts toward environmentally enhancing community economic development, the Central American solidarity movement, and the Citizens Trade Campaign's opposition to the current version of the NAFTA and GATT agreements.

Jonnie G. Guerra is dean of the College and professor of English at Randolph Maun Women's College in Lynchburg, VA. She is the author of articles on Emily Dickinson and American theater and serves on the board of directors of the Emily Dickinson International Society.

Janet Varner Gunn is the author of *Second Life: A West Bank Memoir* (University of Minnesota Press, 1995) and *Autobiography: Toward a Poetics of Experience* (University of Pennsylvania Press, 1982). Having recently returned from a Fulbright Lecturership in South Africa, she is currently writing a book on women's autobiographical writing, including Bessie Head and Rigoberta Menchú, under the title *Survivor Knowledges*. She is currently a research associate in women's studies at the University of Pittsburgh.

Laura G. Gutiérrez is a graduate student of Mexican origin. She is currently enrolled in the Ph.D. program in the Department of Spanish and Portuguese at the University of Wisconsin–Madison. Her area of interest is Contemporary Spanish American Literature.

Tace Hedrick received her Ph.D. in Comparative Literature from the University of Iowa in 1992, specializing in Twentieth-Century Latin American and French Literature and literary theory. She teaches Comparative Literature at Penn State Harrisburg's Humanities Division. She has recently published on the place of the feminine in the poetry of César Vallejo in *Latin American Literary Review* and is currently working on a book-length study of the ways in which gender and the domestic intersect with Vallejo's appropriation of *modernista*, Symbolist, and French avant-garde artistic movements.

Robin Jones received her Ph.D. from the University of Colorado at Boulder. She has written articles about women writers as well as pedagogy. Her current project focuses on social protest novels and testimonies by women.

June Kuzmeskus received her Master in Education degree from the University of Massachusetts in Amherst, Massachusetts. She has taught English on the junior/senior high school level for seven years. In 1990–91, a Lucretia Crocker Fellowship for "best practices" in the teaching of writing brought her into the classrooms of many Massachusetts schools to instruct in and model successful practices. She coordinated the English Fellows of the Massachusetts Academy for Teachers and co-directed the Western Massachusetts Writing Project. She recently became the associate director of the Massachusetts Field Center for Teaching and Learning at the University of Massachusetts Boston.

Teresa Longo is associate professor of Spanish at the College of William and Mary where she teaches Rigoberta Menchú in a course on Latin American Cultural History. Professor Longo is particularly interested in transcultural communication, linguistic or rhetorical authority, and identity, ethnicity, and revolution.

Steve Mathews has taught courses on Mexican cinema and Latin American narrative at the University of Iowa. In 1994, he was visiting professor at the *Universidad Nacional Mayor de San Marcos* in Lima, Peru, where he taught a course on cultural theory. He is currently completing his dissertation on the cultural politics of modernity in Peruvian literary magazines for the Comparative Literature Program at Iowa. With the support of a Fulbright-Hays fellowship, he spent the 1994–1995 academic year as research associate at the *Institute de Estudios Peruanos* in Lima..

Clyde Moneyhun is assistant professor of English at New Mexico Highlands University in Las Vegas, New Mexico. He has taught composition for nearly twenty years in the United States and Japan. His publications have included articles in *Rhetoric Review,* the *Journal of Teaching Writing,* and *NCTE Classroom Practices* and in the *Encyclopedia of Rhetoric* and *Keywords in Composition Studies.* He has written textbooks and manuals for Prentice-Hall, Harcourt Brace, and Holt, Rinehart, and Winston.

Angela Wilcox Moroukian is a teacher at the University Day Community, a day treatment center for adolescents in Minneapolis, Minnesota. She holds degrees from Carleton College and the University of Minnesota in English Literature, and is certified in English Education from the University of St. Thomas.

Myriam Osorio is teaching assistant in the Department of Spanish and Portuguese at the University of Wisconsin–Madison and is a candidate for a doctoral degree in Contemporary Latin American Literature. She is currently working on a dissertation that analyzes the novels of Alba Lucia Angel and Fanny Buitrago.

Judith E. Petersen has been teaching for twenty-five years in both public and private schools, presently at Creighton Preparatory School. She has a M.S. from the University of Nebraska at Omaha. She is currently developing interdisciplinary multicultural and multinational curricula for secondary students. Her curricula have been the focus of an article in *The English Journal* and for presentations at national conventions of the National Council of Teachers of English.

Mary Louise Pratt teaches in the Departments of Spanish and Portuguese and Comparative Literature at Stanford University. She has written extensively on the history of women and print culture in Latin America as well as on the subject of writing and imperialism. She is author of *Imperial Eyes: Travel Writing and Transculturation* (1992) and coauthor of *Women, Culture, and Politics in Latin America* (1990). She is currently writing a book on authoritarianism, democratization, and the politics of culture in Chile.

Meri-Jane Rochelson is associate professor of English at Florida International University, with research and teaching specializations in nineteenth-century British literature, and a faculty member of the interdisciplinary Honors Program. She is co-editor (with Nikki Lee Manos) of *Transforming Genres: New Approaches to British Fiction of the 1890s* (St. Martin's, 1994), and is at work on an edition of Israel Zangwill's 1892 novel *Children of the Ghetto.* She is on the

Advisory Board of the FIU Women's Studies Center and the Coordinating Committee of the Judaic Studies Certificate Program.

Geraldine T. Rodriguez has taught for eighteen years in suburban Chicago, New Jersey, and Michigan at elementary, middle, secondary, and college levels. She has an MA in Speech and Performing Arts from Northeastern Illinois University. Winner of several teaching awards, she has an interest in interdisciplinary studies, theater, and photography. She lived in Guatemala during 1986–87.

Stacey Schlau directs the Women's Studies Program and teaches Latin American literatures and cultures and women's studies at West Chester University (PA). Co-author (with Electa Arenal) of *Untold Sisters: Hispanic Nuns in Their Own Works* (Albequerque: University of New Mexico Press, 1989), she has published on a wide variety of Latin American and Spanish women's narratives from the seventeenth through the twentieth centuries. She is currently writing a study of women's narrative tradition in Latin America, entitled, *The Use of the Word: Women, Narrative, and Politics in Latin America.*

Stacey D. Skar is a graduate student in the Department of Spanish and Portuguese at the University of Wisconsin–Madison. She has published on Diamela Eltit and Sonia Guralnik and will write her dissertation on the problematics of (re)presenting torture in Contemporary Latin American Literature.

Patricia Varas was born in Ecuador and is Assistant Professor of Spanish, Willamette University. She has a Ph.D. in Latin American Literature from the University of Toronto. Her publications include *Narrativa y cultura nacional* (Quito: Abrapalabra, 1993) and articles in *Journal of Hispanic Philology, Hispanic Journal, Hispanófila,* and others. She is carrying out research on modernity, culture, and gender in the Southern Cone and was co-director the World Views program in 1993.

Angela G. Wasia is a graduate student in the Department of Spanish and Portuguese at the University of Wisconsin–Madison with a special interest in Contemporary Latin American Literature.

William Westerman is coordinator of the Program for Immigrant Traditional Artists at the International Institute of New Jersey in Jersey City and a freelance folklike specialist, curator, and cultural worker. In 1995 he completed his Ph.D. in Folklore and Folklife from the University of Pennsylvania in Philadelphia, where he served for two years as co-chair of Central American Refugee Action.

John Willinsky is professor of education and director of the Centre for the Study of Curriculum and Instruction at the University of British Columbia. He has worked as a teacher both in the schools of northern Ontario and universities of western Canada. His scholarship is focused on questions of teaching literature and literacy, and more recently on curriculum and postcolonial theory. His most recent book is *The Empire of Words: The Reign of the OED.*

BIBLIOGRAPHY

Adams, R. N. 1989. "Internal and External Ethnicities: With Special Reference to Central America." Austin: Texas Papers on Latin America, Institute of Latin American Studies, No. 3.

Adorno, R. 1986. *Guaman Poma: Writing and Resistance in Colonial Peru.* Austin: University of Texas Press.

Alcoff, Linda. 1988. "Cultural Feminism vs. Poststructuralism: The Identity Crisis in Feminist Theory." *Signs* 13, 3:405–36.

Allen, Virginia, and Terri Paul. 1986. "Science and Fiction: Ways of Theorizing about Women." *Erotic Universe.* Ed. Donald Palumbo. New York: Greenwood Press.

Allende, Isabel. 1982. *La casa de los espiritus.* Barcelona: Plaza & Janes.

Alvarado, E., with M. Benjamin. 1988. *Don't Be Afraid Gringo: A Honduran Woman Speaks from the Heart.* New York: Harper and Row.

Alvarado, Pedro de. 1924. *An Account of the Conquest of Yucatan in 1524.* Ed. Sedley J. Mackie. New York: Cortes Society.

Amlin, Patricia. 1988. *Popol Vuh: Creation Myth of the Maya.* University of California Extension Center for Media.

Arèvalo, Juan Josè. 1963. *The Shark and the Sardines.* New York: Lyle Stuart.

Arias. A. 1990. "Shifts in Indian Identity: Guatemala's Violent Transition to Modernity." In *Guatemalan Indians and the State, 1521–1988.* Ed. Carol Smith. Austin: University of Texas Press.

Arias. A. 1990. "La cultura, la política y el poder en Guatemala." In *Cultura y política en América Latina.* Ed. Hugo Zemelman. Mexico: Siglo XXI.

Arnold, M. 1969 [1869]. *Culture and Anarchy.* Ed. G. Dover Wilson. Cambridge: Cambridge University Press.

Aufderheide, Patricia. 1992. *Beyond PC: Toward a Politics of Understanding.* Saint Paul, Minn.: Graywolf.

Barnet, Miguel. 1986. "La novela testimonio. Socio-literatura." In *Testimonio y literatura.* Ed. René Jara and Hernán Vidal. Minneapolis, Minn.: Institute for the Study of Ideologies and Literature, 280–302.

Barnouw, Erik. 1993. *Documentary: A History of the Non-Fiction Film.* New York: Oxford University Press.

Barrios de Chungara, Domitila. 1982. *Si me permiten hablar: testimonio de Domitila, una mujer de las minas de Bolivia, 7a.ed.* Mexico: Siglo Veintiuno Editores.

Barrios de Chungara, Domitila, and Moema Viezzer. 1991. *'Si me permiten hablar . . . ' Testimonio de Domitila una mujer de las minas de Bolivia.* Madrid: Siglo Veintiuno.

Barthes, R. 1972. "The Great Family of Man." In *Mythologies.* Trans. A. Lavers. London: Paladin.

———. *S/Z: An Essay.* Trans. Richard Miller. New York: Hill & Wang, 1974.

Bell-Villada, Gene H. 1982. "Two Americas, Two World Views, and a Widening Gap." *Monthly Review* 34, 5 (October):37–43.

Benhabib, Seyla. 1992. "The Generalized and the Concrete Other." *Ethics: A Feminist Reader.* Ed. Elizabeth Frazer, Jennifer Hornsby, and Sabina Lovibond. Oxford, England, and Cambridge, Mass.: Blackwell, 267–300.

Benouis, M. 1986. "French for Special Purposes: The Hawaiian Experience." *Foreign Language Annals* 19, 1: 13–17.

Bercovitch, Sacvan. 1986. "The Problem of Ideology in American Literary History." *Critical Inquiry* 12, 1 (Summer).

Berger, John. 1972. *Ways of Seeing.* London: Penguin.

Berger, S. 1993. "Guatemala: Coup and Countercoup." In *NACLA Report on the Americas* 27, 1 (July/August).

Beverley, John. 1992. "The Margin at the Center: On *Testimonio* (Testimonial Narrative)." In *De/Colonizing the Subject: The Politics of Gender in Women's Autobiography.* Ed. Sidonie Smith and Julia Watson. Minneapolis: University of Minnesota Press.

———. 1993. "'Through All Things Modern': Second Thoughts on *Testimonio.*" In *Critical Theory, Cultural Politics, and Latin American Narrative.* Ed. Steven M. Bell, Albert H. LeMay. and Leonard Orr. Notre Dame, Ind.: University of Notre Dame Press.

Bhabha, Homi. 1983. "The Other Question." *Screen* 24, 6:18–35

Blaut, J. M., with A. Frank, S. Amin, R. Dodgson, and R. Palan. 1992. *1492: The Debate on Colonialism, Eurocentrism and History.* Trenton, N.J.: African World Press.

Bonner, Raymond. 1984. *Weakness and Deceit: U. S. Policy and El Salvador.* New York: Times Books.

Brinton, Donna. 1989. *Content-Based Second Language Instruction.* New York: Newbury House.

Brittin, A. 1993. "Close Encounters of the Third World Kind: Rigoberta Menchú and Elisabeth Burgos." San Francisco: unpublished.

Brittin, A., and K. Dworkin. 1993. "Rigoberta Menchú: 'Los indígenas no nos quedamos como bichos aislados, inmunes desde hace 500 años. No, nosotros hemos sido protagonistas de la Historia." In *Nuevo Texto Crítico* 6, 11:207–20.

Brown, Cynthia Stokes, ed. 1990. *Ready from Within: Septima Clark and the Civil Rights Movement.* Trenton, N.J.: Africa World Press.

———. 1988. *Like It Was: A Complete Guide to Writing Oral History.* New York: Teachers and Writers Collaborative.

Burgos-Debray, E. 1983. *Me llamo Rigoberta Menchú y así me nació la conciencia.* La Habana: Casa de las Américas.

Cachin, F. 1992. *Gaugin: The Quest for Paradise.* Trans. I. M. Paris. New York: Harry N. Abrams.

Cantoni-Harvey, G. 1987. *Content-Area Language Instruction: Approaches and Strategies.* Reading, Mass.: Addison-Wesley.

Carey-Webb, Allen. 1991. "Autobiography of the Oppressed: The Power of Testimonial." *English Journal* 80, 4 (April):44–47.

Carmack, Robert, ed. 1988. *Harvest of Violence.* Norman: University of Oklahoma Press.

Carney, W. 1986. "Integrating Commercial French into the Traditional Foreign Language Curriculum: A Marriage of Convenience That Works." *ADFL Bulletin* 17 (July):43–46.

Castillo, Debra A. 1992. *Talking Back: Toward a Latin American Feminist Literary Criticism.* Ithaca, N.Y.: Cornell University Press.

Chávez, Rebecca. 1992. *Rigoberta.* Havana: El Instituto Cubano de Arte e Industria Cinematográficos.

Child, L. Maria. 1987. Introduction by the Editor. In *Incidents in the Life of a Slave Girl, Written by Herself,* by Harriet A. Jacobs. Ed. Jean Fagan Yellin. Cambridge, Mass.: Harvard University Press, 3–4.

Chilsen, Liz, and Sheldon Rampton. 1988. *Friends in Deed: The Story of U. S.-Nicaragua Sister Cities.* Madison: Wisconsin Coordinating Council on Nicaragua.

Clements, Charles. 1984. *Witness to War: An American Doctor in El Salvador.* New York: Bantam.

Clifford, J. 1986. "Introductions: Partial Truths." In *Writing Culture: The Poetics and Politics of Ethnography.* Ed. J. Clifford and G. E. Marcus. Berkeley: University of California Press, 1–26.

Code, Lorraine. 1991. *What Can She Know?: Feminist Theory and the Construction of Knowledge.* Ithaca, N.Y., and London: Cornell University Press.

Coe, Michael D. 1992. *Breaking the Maya Code.* New York: Thames and Hudson.

———. 1993. *The Maya.* 5th ed. New York: Thames and Hudson.

Colón, Cristóbal. 1991. *Los cuatro viajes del Almirante y su testamento.* Madrid: Espasa-Calpe.

Coutin, Susan B. 1993. *The Culture of Protest: Religious Activism and the U. S. Sanctuary Movement.* Boulder, Colo.: Westview.

Culley, Margo, and Catherine Portuges, eds. 1985. *Gendered Subjects: The Dynamics of Feminist Teaching.* Boston: Routledge.

Culley, Margo, Arlyn Diamond, Lee Edwards, Sara Lennox, and Catherine Portuges. 1985. "The Politics of Nurturance." In *Gendered Subjects: The Dynamics of Feminist Teaching.* Ed. Margo Culley and Catherine Portuges. Boston: Routledge, 11–20.

Darwin, C. 1962. [1859]. *The Origins of Species and the Descent of The Man.* New York: Modern Library.

Davis, Charles P., and Henry Louis Gates, Jr., eds. 1985. *The Slave's Narrative.* New York: Oxford University Press.

De Certeau, Michel. 1986. *Heterologies: Discourse on the Other.* Trans. Brian Massoni. Minneapolis: University of Minnesota Press.

Dillard, Annie. 1987. *An American Childhood.* New York: Harper and Row.

Dingwaney, Anuradha, and Carol Maier. 1992. "Translation as a Method for Crosscultural Teaching." In *Understanding Others.* Ed. Joseph Trimmer and Tilly Warnock. Urbana, Ill.: NCTE, 47–62.

Dinnerstein, Dorothy. 1977. *The Mermaid and the Minotaur: Sexual Arrangements and Human Malaise.* New York: Harper Colophon.

Donald, J., and A. Rattansi, eds. 1992. *Race, Culture and Difference.* London: Sage.

Dorfman, Ariel. 1991. *Some Write to the Future: Essays on Contemporary Latin American Fiction.* Trans. George Shivers. Durham: Duke University Press.

D'Souza, Dinesh. 1984. *Falwell: Before the Millennium, A Critical Biography.* Chicago: Regnery Gateway, 205.

———. 1991. *Illiberal Education: The Politics of Race and Sex on Campus.* New York: Random House.

———. 1991. "The Politics of Force-Fed Multiculturalism." *The Christian Science Monitor.* (April 22) 19.

Eagleton, Terry. 1983. *Introduction To Literary Theory.* Minneapolis: University of Minnesota Press.

Edmonson, Munro S. 1965. *The Book of Counsel: The Popol Vuh of the Quiché Maya of Guatemala.* Middle American Research Institute Publication 35. New Orleans: Tulane University.

Fabri, A. 1991. "The Silences and Discourses of Bodies: Women, Medicine and Violence in Guatemala." Paper presented to the American Anthropology Association meeting, Chicago.

————. 1992. "Memories of Violence, Monuments of History." Paper presented to the American Anthropology Association meeting, San Francisco.

Fagen, Patricia Weiss. 1992. "Victims of Fear: The Psychology of Repression." In *Fear at the Edge: State Terror and Resistance in Latin America.* Ed. Juan Corradi et al. Berkeley: University of California Press.

Fairness and Accuracy in Reporting (FAIR). 1987. "Nicaragua and the U. S. Media—A History of Lies. Extra!" 1, 4 (October/November).

Fanon, F. 1965. *The Wretched of the Earth.* Trans. C. Farrington. Harmondsworth: Penguin.

Feal, Rosemary Geisdorfer. 1990. "Spanish American Ethnobiography and the Slave Narrative Tradition: *Biografía de un cimarrón* and *Me llamo Rigoberta Menchú. Modern Language Studies* 20, 1:100–11.

Felman, Shoshana, and Dori Laub. 1992. *Testimony: Crises of Witnessing in Literature, Psychoanalysis, and History.* New York: Routledge.

Fetterley, Judith. 1993. "Class Consciousness." Revision of "Calling: Essays on Teaching in the Mother Tongue." *Women's Review of Books* 10, 12 (September):21.

Fine, Michelle. 1992. *Disruptive Voices: The Possibilities of Feminist Research.* Ann Arbor: University of Michigan Press.

Foucault, Michel. 1973. *The Order of Things: An Archaeology of the Human Sciences.* New York: Vintage.

————. 1977. *Discipline and Punish: The Birth of the Prison.* Trans. Alan Sheridan. New York: Pantheon.

Freidel, David, Linda Schele, and Joy Parker. 1993. *Maya Cosmos.* New York: William Morrow.

Freire, Paulo. 1985. "Cultural Action and Conscientization." *The Politics of Education: Culture, Power, and Liberation.* South Hadley, Mass.: Bergin and Garvey.

————. 1992. *Pedagogy of the Oppressed.* Trans. Myra Bergman Ramos. New York: Continuum.

Frye, Northrop . 1968. *Anatomy of Criticism.* New York: Atheneum, 307–8.

Galeano, Eduardo. 1985. *Memory of Fire: Genesis.* Trans. Cedric Belfrage. New York: Pantheon.

García Márquez, Gabriel. 1986. *La aventura de Miguel Littín clandestino en Chile.* Colombia: Editorial La Oveja Negra Ltda.

————. 1986. *Cien años de soledad.* México: Editorial Diana.

————. 1983. "La soledad de América Latina." Trans. Marina Castañeda. *The New York Times* (February 6).

García-Ruiz, Jesus. 1992. *Historias de nuestra historia: La construccion social de las identificaciones en las sociedades mayas de Guatemala.* Guatemala: IRIPAZ Ediciones.

————. n.d. "Lenguaje y cultura: elementos de reflexión." Paris: unpublished.

Garcia Márquez, Gabriel. 1970. *One Hundred Years of Solitude.* New York: Harper and Row.

————. 1986. *La aventura de Miguel Littín clandestino en Chile.* Bogotá: La Oveja Negra Ltda.

Garrison, William Lloyd. 1968. Preface. *Narrative of the Life of Frederick Douglass, An American Slave, Written by Himself* (1845); New York: New American Library, v–xiv.

Gates, Henry Louis, Jr., ed. 1987. *The Classic Slave Narratives.* New York: New American Library.

Geertz, C. 1973. "The Impact of the Concept of Culture on the Concept of Man." In *The Interpretation of Cultures: Selected Essays.* New York: Basic, 33–54.

————. 1994. "Life on the Edge." *New York Review of Books* (April 7):3–4.

Giauque, Gerald. 1987. "Teaching for Content in a Skills Course: Greek Mythology in French." *Foreign Language Annals* 20:565–69.

Giroux, Henry A., ed. 1991. *Postmodernism, Feminism, and Cultural Politics: Redrawing Educational Boundaries.* Ed. Henry A. Giroux. Albany: State University of New York Press, 1–59.

————. 1993. "Living Dangerously: Identity Politics and the New Cultural Racism: Towards a Critical Pedagogy of Representation." *Cultural Studies* 7, 1 (January).

Gisbert, T. 1992. "Art and Resistance in the Andean World." In *Amerindian Images and the Legacy of Columbus.* Ed. R. Jara and N. Spadaccini. Minneapolis: University of Minnesota Press, 629–77.

Golden, T. 1992. "Guatelama Indian Wins the Nobel Peace Prize." *The New York Times* (October 17):Y1, Y5.

Goldrich, Daniel. 1987. *"Virtual Genocide" or Working toward Regional Autonomy? Totalitarianism or Politics in Sandinista-Ethnic Community Relations in Nicaragua.* Eugene, Ore.: Witness for Peace North Pacific.

Graff, Gerald. 1992. "Point of View." *Chronicle of Higher Education* (12 February):47–48.

Greenblatt, S. I. 1991. *Marvelous Possessions: The Wonder of the New World.* Chicago: University of Chicago Press.

Griffin, Gail B. 1993. *Calling: Essays on Teaching in the Mother Tongue.* Pasadena, Calif.: Trilogy.

Griffin-Nolan, Ed. 1991. *Witness for Peace: A Story of Resistance.* Louisville, Ky.: Westminster/John Knox.

Gugelberger, Georg, and Kearney, Michael. 1991. "Voices for the Voiceless: Testimonial Literature in Latin America." *Latin American Perspectives* 18, 3:3–14.

Gunn, Janet Varner. 1982. *Autobiography: Toward a Poetics of Experience*. Philadelphia: University of Pennsylvania Press.

———. 1992/1993. "'A Window of Opportunity': An Ethics of Reading Third-World Autobiography." *College Literature* 19/20 (October/February):162–69.

Gutiérrez, G. 1973. *A Theology of Liberation: History, Politics, and Salvation*. Ed. and trans. C. Inda and J. Eagleson. Maryknoll, N.Y.: Orbis Books.

Handy, Jim. 1984. *Gift of the Devil: A History of Guatemala*. Boston: South End.

Harlow, B. 1987. *Resistance Literature*. London: Methuen.

Harris, John J., and Stephen K. Stearns. 1992. *Understanding Maya Inscriptions. A Hieroglyph Handbook*. Philadelphia: The University Museum of Archeology and Anthropology, University of Pennsylvania.

Harrison, Beverley Wildung. 1985. *Making the Connections: Essays in Feminist Social Ethics*. Ed. Carol S. Robb. Boston: Beacon.

Hazelfield-Pipkin, N., and J. McCarrick. 1985. *Exploring the United States*. Englewood Cliffs, N.J.: Prentice-Hall.

Herbert, C. 1991. *Culture and Anomie: Ethnographic Imagination in the Nineteenth Century*. Chicago: University of Chicago Press.

Herman, Edward, and Noam Chomsky. 1988. *Manufacturing Consent: The Political Economy of the Mass Media*. New York: Pantheon.

Hogan, Patrick Colm. 1992. "Mo' Better Canons: What's Wrong and What's Right About Mandatory Diversity." *College English* 54:182–92.

hooks, bell. Keynote Address. Interdisciplinary and Identity Conference. Newark Dela., 15 Apr. 1994.

Immerman, Richard H. 1982. *The CIA in Guatemala*. Austin: University of Texas Press.

Jacobs, Harriet A. 1987. *Incidents in the Life of a Slave Girl*. Ed. Jean Fagan Yellin. Cambridge, Mass.: Harvard University Press.

Jara, R., and N. Spadaccini. 1992. "The Colonial Imaginary: Columbus's Signature." In *Amerindian Images and the Legacy of Columbus*. Ed. R. Jara and N. Spadaccini. Minneapolis: University of Minnesota Press, 1–95.

Jonas, S. 1991. *The Battle for Guatemala: Rebels, Death Squads, and U.S. Power*. Boulder, Colo.: Westview.

Jordania, R. 1981. *Life in the U.S.A.: A Simplified Reader on American Culture*. Chicago: Science Research Associates.

Kaplan, Caren. (forthcoming). "Resisting Autobiography: Out-Law Genres and Transnational Feminist Subjects." Smith and Watson.

Kaye/Kantrowitz, Melanie. 1986. "To Be a Radical Jew in the Late Twentieth Century." *The Tribe of Dina: A Jewish Women's Anthology*. Special issue of *Sinister Wisdom* 29/30:264–88.

Keck, Margaret, and Kathryn Sikkink. 1992. "International Issue Networks in the Environment and Human Rights." Paper presented at the XVII International Congress of the Latin American Studies Association. Los Angeles (24–27 September).

Kirkpatrick, Jeane. 1979. "Dictatorship and Double Standards." *Commentary* 68, 5 (November):34–45.

———. 1981. "U.S. Security and Latin America." *Commentary* 71, 1 (January):29–40.

Kissinger, Henry A., et al. 1984. Report of the National Bipartisan Commission on Central America. Washington, D.C.: U.S. Government Printing Office.

Krashen, Stephen D. 1988. *Second Language Acquisition and Second Language Learning.* New York: Prentice-Hall.

Labarca, Angela, and Raquel Halty Pfaff, eds. 1991. *Convocación de palabras.* Boston: Heinle and Heinle.

Las Casas, B. de. 1992. *The Devastation of the Indies: A Brief Account.* Trans. H. Briffault. Baltimore: Johns Hopkins University Press.

Leaver, Betty Lou, and Stephen B. Stryker. 1989. "Content-Based Instruction for Foreign Language Classrooms." *Foreign Language Annals* 22:269–75.

LeoGrande, William M. 1984. "Through the Looking Glass: The Kissinger Report." *World Policy Forum* 2, 1:3–7.

Lewis, Norman. 1988. *The Missionaries.* New York: McGraw Hill.

Lifton, Robert J. 1973. *Home from the War. Vietnam Veterans: Neither Victims nor Executioners.* New York: Simon and Schuster.

Longo, Teresa. 1993. "Authority and Reconquest in *Me llamo Rigoberta Menchú y así me nació la conciencia.*" Revista Interamericana de Bibliografía. Vol. XLIII, No. 2.

———. forthcoming. "*When the Mountains Tremble:* Images of Ethnicity in a Transcultural Text." In *Hispanic Issues.* Minneapolis: University of Minnesota Press.

Lorde, Audre. 1984. "Age, Race, Class, and Sex: Women Redefining Difference." *Sister Outsider: Essays and Speeches.* Trumansburg, N.Y.: Crossing, 114–23.

MacGregor, Eleanor. 1990. "Organizing in Guatemala." *Z Magazine* (July/August):129–34.

Maher, Frances. 1985. "Classroom Pedagogy and the New Scholarship on Women." In *Gendered Subjects: The Dynamics of Feminist Teaching.* Ed. Margo Culley and Catherine Portuges. Boston: Routledge.

Martin, G. 1981. *Journeys through the Labyrinth.* New York: Verso.

Martín-Baró, Ignacio, S.J. 1991. "Violence in Central America: A Social Psychological Perspective." In *Towards a Society That Serves Its People: The Intellectual Contribution of El Salvador's Murdered Jesuits.* Ed. John Hassett and Hugh Lacey. Trans. Anne Wallace. Washington, D.C.: Georgetown University Press, 333–46.

Marx, Karl, and Friedrich Engels. 1992 [1847]. *The Communist Manifesto.* Oxford: Oxford University Press.

Mathews, Steve. 1992. "Multiculturalism and the 'Family of Man.'" *Toronto South Asian Review* 10, 3 (Spring).

Mauriac, François. 1982. Foreword. In *Night,* by Elie Wiesel (1960); New York: Bantam, vii–xi.

McCurdy, J. 1988. "Bennett Calls Stanford Curriculum Revision Capitulation to Pressure." *The Chronicle of Higher Education* (27 April):A–2.

McGrane, B. 1989. *Beyond Anthropology: Society and the Other.* New York: Columbia University Press.

Meese, Elizabeth A. 1990. "(Dis)Locations: Reading the Theory of a Third-World Woman in *I . . . Rigoberta Menchú." (Ex)Tensions: Re-Figuring Feminist Criticism.* Urbana: University of Illinois Press, 97–128.

Meese, Elizabeth. 1990. *(Ex)Tensions: Re-Figuring Feminist Criticism.* Urbana: University of Illinois Press.

Menchú, Rigoberta. 1984. *I, Rigoberta Menchú. An Indian Woman in Guatemala.* Ed. Elisabeth Burgos-Debray. Trans. Ann Wright. London: Verso.

———. 1985. *Me llamo Rigoberta Menchú y así me nació la conciencia.* Ed. Elisabeth Burgos. Mexico: Siglo Veintiuno Editores.

———. 1993. *El clamor de la tierra.* Donostia: Tercera Prensa.

Miller, Mary, and Karl Taube. 1993. *The Gods and Symbols of Ancient Mexico and the Maya.* New York: Thames and Hudson.

Mlynarczyk, R., and S. Haber. 1991. *In Our Own Words: A Guide with Readings for Student Writers.* New York: St. Martin's.

Mohan, Bernard. 1986. *Language and Content.* Reading, Mass.: Addison-Wesley.

Montejo, Victor. 1987. *Testimony: Death of a Guatemalan Village.* Willimantic, Conn.: Curbstone.

Mörner, M. 1957. *Race Mixture in the History of Latin America.* Boston: Little, Brown.

Moya-Raggio, Eliana. 1987. "Three Testimonies from Latin America." *Michigan Quarterly Review* 26:272–77.

Nabokov, Peter. 1991. *Native American Testimony: A Chronicle of Indian-White Relations from Prophecy to the Present—1492–1992.* New York: Penguin.

National Clearinghouse for Bilingual Education. 1991. "Integrating Language and Content." *Forum* 14:1–3.

Nava, Gregory, and Anna Thomas. 1983. *El norte.* American Playhouse Independent Productions.

Nelson, Cary. 1993. "Multiculturalism without Guarantees: From Anthologies to the Social Text." *Journal of the Midwest Modern Language Association* 26, 1 (Spring).

Neustadt, B. 1981. *Speaking of the U.S.A.: A Reader for Discussion.* 2d ed. New York: Harper and Row.

Panyella, August, ed. 1981. *Folk Art of the Americas.* New York: Abrams.

Partnoy, Alicia, ed. 1988. *You Can't Drown the Fire: Latin American Women Writing in Exile.* Pittsburgh: Cleis.

Paschke, Barbara, and David Volpendesta, eds. 1988. *Clamor of Innocence: Stories from Central America.* San Francisco: City Lights Books.

Perera, V. 1994. "The Mayans: A New Force in Guatemalan Politics." In *Los Angeles Times* (6 February).

Petras, James. 1981. "White Paper on the White Paper." *The Nation.* Cover (28 March):367–72.

Poff, S. 1992. "Rigoberta Menchú Visits Guatemala." In *Report on Guatemala* Vol. 13, No. 3:11.

Poniatowska, Elena. 1975. *La noche de Tlatelolco.* México: Ediciones Era.

———. 1980. *Fuerte es el silencio.* México: Ediciones Era.

Popol Vuh. 1985. Trans. Dennis Tedlock. New York: Simon & Schuster.

Pratt, Mary Louise. 1990. "Women, Literature, and National Brotherhood." In *Women, Culture, and Politics in Latin America: Seminar on Feminism and Culture in Latin America.* Ed. E. Bergman, J. Greenberg, G. Kilpatrick, F. Masiello, F. Miller, M. Morello-Frosch, K. Newman, M. L. Pratt. Berkeley: University of California Press, 48–73.

———. 1991. "Arts of the Contact Zone." *Profession 91.* New York: MLA, 33–40.

———. 1992. *Imperial Eyes: Travel Writing and Transculturation.* London and New York: Routledge.

———. 1994. "Autoethography and Transculturation: Peru 1613/1983." In *Colonial Discourse/Postcolonial Theory.* Ed. Peter Hulme et al. Manchester: Manchester University Press.

Prechtel, M., and R. S. Carlsen. n.d. "Weaving and Cosmos Amongst the Tzutujil Maya of Guatemala." Albuquerque: unpublished.

Rabinovitz, Jonathan. 1994. "Nobel Laureate Rallies a Community." *The New York Times* (6 May).

Raymond, Janice. 1985. "Women's Studies: A Knowledge of One's Own." In *Gendered Subjects: The Dynamics of Feminist Teaching.* Ed. Margo Culley and Catherine Portuges. Boston: Routledge, 49–63.

Reiter, R. R. 1975. *Toward an Anthropology of Women.* New York: Monthly.

Rice-Sayre, Laura P. 1986. "Witnessing History: Diplomacy Versus Testimony." In *Testimonio y literatura.* Ed. René Jar a and Hernán Vidal. Minneapolis: Institute for the Study of Ideologies and Literature, 48–72.

Rich, Adrienne. 1979. "Claiming an Education." In *On Lives, Secrets, and Silence: Selected Prose 1966–1978*. New York: Norton, 231–35.

Rivers, Wilga. 1985. "A New Curriculum for New Purposes." *Foreign Language Annals* 18:37–43.

Rosenthal, Alan. 1988. "*When the Mountains Tremble*: An Interview with Pamela Yates." In *New Challenges for Documentary*. Ed. Alan Rosenthal. Berkeley: University of California Press, 542–53.

Rossdeutscher, D. 1988. "International Protests Help Release RUOG Members." In *Report on Guatemala* 9, 3 (summer):2–3.

Rushdie, S. 1987. *The Jaguar Smile: A Nicaraguan Journey*. New York: Picador.

Said, Edward. 1983. *The World, the Text, and the Critic*. Cambridge, Mass.: Harvard University Press.

———. 1990. "Yeats and Decolonization." *Nationalism, Colonialism, and Literature*. Minneapolis: University of Minnesota Press.

———. 1991. "Narrative, Geography, and Interpretation." *New Left Monthly* (March):81–97.

———. 1993. *Culture and Imperialism*. New York: Knopf.

Salazar, Claudia. 1990. "Rigoberta's Narrative and the New Practice of Oral History." *Women and Language* 13, 1:7–8.

Scarry, Elaine. 1985. *The Body in Pain*. New York: Oxford.

Schele, Linda, and David Freidel. 1990. *A Forest of Kings*. New York: William Morrow.

Schlau, Stacey. 1991. "Rigoberta Menchú, Chronicler." *NWSA Journal* 3, 2:262–77.

Schlesinger, Stephen, and Stephen Kinzer.1983. *Bitter Fruit*. New York: Doubleday and Anchor Books.

Schutte, O. 1993. *Cultural Identity and Social Liberation in Latin America Thought*. Albany: State University of New York Press.

Searle, J. 1990. "The Storm over the University." *New York Review of Books* (6 December):34–42.

Shea, Maureen E. 1993. "Latin American Women and the Oral Tradition: Giving Voice to the Voiceless." *Critique* 34:139–53.

Simon, Jean-Marie. 1987. *Guatemala: Eternal Spring, Eternal Tyranny*. New York: Norton.

Simonson, Rick, and Scott Walker, eds. 1988. *The Graywolf Annual Five: Multi-Cultural Literacy*. Saint Paul, Minn.: Graywolf.

"Sixty Minutes" (CBS Television News). 1993. *Massacre at El Mozote* (14 March).

Skidmore, Thomas E., and Peter H. Smith. 1989. *Modern Latin America*. New York: Oxford University Press.

Smith, Sidonie, and Julia Watson, eds. 1992. *De/Colonizing the Subject: The Politics of Gender in Women's Autobiography.* Minneapolis: University of Minnesota Press.

Snow, Mary Ann, and Donna Brinton. 1988. "Content-Based Language Instruction: Investigating the Effectiveness of the Adjunct Model. *TESOL Quarterly* 22, 4:553–74.

Sölle, Dorothee. 1983. *The Arms Race Kills Even without War.* Trans. Gerhard A. Elston. Philadelphia: Fortress.

Sommer, Doris. 1988. "'Not Just a Personal Story': Women's *Testimonios* and the Plural Self." *Life/Lines: Theorizing Women's Autobiography.* Ed. Bella Brodzki and Celeste Schenck. Ithaca, N.Y.: Cornell University Press.

———. 1991. "No Secrets: Rigoberta's Guarded Truth." *Women's Studies* 20, 1:51–72.

———. 1991a. *Foundational Fictions: The National Romances of Latin America.* Berkeley: University of California Press.

———. 1991b. "Rigoberta's Secrets." *Latin American Perspectives* 18:32–50.

———. 1992. "Sin secretos." *Revista de Crítica Literaria Latinoamericana* 18, 36:135–53.

Sommers, Meredith. 1993. *Rigoberta Menchú: The Prize That Broke the Silence.* Minneapolis: Resource Center of the Americas.

Spanos, George. 1989. "On the Integration of Language and Content Instruction." *Annual Review of Applied Linguistics* 10:227–40.

Spivak, Gayatri Chakravorty. 1988. *In Other Worlds: Essays in Cultural Politics.* New York: Routledge.

———. 1990. *The Post-Colonial Critic.* New York: Routledge.

Stern, Steve J. 1987. *Resistance, Rebellion, and Consciousness in the Andean Peasant World: 18th–20th Centuries.* Madison: University of Wisconsin Press.

Sternbach, Nancy Saporta. 1991. "Re-membering the Dead: Latin American Women's 'Testimonial' Discourse." *Latin American Perspectives* 18, 3:91–102.

Stuart, Gene S., and George E. Stuart. 1993. *Lost Kingdoms of the Maya.* Washington, D.C.: National Geographic Society.

Tedlock, Barbara. 1992. *Time and the Highland Maya.* Rev. ed. Albuquerque: University of New Mexico Press.

Tedlock, D., trans. 1985. *Popul Vuh: The Mayan Book of the Dawn of Life.* New York: Simon and Schuster.

Terkel, Studs. 1975 [Avon ed., 1972]. *Working: People Talk about What They Do All Day and How They Feel about What They Do.* New York: Random House.

They Shoot Children, Don't They? n.d. BBC Productions. (Rented from Resource Center of the Americas).

Tompkins, Jane. 1987. "'Indians': Textualism, Morality, and the Problem of History." In *"Race," Writing and Difference*. Ed. Henry L. Gates. Chicago: University of Chicago Press.

Thompson, E., ed. 1925. "Rabindranath Tagore." *The Augustan Books of Modern Poetry*. London: Ernest Benn.

Todorov, Tzvetan. 1984. *The Conquest of America: The Question of the Other*. Trans. Richard Howard. New York: Harper and Row.

Tozzer, Alfred M., trans. 1941. *Landa's Relación de las cosas de Yucatán*. Papers of the Peabody Museum of American Archaeology and Ethnology, v. 18. Cambridge: Peabody Museum.

Tylor, E. B. 1913 [1881]. *Anthropology, an Introduction to the Study of Man and Civilization*. New York: Appleton.

U.S. Department of State. 1981. Communist Interference in El Salvador (White Paper). Washington, D.C. (23 February).

Valenzuela, Luisa. 1992. "Los censores." In *The Censors: A Bilingual Selection of Stories*. Willimantic, Conn.: Curbstone Press.

Vecchiato, Gianni. 1989. *Guatemala Rainbow*. San Francisco: Pomegranate Artbooks.

Villanueva, Victor. 1993. *Bootstraps: From an American Academic of Color*. Urbana, Ill.: NCTE.

Villegas-Rogers, Carmen, and Frank W. Medley, Jr. 1988. "Language with a Purpose: Using Authentic Materials in the Foreign Language Classroom." *Foreign Language Annals* 21:467–77.

Weiler, Kathleen. 1988. *Teaching for Change: Gender, Class and Power*. Intro. Henry A. Giroux and Paulo Freire. South Hadley, Mass.: Bergin and Garvey.

Welch, Sharon. 1991. "An Ethic of Solidarity and Difference." In *Postmodernism, Feminism, and Cultural Politics: Redrawing Educational Boundaries*. Albany: State University of New York Press, 83–99.

When the Mountains Tremble. 1983. Ed. Peter Kinoy. Cin. Thomas Siegel. Skylight Pictures.

West, Cornel. 1984. "Religion and the Left: An Introduction." *Monthly Review* 36, 3:9–19.

Whisnant, David. 1987. "Revision of *Me llamo Rigoberta Menchú* and *I, Rigoberta Menchú*." Ed. Rigoberta Menchú and Elisabeth Burgos-Debray. *Journal of American Folklore* 100:229–30.

———. 1989. "La vida nos ha enseñado: Rigoberta Menchú y la dialéctica de la cultura tradicional." *Ideologies and Literature* 4, 1:317–43.

Wiener, Jon. 1992. "What Happened at Harvard." In *Beyond PC: Toward a Politics of Understanding*. Ed. Patricia Aufderheide. Saint Paul, Minn.: Graywolf, 97–106.

Willinsky, J. 1994. "Beyond 1492–1992: Toward a Postcolonial Supplement for the Canadian Curriculum." *Journal of Curriculum Studies* 26, 6:613–629.

Willis, M. 1991. "500 Years of Indigenous and Popular Resistance: Report on the Second Continental Meeting." In *Report on Guatemala* 12, 4 (winter):2–5.

Woodward, C. Vann. 1991. "Letter to the Editor." *The New York Review of Books* (26 September):76.

———. 1992. "Freedom and Universities." In *Beyond PC: Toward a Politics of Understanding*. Ed. Patricia Aufderheide. Saint Paul, Minn.: Graywolf, 34.

Wright, R. 1992. *Stolen Continents: The "New World" through Indian Eyes*. Toronto: Pengiun.

Ximénez, Francisco. 1965. *Historia de la provincia de San Vicente de Chiapa y Guatemala*. Biblioteca Guatemalteca de Cultura Popular, vol. 81. Guatemala: Ministerio de Educación.

Yalden, J. 1983. *The Communicative Syllabus: Evolution, Design, and Implementation*. Oxford: Pergamon.

Yáñez, Aníbal, trans. 1992. "The Quincentenary, a Question of Class, Not Race: An Interview with Rigoberta Menchú." *Latin American Perspectives* 19:96–100.

Yates, Pamela, Thomas Sigel, and Peter Konoy. 1993 [1983]. *When the Mountains Tremble*. New York: Skylight Productions.

Yoder, Don. 1974. "Toward a Definition of Folk Religion." *Western Folklore* 33:1–15. Rpt. 1990. In *Discovering American Folklife*. Ann Arbor, Mich.: University Microfilms Inc., Research Press, 67–84.

Yúdice, George. 1989. "Marginality and the Ethics of Survival." *Social Text* 7, 3:214–36.

———. 1991. "*Testimonio* and Postmodernism." *Latin American Perspectives* 18, 3:15–31.

Zimmerman, Marc. 1991. "*Testimonio* in Guatemala: Payeras, Rigoberta, and Beyond." *Latin American Perspectives* 18:22–47.

———. 1992. "El *Otro* de Rigoberta: Los testimonios de Ignacio Bizarro Ujpan y la resistencia indígena en Guatemala." *Revista de Crítica Literaria Latinoamericana* 18, 36:229–43.

INDEX

381